Economic Approaches to Organizations

We work with leading authors to develop the strongest educational materials in Economics, bringing cutting-edge thinking and best learning practice to a global market.

Under a range of well-known imprints, including Financial Times Prentice Hall, we craft high-quality print and electronic publications which help readers to understand and apply their content, whether studying or at work.

To find out more about the complete range of our publishing, please visit us on the World Wide Web at: www.pearsoneduc.com

Economic Approaches to Organizations

Third Edition

Sytse Douma

Tilburg University, The Netherlands

Hein Schreuder

DSM NV and Maastricht University, The Netherlands

FINANCIAL TIMES
Prentice Hall

An imprint of **Pearson Education**

Harlow, England · London · New York · Reading, Massachusetts · San Francisco · Toronto · Don Mills, Ontario · Sydney
Tokyo · Singapore · Hong Kong · Seoul · Taipei · Cape Town · Madrid · Mexico City · Amsterdam · Munich · Paris · Milan

Pearson Education Limited

Edinburgh Gate
Harlow
Essex CM20 2JE
United Kingdom

and Associated Companies throughout the world

Visit us on the World Wide Web at:
www.pearsoneduc.com

First published 1991
Second edition 1998
Third edition 2002

© Prentice Hall Europe 1991, 1998
© Pearson Education Limited 2002

ISBN 0 273 65199 4

British Library Cataloguing-in-Publication Data
A catalogue record for this book is available from the British Library.

Library of Congress Cataloging-in-Publication Data
A catalog record for this book is available from the Library of Congress.

10 9 8 7 6 5 4 3 2 1
06 05 04 03 02

Typeset in 9.5pt Stone Serif by 63
Printed by Ashford Colour Press Ltd, Gosport

Contents

Preface

This book is intended for students of organization and management: an important area of study for students of business administration, sociology and organizational psychology. There is no shortage of textbooks on organization and/or management. However, most standard textbooks do not include even a short introduction to the various economic approaches to organizations that have recently been developed in scientific journals. This book has been written as an auxiliary text that focuses exclusively on economic approaches to organizations. It has been designed as a supplementary text to be used in conjunction with a more conventional textbook on organization and/or (strategic) management. Alternatively, it may be used as an introductory text on the analysis of organizations from an economic perspective.

No prior knowledge of economics is assumed. The economic background needed to understand the arguments made in the text is explained in the text itself, mainly in Chapter 2.

Students of economics will also find this book useful. Most textbooks on microeconomics devote little attention to the field of organization and management. This book offers students in economics a view from their own discipline into a related but usually unknown field.

The book starts by comparing organizations and markets. Why do organizations exist at all? Why are not all economic decisions co-ordinated by the market mechanism? Conversely, why do markets exist at all? Why is not all production carried out by one large firm? Our answer is that information requirements play a crucial role in understanding why markets and organizations coexist.

In Chapter 1 we build step-by-step a conceptual framework to explain the fundamental economic approach to organizations. In this framework information is a concept of vital importance. Chapters 2 and 3 explain how markets and organizations work. In particular these chapters explain how decisions are co-ordinated by various mechanisms such as the price mechanism, direct supervision, mutual adjustment and standardization. Chapter 4 then focuses on the information requirements of different types of co-ordinating mechanism. How players can co-ordinate their decisions in different information settings is also the central theme of the discussion of game theory (Chapter 5). The first five chapters thus explain the fundamental concepts and methods underlying the economic approaches to organizations.

As the title of this book suggests, there are several different but related economic approaches to organizations. These approaches are discussed in Chapters 6 to 10. The approaches are:

■ behavioural theory, which sees the firm as a coalition of (groups of) participants, each with its own interests;

- agency theory, which focuses on delegating decision making to an agent, while the boss (or principal) can only partly observe the agent's behaviour;
- transaction cost economics, which focuses on the sum of transaction costs and production costs as determinants of organizational forms;
- economic contributions to strategic management from the field of industrial organization and game theory;
- evolutionary approaches to organizations, which direct our attention to the development of organizational forms in the interaction with their environments.

Finally, Chapter 11 compares and evaluates these five approaches.

This is the third edition of a book that was first published in 1991. The main differences between the second edition and the third are the addition of sections on corporate governance, hybrid organizational forms, and the role of trust as well as the inclusion of more real-life examples and end-of-chapter questions. These changes should make the book even more useful as a textbook.

An Instructor's Manual containing answers to end-of-chapter questions, together with overhead transparency masters of many of the figures found in this edition, is available at no extra cost to lecturers adopting this textbook. The Manual is available in hard copy on application to the publishers. An electronic version is available for download at www.booksites.net/douma

Sytse Douma
Hein Schreuder

Acknowledgements

No book can be conceived without the assistance of others. We wish to thank first of all our fellow economists who developed and continue to develop the new, exciting field of economic approaches to organizations. We owe a heavy debt to all contributors to this new literature. Their names can be found in the list of references.

Further, we wish to express our thanks to the anonymous referees of the subsequent editions of this book, to Nienke Boelhouwer and Nancy Kanters, who did a great job word-processing the manuscript and to Paula Parish and Ellen Morgan from Pearson Education for their support.

Publisher's acknowledgements

We are grateful to the following for permission to produce copyright material:

Mr. Paul Fuchs of DSM N.V. for DSM organization chart, February 2001 in Box 1.2; The American Society for Engineering Education for an extract from "Creating a learning organization" by P R Nayak, D A Garvin, A N Maira and J L Bragar published in *Prism* 3rd Quarter 1995; and the Economist Newspaper Limited for extracts from "In praise of rules: A survey of Asian business" published in *The Economist* 7th April 2001 © The Economist Newspaper Limited, London 2001, and "The case of Lui and Fung" published in *The Economist* 2nd June 2001 © The Economist Newspaper Limited, London 2001.

In some instances we have been unable to trace the owners of copyright material and we would appreciate any information that would enable us to do so.

1 Markets and organizations

1.1 The economic problem

Imagine a world of abundance – perhaps a tropical island where you are basking in the sun, with lots of food and a tribe of friendly islanders as your companions. Would you have any economic problem on this island? Well, no, you might say, I can't imagine *any* problem on such an island, let alone an economic problem. And you might be right.

However, you might be right for the wrong reason. Many people associate economic problems with money. Since money would either be absent or abundant on our imaginary island, they would see no economic problem. An economist, however, would not be content with this reasoning. She[1] would enquire further, for example whether you felt you had enough time to enjoy all the pleasures of your island. Or whether your needs for housing, education, culture, friendship, etc., had been met. The point is that an economist would

Economic problem

identify an **economic problem** in any situation where needs would not be met as a result of scarcity of resources: and resources are quite broadly conceived as all means that may contribute toward the satisfaction of human needs. So, yes, you might not have an economic problem on your fantasy island, but only if you could truly say that all your needs had been met.

Time to return to the real world, where economic problems abound whether we apply a narrow definition or the broader one presented above. We do not have enough land to meet all our needs for cultivation as well as ecological preservation. We do not manage to feed the world's population properly. Many raw materials come in limited supply. Talent is always scarce. Most people, even in rich countries like the USA, Germany and Japan, do not earn enough money to buy everything that they would like to buy. In short, scarcity is a fact of life in the real world. Given this predicament, the economic problem may be rephrased as the problem of how to make the best use of the available

Optimal allocation

resources. Or in economic jargon: what is the **optimal allocation** of the scarce resources over the alternative uses that can be made of them? Resources that

Efficiency

are optimally allocated are said to be used **efficiently**.

This book is concerned with economic approaches to organizations. Now, economics might not be the first discipline you think of when trying to understand organizational phenomena. Indeed, it will be argued later (in section 1.7) that economics had for a long time hardly any contribution to make to the study of organizations. The approaches that we present in this book have been developed relatively recently, although in some cases their origins are much older. So, you are quite justified in wondering what insights economics has to offer. Our answer is that economic approaches to organizations are fruitful whenever the problem to be studied has an **economic aspect**, that is to say whenever part of the problem deals with the (optimal) allocation of scarce resources.

Economic aspect

Note that we have carefully specified that economics deals with parts and aspects of problems. We believe there are hardly any 'purely economic' problems. Similarly, there are hardly any purely legal, sociological or psychological problems. All these social sciences deal with aspects of real-world phenomena. All illuminate a part of social reality. Whoever believes that economics can explain entirely the 'marriage market' or, for that matter, organizational phenomena is guilty of 'economism' (which, we are informed, is a contraction of economics and colonialism). There is an equal danger of legalism, sociologism, or psychologism, too, whenever the explanatory power of one discipline is exaggerated. Having said this, we do believe that economics has an important contribution to make to the understanding of organizations. From the perspective outlined above, two points follow:

- Economic approaches to organizations focus specifically on the economic problem of optimal allocation of scarce resources (broadly conceived).
- The economic contribution to our understanding of organizational problems increases as the economic problem forms a greater part of the organizational problem that we are trying to understand.

In this book we present the major strands of the current economic approaches to organizations. In addition, we illustrate some of the applications of these approaches to organizational problems. In doing so, we shall avoid technical expositions and instead concentrate on the basic concepts involved. Our aim is to provide a conceptual introduction to these novel approaches. By focusing on the basic concepts, we hope also to present a more coherent picture of organizational economics than has been provided before. In this first chapter we build, step by step, the basic conceptual framework that we use to explain the fundamental economic approach to organizations. This framework is shown in Figure 1.1. The framework will clarify the crucial role of information and the various ways in which information can be mediated. This central role of information will be elaborated further in Chapter 4, where we argue that this is the glue that binds the various economic approaches to organizations together.

1.2 The division of labour

Adam Smith is usually credited as the founding father of modern economics. In his book *An Inquiry into the Nature and Causes of The Wealth of Nations* (1776) he accords great importance to the division of labour: 'The greatest improvement in the productive powers of labour, and the greater part of the skill, dex-

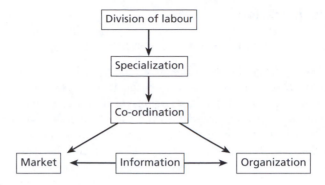

Figure 1.1 **The basic concepts**

terity, and judgment with which it is anywhere directed, or applied, seem to have been the effects of the division of labour.'

His famous example was the pin factory. He showed that a tremendous increase in the productivity of the work of pin-makers could be achieved by splitting this work up into distinct tasks and having each worker perform one specific task rather than making entire pins (see Box 1.1).

Division of labour

Division of labour, therefore, refers to the splitting of composite tasks into their component parts and having these performed separately. It is a pervasive phenomenon in modern societies. Our primeval ancestors were much more self-supporting. They built their own houses, grew or hunted their own food, made their own tools, conducted their own defence, etc. Over the ages these tasks have come to be divided over separate sectors in society (such as the private and the public sector), and within those sectors further divided over separate entities (such as government agencies, industries and firms). An economic system has developed in which we normally buy these goods or services in exchange for money. Most of us work in organizations where we earn our money. Looking inside those organizations we can see that the division of labour extends there as well. We usually perform but a small part of the entire organizational task. In order to accomplish its task the organization itself is split into different parts (such as divisions), levels and functions. As a result we need organization charts (see Box 1.2) as maps to guide us through the organizational territory. These charts are one reflection of the division of labour within organizations.

It was Adam Smith's contention that the progressive division of labour led to productivity increases that constituted the main source of the increasing 'wealth of nations'. In the next section we shall see what the basis was for his contention. Here we want to conclude by emphasizing that we take the division of labour as a fact of life in our kind of society. No matter what position we occupy in society, every time we interact with others to obtain goods or services we need, we might be reminded of this fact. It is this fact of life that forms the starting point for our conceptual framework, which is outlined in Figure 1.1.

Box 1.1 ■ The pin factory

A quotation from Adam Smith, *The Wealth of Nations*, Book I, Chapter 1.

To take an example, therefore, from a very trifling manufacture; but one in which the division of labour has been very often taken notice of, the trade of the pin-maker; a workman not educated to this business (which the division of a labour has rendered a distinct trade), nor acquainted with the use of the machinery employed in it (to the invention of which the same division of labour has probably given occasion), could scarce, perhaps, with his utmost industry, make one pin in a day, and certainly could not make twenty. But in the way in which this business is now carried on, not only the whole work is a peculiar trade, but it is divided into a number of branches, of which the greater part are likewise peculiar trades. One man draws out the wire, another straights it, a third cuts it, a fourth points it, a fifth grinds it at the top for receiving the head; to make the head requires two or three distinct operations; to put it on, is a peculiar business, to whiten the pins is another; it is even a trade by itself to put them into the paper; and the important business of making a pin is, in this manner, divided into about eighteen distinct operations, which, in some manufactories, are all performed by distinct hands, though in others the same man will sometimes perform two or three of them. I have seen a small manufactory of this kind where ten men only were employed, and where some of them consequently performed two or three distinct operations. But though they were very poor, and therefore but indifferently accommodated with the necessary machinery, they could, when they exerted themselves, make among them about twelve pounds of pins in a day. There are in a pound upwards of four thousands pins of a middling size. Those ten persons, therefore, could make among them upwards of forty-eight thousand pins in a day. Each person, therefore, making a tenth part of forty-eight thousand pins, might be considered as making four thousand eight hundred pins in a day. But if they had all wrought separately and independently, and without any of them having been educated to this particular business, they certainly could not each of them have made twenty, perhaps not one pin in a day; that is certainly, not the two hundred and fortieth, perhaps not the four thousand eight hundredth part of what they are at present capable of performing, in consequence of a proper division and combination of their different operations.

1.3 Specialization

Why would an increasing division of labour lead to such great productivity increases and, thus, to a growth in 'the wealth of nations'? Smith gave the following explanation:

This great increase in the quantity of work, which, in consequence of the division of labour, the same number of people are capable of performing, is owing to three different circumstances; first, to the increase of dexterity in every particular workman; secondly, to the saving of the time which is commonly lost in passing from one species of work to another; and lastly, to the invention of a great number of machines which facilitate and abridge labour, and enable one man to do the work of many.

Box 1.2 ■ DSM organization chart February 2001

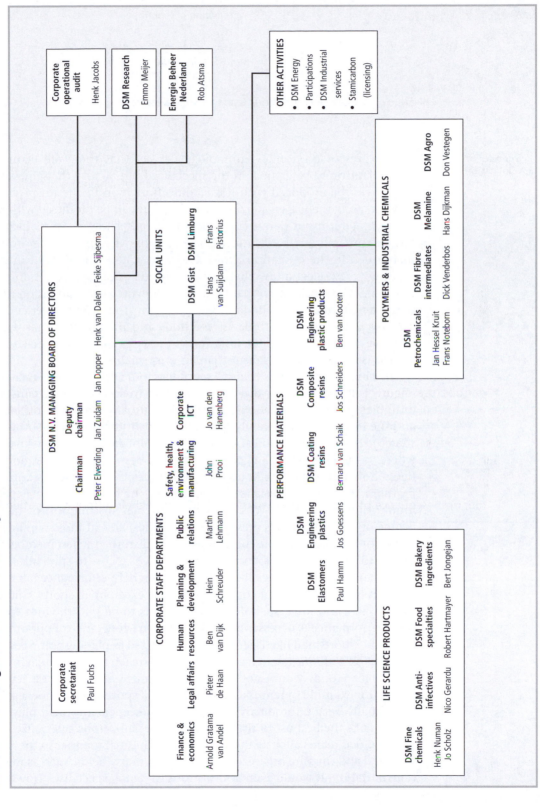

Figure 1.2 **Division of labour leads to specialization**

Economies of specialization

In our present economic terminology we say that there are **economies of specialization** to be gained. In the specialized pin factory the same amount of output can be produced with less labour effort than in the unspecialized factory. Or, conversely, a greater amount of output can be produced with the same level of labour input (ten men), as Smith already showed. Specialized production is thus more *efficient*. Among the reasons why this is true are the ones mentioned in the quotation above. Basically, when work is split into specific tasks, we may select a task that particularly suits our own needs and capabilities. When we specialize in that task, we can devote all our attention to improving our performance of the task. We can learn from more experience and we can use this experience to devise methods and instruments that will further improve our execution of the task. For all these reasons, a specialized economic system is usually more efficient than an unspecialized one.

Division of labour thus leads to specialization, which allows efficiency gains (Figure 1.2). This is a pervasive phenomenon in society. Let us consider some examples. In the family, household work is usually split into different tasks, and the members of the family specialize in distinct tasks (while others may be shared). They become good at these tasks but not at others. Some know exactly where to shop for particular goods and get the best value for their money. Some know how to operate the household appliances; perhaps others know how to fix them. Some have specialized in filling out the tax forms; others perhaps in monitoring the budget. Whatever the particular distribution of tasks, some degree of specialization is present in all families, and in most families the efficiency of running the household is seriously disturbed when members have to switch to unfamiliar tasks. In that sense, there is a cost to specialization.

Similarly in sports, specialization leads to higher performance but comes at a cost. An individual cannot compete, let alone excel, in all sports. Choices have to be made, and long, specialized training has to be put in. Once specialized, high performance is necessarily restricted to a narrow range of options. Even an admirable sportsman like Tiger Woods is restricted to playing golf. Specialization building on a unique talent has allowed him to reach the top in playing golf. But even Tiger Woods would not be able to compete at the highest level in two sports (for example in tennis and golf). In team sports such as hockey or soccer, it is usually very unproductive to switch goalkeepers and field players. Good teams make the best use of their members' specializations. Specialized skills are scarce. Good teams allocate these skills in an optimal manner to the tasks to be executed and thus are organized efficiently. In many fields, such as medicine or transportation, it would even be disastrous to switch specialists. However much we favour variety of work, we are not willing to enter hospitals or board aircraft where the specialists take turns at each other's work.

For the individual, then, specialization has the advantage of allowing higher performance but the disadvantage of restricting choice. At the individual level, the limits of specialization are reached when the satisfaction gained from higher performance (and the consequent rewards) is outweighed by the dissatisfaction from too narrow an area of application of one's skills (with the resulting boredom and frustration). As many organizations have learned over time, the gains from further specialization are easily offset by the costs of dissatisfaction when these individual limits are exceeded. The conveyor belt, for instance, enabled great gains in productivity, but only to the extent that the workers accepted the range of activities required of them. If this range becomes too narrow, the gains are offset and a restructuring of activities (for example, into semi-autonomous workgroups) is called for. Individual limits are thus one boundary to increasing specialization, but there is another boundary, which is the subject of the next section.

1.4 Co-ordination

In the previous paragraphs we have seen that division of labour and specialization are pervasive phenomena in society. As a result, hardly any people are economically self-reliant in the sense that they produce all the goods and services they wish to consume. In order to obtain these goods and services they have to acquire them from other specialized people. In economic terminology

Exchange

we say that **exchange** has to take place. Goods and services are exchanged whenever the right to use them is transferred. Much exchange takes place through markets. On a market, the right to use particular goods and services is bought (and, of course, sold at the same time). When I buy a piece of soap in my local store, I acquire the right to use the soap, while the storeowner acquires the right to use the money I have paid.

Exchange, though, is broader than just market exchange. First, the goods involved need not be only goods that are marketable. Economists speak of goods whenever scarce resources are involved. We can indeed also exchange favours, since favours are very scarce and can be used to get things done. Similarly, we exchange information as soon as the right to use the information has been transferred. Second, the transfer of rights need not be mutual. When I offer you some of my time, I am offering you the right to use a scarce resource. An economist would regard your use of my time as an example of exchange, whether or not you reciprocate in any way.

Transaction

Whenever exchange takes place, we speak of an (economic) **transaction**. Owing to the division of labour and to specialization, innumerable transactions have to occur in society. Since, on the one hand, we are all specialized ourselves and, on the other hand, need the specialized goods and services of others, a vast network of exchange is necessary to allocate the available goods and services. How is this accomplished? How do the parties who are willing to

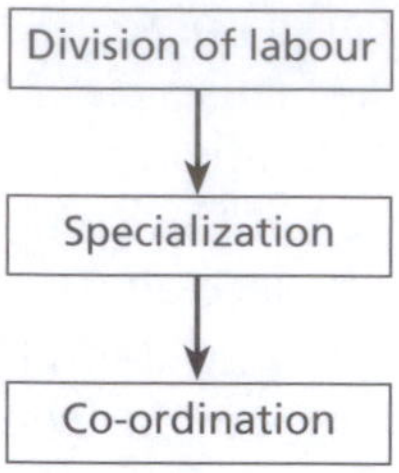

Figure 1.3 **Specialization entails co-ordination**

Co-ordination

engage in a transaction find each other? Phrased in economic terminology, how is the **co-ordination** achieved within an economic system? Specialization leads to a need for co-ordination (Figure 1.3). Basically, we shall submit, there are two types of co-ordination: transactions may take place across markets or within organizations.[2] The next section will discuss this distinction further.

1.5 Markets and organizations

Consider the stock market. Each day on the major stock markets of the world millions of shares and bonds are exchanged. On the New York Stock Exchange alone, as many as 1 million transactions may be carried out on an average trading day, involving more than 100 million shares with a total value of more than $5 billion. (Box 1.3 shows an extract from a New York Stock Exchange listing.) Buyers and sellers are not only American but include private and institutional investors from all over the world. How do all these parties find each other to sort out the opportunities for transactions? How, for instance, does a Japanese buyer find out who (from the USA, Germany or Hong Kong) wants to sell the stocks in which he is interested? The answer is: he does not.

Price system

He does not, because the stock market comes close to that ideal type of market in which it is not necessary for buyers and sellers to have any kind of personal contact. The reason is that the **price system** is the co-ordinating device that takes care of allocation. Suppose you are a potential buyer or seller of IBM stock. All you have to do is inform yourself of the current price of IBM shares, make up your mind whether you want to transact at that price level and, if so, instruct your bank or broker to carry out the transaction. You will never know the party with whom you exchanged the stock. It is not necessary to know the other party. The price contains all the information you need to base your trans-

Sufficient statistic

action on: it is a '**sufficient statistic**' (Hayek, 1945).

No wonder economists marvel at the functioning of these types of market. Through the interlinked system of stock exchanges in the world all potential buyers and sellers of our example IBM stock are connected with each other. What is more, if globally there are more potential buyers than sellers, the price goes up; some buyers are discouraged at that price level and some new sellers are interested in entering the market. This goes on until demand and supply of

Box 1.3 ■ New York Stock Exchange prices

Thursday, July 26, 2001
4:00 P.M. New York Time

52 week High	52 week Low	Stock	Div.	Yld %	PE	Vols. 100s	Hi	Lo	Close	Net Chg.

-A-A-A-

High	Low	Stock	Div.	%	PE	100s	Hi	Lo	Close	Net Chg.
17.10	9.75	AAR	.34	2.2	22	504	15.50	15.00	15.50	+ 0.05
38.20	23.94	ABM Indus	.66	1.8	19	588	36.47	35.80	35.90	– 0.53
26.50	16.81	ABN Am ADR	.81e	4.7	...	648	17.25	16.95	17.25	+ 0.01
25.60	21.69	ABN Am pfA	1.88	7.5	...	395	25.28	25.16	25.17	+ 0.01
25.65	20.50	ABN Am pfB	1.78	7.2	...	431	24.74	24.65	24.70	+ 0.04
43.94	31.59 ♣	ACE Ltd	.60f	1.8	16	11622	33.82	33.00	33.42	+ 0.31
39.55	18.75	ACLN Ltd			11	422	35.80	35.10	35.71	+ 0.74
8.89	7.13	ACM GvtFd	.84	9.7	...	2047	8.70	8.57	8.70	+ 0.06
9.38	6.19	ACM MgdDlr	1.02	12.7	...	271	8.10	8.01	8.04	– 0.01
6.56	4.35	ACM MgdInco	.51	11.0	...	317	4.69	4.62	4.64	+ 0.02
72.81	33.60 ♣	AES Cp			28	49948	35.40	33.63	34.10	– 0.85
37.47	23.38	AFLAC	.20f	.7	24	58014	29.79	28.85	29.48	+ 1.28
13.19	7.90	AGCO Cp	.04	.4	71	1626	9.94	9.30	9.94	+ 0.29
25.45	24.85	AGL Cap TruPs	.47p		...	208	25.40	25.20	25.38	+ 0.03
24.25	17.13	AGL Res	1.08	4.6	12	1266	23.70	22.90	23.68	+ 0.88
46.75	15.00	AIPC			28	635	42.75	41.03	42.75	+ 1.80
15.00	7.50 ♣	AK Steel	.25	2.1	29	1359	12.37	11.82	12.10	– 0.09
26.06	22.50 ♣	AMB Prop	1.58	6.2	17	1378	25.80	25.40	25.69	+ 0.34
7.81	2.88	AMCOL	.06f	1.0	38	973	6.10	5.98	6.09	+ 0.11
25.31	20.13 ♣	AMLI Resdntl	1.88	7.9	9	316	23.77	23.65	23.75	– 0.02
43.94	27.63	AMR	stk	...	dd	5425	35.91	35.17	35.80	+ 0.25
25.69	22.44	ANZ pf	2.00	7.9	...	360	25.25	25.14	25.25	+ 0.10
25.75	22.75	ANZ ll pf	2.02	8.0	...	318	25.40	25.25	25.30	– 0.01
62.27	31.50	AOL Time			dd	125094	45.08	42.93	44.91	+ 1.16
49.88	5.00 ♣	APW			...	1139	8.65	8.50	8.50	– 0.15
22.90	14.06 ♣	ASA	.60	3.4	...	712	18.29	17.60	17.74	– 0.61
29.56	15.29	AT&T Wrls			...	116891	17.79	17.11	17.56	+ 0.24
25.52	12.41	AT&T	.15	.7	dd	81929	20.60	20.01	20.52	+ 0.37
31.75	15.13	AVX Cp	.15l	.7	8	1935	21.97	20.65	21.80	+ 1.05
39.88	24.58	AXA ADS	.50e	1.8	...	2529	27.85	27.00	27.76	+ 0.20
18.95	10.51	ABB ADS			...	484	10.55	10.22	10.48	– 0.52
25.09	20.63	AbbeyNtl	1.75	7.2	...	392	24.52	24.35	24.44	– 0.09
25.25	21.75	AbbeyNtl 7 1/4%	1.81	7.3	...	547	24.87	24.76	24.79	+ 0.02
56.25	39.31	AbbottLab	.84	1.6	47	20817	51.85	51.01	51.85	+ 0.35
47.50	14.06	Abercrombie A			25	20062	42.75	39.79	40.50	– 0.90
11.44	7.00	Abitibi g	.40g		...	1799	7.85	7.70	7.71	– 0.06
15.29	14.55	Accenture			...	61716	14.99	14.50	14.50	– 0.45
6.94	3.70 ♣	Acceptns			dd	1100	5.99	5.85	5.89	+ 0.14
15.06	7.88	AckrlyGp	.02	.2	dd	561	13.74	13.10	13.22	+ 0.02
27.04	16.01 ♣	AdamsExp	1.85e	10.7	...	957	17.23	16.90	17.23	+ 0.07
21.48	10.89	Adecco			...	4178	11.86	11.60	11.77	+ 0.62
44.56	15.40	Administaff			46	861	23.40	22.80	22.99	+ 0.04
20.95	9.63 ♣	AdvMktg	.03	.2	17	838	17.86	16.75	17.80	– 0.19
39.34	13.56 ♣	AdvMicro			8	74232	17.51	16.13	17.45	+ 1.15
48.00	30.05	Advo			16	1767	40.15	38.75	39.80	+ 1.05
43.00	25.92 ♣	AEGON	.68e	2.6	19	1902	26.85	26.15	26.66	– 0.15
42.89	23.01	Aetna			dd	7019	26.15	25.40	26.13	+ 0.13
25.85	25.08	Aetna8.5%			...	1153	25.91	25.65	25.80	+ 0.15
83.12	41.25	AffilCmptr A			35	3991	81.95	79.45	81.81	+ 1.52
65.00	41.20	AffilMangr			26	2795	63.70	60.50	62.91	+ 4.41
9.50	4.10	AgereSys A			...	69636	5.75	5.05	5.55	+ 0.20
68.00	25.00	AgilentTch			18	18174	29.55	27.65	29.21	+ 1.37
9.63	4.88 ♣	AgnicoEgl	.02	.2	dd	1890	8.27	8.13	8.25	+ 0.05
14.75	8.19	Agrium	.11	1.0	15	1026	10.83	10.61	10.75	+ 0.02
33.49	26.31	Ahold	.56e	1.8	...	699	30.37	30.02	30.36	– 0.31
7.59	3.06	AirNetSys			11	274	7.65	7.35	7.54	+ 0.02
49.00	30.50	AirProduct	.80f	1.9	16	12633	42.14	41.02	41.54	– 0.54
16.50	8.25	AirborneInc	.16	1.3	dd	1952	12.12	11.55	12.11	+ 0.31
12.85	5.06	Airgas			28	1947	12.20	11.50	12.20	+ 0.38
35.25	19.50	AlaskaAir			dd	967	31.00	30.48	30.87	+ 0.07
23.00	9.63 ♣	AlbanyInt	.j		15	2335	19.49	17.57	19.49	+ 1.62
26.13	18.50	Albemarle	.52	2.5	13	901	20.98	20.26	20.98	+ 0.32
50.90	34.00 ♣	AlbEngy g	.60fg		...	1266	39.41	38.29	39.14	+ 0.32
44.70	27.38	AlbertoCl	.33	.8	24	997	43.85	43.42	43.70	+ 0.02
37.40	23.50	AlbertoCl A	.33	.9	20	515	36.11	35.60	35.97	– 0.03
34.05	20.06	Albertsons	.76	2.4	17	11065	32.34	31.86	32.12	– 0.16
48.75	28.19 ♣	Alcan	.60g	1.6	20	12567	37.35	35.84	37.19	+ 0.16
86.25	14.75	Alcatel ADS	.43e	2.7	...	20269	15.93	15.15	15.82	+ 0.82
45.71	23.13	Alcoa	.60	1.5	23	26631	39.56	38.11	39.54	+ 0.48
55.09	30.88	AlghnyEngy	1.72	3.9	15	8784	44.00	42.65	43.85	+ 1.35
22.63	12.50	AlghnyTch	.80	4.4	24	1987	18.42	18.00	18.17	+ 0.12
24.00	10.80	AllenTele			31	359	13.97	13.27	13.97	+ 0.51
101.13	59.00 ♣	Allergan	.36	.5	44	36029	76.50	70.15	74.55	+ 5.55
26.13	20.13 ♣	ALLETE	1.07	4.6	13	1494	23.50	22.86	23.37	+ 0.42
59.35	37.40	AllncCapMgt	3.05e	6.1	17	1670	50.22	47.40	50.15	+ 2.18
17.40	12.50	AllianceData			...	6531	13.90	13.50	13.75	+ 0.25
16.80	9.00	AllncFrstPdt			12	637	15.20	15.02	15.05	– 0.17
11.00	8.00	AllncWrld ll	1.38	13.8	...	1959	10.04	9.86	9.99	+ 0.04
33.20	26.19	AlliantEngy	2.00	6.9	6	1801	29.10	28.60	29.00	+ 0.46
102.00	46.67	AlliantTech			20	585	98.10	96.48	97.57	+ 0.78
25.72	17.75	AldCap	2.04f	8.7	11	2593	23.50	22.91	23.49	+ 0.49
25.81	15.75	AldIrishBk	.71e	3.2	...	272	22.06	21.70	21.93	– 0.46
19.90	7.50	AlliedWaste			cc	5501	18.37	17.55	18.20	+ 0.19

Source: The Wall Street Journal Europe, 26 July 2001

Explanatory notes

Boldfaced quotations highlight those issues whose price changed by 5% or more if their previous closing price was $2 or higher.

Underlined quotations are those stocks with large changes in volume, per exchange, compared with the issue's average trading volume. The calculation includes common stocks of $5 a share or more with an average volume over 65 trading days of at least 5,000 shares. The underlined quotations are for the 40 largest volume percentage leaders on the NYSE and the Nasdaq National Market. It includes the 20 largest volume percentage gainers on the Amex.

The 52-week high and low columns show the highest and lowest price of the issue during the preceding 52 weeks plus the current week, but not the latest trading day. These ranges are adjusted to reflect stock payouts of 1% or more, and cash dividends or other distributions of 10% or more.

Dividend rates, unless noted, are annual disbursements based on the last quarterly, semiannual, or annual declaration. Special or extra dividends, special situations or payments not designated as regular are identified by footnotes.

Yield is defined as the dividends paid by a company on its securities, expressed as a percentage of price.

The P/E ratio is determined by dividing the closing market price by the company's primary per-share earnings for the most recent four quarters. Charges and other adjustments usually are excluded when they qualify as extraordinary items under generally accepted accounting rules.

Sales figures are the unofficial daily total of shares traded, quoted in hundreds (two zeros omitted).

stock is in equilibrium. At that point we can say that an optimal allocation of that stock has been achieved, since the buyers who are most interested in that stock have been satisfied (while the sellers who were least interested have sold). This optimal allocation obtains without any personal contacts between the transacting parties.

There are a number of such markets. Markets for raw materials often approximate ideal markets. Let us borrow an example from Hayek (1945) to emphasize how efficiently such markets operate:

> Assume that somewhere in the world a new opportunity for the use of some raw material, say tin, has arisen, or that one of the sources of the supply of tin has been eliminated. It does not matter for our purpose – and it is very significant that it does not matter – which of these two causes has made tin more scarce. All that the users of tin need to know is that some of the tin they used to consume is now more profitably employed elsewhere, and that in consequence they must economize tin. There is no need for the great majority of them even to know where the more urgent need has arisen, or in favor of what other needs they ought to husband the supply. If only some of them know directly of the new demand, and switch resources over to it, and if the people aware of the new gap thus created in turn fill it from still other sources, the effect will rapidly spread throughout the whole economic system and influence not only all the uses of tin, but also those of its substitutes and the substitutes of these substitutes, the supply of all the things made of tin, and their substitutes, and so on; and all this without the great majority of those instrumental in bringing about these substitutions knowing anything at all about the original cause of these changes.

Again, the adjustment of the price levels of tin and its substitutes is sufficient for a worldwide communication of all the necessary information to all relevant parties. As if led by the famous 'invisible hand' of Adam Smith, the individual decisions made by these parties will lead to new aggregate equilibrium levels of supply and demand of tin.

Assuming you are now convinced of the efficiency properties of ideal markets, we may proceed to ask, why is not all exchange executed across markets? In fact, this is a rather old question. It was raised most effectively by Coase in 1937, who put it this way:

> If a workman moves from department Y to department X, he does not go because of a change in relative prices, but because he is ordered to do so . . . The example given above is typical of a large sphere in our modern economic system . . . But in view of the fact that it is usually argued that co-ordination will be done by the price mechanism, why is such organization necessary?

Coase went on to provide an answer along the following lines. Contrary to the standard assumptions for ideal markets, Coase maintained that usually there is a *cost* to using the price system. First of all, there is usually a cost (if only in time) to finding out what the relevant prices are. Next, for important transactions a *contract* is usually drawn up to provide the basis for a market transaction. For instance, on the labour market, labour contracts are necessary to specify the conditions under which most exchange takes place. It is costly to draw up these contracts. Finally, there may be conditions under which it is hardly possible (or extremely costly) to reach a contractual agreement that may serve as a basis for market exchange.[3] In those cases, too, *organization* may provide an alternative.

Therefore, Coase posited markets and organizations as alternatives for the execution of transactions. On markets, the price system is the co-ordinating device. Within organizations, the price system is replaced by authority as a co-ordinating mechanism.[4] The question remains as to the circumstances under which the market will be employed for exchange transactions and the conditions under which organizations will be preferred. Coase's answer was that this is determined by the relative cost of transacting under these two alternatives. Transactions will typically be executed at the lowest cost. As a consequence, transactions will shift between markets and organizations as a function of the *transaction costs* under these two alternatives. This answer was taken up much later by Williamson (1975) to establish 'transaction cost economics', as we shall see in Chapter 8. Here we conclude by noting that Coase's analysis allowed standard economic reasoning to be employed in analyzing both the nature and the size of the firm:

> When we are considering how large a firm will be, the principle of marginalism works smoothly. The question always is, will it pay to bring an extra exchange transaction under the organizing authority? At the margin the cost of organizing within the firm will be equal either to the cost of organizing in another firm or to the costs involved in leaving the transaction to be 'organized' by the price mechanism.

We adopt Coase's original distinction between markets and organizations as two ideal types of co-ordination for exchange transactions. In the next section we argue that markets and organizations differ most essentially in the way that information is communicated between the transacting parties. The argument developed above entails that an **ideal market** is characterized by the fact that prices act as 'sufficient statistics' for individual decision-making. If we adopt this characterization, **ideal organizations** can be characterized as all those forms of co-ordination of transactions that do *not* use prices to communicate information between the transacting parties. In fact, we argue in Chapter 3 that most transactions in the real world are governed by hybrid forms of co-ordination. Most markets are to some extent 'organized'. Most organizations do use prices (like transfer prices) to communicate information within the organization. As a summary of the argument so far, we may present the conceptual framework in its present stage of development (Figure 1.4).

Ideal market

Ideal organizations

1.6 Information

We now arrive at the final step in the development of our conceptual framework. We have seen that the division of labour, leading to economies of specialization, necessitates the co-ordination of transactions. We have seen that

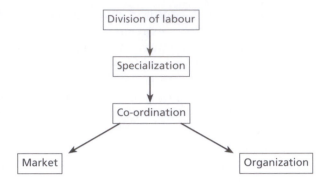

Figure 1.4 **There are two types of ideal co-ordination: market and organization**

there are two ideal types of co-ordination: market and organization. Finally, we shall argue that the actual (mix of) co-ordination mechanism(s) that we will observe in any situation will depend mainly on the information requirements that are inherent in that situation. Thus we present *information* as the final concept in our framework (Figure 1.5). We introduce this concept below and elaborate on its significance in Chapter 4.

Recall that ideal markets are characterized by the operation of prices as sufficient statistics: that is to say the price contains all the information needed for the co-ordination of transactions. The price mechanism is therefore a perfect channel of information to all parties potentially interested in transacting. In situations where the price mechanism is applicable as a co-ordination device it is, therefore, hard to beat its efficiency properties. However, we have also argued that in many situations the price mechanism is complemented or substituted by organizational co-ordination mechanisms. There are many situations in which the price cannot absorb all the information necessary to enable the execution of transactions. When Volkswagen buys ignition systems for the Audi A6 it will probably use a long-term contract containing many details with respect to quality and quantities with one or a few suppliers. In such a situa-

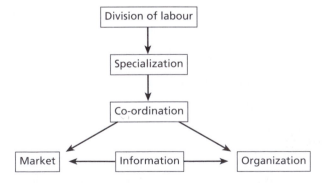

Figure 1.5 **The market/organization mix depends on the particular information requirements of the situation**

Box 1.4 ■ Organizations and the Internet

We argue in this book that organizations arise as solutions to information problems. A similar line of reasoning was followed recently by *The Economist* in analyzing the effects that the rise of the Internet and other new communication technologies may have on the shape of firms:

A prime reason why economic activity is organized within firms rather than in open markets is the cost of communication. The costlier it is to process and transmit information, the more it makes sense to do things in firms; the cheaper communication becomes, the more efficient (relatively) markets will be. Because the Internet and other inventions have cut the cost of communication so much, firms ought to be able to do less in-house and to outsource more. In 1999, General Motors, a byword for vertical integration, spun off Delphi Automotive Systems, one of its supply divisions, for instance.

In Chapter 9 we shall discuss vertical integration and show that more factors are involved in the decision of General Motors than only the cost of communication. However, the basic reasoning of *The Economist* is sound, and well in line with the approach taken in this book:

■ markets and organizations represent alternative ways to co-ordinate transactions,
■ and information will determine their relative efficiency.

Source: 'Electronic glue', *The Economist,* 2 June 2001

tion, where Volkswagen buys ignition systems rather than making ignition systems itself, we still have market transactions. But we cannot say that price is a sufficient statistic. Rather we have a situation in which the price mechanism (which is still important; Volkswagen will try to buy from the cheapest source) is supplemented by a form of planning not unlike the planning used within organizations.

There are also many situations in which the price mechanism is totally incapable of performing its co-ordination function. In Chapter 4 we delve into the reasons for this. We show that there are fundamental information problems that cannot be resolved by the price system. A number of these problems can, however, be dealt with through organizational co-ordination. Thus, from the perspective developed in this book, *organizations arise as solutions to information problems.*[5] Organizations are more suited to deal with certain information problems than are markets.

As Figure 1.5 indicates, the market/organization mix depends on the particular information requirements of the situation. Information and communication costs determine to a large extent the relative efficiency of the two broad co-ordination mechanisms (markets and organizations). This is also illustrated in Box 1.4.

1.7 Historical perspective

One may wonder why the economic approaches to organizations have been only fairly recently developed. Why did it take so long, for instance, to pick up the fundamental question raised by Coase in 1937: why do we observe so many organizations if markets are so efficient? The main reasons, as we see them, are summarized in the following two statements:

- Until recently, most (but not all) economists focused their attention on how the market achieves co-ordination *between organizations* (and individuals).
- Most (but not all) organization theorists studied co-ordination *within organizations*.

We briefly illustrate these statements below.

While the older economic writers, such as Adam Smith and Alfred Marshall, still had a lot to say about the functioning of organizations, over time economists' fascination with the functioning of markets led them to study market co-ordination almost exclusively. The mainstream economists of the twentieth century elaborated a theory of markets. That theory is now highly developed. Meanwhile, however, there were some exceptional economists, such as Ronald Coase, who recognized that an important and growing share of the economic transactions within society were executed not across markets but within organizations. It was only fairly recently that more economists became interested in the economic processes and the resulting allocation within organizations, such as business firms. One of the reasons was that new theoretical approaches were developed that were more satisfactory than the older ones. It is the purpose of this book to introduce these approaches.

Organization theory, on the other hand, was interested primarily in what goes on within organizations. The first writers on organization focused on 'scientific management': that is, discovering principles of work organization that would enhance productivity. Many of these early writers had a technical or engineering background and had management experience to draw upon. Later on, social and psychological considerations were introduced by writers in the 'human relations' school. Many of the early contributions to the field of organization studies attempted to formulate the 'one best way to organize'. Only since the 1950s and 1960s has it been recognized that the best way to organize is dependent upon the particular situation the organization is in. The 'contingency theories' of organization were developed. These theories emphasized the technological and environmental factors that were important in shaping the organization. Still later, since the 1970s, organization studies have become even more multi-disciplinary. Some would maintain that the subject has become increasingly fragmented. Diverse perspectives and approaches coexist. Contributions are made from the disciplines of sociology, psychology, political science, management, anthropology, etc. Perhaps it is inevitable that such a multifaceted phenomenon as organizations is studied from many different angles and backgrounds.[6]

To these various contributions an economic perspective has been added since the 1970s. Initially, this occurred because economists became interested in organizations and exported their newly developed theories into the field of organization studies. As such, the economic perspective simply came to coexist alongside the other disciplinary perspectives on organizations. Organization theorists, however, became interested in those theories too. One reason for their interest was that some of the economic approaches incorporated concepts that had been borrowed by economists from earlier work within organization theory.

Transaction cost economics, for example, makes extensive use of the concept of *bounded rationality*, developed in organization theory. Through such common use of concepts the integration of economic theories within organization studies is facilitated.[7] Another reason for the growing interest in economic perspectives on organizations is that these allow the analysis of organizational problems different from those studied in the other disciplines. As mentioned in section 1.1, these problems always deal with the economic aspect of organizations: how to allocate the scarce organizational resources efficiently.

We conclude this section with a final introductory observation: that there is currently a *family* of economic approaches to organizations. The family is bound together by their focus on the economic aspect of organizations. This identifies them as *economic* theories of organization. Within this common family resemblance, however, the various theories to be introduced differ in many respects. They differ, for instance, in the problems identified and in their basic modes of analysis, as will become clear as they are introduced. In the following chapters, therefore, the differences within the family may stand out more clearly than the similarities. In the final chapter we return to this observation and discuss the question of how tightly knit the family currently is, and what the prospects are for their future development.

1.8 Summary: the conceptual framework of this book

This chapter introduces the basic conceptual framework we use to explain the fundamental economic approach to organizations (Figure 1.1). The framework takes the division of labour in society as its starting point. The division of labour leads to specialization, which allows efficiency gains. However, with increasing specialization there is a corresponding need for co-ordination. Co-ordination is necessary to arrange the vast network of exchange between specialized economic actors. This is illustrated in a modern, international context in Box 1.5.

We have argued that there are two ideal types of co-ordination of exchange transactions: markets and organizations. Markets use the price system as the co-ordinating device. Organizations use non-price systems, such as authority. In practice, both ideal types of co-ordination are usually mixed. We have argued that the actual mix found in any situation will depend on the information requirements of that situation. Markets and organizations are different solutions to information problems that are inherent in (economic) transactions. From an economic perspective, they have different efficiency properties. They are efficient co-ordination mechanisms for different sets of transactions, dependent upon the information requirements involved. This basic perspective is further elaborated and illustrated in this book.

1.9 Outline of the book

This first chapter has introduced some basic concepts in a preliminary way. These concepts will be elaborated in Chapters 2 to 10. Equipped with this

Box 1.5 ■ Globalization, specialization and co-ordination: the case of Li & Fung

In this chapter we have used Adam Smith's original example of the pin factory as an illustration of the concepts of division of labour, specialization and co-ordination. However, these forces play not only at the local level of a factory, but also at the global level. This is shown by the case of Li & Fung, a Chinese firm that was called 'a surprising world leader in supply-chain management' by *The Economist*:

Li & Fung used to introduce Western retailers of clothes, toys and the like to the sweatshops of China. As such, it was no different from countless Chinese firms. . . But when Victor and William Fung, the brothers who today run the family business, sat down to think about globalization and what it means for Asia, they came up with a winning new strategy for their company.

To them, globalization meant above all *specialization*, and specialization brings complexity. If supply chains of companies once consisted of five links, they might soon have dozens, or even hundreds, they surmised. 'Somebody's got to pick up the pieces and bring them back together' says William Fung, the younger brother – which is what Li & Fung is now doing, to all appearances better than its rivals in the West.

It works like this. Say, a European clothes retailer wants to order a few thousand garments. The optimal *division of labour* might be for South Korea to make the yarn, Taiwan to weave and dye it, and a Japanese-owned factory in Guangdong Province to make the zippers. Since China's textiles quota has already been used up under some country's import rules, Thailand may be the best place to do the sewing. However, no single factory can handle such bulk, so five different suppliers must share the order. The shipping and letters of credit must be seamless, and the quality assured.

Co-ordinating all this is the challenge of globalization. . . And this requires knowledge. Village women with sewing-machines in Bangladesh are not on the Internet. Finding the best suppliers at any given time, therefore, takes enormous research – so much, indeed, that companies are increasingly deciding that it no longer pays to do it in-house. Instead, they outsource the knowledge gathering to Li & Fung, which has an army of 3,600 staff roaming 37 countries ('a machete in one hand, a laptop in the other', as Victor Fung likes to caricature them) for the purpose.

In this sense, Li & Fung is itself a product of *specialization*. A company that focuses entirely on optimizing supply chains for other companies is a recent phenomenon.

Source: The Economist, 2 June 2001

further knowledge, we return to the common perspective in the final chapter. There we can discuss it more thoroughly and contrast various ways of highlighting the similarities and the differences in the economic approaches to organizations.

In Chapters 2–4, the general ideas introduced so far are explored in more depth. Chapter 2 focuses on markets. Standard microeconomic theory is used to explain how co-ordination is achieved in an (ideal) market. This theory illustrates the role of the price mechanism in equating demand and supply for goods and services. The chapter serves two purposes: first, to introduce some basic economic concepts and modes of analysis, and secondly to serve as a benchmark against which other economic approaches can be measured. If you are already familiar with standard microeconomics, you can either glance quickly through Chapter 2 or skip it entirely.

To conclude this introductory chapter, we borrow from the economist A.C. Pigou the following quotation: 'When a man sets out upon any course of inquiry, the object of his search may be either light or fruit – either knowledge for its own sake or knowledge for the sake of good things to which it leads.'[8] Upon your course of inquiry through this book, we wish you occasional light and fruit, as well as some fun along the way.

Questions

1 Suppose you are a Saudi prince and you are studying economics at Oxford University in the UK. Your family sends you a very large monthly allowance to cover tuition and other expenses. In fact this allowance is more than ten times the average allowance of the other students. Do you think you would still have an economic problem? Why?

2 Suppose you are an American student and you are about to obtain your MBA and start looking for a job. An economist would say that you are about to enter the job market. Compare this market with the tin market that is described in the text. Is the job market for MBAs also an example of an ideal market? Is price a sufficient statistic for this market? Discuss the latter question from the point of view both of employers and of persons seeking employment.

3 What might be the economic aspect of (partner matching on) the 'marriage market'?

4 Box 1.5 describes the success of a company named Li & Fung. What exactly is Li & Fung's business? Who are Li & Fung's customers? After having read Chapter 1 including Box 1.5, what do you think is the main point that the case brings forward?

5 In Box 1.4 it is argued that the rise of the Internet has cut the cost of communication so much that firms will be inclined to outsource more than before. Do you think this is true? Do you see an implicit assumption, made by the journalists of *The Economist*, that is highly relevant but which is not mentioned in Box 1.4? Discuss.

Suggested further reading

Barney, J.B. and W.G. Ouchi (eds) (1986), *Organizational Economics*, San Francisco: Jossey Bass.

FitzRoy, F.R., Z.J. Acs and D.A. Gerlowski (1998), *Management and Economics of Organization*, Harlow: Prentice Hall.

Milgrom, P. and J. Roberts (1992), *Economics, Organization and Management*, Englewood Cliffs, NJ: Prentice Hall.

Putterman, L. (ed.) (1986), *The Economic Nature of the Firm: A Reader*, Cambridge: Cambridge University Press.

Notes

1. We use he and she intermittently in this book.
2. These two types of co-ordination should be regarded as ideal types in the Weberian sense. That is to say, they are theoretical notions that are hardly observable in the real world in any 'pure' form. This is discussed further in Section 1.5.
3. This is further elaborated in Chapter 8.
4. As we argue in Chapter 3, authority (or direct supervision) is only one of several co-ordinating mechanisms employed within organizations.
5. We consider it fruitless to discuss the question whether 'in the beginning there were markets' (as Williamson has posited as an analytical device) or whether organizations 'came first' (as an historical analysis would probably reveal). We are concerned here with the explanation of present-day phenomena.
6. See, for example, Morgan (1997) or Clegg *et al.* (1996).
7. In this book we use the terms 'economic theories of organization' and 'economic approaches to organizations'. Examples of economic theories of organization are the behavioural theory of the firm, agency theory and transaction cost economics (Chapters 6, 7 and 8 respectively). 'Economic approaches to organizations' is a broader term encompassing also the economic contributions to strategic management that are described in Chapter 9.
8. Pigou (1920), p.3.

2 Markets

2.1 Introduction

Standard microeconomic theory focuses on how economic decisions are co-ordinated by the market mechanism. Economic decisions have to be made both by consumers and by producers. Consumers can choose between a large number of goods. For each good they must decide how much they are going to consume. Producers must decide how much they are going to produce and how they are going to produce. Consumers and producers meet each other on the market. Co-ordination between the total quantity demanded by consumers and the total quantity supplied by producers is achieved through interaction on the market. Thus the quantity of tomatoes that is to be shipped to London on a certain day is determined not by a planning authority but by '**the process of market interaction**' (see Box 2.1). This process of market interaction is explained in section 2.2. In competitive markets, prices are determined by the process of market interaction, not by individual buyers or sellers.

The process of market interaction

How does an individual consumer choose between different goods when the prices of those goods are given? That is the central question of the theory of demand that we discuss in section 2.3.

How does an individual producer decide how much he is going to produce? And how does he decide how he is going to produce that quantity? Those are the central questions of the theory of production that we discuss in section 2.4.

Having thus outlined the main characteristics of standard microeconomic theory, section 2.5 concludes this chapter with a number of comments on the theory.

Box 2.1 ■ The London vegetable market

In rich countries, markets are too familiar to attract attention. Yet a certain awe is appropriate. When Soviet planners visited a vegetable market in London during the early days of *perestroika*, they were impressed to find no queues, shortages, or mountains of spoiled and unwanted vegetables. They took their hosts aside and said: 'We understand, you have to say it's all done by supply and demand. But can't you tell us what's really going on? Where are your planners, and what are their methods?'

Source: The Economist, 17 February 1996

2.2 Market interaction: analysis of demand and supply

Law of demand

Demand curve

Law of supply

Supply curve

The total demand for a certain good depends on the price for that good. Take for example TV sets. When the price of a TV set is €500, total demand in the European Union (EU) market may be 10 million sets annually. If the price of TV sets goes down (and nothing else changes), some families that now have only one set may decide to buy a second set. Other families may decide to replace their existing set by a new one sooner. Hence we would expect total demand to go up if the price goes down. This is the **law of demand**. The relation between price and quantity demanded is shown in Figure 2.1. The **demand curve** D in Figure 2.1 is presented as a straight line only for simplicity: there is no reason to expect a linear relationship between price and quantity demanded. From the demand curve we can read, for every price, the quantity demanded. For a price of €500, the quantity demanded is 10 million sets.

Television sets are supplied to the market by TV manufacturers. The total quantity supplied also depends on the price. If prices go up (and everything else remains the same), then TV manufacturers will find it more profitable to make TV sets and they will supply more sets in order to take advantage of increased profit opportunities. Therefore we expect supply to go up as the price goes up. This is the **law of supply**. The **supply curve** S in Figure 2.2 depicts the relationship between price and quantity supplied. For example, if the price is €500, all manufacturers will together produce 24 million sets. The supply curve need not be a straight line as it is shown in the figure.

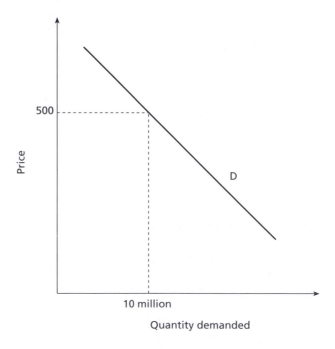

Figure 2.1 **Demand for TV sets within the EU**

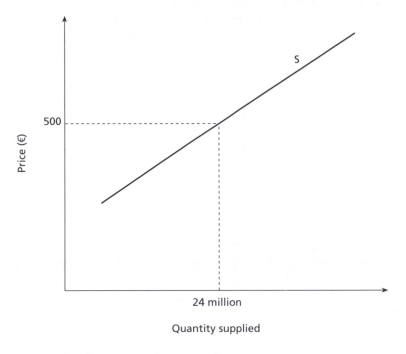

Figure 2.2 **Supply of TV sets to the EU market**

Market equilibrium

Market equilibrium occurs where the demand curve D and the supply curve S intersect. The equilibrium price is €400 per set (see Figure 2.3). At that price, total supply is 14 million sets, while total demand is also 14 million sets. At the equilibrium price of €400 per set, all sets manufactured by producers are sold to consumers. Moreover, all consumers who want to buy at €400 per set actually buy a set.

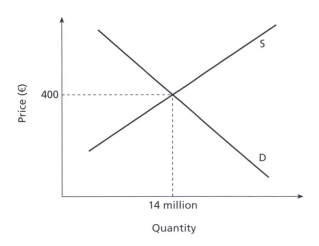

Figure 2.3 **Supply and demand**

Suppose there is an increase in the demand for TV sets in the EU. This may occur as a result of population growth or because of an increase in per capita income. It will result in a new market equilibrium. Box 2.2 illustrates how an increase in the demand for tin leads to an increase in price and an increase in the quantity supplied.

Box 2.2 ■ An increase in the demand for tin

In Chapter 1 we quoted Hayek (1945): 'Assume that somewhere in the world a new opportunity for the use of some raw material, say tin, has arisen. . .'. A new opportunity for the use of tin means an increase in the demand for tin, which will lead to higher prices. This in turn will encourage users of tin to economize on the use of tin. In terms of the analysis presented in section 2.2 an increase in the demand for tin is simply a shift in the demand curve. This is illustrated in Figure 2.4. The fact that a new opportunity for the use of tin is discovered means that the demand curve shifts from D_1 to D_2. As a result, the price of an ounce of tin increases from p_1 to p_2 and quantity supplied (and used) increases from q_1 to q_2.

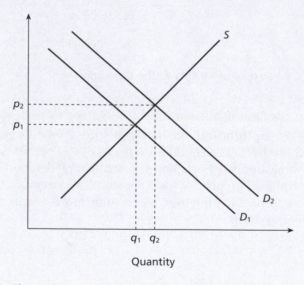

Figure 2.4 **An increase in the demand for tin**

2.3 The theory of demand

How does an individual consumer choose between the goods he or she can buy? Suppose a consumer is confronted with several different baskets of goods. Standard microeconomic theory assumes that each person can rank these baskets in the order that reflects his preferences. These preference rankings are

Transitive

assumed to be **transitive**. This means that if a person prefers basket A to basket B and prefers basket B to basket C, then he also prefers basket A to basket C. Finally, it is assumed that each person prefers more of a certain good to less of it.

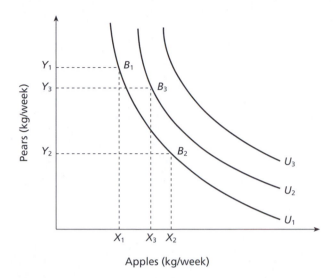

Figure 2.5 Indifference curves

Indifference curves

With these assumptions about consumers' preferences it is possible to represent the preferences of a certain consumer by a set of **indifference curves**. Figure 2.5 gives the indifference curves for a consumer who can choose among baskets containing different quantities of apples and pears.

The consumer whose preferences are depicted in Figure 2.5 is indifferent between baskets B_1 and B_2. Basket B_1 means having X_1 kilograms of apples per week and Y_1 kilograms of pears per week; basket B_2 means having X_2 kilograms of apples and Y_2 kilograms of pears per week. Points B_1 and B_2 lie on curve U_1. A curve like U_1 is called an indifference curve: this consumer is indifferent between the baskets represented by points on U_1. He is not indifferent between baskets B_1 and B_3: on the contrary, he prefers B_3 over B_1. This is represented in Figure 2.5 by the fact that B_3 lies on an indifference curve that is farther from the origin. This consumer prefers all baskets represented by points on indifference curve U_2 to all points on indifference curve U_1.

Utility

The satisfaction that consumers derive from having goods is usually called **utility** by economists. Instead of saying that a consumer is indifferent between baskets B_1 and B_2, we can say that this consumer derives the same utility from both basket B_1 and basket B_2. Thus an indifference curve is a curve representing points with the same level of utility. Curve U_2 represents all points that give our consumer a level of utility equal to U_2, whereas curve U_1 indicates all points that give him a level of utility U_1. It is not possible to measure utility. Standard microeconomic theory assumes only that consumers can rank different baskets of goods. Therefore the assumption is that our consumer can indicate that he prefers basket B_3 to basket B_1, not that he can indicate how great the difference in utility is between those two baskets.

The amounts of apples and pears that our consumer will buy depend not only on his preferences as given by his set of indifference curves but also on his

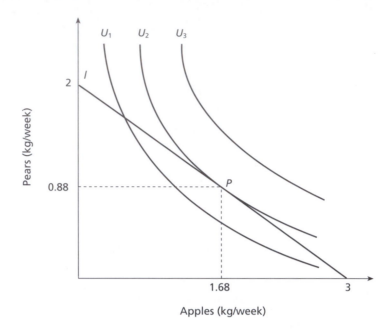

Figure 2.6 **A model of consumer choice: a budget line and a set of indifference curves**

budget. Suppose that this consumer has €3.00 per week available for buying fresh fruit and that apples are €1.00/kg and pears €1.50/kg (for simplicity assume that it is possible to buy every quantity you want, such as 0.683 kg). The quantities of apples and pears that our consumer can buy with this budget are given by line *l* in Figure 2.6. Line *l* is called the **budget line**. We assume that every consumer wants to maximize his level of utility, so he will choose the point on line *l* that gives him the highest possible level of utility. This is point *P* on line *l*, where line *l* is tangential to indifference curve U_2. Point *P* represents a basket of 1.68 kg of apples and 0.88 kg of pears. Looking at the set of indifference curves we see that some indifference curves (such as U_1) intersect with line *l*, while other indifference curves (such as U_3) do not. There is one, and only one, indifference curve that is tangential to the budget line: this is U_2. The point of tangency indicates the basket that the consumer will actually buy, given this budget constraint. This basket provides him with the highest attainable utility.

Budget line

2.4 The theory of production

How does a producer of a certain good decide *how much* she is going to produce? And how does she decide *how* she is going to produce that quantity? These are the two main questions of the theory of production in standard microeconomic theory. In order to answer these questions we need a description of the firm. In standard microeconomics the firm is described as an entity

Objective function

that maximizes an **objective function**. The objective function of a firm describes the goal(s) that the firm pursues (usually profit or the value of the firm on the stock market). The objective function can be maximized only within the constraints given to the firm by its production function. In this paragraph we shall first describe the concept of a production function, and then discuss how the firm, in trying to maximize profits, decides how much and how to produce.

2.4.1 The production function

Production function

A **production function** describes the relationship between any combination of inputs and the maximum output that a firm can produce with those inputs. As an example, consider a firm producing pencils. In order to make pencils the firm needs machines, labour and raw materials. Assume for the sake of simplicity that the firm needs only one kind of machine, only one kind of labour and only one kind of raw material. This assumption is not very realistic, but it has no influence at all on what follows. Standard microeconomic theory can easily handle several kinds of machine, several kinds of labour and several kinds of raw material – it just makes the mathematics a little bit more complicated.

Let K be the amount of capital, L the amount of labour and M the amount of raw materials the firm has at its disposal. K may be measured as the number of machines, L as the number of labour hours per period (number of employees times the number of hours worked per period) and M as the volume or weight of raw materials. Let Q be the maximum quantity of pencils that the firm can produce for a given combination of K, L and M. The production function is the relationship between Q and K, L, M and is expressed as

$$Q = Q(K, L, M)$$

The production function describes how much output can be produced with any combination of inputs. For given values of K and M, Q generally increases when L is increased. This implies that, for a factory with a given number of machines and a given amount of raw materials, output can be increased by hiring more employees or by working overtime. However, output cannot be increased indefinitely in this way: either the amount of raw materials available per period or the amount of capital goods will prevent a further increase in production by adding more and more labour.

To increase or decrease the inputs that are available for production takes time. It is useful to make a distinction between the *short run* and the *long run*. In the short run only some inputs can be varied. In the long run all inputs can be varied. In most cases it is fairly easy to vary the amount of raw materials that the firm buys per period. This means that M can be varied in the short run. To build a new factory usually takes more time, so it seems reasonable to assume that K can vary only in the long run. Labour may fall somewhere between, depending on how easily employees can be hired and fired or induced to work overtime. Whether or not it is possible to vary the amount of labour may also depend on the type of labour: perhaps it is easier to hire and fire unskilled workers at short notice than highly skilled workers.

The distinction between input factors that can be varied in both the short run and the long run and input factors that can be varied only in the long run is an important one. In fact we need only two kinds of input to develop the theory further: those inputs that can be varied in the short run as well as in the long run and those inputs that can vary only in the long run. It is customary to denote input factors that can be varied in the short run by L and input factors that can be varied only in the long run by K, so from now on L stands for all input factors that can vary both in the short run and in the long run, such as raw materials and perhaps certain kinds of labour, while K stands for all inputs that can vary only in the long run, such as capital goods and other kinds of labour. Despite this new interpretation of L and K we shall still refer to L as labour and to K as capital, so labour now means those inputs that can be varied in the short run as well as in the long run, while capital means those inputs that can be varied only in the long run.

The production function with two inputs is

$$Q = Q(K, L)$$

This production function is depicted in Figure 2.7.

The curve Q_1 in Figure 2.7 represents all possible combinations of K and L that the firm can choose from if it wants to produce quantity Q_1. The points on Q_1 thus represent combinations of K and L leading to the same volume of output. The curves Q_1, Q_2, Q_3 and Q_4 are called **isoquants**. In Figure 2.7 the four isoquants are such that $Q_4 > Q_3 > Q_2 > Q_1$.

Isoquants

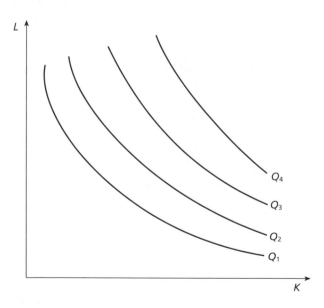

Figure 2.7 **An isoquant map as a graphical representation of a production function**

2.4.2   Profit maximization in competitive markets

Suppose we have a firm with a given production function. How does this firm decide how and how much to produce? In order to answer this question we need an assumption about the firm's objective function. In standard microeconomics it is usually assumed that the firm wants to maximize profits.

How can a firm with a given production function maximize profits? The answer depends on whether or not the firm has some freedom to determine the price of its products. In a competitive market – that is, a market with many sellers and buyers and with free entry and exit of firms – the firm cannot set its own prices. In competitive markets, prices are determined by the process of market interaction. The price resulting from this process is then given for each individual firm. In what follows we discuss only profit maximization in competitive markets.

We first need a definition of profit. *Profit* is defined as revenue minus total cost, or

$$\pi = pQ - KP_K - LP_1$$

where

π = profit
p = market price of the firm's product pQ = total revenue
Q = quantity produced (and sold)
K = amount of capital used
L = amount of labour used $KP_K + LP_1$ = total cost
P_K = price of one unit of capital
P_1 = price of one unit of labour

Here Q is a function of K and L (remember that profit can be maximized only within the constraint given by the firm's production function), $Q = Q(K, L)$.

We now have all that we need in order to discuss the two main questions of the theory of production: how much to produce and how to produce. How much to produce means choosing a value for Q. How to produce means choosing values for K and L. The two questions are not independent since $Q = Q(K, L)$. So the firm cannot choose Q, K and L independently: it can choose only two of those three variables independently. The third variable is then determined through $Q = Q(K, L)$. We shall assume that K and L are the two decision variables and that Q is then determined through $Q = Q(K, L)$.

In the *short run*, K is fixed, so the firm can choose only L. By choosing a value for L (with a fixed value for K), Q is also determined through $Q = Q(K, L)$. This is illustrated in Figure 2.8. Here K^* is the amount of capital that the firm has installed. In the short run it cannot add or scrap capital goods, so it can choose only values for K and L that lie on the vertical line l. If the firm chooses a value for L, say L_1, then it has also decided to produce quantity Q_1 (Q_1 is the isoquant through point (K^*, L_1)).

We can now formulate the problem of short-run profit maximization in mathematical terms. Total profit as a function of L is

$$\pi = pQ(K, L) - KP_K - LP_1$$

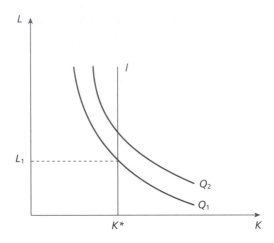

Figure 2.8 In the short run, K is fixed. By choosing a level of L, the firm also chooses a level Q

For a maximum, the first-order derivative with respect to L must equal zero, so we have:

$$p\frac{dQ}{dL} - P_1 = 0$$

or, alternatively:

$$\frac{dQ}{dL} = \frac{P_1}{p}$$

Solving this equation gives a value for L. Quantity Q is then determined through $Q = Q(K, L)$. This procedure can be illustrated by an example. Suppose the firm is producing pencils. The market price of pencils is 25 cents per item and the wage rate is \$20.00 per hour. So we have $p = 0.25$ and $P_1 = 20$.

Suppose further that the production function is such that its first-order derivative with respect to L is a decreasing function of L. In Figure 2.9 we have sketched dQ/dL, which is called the **marginal productivity of labour**, as a function of L. The economic interpretation of dQ/dL is the additional quantity of pencils that the firm can produce if it adds one hour of labour. Given this interpretation it is quite reasonable to assume that dQ/dL is a decreasing function of L. In our example, the firm will choose that value of L for which

| Marginal productivity of labour |

$$\frac{dQ}{dL} = \frac{P_1}{p} = \frac{20}{0.25} = 80$$

This is L_{opt} in Figure 2.9.

We can summarize this discussion on profit maximization in the short run as follows. In the short run the firm can choose only L. By choosing a value for L, Q is also determined. The firm will choose L such that the marginal productivity of labour (dQ/dL) is equal to P_1/p.

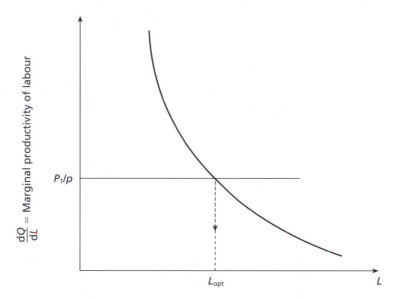

Figure 2.9 How the firm chooses _L_ in short-run profit maximization

In the *long run* both K and L can be varied. The problem of profit maximization now is a problem with two decision variables K and L. The problem now is to maximize the expression

$$\pi = pQ(K, L) - KP_K - LP_1$$

with respect to both K and L.

For a maximum both partial derivatives $\partial\pi/\partial K$ and $\partial\pi/\partial L$ must equal zero. This gives

$$p\partial Q/\partial K - P_K = 0$$

or, alternatively,

$$\frac{\partial Q}{\partial K} = \frac{P_K}{p}$$

and

$$p\partial Q/\partial L - P_1 = 0$$

or, alternatively,

$$\frac{\partial Q}{\partial L} = \frac{P_1}{p}$$

Solving these two equations gives the optimal values for K and L. With $Q = Q(K, L)$, Q is also determined. The firm will choose K and L such that the marginal productivity of capital, $\partial Q/\partial K$, is equal to the ratio P_K/p, and the marginal productivity of labour, $\partial Q/\partial L$, is equal to the ratio P_1/p. The interpretation of this result is analogous to the interpretation given above for the short-run case.

We can summarize these results as follows:

- In the short run the firm can only decide how much labour to use. This is equivalent to deciding how much to produce. Once L and thus Q are determined, the firm has no freedom left. So the firm can, in the short run, decide only how much to produce, not how to produce. It decides how much to produce by choosing L such that the marginal productivity of labour equals P_1/p.
- In the long run the firm can decide how much to produce and how to produce. This is equivalent to choosing both K and L independently. It will choose K and L such that the marginal productivity of capital equals P_K/p and the marginal productivity of labour equals P_1/p.

2.4.3 The paradox of profits

In a competitive market (that is, a market with large numbers of sellers and buyers and with free entry and exit of firms) the firm can earn no economic profit in the long run. Here economic profit means profit in excess of normal profit, where normal profit is defined as the profit that a firm needs to make in order to stay in business. Normal profit is equal to the opportunity cost[1] of the equity capital provided by the owner(s) of the firm. If profit is lower than the opportunity cost of equity capital, the owners will decide to take their capital out of this firm and employ it elsewhere (in a competitive market there is free – that is, costless – exit). In the long run, no firm can earn an economic profit in a competitive market. It is easy to see why this is true: if there were economic profits, entry would occur, supply would increase, price would go down and economic profits would vanish. Hence, while each firm tries to maximize profits, no firm can make any economic profit in the long run.

2.5 Comments on standard microeconomic theory

The model of a competitive market is an important benchmark for understanding how markets operate. It shows how co-ordination between quantities demanded by buyers and quantities supplied by sellers is achieved by the price mechanism. It introduces some basic concepts and techniques of economic analysis. It also shows that, although every firm has maximization of profits as its objective, no firm can earn an economic profit in the long run. If all industries were adequately described by the model of perfect competition, we should live in a maximally efficient world. The result of free competition would then be an allocation of resources in the economy that is called Pareto-optimal. A

Pareto-optimal allocation of resources

Pareto-optimal allocation of resources is such that no one can be made better off by changing the allocation of resources without anyone becoming worse off. It does not mean that everyone's wants are satisfied to the same extent. Some people may be able to buy many more goods than others, depending on the initial distribution of wealth and talents. A Pareto-optimal allocation of resources means only that there is no other allocation of resources that can make someone better off while making no one worse off.

This result of the model of competitive markets has led economists and policymakers alike to the conclusion that competition between firms should be encouraged. This is the general idea behind antitrust policy.

Perfect competition

While recognizing the importance of the model of **perfect competition** we should also point out some of its limitations. We should start by summarizing the basic assumptions on which the model of perfect competition is based. There are three assumptions that, when relaxed, lead to other models within the context of standard microeconomics:

- There are a *large number of small buyers and sellers*. That is, each seller and each buyer is so small that their decisions do not affect the market price. This assumption is relaxed in other models of standard microeconomics such as models of monopoly and oligopoly.
- There is *free entry and exit of firms*. That is, there are no barriers to entry and no barriers to exit. This assumption is also relaxed in other models of standard microeconomics such as models of monopoly and oligopoly.
- Each industry is characterized by *standardized products*. That is, consumers do not care whether they buy from firm A or firm B. The products of firms A and B are perfect substitutes in the eyes of the consumer. This assumption is relaxed in the model of monopolistic competition. This is another extension of standard microeconomics.

We shall not discuss these other models of standard microeconomics here. If you would like to know more about these models, you should consult a textbook on microeconomics (see the further reading at the end of this chapter). Instead we want to point out four other assumptions underlying all models of standard microeconomics:

Holistic entities

- Firms are viewed as **holistic entities**. This means that the firm is considered to be a single unified entity. There is in fact no difference in standard microeconomics between the concept of a producer (one person working alone) and a firm (several persons co-operating to produce outputs). When, for example, profit maximization is the firm's objective, then it is assumed that everyone inside the firm takes all decisions solely with that objective in mind. In standard microeconomics the firm is really no more than a production function with an objective function (profit maximization). When the purpose of the analysis is to explain how competitive markets work, this may be an adequate description of a firm. When, however, the purpose of the analysis is to explain how a firm makes decisions to co-ordinate the work of its employees, we need another description of the firm.

Single objective

- Firms are supposed to have a **single objective**. Standard microeconomics assumes that firms have only a single objective. Usually it is assumed that the objective is to maximize either profits or the value of the firm on the stock market. Now imagine a firm having two objectives: to maximize profits and to maximize employee satisfaction. Suppose it is impossible to measure profits and employee satisfaction with the same yardstick: there is no common *numéraire*, no unit in which both objectives can be expressed. In standard microeconomics this situation can be handled in one of two ways: one can assume that the firm's objective is to maximize profits and introduce a minimum level of employee satisfaction as an additional constraint, *or* one can assume that the firm's objective is to maximize employee satisfaction and introduce a minimum profit level as an additional constraint.

Suppose now, for the sake of argument, that all producers are able to say, 'for me, every unit of employee satisfaction is worth €3.00 of profits'. It would then be possible to combine both objectives into one single objective: (profits in € + units of employee satisfaction × €3.00). Standard microeconomics can handle firms with two objectives only when these two objectives can be combined into a single one. With objectives such as maximization of profits and maximization of employee satisfaction, this seems unlikely.

Perfect information

■ There is **perfect information**. Another important assumption of standard microeconomics is that everyone has perfect information: everyone knows everything. Here, 'everything' means everything that is relevant for making decisions on how much and how to produce (producers) and on how much to buy of each finished consumer good (consumers). Hence each producer is assumed to know the production functions of all goods and prices of all finished consumer goods, component parts, raw materials, wages and capital goods, while all consumers are supposed to know all prices of all consumer goods.

In modern microeconomics this assumption of perfect information is relaxed. In section 4.2 we illustrate this by discussing the market for health insurance. Here an individual considering whether or not to take out a policy has more information about his risk profile than the insurance company does. We show that such a market cannot exist (that is, no transactions in health insurance policies can take place) unless there is a solution for this information problem.

Another example is the market for the services of a travelling salesman. Here the salesman has more information about his level of effort than his boss back in the office. As we explain in section 4.3, the problem now is to write a contract that gives the travelling salesman a strong incentive to put in a real effort without allocating all the risk to him. This is an example of an agency relation. Agency theory is discussed in Chapter 7.

Maximizing behaviour

■ Behaviour of producers and consumers is described as **maximizing behaviour**. Producers are assumed to maximize a given objective function, usually profit. The essential assumption is that producers know all alternatives (for example, they know the complete isoquant map of Figure 2.7) such that they are able to compare all decision alternatives and choose the one that maximizes the objective function. For some types of decision, such as the decision on how much to produce in the short run, this assumption may not be very unrealistic. For other types of decision, for example decisions concerning which new products to develop, this assumption does seem unrealistic. Such decisions can be so complex that it is difficult or costly to evaluate fully even one alternative. Moreover, ideas for new products do not all come at the same time. Firms have to decide on one idea without knowing any other which may come up the next day. Therefore not all decision alternatives may be known at the time a decision must be taken.

2.6 Summary: how economic decisions are co-ordinated by the market

In a competitive market economic decisions are co-ordinated by the laws of supply and demand. The law of supply states that supply will increase as the price of a product goes up. The law of demand states that demand will decrease as the price of a product goes up. This means that there is only one price at which total demand equals total supply. This is the market (or equilibrium) price. The market price is determined by the point of intersection of the supply curve and the demand curve. Let us take another look at Figure 2.3. The supply curve for TV sets and the demand curve for TV sets intersect at a price of €400. At that price all manufacturers of television sets in the EU will together produce exactly 14 million sets without any planning authority telling them how much to produce. Each manufacturer of television sets will take the price of €400 as given. Given this price, he will determine how many sets to produce. There are many manufacturers of TV sets in the EU. With a price of €400, total production by all these manufacturers is 14 million sets. Also, with a price of €400, total demand by all consumers in the EU is equal to 14 million sets. This means that all sets will be sold and that every consumer that wants to buy at €400 can do so. The quantity of sets to be produced is determined not by a planning authority but by the laws of supply and demand.

Consumers buy not only TV sets but many other products as well. Consider a consumer who likes apples as well as pears. Given a certain budget, how many apples and how many pears will he buy? That depends on his tastes and on the prices of apples and pears. In order to explain how a consumer makes this type of decision economists use the rather abstract concept of utility. Consumers act as if they are maximizing their utility. This enables us to draw indifference curves like those in Figure 2.6. All points on the same indifference curve give the consumer the same level of utility. The concepts of utility and indifference curves belong to the standard toolbox of a microeconomist. These tools are used again in Chapter 7.

How does a manufacturer decide how much to produce? Here we have to make a distinction between the short run and the long run. In the short run (days or weeks), the manufacturer cannot add another assembly line or close one of the existing assembly lines. However, in the short run the firm can add labour, for example by working overtime or by hiring temporary employees (perhaps students). It is standard economic theory to assume that, as the firm adds more and more labour, the output will not increase linearly. This is because employees get tired if they work long hours, and because the factory becomes crowded as the number of employees increases. The additional output as a result of an additional hour of labour decreases as the firm adds more and more labour. In the language of economists: the marginal productivity of labour decreases as the amount of labour increases. Given a market price, the firm will choose the amount of labour in such a way that its profits are maximized.

In the long run the firm can vary both capital and labour. For example, the firm can invest in additional assembly lines and also hire additional employees. In the long run the firm has more freedom than in the short run. In the long run it can decide not only how much to produce but also how to produce: that is, how much capital and labour to use in order to produce a given quantity.

The standard microeconomic theory that is explained in this chapter is based on four assumptions:

- Firms are holistic entities. This means that a firm is assumed to be a single, unified entity. The result is that in standard microeconomics one does not consider what goes on inside the firm: it is as if the firm is simply a black box that we cannot look into. This first assumption is relaxed in more modern approaches that are discussed in subsequent chapters. It is quite obvious that if we want to discuss organizations we have to look inside those organizations.
- Firms have a single objective function, such as to maximize profit or to maximize the value of the firm. This assumption means that the objectives of the owner(s) of the firm are the only objectives that matter. In later chapters, especially in Chapters 6 and 7, this assumption will be relaxed.
- Everyone has perfect information. This is a very important assumption underlying standard microeconomics. However, as we have stated in Chapter 1, organizations arise mainly as solutions to information problems. If we want to understand why not all economic decisions are co-ordinated by the price mechanism of standard microeconomics, then we have to relax this crucial assumption. This is done in all subsequent chapters.
- The behaviour of producers and consumers can be described as maximizing behaviour. This assumption typifies the 'homo economicus', who knows everything and makes decisions solely on the basis of calculating the solution of some maximizing problem. This homo economicus reappears in Chapters 5 and 7. In several other chapters, however, we assume that human beings may try to maximize something but that they are unable to calculate optimal solutions in all circumstances.

Questions

1   Prove that two indifference curves can never intersect. *Hint*: sketch a situation in which two indifference curves do intersect and show that this leads to a contradiction.

2   Prove that two isoquants can never intersect.

3   Box 2.2 illustrates the increase in the demand for tin as a result of the fact that a new opportunity for the use of tin has arisen. As you can see in Figure 2.4, the quantity supplied increases (from q_1 to q_2) as a result of the shift in the demand curve. Does this contradict Hayek's conclusion that a new opportunity for the use of tin will cause existing users of tin to economize on the use of tin?

4 Consider Figure 2.9. This figure gives the marginal productivity of labour, dQ/dL, as a function of L. According to the text, the firm should choose L such that dQ/dL equals P_1/p, where P_1 is the price of labour, and p is the price of pencils. In the example given in the text, $P_1 = \$20$ and $p = \$0.25$, so L must be chosen such that $dQ/dL = 80$.

   Show that the firm can increase profits by adding labour when $dQ/dL > 80$. Also show that the firm can increase profits by reducing the amount of labour when $dQ/dL < 80$.

5 Consider a very large firm such as Royal Dutch/Shell. Do you think that it is realistic to treat such a firm as an holistic entity? Can you give an example of a situation in which conflicts between different parts of such a firm can arise?

Suggested further reading

Katz, M.L. and H.S. Rosen (1998), *Microeconomics*, Boston, MA: Irwin/McGraw-Hill.

Perloff, J.M. (2001), *Microeconomics*, Boston, MA: Addison-Wesley.

Note

1. If you are unfamiliar with the notion of opportunity cost, consider the following example. Suppose a dentist decides to take a day off in order to fish. Suppose that on a normal working day he earns €800. The opportunity cost of his day off is then €800. To put it more generally, the opportunity cost of a resource (a dentist's day, an amount of capital) is equal to the revenue that could have been generated in the best alternative use.

3 Organizations

3.1 The world of organizations

We live in a world of organizations. Think about it for a moment. When you were born, it was perhaps in a hospital: an organization for health care. Growing up, you attended school: an educational organization. In your adult life, you probably earn your living in work organizations. You are a member of recreational organizations. You may belong to a religious organization. You buy the goods and services you need from organizations, such as business firms. You pay your taxes to government organizations. Culture is preserved in organizations such as museums and libraries. Communication is made possible through organizations such as publishers, television networks and telecom services. Discovery is organized in research laboratories and universities. Resocialization is arranged through psychiatric hospitals and prisons. And finally: when you die, your funeral will probably be supervised by an undertaker's business.

A moment's reflection will make it clear that organizations are a pervasive phenomenon in the contemporary world. So pervasive that some people will be surprised (or even mildly shocked) by the realization of their ubiquity. Organizations perform many of the pleasant and unpleasant tasks that we usually take for granted in our societies. They are the main vehicles by which individuals may collaborate in the pursuit of specified goals. As a well-known sociologist has observed: 'the development of organizations is the principal mechanism by which, in a highly differentiated society, it is possible to "get things done", to achieve goals beyond the reach of the individual'.[1] If we state this in the terms introduced in our opening chapter, in a world characterized by a high division of labour, in which we are all specialized, organizations are the principal means to co-ordinate for collective action. We can hardly imagine a world in which individuals would have only the market mechanism to co-ordinate their actions.

How is organizational co-ordination achieved? How does it differ from market co-ordination by the price mechanism, as introduced in the previous chapter? This is the subject of the next section, where six co-ordination mechanisms will be identified. In section 3.3 we build on this distinction to identify six ideal types of organization. Then we relax somewhat the sharp distinction between organizational and market co-ordination in sections 3.4 and 3.5. In the concluding section we summarize the argument so far.

3.2 Organizational co-ordination

Let us first examine what economists have had to say about organizational co-ordination. When Coase posited organizations and markets as alternative co-ordination devices, he assumed that, within organizations, *authority* directed the allocation of resources instead of the price mechanism:

> Outside the firm, price movements direct production, which is co-ordinated through a series of exchange transactions on the market. Within a firm, these market transactions are eliminated and in place of the complicated market structure with exchange transactions is substituted the entrepreneur/co-ordinator, who directs production . . . We may sum up this section of the argument by saying that the operation of a market costs something and by forming an organization and allowing some authority (an 'entrepreneur') to direct the resources, certain marketing costs are saved.

Similarly, when Hayek (1945) praised the virtues of the market, he compared a market system with a central planning authority for an entire economic system:

> The various ways in which the knowledge on which people base their plans is communicated to them is the crucial problem for any theory explaining the economic process. And the problem of what is the best way of utilizing knowledge initially dispersed among all the people is at least one of the main problems of economic policy – or of designing an efficient economic system. The answer to this question is closely connected with that other question which arises here, that of *who* is to do the planning. It is about this question that all the dispute about 'economic planning' centers. This is not a dispute about whether planning is to be done or not. It is a dispute as to whether planning is to be done centrally, by one authority for the whole economic system, or is to be divided among many individuals.

We show in this section that Hayek's problem diagnosis was right: the best use of dispersed knowledge is indeed one of the main problems in economic co-ordination. However, by comparing a market system with a central planning system Hayek overlooked the fact that there are various other ways of communicating knowledge and co-ordinating economic activities than through prices or authority. It is to these alternatives that we now turn.

Mintzberg (1979, 1989) has synthesized the organizational literature on the structure of organizations. He has shown how the various elements of the structure of organizations (such as the size of its parts, or the extent of decentralization) 'configure' with determinants of organizational structure (such as the type of environment). He has thus developed a typology of organizational configurations. This typology is described in the next section. For now, we focus on the basis of this typology: a distinction between various types of co-ordination mechanism. These six mechanisms are reproduced in Figure 3.1. Here is a description of each of them:[2]

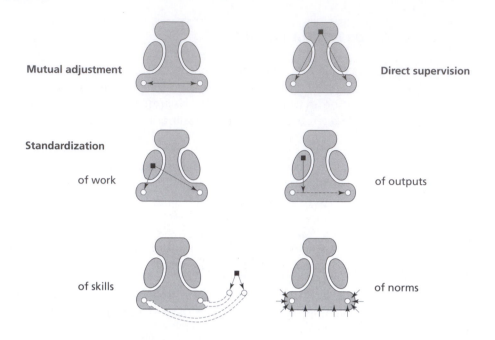

Figure 3.1   **The co-ordinating mechanisms**
Source: Mintzberg (1989), p.102

Mutual adjustment	■ **mutual adjustment**, which achieves co-ordination by the simple process of informal communication (as between two operating employees);
Direct supervision	■ **direct supervision**, in which co-ordination is achieved by having one person issue orders or instructions to several others whose work interrelates (as when a boss tells others what is to be done, one step at a time);
Standardization of work processes	■ **standardization of work processes**, which achieves co-ordination by specifying the work processes of people carrying out interrelated tasks (those standards usually being developed in the technostructure[3] to be carried out in the operating core, as in the case of the work instructions that come out of time-and-motion studies);
Standardization of outputs	■ **standardization of outputs**, which achieves co-ordination by specifying the results of different work (again usually developed in the technostructure, as in a financial plan that specifies sub-unit performance targets or specifications that outline the dimensions of a product to be produced);
Standardization of skills	■ **standardization of skills** (as well as *knowledge*), in which different work is co-ordinated by virtue of the related training the workers have received (as in medical specialists – say a surgeon and an anaesthetist in an operating room – responding almost automatically to each other's standardized procedures);
Standardization of norms	■ **standardization of norms**, in which it is the norms determining the work that are controlled, usually for the entire organization, so that everyone functions according to the same set of beliefs (as in a religious order).

These six mechanisms are all ways in which work is co-ordinated within organizations. They are thus also the ways in which people in organizations can communicate knowledge and expectations. Conversely, they are the ways in which people in the organization may learn from others what they need to know to carry out their tasks as well as what is expected from them. In short, all six mechanisms are alternatives to the price mechanism for communicating information and for co-ordinating economic activities. Authority (direct supervision by an entrepreneur or a boss) is but one of the organizational co-ordinating mechanisms.

Only in relatively small organizations can authority be used as the primary co-ordination mechanism, as we emphasize in the next section. Almost all large organizations use a variety of co-ordination mechanisms, including mutual adjustment and standardization of work processes, skills, outputs and norms. Standardization of work processes, skills, outputs and norms may be fostered by training. Box 3.1 explains how Disney uses training of new employees at 'Disney University' to standardize norms.

To illustrate how organizations use a variety of co-ordinating mechanisms let us take an example from our own experience. When you move to a new university, you learn in various ways how to co-ordinate your work with others. First, you receive several rule books, such as computer manuals, administrative procedures, faculty regulations and library instructions. These tell you the formal rules that govern the co-ordination of work (standardization of work processes). However, although universities are definitely bureaucracies, they are not so bureaucratic that all work is co-ordinated 'by the book'. Some of the formal rules are not upheld (they might, for instance, be outdated and nobody has bothered to update them). Moreover, much co-ordination is not formalized, so you negotiate with co-workers how to work with each other (mutual adjustment). With your fellow professors you co-ordinate your courses; with the administrative staff you schedule them, and with the secretaries you negotiate to get them typed. In your research work you might look for co-workers who understand your type of work and have complementary knowledge or skills. In the doctoral courses you teach the skills required from future colleagues (standardization of skills). Finally, you try to find out what is really regarded as important at your new institution: how important research is versus teaching, how important the fulfilment of administrative duties or the rendering of community service is, how sociable you are expected to be, etc. (standardization of norms). In all of these ways and more you learn how to co-ordinate your work with that of your new colleagues.

Similar accounts could be given about learning to deal with other types of organization. The point is that each organization has an array of communication and co-ordination mechanisms available. Through these mechanisms, knowledge and information are transported. In certain types of organization certain mechanisms dominate, but hardly any organization uses just one mechanism – and we shall see in the next section that it is only in relatively small, entrepreneurial organizations that authority (direct supervision) is dominant. Therefore, it is too simple a view to assume that the price mechanism is substituted by authority when markets give way to organizations. The price

Box 3.1 ■ Disney training: the standardization of norms

The Disney company is well known for the rigorous training it offers to every new employee. The courses are taught by the faculty of Disney University, the company's own training organization. The introductory course is called *Disney Traditions* and is designed so that 'new members of the Disney team can be introduced to our traditions, philosophies, organization, and the way we do business' (company brochure). The trainers drill new employees with questions about Disney characters, history, and mythology. They also constantly emphasize the values and norms that Disney holds dear:

TRAINER: What business are we in? Everybody knows that McDonald's makes hamburgers. What does Disney make?

NEW HIRE: It makes people happy.

TRAINER: Yes, exactly! *It makes people happy*. It doesn't matter who they are, what language they speak, what they do, where they come from, what colour they are, or anything else. We're here to make them happy. . .

In the University textbooks the values and norms are reinforced:

At Disneyland we get tired, but never bored, and even if it's a rough day, we appear happy.

You've got to have an honest smile. It's got to come from within. . . If nothing else helps, remember that you get paid for smiling.

The culture even comes with its own language, which is designed to convey that work at Disney should be seen as 'play', a theatrical performance:

Employees	=	cast members
Customers	=	guests
A crowd	=	audience
A work shift	=	performance
A job	=	part
A uniform	=	costume
On duty	=	onstage
Off duty	=	backstage

Sources: Collins and Porras (1998); Tom Peters Group, *In Search of Excellence*, video

mechanism is certainly substituted when we move away from ideal markets, but the alternatives are manifold.

In concluding this section, let us restate what we indicated by way of a preview in Chapter 1. If we adopt the definition of an ideal market as the co-ordination device that uses the price mechanism *only*, then we may define ideal organizations as the co-ordination devices that do *not* use the price mechanism at all for (internal) co-ordination. This leaves, however, a number of organizational forms, each depending on which mechanism is primarily used for co-ordination purposes. The next section is devoted to these forms.

3.3 Types of organization

We have introduced six alternative co-ordination mechanisms to the price system. The description of these six mechanisms was based on Mintzberg's (1979, 1989) work, which integrates much previous organizational research into a typology of organizational configurations. The purpose of this section is to introduce the organizational configurations that correspond to the dominant use of any one of these six mechanisms. Since real organizations are often hybrid forms of these six 'pure' types, this section provides an overview of the variety of organizational forms we are dealing with as alternatives to market co-ordination.

The six co-ordination mechanisms introduced in the previous section correspond with six organizational configurations as presented in Figure 3.2. That is to say, when, for instance, direct supervision is the prime co-ordinating mechanism, we are dealing with a configuration called the **entrepreneurial organization**.[4] This type corresponds well to the firm that Coase envisaged as substituting for market co-ordination. In this firm, an entrepreneur (who may or may not be an owner-manager) directs production and the allocation of resources. The firm is simple enough for the entrepreneur to control personally the organizational activities through direct supervision. Its structure is thus flexible, informal, and not elaborated. It operates in environments that are simple and dynamic. Simple enough for one person at the top to be able to co-ordinate activities; dynamic enough to require organizational flexibility and not to turn into a bureaucracy. Think of retail stores or young computer companies as good examples of this type.

Take Apple Computer Company. In the early stages of its existence it was an entrepreneurial organization under the direct supervision of Steven Jobs. Jobs was a charismatic leader with a clear vision of the company that he wanted Apple to be. Under his personal leadership and supervision, Apple developed the Macintosh and became a credible, aggressive player on the market for personal computers. As the company grew, however, co-ordination solely from the top became problematic. One man could no longer oversee all the operations. Choices had to be made on how to reshape Apple in order to allow it to develop further. Jobs appointed a manager, John Sculley. At first, the two

Entrepreneurial organization

CONFIGURATION	PRIME CO-ORDINATING MECHANISM
Entrepreneurial organization	Direct supervision
Machine organization	Standardization of work processes
Professional organization	Standardization of skills
Diversified organization	Standardization of outputs
Innovative organization	Mutual adjustment
Missionary organization	Standardization of norms

Figure 3.2 **The six configurations**

sought solutions together, but over time their differences of opinion grew and in the end Jobs was forced to leave the company (see Sculley, 1987).[5]

From a configuration point of view, the dilemmas could be described as follows. Apple had grown too large to be run as a simple entrepreneurial organization. Direct supervision broke down as the prime co-ordinating mechanism. The organization should be taken through a transition phase in which one or more of the alternative co-ordinating mechanisms shown in Figure 3.2 would become more prominent. Which one(s) would depend on the circumstances. To the extent that Apple's environment had stabilized, standardization of work processes would be most feasible. If, for instance, technological developments had slowed down and basic technical designs had been developed, more routinization of production would be possible than in the early stages when no-one really knew what technological horse to bet on. Once production is routinized, other functions can be standardized too. Standard products generate standard purchasing requirements, standard packaging instructions, etc. The more Apple standardized its work processes, the more it would turn into a

Machine organization

machine organization.

This is not the only possibility, though. Also important is the amount of professional work in the company's operations. Professional work (such as R&D and systems design) cannot be standardized: all an organization can do is standardize the skills required for executing this work, for instance by demanding a certain type of training. The more professional work an organization requires, the more it has to rely on well-trained individuals to execute their work with considerable discretion and to co-ordinate their work through the professional standards acquired during their long training. Universities and hospitals are

Professional organizations

examples of **professional organizations**, but certain parts of Apple would probably show these features as well.

Similarly, the other three co-ordinating mechanisms listed in Figure 3.2 could be employed. If the company wanted to diversify into other markets or market niches, it could aim for standardization of outputs, in terms of both product specifications and financial results of its divisions. It would then move

Diversified organization

towards the **diversified organization**, which specifies the output expected from its divisions and then leaves them considerable autonomy in how to attain these goals. Many of the large corporations in the world, such as General Electric, Unilever and Mitsubishi, are diversified organizations, which operate on diverse markets with different families of products.

It is important to remain innovative in the computer market, which requires the collaboration of hardware and software specialists, marketing and production people through mutual adjustment. Organizations that rely primarily on

Innovative organizations

this co-ordination mechanism are called **innovative organizations**.[6] As organizations grow larger, it becomes harder to retain mutual adjustment as the dominant co-ordination mechanism. This point is illustrated in Box 3.2 about Hewlett-Packard (HP). HP has found it difficult to maintain the entrepreneurial and innovative spirit that brought the company enormous growth and success.

Smaller organizations, though, such as consultancy firms or architectural bureaux, can rely on mutual adjustment as the main co-ordination mechanism and thus maintain a spirit of innovation. For larger organizations such as Apple

Box 3.2 ■ The HP Way

In 1939 Bill Hewlett and Dave Packard, two engineers aged 26, founded the Hewlett-Packard company in a garage in Palo Alto, California. That garage is regarded by many as the birthplace of Silicon Valley. The founders instilled an entrepreneurial, innovative spirit in their company. HP became a symbol of inventiveness. It also became well known for its business principles, encoded in 'the HP Way'. The HP way of doing business emphasized (1) making a technological contribution to society, (2) respect and opportunity for its employees, (3) being a responsible citizen in its communities, and (4) profitable growth as a means to achieve these other values and goals.

The HP Way brought the company enormous success. Its famous products included hand-held calculators and printers. By the end of the century it was approaching $50 bn revenues and employed 80,000 people. However, as our organizational framework predicts, HP had found it increasingly difficult to maintain its entrepreneurial and innovative spirit as it grew to this huge size. New product development was disappointing, growth was faltering, and profitability was decreasing rapidly. Moreover, it had developed the image of a slow, stumbling giant and was dubbed the Gray Lady of Silicon Valley.

In 1999 the HP Board took the radical step of looking outside the company for a new President and CEO. They appointed Carly Fiorina, the first woman to head a company listed on the Dow Jones Industrial Average. She found a company that still lived up to 'the core values of the firm: respect, integrity, teamwork, contribution', but had also become 'a gentle bureaucracy of entitlement and consensus', consisting of 'a collection of tribes'. In order to revitalize this company she launched the slogan 'preserve the best, reinvent the rest'. Reaching back to the origins of the company, HP issued new 'Rules of the Garage', including:

■ Believe you can change the world.
■ Share tools, ideas. Trust your colleagues.
■ No politics. No bureaucracy. (These are ridiculous in a garage.)
■ Radical ideas are not bad ideas.
■ Make a contribution every day. If it doesn't contribute, it doesn't leave the garage.
■ Believe that together we can do anything.

She streamlined the company, slashing the number of product divisions from 83 to 16. In addition she cut costs and jobs (5% of the workforce) and reoriented the company towards being a service-centred company rather than a hardware-centred company.

In 2000 a bold attempt to expand the service-centred concept by acquiring the management consultancy and IT-related services of PricewaterhouseCoopers failed. By the end of 2000 the economy slowed, and in particular the demand for computers and computer-related services fell. It turned into a real slump in 2001. On 4 September 2001 Carly Fiorina announced that HP would acquire Compaq, a large maker of personal computers, for about $20 bn. 'For the first time in a very long time, IBM will have a competitor that is strong enough to take it head-on,' she said. Analysts, however, dubbed this step 'a classical defensive move in a consolidating industry'. HP's share price was almost down by a quarter on 5 September, jeopardizing the success of the all-share bid. While we were finalizing the manuscript of this third edition it was unclear where the HP Way would lead. However, it was clear once again how difficult it is for successful firms to retain their success, a theme we shall return to in Chapters 10 and 11.

Sources: Collins and Porras (1998): 'The HP Way forward', interview with Carly Fiorina in *Worldlink*, the magazine of the World Economic Forum, Jan/Feb 2001; 'Rebuilding the HP way', *Information Week*, 23 July 2001; 'Hewlett-Packard and Compaq: sheltering from the storm', *The Economist*, 8 September 2001

and HP the challenge is to combine mutual adjustment, which is especially suited to bringing together specialists collaborating under dynamic and complex circumstances, with other co-ordination mechanisms.

Finally, Apple could rely on the standardization of norms (or ideology), to the extent that its workforce shares a common system of values and beliefs that direct their activities. A strong sense of mission, *esprit de corps* or ideology, which individuals share, tells them how to act together and dispenses the need for other forms of co-ordination. Religious orders may depend to a large extent on standardization of norms – they are prime examples of *missionary organizations* – but other organizations often have their own culture too. If that culture is strong, and tells organizational members what to do in certain situations, the culture acts as a co-ordination mechanism.

Which course(s) Apple takes depends on the actual circumstances at the time. In all cases, however, the pressures of the situation would force it to replace direct supervision as its prime co-ordinating mechanism. One or more other mechanisms would take over. To the extent that Apple would, after some time, show a new *prime* co-ordinating mechanism, it would have been transformed into a new configurational type. If it were to employ a mixture of these mechanisms, with no single one being prominent, it would be a hybrid form between the relatively 'pure' types. This is the common case. Most organizations combine several types of co-ordination mechanisms – an example is given in Box 3.3.

Box 3.3 ■ An insurance brokerage firm

Real organizations are often hybrid forms of two or more of the six pure organizational configurations. As an example, consider an insurance brokerage firm. An insurance brokerage firm is often a combination of a professional organization and a machine organization.

An important element that characterizes an insurance brokerage firm as a professional organization is the extensive training that insurance brokers receive before they are allowed to work independently. As a result, standardization of skills is an important coordinating mechanism in these firms.

On the other hand, administrative procedures tend to be very much standardized in an insurance brokerage firm. When a client requires a certain type of policy, all brokers within the firm use exactly the same administrative method and routing for that type of policy. This is an example of standardization of work processes, and, as mentioned in the text, standardization of work processes is the prime co-ordinating mechanism for a machine organization.

Figure 3.3 summarizes the space available for organizational forms. The relatively pure configurations are located toward the corners of the pentagon. Within the pentagon, all kinds of hybrid forms are possible. What form a particular organization will tend to take is a complex issue. For a discussion of the forces involved, you are referred to Mintzberg (1989). For our purposes, it is sufficient if the main point has come across: when markets are replaced by organizations, co-ordination by the price mechanism gives way to co-ordination by a set of other mechanisms. Organizations can take many forms, and each form is specifically adapted to particular circumstances – it can handle different

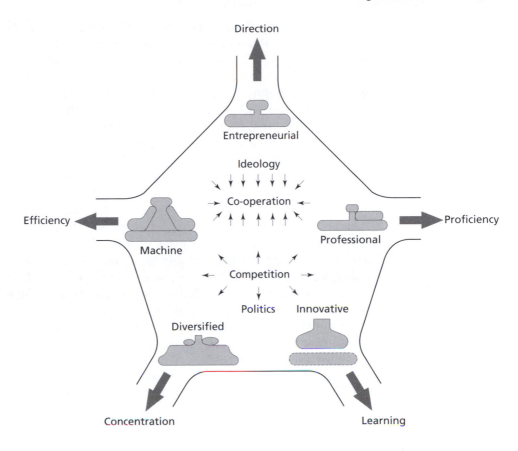

Figure 3.3 **An integrating pentagon of forces and forms**

Note: in this figure you do not see the missionary organization, which is the organizational form relying primarily on the standardization of norms or ideology.

Source: Mintzberg (1989), p.256

types of transaction. No wonder we see so many organizations and that such a large part of economic life is conducted within them.

3.4 Organizational markets

Until now we have argued as though market co-ordination and organizational co-ordination were mutually exclusive: that is, as if these two types of co-ordination cannot be combined. We now take the argument one step further and show that markets may exist within organizations as well. In the next section, we briefly show that markets may be organized to some extent too. Hence, in practice, market and organizational co-ordination may often be found in combination.

Take the example of a large, diversified organization like Royal Dutch/Shell. Within that organization, transactions between divisions may take place, such as when the oil division delivers oil to the petrochemical division, which processes it further into commodity chemicals. Within the petrochemical division similar exchanges may occur, for instance when the commodity chemicals are produced by one business unit and delivered to the next to be processed further into specialty chemicals. Often such transactions are effected against an internal price, the transfer price. In such a case, Shell may be said to have an **internal market for goods**. Decisions on whether to sell or procure internally will be based on the transfer price as compared with external prices.

Internal market for goods

Similarly, Shell has an **internal capital market** since corporate management allocates its funds among the divisions on the basis of those divisional plans that fit best in corporate policy and generate the highest return. Internally, Shell's corporate management takes over the function of the external capital market in directing financial resources to their best use. The internal and external capital markets remain linked. Management may decide not to invest all its available resources internally if the internal returns are insufficient. It may then seek temporary outside investment of its superfluous funds, perhaps in anticipation of the acquisition of another firm. On the other hand, it may want to attract new (external) capital when it can meet the required external conditions and earn an additional profit.

Internal capital market

Similarly, an **internal labour market** may be said to exist where divisions compete for the best human resources, also by bidding up their potential salaries.[7] Organizational members may seek career advancement by applying internally for better positions with higher salaries. If the allocation of human resources is primarily an internal affair, the function of the external labour market is taken over by the organization. Again, the internal and external markets remain linked, however. New people enter the organization through its ports of entry. Others leave the organization and seek new employment on the external labour market.

Internal labour market

Within organizations, then, several types of market may be operative. This implies that market and organizational co-ordination may be mixed. It further implies that there is no sharp demarcation between markets and organizations. In our conceptual framework we distinguish between the two ideal types: 'pure' market co-ordination (solely by the price mechanism) and 'pure' organizational co-ordination (solely by other mechanisms). Most real cases fall between these two pure types, and will be characterized by mixed co-ordination systems. This is shown below for the operation of most markets.

3.5 Organized markets

Pure market co-ordination, solely by means of the price mechanism, is an exceptional case. Let us return to the example of the stock market, discussed in Chapter 1. This example was taken since this market conforms closely to the model of perfect competition. The numerous buyers and sellers of IBM stock individually have no effect on the stock price. IBM's common stock is standardized: there is no product variation. The market for IBM stock has no barriers to entry or exit. This market therefore meets the main assumptions specified in Chapter 2 for the operation of perfect competition.

Yet, when we look more closely at the operation of this market, we see that at least two organizational co-ordination mechanisms operate as well. First, the market is regulated. It is regulated both by governments (through Securities Acts) and by stock exchange boards (through conditions for listing). These regulations specify the rules with which the various market parties must comply. For example, in most countries, buyers are prohibited from acquiring a controlling interest in listed firms without prior notification of their intentions. Similarly, IBM has to comply with a number of regulations and restrictions before it is permitted to issue new stock. Such regulations standardize the work processes of the market parties. The Securities Acts and the stock exchange regulations function just as operating manuals do in organizations. The market parties can use them to see what behaviour is required in particular situations. The stock market is organized in this sense. It is organized in the further sense that direct supervision is operative as well. The stock markets are supervised by bodies such as the Securities and Exchange Commission in the USA and by stock market boards. These bodies have the power to interfere with free market interaction, for instance by suspending the listing of a firm when there are strong indications of irregularities or misconduct.

Let us take another of the six organizational co-ordination mechanisms: mutual adjustment. As explained above, this mechanism achieves co-ordination through the process of informal communication. Such informal communication is a common feature in many markets. One pernicious form of it is

Collusion

called **collusion** by economists. It refers, for example, to conspiracies by the few suppliers in oligopolistic markets to set prices higher than would result under free market interaction. Alternatively, informal cartels may divide markets between them and thus collude to restrain competition. Collusion may be

Tacit collusion

rather overt or it may be tacit. **Tacit collusion** is a prime example of mutual adjustment since it involves the informal development of rules regulating market behaviour. One such rule may be that a particular supplier acts as price leader. If that supplier changes its price level, the other suppliers follow. No formal communication is required to organize an oligopolistic market in this way.

Finally, consider two examples of the influence of culture (standardization of norms) upon the operation of markets. First, the Islamic prohibition on charging interest. This prohibition derives from the Koran. As a result, the Islamic banking system has to organize some of its transactions differently than customary in the Western world. Secondly, take the common Asiatic practice of charging a different price to the 'in-group' of family, friends and long-standing business associates from that charged to outsiders. These examples illustrate how economic transactions are embedded in cultural norms.[8] If some foreign practices seem strange to us, we should realize that our norms, too, are standardized to allow us to engage in economic transactions with roughly the same expectations of what is fair and what is not. One illustration of this is provided by Stewart Macaulay[9]:

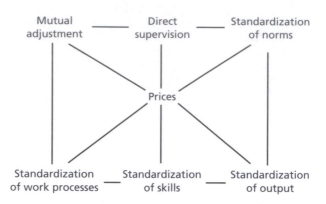

Figure 3.4 **The seven co-ordinating mechanisms**

One purchasing agent expressed a common business attitude when he said, 'if something comes up, you get the other man on the telephone and deal with the problem. You don't read legalistic contract clauses at each other if you ever want to do business again. One doesn't run to lawyers if he wants to stay in business because one must behave decently.'

These few examples will suffice to show that combination of market and organizational co-ordination is the rule rather than the exception.[10] Analytically, it is necessary to distinguish carefully between the price system as the market co-ordination device and the six organizational mechanisms. We shall continue to do so in the following chapters. Only by a clear analytical separation can we examine which device is most efficient under what circumstances. The foregoing discussion will have made it clear, however, that when we move from the analytical world (with its sharp distinctions) to the messy real world we shall often find bundles of co-ordination mechanisms operating together. This is illustrated in Figure 3.4.

3.6 Summary: how organizations achieve co-ordination

Market and organizational co-ordination are the two ideal types of co-ordination device for economic transactions. Pure market co-ordination is effected by the use of the price mechanism only. Pure organizational co-ordination is characterized by the use of non-price mechanisms only. In this chapter we have introduced six of those non-price mechanisms. All six mechanisms can communicate the knowledge necessary for organizational members to engage in economic transactions. All six may substitute for the price mechanism in co-ordinating economic action.

Associated with the dominant use of each of these six mechanisms are six pure types of organizational configuration: for instance, the entrepreneurial organization in which direct supervision is the prime co-ordinating mechanism. The entrepreneurial organization thus conforms closely to the type of organization that Coase had in mind when he posited authority as the alternative to the price mechanism in co-ordinating economic transactions. However, organizational theory shows that four types of standardization (of work processes, skills, outputs, or norms) and mutual adjustment can act as co-ordinating mechanisms as well. If organizational co-ordination is dominated by one of these six mechanisms we shall observe one of the relatively 'pure types' of organizational configuration. It was shown, however, that most organizations use a combination of these mechanisms. In the real world, therefore, we usually encounter hybrid types of organization. Moreover, it was shown that many organizations (such as business firms) also use the price mechanism to some extent for internal purposes. Within those firms, market and organizational co-ordination are then combined.

Finally, it was briefly shown that the opposite occurs frequently as well: markets are often organized to some extent. That is to say, market co-ordination by the price mechanism is often combined with one or more of the organizational mechanisms. We conclude, therefore, that in practice we shall often find that economic transactions are co-ordinated by a bundle of co-ordination mechanisms. It is the exception when one mechanism suffices; it is the rule where two or more are combined.

Questions

1 Did you see the movie *A Few Good Men*? This is a movie about an American élite corps of marines. What do you think is the main co-ordinating mechanism in such an élite unit? What other co-ordinating mechanisms will probably be employed?

2 Section 3.4 gives two examples of internal markets: an internal capital market and an internal labour market. Read these two examples again carefully. Do you feel that the example of the internal labour market is a better example of an internal market than the internal capital market? Discuss the possible differences between the internal capital market and the internal labour market.

3 Linklaters & Alliance is a large international law firm with more than 1,900 lawyers, including 429 partners, based in 26 offices in Europe, Asia and North and South America. The firm is headed by a senior partner, who is elected by the partners for a five-year term. Lawyers who are not (yet) partners work under the supervision of one of the partners, often as a member of a client team. The firm also has 16 key practice areas, such as EU and competition law, litigation and arbitration, intellectual property, and corporate and M&A, as well as a number of business groups, drawing together lawyers from across the firm specializing on certain sectors of the economy.

Which type(s) of co-ordination mechanism(s) is/are likely to be used by Linklaters? Would you say that Linklaters corresponds closely to one of Mintzberg's six configurations, or would you say that Linklaters corresponds more closely to a hybrid form?

4 SNCF is the French state-owned railway company, made up of the parent company SNCF and over 500 consolidated subsidiaries. In 1999 it employed 211,265 employees, 178,893 of whom were working for the parent company. More than 70 per cent of its annual income is from the railway itself. SNCF's ambition is to become the model for public service companies in Europe. It is firmly committed to guaranteeing a high level of traffic safety, punctuality, reliability, security of people and goods, and cleanliness.

Which type(s) of co-ordination mechanism(s) is/are likely to be used by SNCF? Would you say that SNCF corresponds closely to one of Mintzberg's six configurations, or would you say that SNCF corresponds more closely to a hybrid form?

Suggested further reading

Mintzberg, H. (1983), *Structure in Fives: Designing Effective Organizations*, Englewood Cliffs, NJ: Prentice Hall.

Mintzberg, H. (1989), *Mintzberg on Management*, New York: Free Press.

Schreuder, H. (1993), 'Coase, Hayek, and hierarchy', in: Lindenberg, S. and H. Schreuder, *Interdisciplinary Perspectives on Organization Studies*, Oxford (UK): Pergamon Press.

Notes

1. Parsons (1960), p.41.
2. Based on Mintzberg (1989), p.101.
3. The technostructure is that part of the organization where the analysts are located. They are the staff, outside the hierarchy of line authority, who plan and control the work of others. Examples are work-study analysts, schedulers, quality control engineers, planners, budgeters, accountants and operations researchers.
4. In Mintzberg (1979), called the simple structure. In Figure 3.2 we show only the correspondence between the prime co-ordinating mechanism and the organizational configuration. For other elements of each configuration (such as the key parts, the type of decentralization, contextual variables, etc.) see Mintzberg, 1979, 1989. The political organization has been left out of Figure 3.2 since it is characterized by lack of co-ordination and absence of clear structure.
5. Many years later Steven Jobs returned to be CEO of Apple when the company was at the brink of failure.
6. Formerly called the adhocracy by Mintzberg (1979).
7. Interestingly, from an economist's perspective, internal labour markets are characterized by the existence of formalization (see Doeringer and Piore, 1971). However, given that we are dealing with markets that are internal for organizations, and that organizations are generally characterized by some degree of formalization, for an organization theorist the distinguishing characteristic of internal markets is that competition is allowed, partly by price.
8. On the embeddedness of economic behaviour, see Granovetter (1985).
9. Macaulay (1963), p.61.
10. As also argued by Imai and Itami (1984) and Schreuder (1993a).

4 Information

4.1 Co-ordination and information

In Chapter 1 we developed a basic conceptual framework that represents a fundamental economic approach to organizations. This approach starts from the division of labour within society, which necessitates co-ordination between specialized economic entities. We have argued that there are two ideal types of co-ordination mechanism for economic transactions: markets and organizations. We have also indicated that the information requirements present in any situation will determine the actual (mix of) co-ordination mechanism(s) that we shall observe in that situation. In this chapter we explore these information requirements, indicate some fundamental information problems, and discuss how organizations may be seen as solutions to such problems. In this first section we explore some differences between information requirements in various situations, and show how these are related to market and organizational co-ordination. The purpose is to give you a feel for these situations. In the course of this chapter we gradually use more precise language and distinctions, and thus introduce the main concepts involved in the economic analysis of information problems.

Let us again take an ideal market as a point of departure. Hayek's example of the tin market (see Chapter 1) may come reasonably close. On the tin market numerous buyers and sellers operate. Let us assume that each one of them has no appreciable effect on the market price for tin, since all buyers and sellers are small. That is to say, their individual transactions will not have an effect on the market price since there is such a huge volume of transactions that no individual transaction can make a difference. Only the collective (in economic terms, aggregate) effect of all those individual transactions becomes noticeable in changes of the market price. As discussed in Chapter 2, we say that under these circumstances *perfect competition* exists. Under perfect competition each

Price-taker   individual economic entity is necessarily a **price-taker**: it has to accept the prevailing market price and cannot hope to influence the price level. Only in such circumstances can we say that prices act as sufficient statistics that convey all the necessary information to the market parties.

Prices act as sufficient statistics under conditions of perfect competition because the decisions that the economic entities can make are really very limited. Given the prevailing market price, each seller can only decide *how much* to (produce and) sell. Each buyer can only decide *how much* to buy. Hence each party can only make decisions as to *quantities* of tin. Under conditions of perfect competition many other types of decision are irrelevant owing to the assumptions that underlie the model of perfect competition. One of those assumptions is indeed that there are numerous buyers and sellers. So many, in fact, that we are always assured of a counterparty when we want to transact at the market price. Another crucial assumption is that we are dealing with a **homogeneous good**: a good that comes only in one standardized form. Therefore we do not have to be concerned what variety of the good to make or buy. There are no quality differences: it does not matter to whom we sell or from whom we buy. Moreover, as buyers of those goods, we can easily observe whether we have obtained what we expected: all we have to do is check the quantity delivered. As we shall see, these conditions alone (numerous buyers and sellers, homogeneous goods) are not met in most situations in the real world. As Samuelson notes in his well-known introduction to economics[1]:

> A cynic might say of perfect competition what Bernard Shaw said of Christianity: The only trouble with it is that it has never been tried.

The price mechanism, then, is a sufficient co-ordination mechanism only in circumstances where the economic entities involved have quite limited information requirements. Basically, only when all the necessary information can be 'absorbed' in the price can we rely on the price mechanism as the sole communication device. Let us examine some situations in which the price mechanism is *not* sufficient to communicate all the necessary information – and let us take situations that are quite close to the model of perfect competition as a starting point of the examination.

First, let us have a look at retail markets, for instance groceries and supermarkets. Have you ever wondered why the various products are displayed so differently? Some products are packaged, others are not. Some have brand names, others do not. Some can be inspected by the customer, others cannot. We submit that a major reason for these differences is the variation in *quality* that may be expected in these different goods. Sugar, for instance, is such a standardized product that most people are interested only in its price per kilo. They have no desire to inspect the product before purchasing it, and they do not care much about brand names. Now compare this with, for instance, fruit. Fruit is normally on display for the customers. Often customers are also able to inspect the fruit and even to choose the particular pieces they would like to buy. The major reason for this, we submit, is that fruit quality varies (with season, region, delivery times, etc.). The customer wants to be able to form a first-hand judgment of its quality before purchase. The fruit price is insufficient as a communication device to transmit the quality dimension. A higher price should reflect a higher quality, but not many of us trust the flawless operation of this mechanism.

For many retail products an intermediate solution is to standardize quality as much as possible. Soup, for example, is a product that may also vary in quality. It is difficult, however, to give the potential buyers a first-hand experience of the product before purchase. The solution to this information problem is

Homogeneous good

usually the creation of *brand names* that are supposed to reflect the quality class of particular soups. Through advertising, through the accumulation of consumer experience, and through joint use of common brand names for different products (soups and sauces), we learn to identify certain brand names as signals of particular quality classes. We may rely on that signal as an accurate indicator of quality, at least for the first purchase of a particular soup. If our quality expectation is met, our confidence in the accuracy of the brand name signal is increased. Brand names can thus be seen as solutions to information problems. These solutions are available for organizations that are willing to invest in the creation and maintenance of their brand name reputation.[2]

The above examples assume that there is one true quality of the product and that the information problem is to communicate this true quality to the consumer. Suppose, however, that the quality of the product is not yet known (to anyone). This might be the case for the supermarket that wants to be assured of a good supply of next year's crop of fruit. In this situation the supermarket might contemplate a long-term contract with a supplier. The quality of next year's crop, however, is dependent on the future weather, which is unknown to both the supermarket and the supplier. In this case we say there is *uncertainty* as to the quality of the fruit. Markets can deal with uncertainty, at least to some extent. In this case, the supermarket and the supplier will have difficulty in agreeing on a contract that specifies only the quantities of fruit to be delivered next year (at a certain price). Both will want to feel assured that the price is fair given the quality of next year's fruit. They have opposing interests in setting a particular price level, given the uncertainty involved. They might agree, however, on a specification of quality levels and on prices that are dependent on

Contingent claims contract

the actual quality levels of next year's fruit. Such a contract is called a **contingent claims contract**. The specific terms of the contract are made contingent upon the uncertainty involved. Note that such a contract is possible only if there is a way to determine next year's fruit quality that is acceptable to both parties. If such quality measurement is not possible, the transaction will probably not come to pass.

While markets may thus handle some such uncertainty, they are not able to handle very much of it. The simple reason is that it is not possible for human minds to juggle with very many uncertain factors simultaneously: therefore we are not able to write contingent claims contracts in situations with numerous uncertain factors. Suppose the fruit supplier wants to research and develop a new strain of fruit, say a cross between apples and pears: appearls. Imagine that this requires large amounts of investment, for instance in a laboratory and in specialized biologists. If the supplier wanted to cover part of this investment by offering the supermarket a contract for the delivery of appearls (for an advance payment), it is questionable whether the supermarket would take it. The reason is that there are so many uncertain factors (the technology required, the mass production possibilities, consumer tastes, etc.) that it would be almost impossible to specify all the possible (combinations of) contingencies. Hence the contract could not be written, and the basis for the transaction would thus remain lacking. One organizational solution in this case might be vertical integration between the supermarket and the fruit supplier: the one taking over the other. This organizational solution is again a remedy for the fact that the price mechanism and, hence, market co-ordination cannot absorb all the uncertainty involved. (We return to this issue in Chapter 8.)

Finally, let us explore the situation where information is available but it is unevenly distributed. There is an **information asymmetry**. Say the supplier has developed his appearls in the laboratory, but is unable to grow them on any scale large enough himself. Then there are two routes he can follow. One is to sell his knowledge on the market, for instance to other suppliers. However, there is a fundamental difficulty here. These other suppliers will want to know what exactly they are buying. How are appearls grown? What steps are to be followed in the appearl-growing process, and which investments are necessary for each step? How sensitive are appearls to weather conditions? Are they resistant to the common apple and pear diseases? All such questions have to be answered before potential buyers are able to determine the value of the new appearl-growing recipe they are offered. If, however, all these questions are answered, they already have all the information they need to grow appearls themselves. This is the **fundamental paradox of information**: the value of information can only be revealed to another party by disclosing that information, while such disclosure destroys its value.

The second route the appearl-grower can take is again an organizational route. He can, for example, enter into joint venture agreements with other producers. Such agreements can be efficient risk-sharing arrangements, as we discuss further in section 7.6.

We have now discussed situations in which:

- the price cannot reflect all the dimensions of the good,
- uncertainty is present, and
- information asymmetries exist.

It is especially in situations with information asymmetries that all kinds of interesting problems occur. The reason is that information asymmetries may give rise to *opportunistic behaviour*. The notion of opportunistic behaviour (also called *strategic behaviour*) is more fully described in Chapter 8. Here we shall illustrate this by an example derived from Milgrom and Roberts[3]. The example also introduces the distinction between information (in)completeness, uncertainty, and asymmetry:

> To get an idea of the role of informational asymmetries in strategic behavior, consider three simple card games. In the first, each player is dealt five cards face up, the players make any bets they want, and then the best hand wins. In the second, each player receives five cards, some of which are dealt face up and the rest face down. Without looking at their hole cards, the players make their bets, then the cards are turned face up and the best hand wins. Finally, the third game is like the second except that the players can look at their hole cards. Again there is betting, the hidden cards are revealed, and the best hand wins.
>
> The first game is one of complete (and perfect) information. Everyone knows everything, and as long as we assume that people prefer more money to less, it is fairly trivial to figure out what will happen: there will certainly be no betting, and probably no one will bother to play! . . .

(Margin notes:)

Information asymmetry

Fundamental paradox of information

> The second game has uncertainty/informational incompleteness, but no information asymmetries . . . Games of this sort are useful models for studying such issues as insurance, risky investments, and learning (especially if we revise the game to have the hole cards revealed one at a time, with betting after each is shown). However, its play would not generate any interesting forms of strategic behavior.

> The third game involves informational asymmetries: while there is some publicly available information, each player is privately informed of his or her hole cards . . . The existence of this private information can obviously lead to interesting strategic play: bluffing, signaling, reputation building, etc. It is also the reason why poker is of enduring popularity.

In the next sections we continue the exploration of the consequences of information problems, particularly of information asymmetries. From the examples above we hope that you have gained the intuition that information problems might be significant in explaining the type of co-ordination that is appropriate for particular transactions. All co-ordination requires information. When two parties wish to enter into a transaction, they must both be able to receive the necessary information. Markets and prices are able to transmit certain types of information, but often not all the necessary information. Through organizational co-ordination other types of information can be communicated. In the following sections we shall develop this basic notion further by introducing some concepts from the economics of information.

4.2 Hidden information

The economics of information is a young branch of economics. It studies the implications of information problems and characteristics for economic theory. Some of its main inspirations have come from the analysis of insurance problems. We shall use some of these classic examples to introduce the concepts of *hidden information* (or *adverse selection*) and *hidden action* (or *moral hazard*) below and in section 4.3.

First, hidden information. To illustrate, imagine a country with no health insurance. Let us call this country Riskaria. You have emigrated to Riskaria and you have determined that no health insurance coverage is yet available, so you decide to go into the insurance business to fill this market niche. How do you proceed? The normal procedure is to employ an actuary.[4] The actuary will determine the health risks among the population of Riskaria. She might come up with a bell-shaped curve (a normal distribution) as shown in Figure 4.1.

We can observe from Figure 4.1 that the population of Riskaria contains people with very low health risks (represented towards the left of the figure) as well as people with high risks (on the right). Probably, older people will tend to be located on the right since health risks increase with age. Also people with, for instance, hereditary health risks or who smoke will be located further to the right than one would expect from their age. On the other hand, there will be

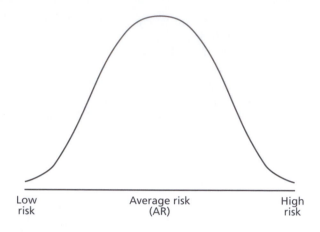

Figure 4.1 **The health risks in the population of Riskaria**

older people who are in good shape and thus represent lower health risks than the average of their age group. In Riskaria most people know more or less what risk class they belong to.

On the basis of risk distributions such as Figure 4.1, an actuary can calculate the insurance rate you would have to ask in order to be able to provide the specified coverage. Say this rate is calculated on the basis of Figure 4.1, which represents the entire population of Riskaria. In essence, the rate will then reflect the average risk. You now enter the market and offer your new product, a health insurance policy. Which members of the population of Riskaria will take it? The prediction is that members of the population with higher than average risks will be particularly keen to take your offer. The reason is simple: at a rate reflecting average risks your product is an attractive offer to those with higher risks. Very few people with lower than average risks will take out your insurance policy. For them, the required rate is unattractive.

Adverse selection   This phenomenon is called **adverse selection** in insurance economics. It refers to the expected outcome of this scenario: you will end up with a set of clients in which the high-risk part of the population is over-represented. The high risks have self-selected themselves in response to your product offer. They alone have been offered an attractive incentive to apply for health insurance. As a consequence of this adverse (client) selection, you will be forced to raise your rates – but this has an adverse effect as well. At this higher rate, the insurance policy has become unattractive even to the average-risk groups. These will cancel their policies and you are left with an even worse selection of clients. Driven to the extreme, adverse selection could become a self-reinforcing mechanism that would make a health insurance policy an impossible product to offer on the market. Before delving into the possible solutions to this problem, let us first consider the basic characteristics of the adverse selection phenomenon.

Hidden information   Adverse selection is basically a type of information asymmetry. It is a problem of **hidden information** (Arrow, 1985) in which one party in a potential transaction (here, the population of Riskaria) is better informed about a relevant variable in the transaction (here, the individual member's health) than the other party (here, your insurance company). It is an information problem that already exists *before* the insurance contract is written. In the language of the economics of information, it is an ***ex ante* information problem**. The problem for your insurance company is how to determine the actual risks that your potential clients represent: you will want to know whether your potential clients are indeed a fair representation of the Riskaria population. If not, you may want to adjust your rates or introduce risk-dependent rates (for instance, partly dependent on age). To some extent, the company can use available information, such as age, to determine these risks. On the other hand, those seeking insurance will have better knowledge about risk factors, such as hereditary risks and smoking habits, than the insurance company. They have no *incentive* to reveal this knowledge truthfully if it would be harmful to them. On the contrary, those who have private knowledge that they are higher risks than is observable have an incentive both to apply for the insurance *and* to keep quiet their private information. The company has hardly any means to find out what this knowledge is without the co-operation of the potential clients. In its information structure, this example corresponds with the third card game discussed in the previous section. The adverse selection phenomenon arises because one party has *private information* that is relevant to a potential transaction. This private information is basically unobservable to the other party. It is this *unobservability* of the private information that constitutes the essence of the information problem and introduces the risks for the other party.

Adverse selection problems abound in society. One example is given in Box 4.1. Another example comes from the market for used cars, as analyzed by Akerlof (1970). Akerlof set out to explain why there is such a large price difference between brand new (i.e. unregistered) cars and those that have just left the showroom. Suppose you have just bought a new car (say, a Ford) and have driven it for only a short time, when you find out that you have won a Mercedes in a lottery. You decide to sell the Ford. Then you will normally have to accept a loss of up to 20 per cent of the original purchase price of the Ford. Why is this? Akerlof's answer starts from the assumption that there are good cars and bad cars. The latter may have been assembled on a Monday morning. They are referred to as 'lemons'. When buying a new car, we all run the risk of buying a 'lemon'. All parties involved are unaware which of the new cars is a lemon. Your Ford dealer was unaware whether he sold you a good car (the normal case) or a lemon (the exception). Similarly, you, as a buyer, cannot tell the difference after just one test drive. So, we all face the same probability of ending up with a new car that is a lemon. After owning the car for some time, however, the owner can form a revised opinion about the quality of his automobile. He may have become aware of some (potential) problems. An information asymmetry develops: the sellers of used cars now have more knowledge about the true quality of their vehicles than the potential buyers. The buyers, however, have no way to discriminate between good and bad used cars. Since they are unable to tell the difference, good cars and bad cars must sell at the same market price. However, at this price there is little incentive for owners of good used cars to sell their vehicles. For owners of lemons, selling is attractive. As a

Ex ante information problem

Box 4.1 ■ Blood donorship

In various parts of the world there is a serious shortage of good-quality blood that can be used for blood transfusion purposes. As a potential recipient of such blood, you can imagine that you want it to be of the best quality, that is to say totally uncontaminated (e.g. by hepatitis or HIV viruses). It would be very beneficial if more people could be convinced to donate such blood. In principle, this blood could command a high price. Yet, we observe that most of the blood collection is still organized on a voluntary basis: the problem of increasing the blood supply is the problem of finding more voluntary donors. Why do we not observe more commercial transactions? Why is blood collection not governed by the price mechanism?

One reason is the adverse selection problem introduced by offering money for blood. The incidence of hepatitis and HIV among drug addicts is high because they tend to infect one another by sharing needles. At the same time, their need for cash is high. For these individuals 'cash for blood' is therefore a particularly attractive offer. Any attempt to purchase blood in the market, then, is likely to attract a relatively large proportion of carriers. This adverse selection is unacceptable if we cannot be 100 per cent certain that our blood-testing procedures will capture all contaminations, including possible new strains of viruses.

Conversely, a voluntary system presents no incentive whatsoever to people who know or suspect that they are carriers to volunteer for blood donation (Titmuss, 1971).

Another reason is given in Box 8.2.

consequence, the probability of buying a lemon is much higher on the used car market than on the new car market. This risk is reflected in the market price. Even though your Ford has given you no problem at all, its selling price will reflect the higher probability of used cars being lemons. Again, the basic problem is the unobservability of the true quality of the used cars for the buyers. Sellers have private information and they have no incentive to share bad news with the buyers. Bad risks self-select into the used car market. Buyers have few means at their disposal to identify bad risks. If there were no means at all, the market for used cars would conceivably not exist. The 'lemon effect' can also occur in the labour market. This is illustrated in Box 4.2.

Fortunately, in many cases there are some solutions to problems of hidden information, although these are often only partial solutions. Since the essential problem is one of unobservability, we may try to increase the observability of the hidden information. In the case of health insurance, we may require a medical examination. This would at least reveal already observable problems, but it would not reveal hereditary risks. Similarly, a used car buyer may insist on an inspection of the vehicle. Such an inspection can be done by a qualified dealer, although he has some interest in an active used car market for his brand of cars. In some countries, automobile associations arrange for independent inspections. In these countries the consumers have thus organized to struggle with the information problem. Again, an inspection can reveal apparent problems but cannot guarantee that the car is not a lemon.

There are other strategies to deal with hidden information. A number of these strategies aim at the risk involved. For the adverse selection problem in

Box 4.2 ■ Layoffs and lemons

Suppose you are working for a company fiercely threatened by international competition. During the imminent company restructuring about 10 per cent of all white-collar workers are to be fired. However, it is also possible that the company will go bankrupt: if that happens every worker will lose his or her job. Do you think it will make any difference to you whether you lose your job as a result of a restructuring or as a result of bankruptcy?

In a world of asymmetric information it is reasonable to assume that your current employer has better information on your productivity than potential future employers. If you are fired as a result of restructuring then future employers will probably think that, in the opinion of your current employer, you belong to the 10 per cent of workers with the lowest productivity. It will not be easy for you to find a new job, and you may be forced to accept a wage that is much lower than your current wage. The fact that you are fired is a negative signal to future employers. There is no such negative signal if the company goes bankrupt, since all workers then have to leave. So it should be easier for you to find a job if the company goes bankrupt.

This effect has been confirmed in statistical research: the earnings of white-collar workers who have been displaced by layoffs are significantly lower than those of white-collar workers displaced by plant closings. Also, white-collar workers displaced by layoffs endure longer unemployment spells than white-collar workers displaced by plant closings (Gibbons and Katz, 1991).

Hence you are probably better off when you are fired as a result of bankruptcy rather than when you are fired as a result of restructuring.

health insurance one solution is to pool the risks. If the insurance policy can be made a collective one for all inhabitants of Riskaria, the problem is dealt with, since the actuarial rates would reflect the true risks of the population. This is, of course, the solution adopted in the case of mutual insurance companies or insurance provided by the state. An alternative strategy is to redistribute the risks involved. In a used car transaction, all the risk that the car is a lemon is located with the buyer. Part of that risk can be relocated if the seller can provide a warranty that specifies risks that will remain with the seller for some period of time. Often, garages will provide such a warranty. The credibility of that arrangement is strongly dependent on the type of organization that provides it. You will not as easily believe the junkyard garage as the approved dealer. Finally, risks can sometimes be *segmented* (if only crudely) and dealt with in separate ways. In many countries, health risks are segmented into one portion that is dealt with privately and another that is covered collectively (by social security). On the used car market, you indeed have a choice between buying from another individual, from the junkyard garage, or from approved dealers. You know that the risk characteristics of these market segments as well as the terms of trade will be different.

To conclude this section it is probably useful to emphasize that hidden information is a problem that may be manifest across markets as well as within organizations. It can prevent the development of a market for health insurance as well as the establishment of a mutual insurance company. Private information, unobservable to other parties, may preclude transactions across markets as well as within organizations. It does not matter whether you, as an individual, are trying to sell your Ford to another individual or whether you are acting in your capacity as the head of a department trying to sell a car, a person or an idea to another department. Hidden information, or only the suspicion of it, may hinder both kinds of transaction. From the examples above, however, we hope you have gained the insight that markets and organizations do differ in the kinds of solution they may provide for particular problems of hidden information. For some types of problem the market has an appropriate solution, such as market segmentation. For other types we need organizations, such as mutual insurance companies or consumer associations. Hence problems of hidden information lead us to the basic perspective of this book: markets and organizations provide differential solutions for the information problems involved in economic transactions. Which (mix of) co-ordination mechanism(s) is most appropriate depends on the kinds of information problem involved and the kinds of solution offered by both mechanisms. We develop this perspective further in the next section, which deals with problems of hidden action.

4.3 Hidden action

Hidden action

Hidden action (or moral hazard) is an information asymmetry that can also develop in both market and organizational settings. It is, however, not an *ex ante* but an *ex post* phenomenon. That is to say, it refers to actions that parties in a transaction may take *after* they have agreed to execute the transaction. If these actions are unobservable to the other party in the transaction, and if they may harm this other party's interest, then these hidden actions may prevent the successful completion of the transaction. Worse still, the *anticipation* that such hidden action is possible may prevent the transaction altogether. We illustrate these ideas with some examples, first from the insurance field again.

Take fire insurance. In the Netherlands, personal fire insurance policies used to extend to damage to personal belongings from contact with burning objects, such as cigars and cigarettes. The latter coverage has been terminated now. The reason is that the insurance companies were confronted with a rising tide of claims for such coverage. An increasing amount of damage to, for instance, clothes and furniture was claimed to be the result of accidental contact with cigarettes, etc. Interestingly, the clothes tended not to be brand new, but rather last year's models. Here we have a typical problem of hidden action. Once insurance is provided for such accidents, there is an *incentive effect* on the behaviour of the insured. They may start to behave with less caution, perhaps with some sloppiness, or in extreme cases even with malicious intent.

Moral hazard

Examples of this kind gave rise to the term **moral hazard**. For the insurance company it is impossible to observe whether the damage has indeed been caused by uncontrollable accidents or whether the behaviour of the insured had anything to do with the damage. When, as a result, the number of claims becomes too high, the coverage cannot be continued.[5]

Travel insurance is a similar case in point, which also indicates one type of organizational solution. Under travel insurance we may claim personal belongings that we have lost while travelling abroad. Such claims have also risen enormously. It is hard to believe that we have collectively become much more accident-prone. Some degree of deception and fraud must be present. Apparently, a growing number of insured persons try to finance their trip partly by making false travel insurance claims. In order to counter this trend Dutch insurance companies have set up a joint venture that supervises a collective databank to register such claims. In addition, they have agreed on measures to take against possible fraud, such as joint exclusion of people who make an exceptionally high number of claims. Through the databank they share information and may prevent some frauds such as those involving one lost item being claimed twice under different policies, and people with fraudulent behaviour going unnoticed as long as they 'hop' from one company to the other. It will be clear that these organizational arrangements are (partial) countermeasures against the problem of the unobservability of hidden action.

When we leave the field of insurance we find that problems of hidden action are plentiful. Take the travelling salesman as an example. He may be assigned by his company to a particular new region. Assume that he returns with a disappointing number of orders. Perhaps he has not put in enough effort and has chosen to pursue other interests. Perhaps also the competition is stiffer in that region, consumer tastes are different, the time of year was not right, etc. The point is that the company is unable to differentiate between these reasons because of a lack of observability. One strategy, as discussed above, is to increase observability. This can be done by rotating the salesmen or conducting market research. Another strategy is to consider risk-sharing arrangements. If the salesman is paid a fixed salary, the risk is entirely on the company. Whatever amount of effort the salesman puts in, he always receives the same salary. So he bears no risk in this transaction.[6] At the same time, there is little incentive for him to put in the required effort, let alone that extra bit of work. As a consequence, the entire risk of disappointing outcomes is on the company. If, on the other hand, the salesman is paid an entirely variable salary (say, on a percentage basis), all the risk is on him: no orders, no salary. This will probably not be acceptable to him. Hence the company may negotiate a salary schedule with him that contains fixed as well as variable elements. The mix of these elements determines the specific allocation of risks (and incentives). In Chapter 7 we return to these kinds of solution when we discuss agency theory.

As a final example, assume that you cannot even determine whether actions have been correct, even if you could observe them. The relation between a physician and a patient is a case in point. The very basis of this relation is the superior knowledge of the physician in medical affairs. Even if the physician were to disclose every step he took in treating you as a patient, you would normally not be able to determine whether his actions were as diligent and as responsible as they could be. There is a fundamental information asymmetry owing to the existence of professional knowledge. You simply do not have the knowledge to interpret the signals about the physician's actions correctly. You will want some assurance that this asymmetry is not exploited against your best interests: you want the best treatment you can get. In this case the medical associations try to provide you with some such assurance by the development of professional codes of conduct, by requiring continuous education of their members, and by reviewing complaints that are brought to their attention (with sanctions in case of professionally substandard behaviour). While these organizational arrangements may give you some assurance, they are not able to guarantee high performance in all cases. In the end, professional ethics and individual responsibility are the only solutions for the considerable discretion that the doctor has as a consequence of this fundamental information asymmetry (Arrow, 1963, 1973).[7]

To summarize this section, we may list some similarities and some differences between the concepts of hidden information (adverse selection) and hidden action (moral hazard). One basic similarity is that they are both a consequence of problems of unobservability. If, at any time, all parties in a transaction were able to observe all the information they needed to prepare and execute the transaction, both concepts would be irrelevant. A second similarity is that the information is unevenly distributed. One party has private information that is unobservable to the other party. That private information is valuable, in the sense that it would affect the terms of trade in the transaction. Since the information is private, the owner can decide whether to disclose it or not. There is no incentive to do so when disclosure would harm the owner's private interest. A final similarity is that both problems may occur in both market and organizational settings. However, markets and organizations offer different solutions for these problems, albeit often partial solutions.

Hidden information

Hidden action

Differences between both concepts are the following. **Hidden information** is an *ex ante* concept: it refers to private information that exists before parties agree on a transaction. **Hidden action** is an *ex post* concept: it pertains to private information that may develop during the execution of a transaction. Moreover, it denotes a particular type of private information: information about the unobservable behaviour of one of the parties in the transaction. Again, that behaviour is valuable in the sense that it affects the terms of trade in the transaction. If an insurance company knows negligence or fraud is involved, it will provide no coverage. There is no incentive for the insured party to disclose such information. The similarity and the differences between the concepts of moral hazard and adverse selection are also illustrated in Box 4.3.

Assuming that these concepts have now been sufficiently clarified by the use of examples, we proceed now to introduce the basic concepts in the economics of information somewhat more formally. This will help to define their exact meaning, and it will also allow us to use them in subsequent chapters in these precise terms.

4.4 The value of information

In a world in which everybody knew everything the economics of information would have no place. Information would not be scarce, and hence economics

Box 4.3 ■ An insurer's worst nightmare

Insurance can reduce the devastating financial fallout from accidents. But it can also increase the risk of them happening.

Aeroplane crashes, oil spills and product failures are generally unpredictable events. But they are not totally random: their occurrence can sometimes be influenced by human actions. And although insurance can help to protect people from the financial impact of accidental misfortune, it may also inadvertently make them more accident-prone.

Insurance works on the principle of pooling risks, and charging each customer a premium based only on the average risk of the pool. This approach has much appeal. But it also presents two problems, which economists call 'adverse selection' and 'moral hazard'.

Customers who have the greatest incentive to buy insurance are likely to be those who pose the worst risk for insurers, hence adverse selection. A person will be keener to buy health insurance, for example, if he is already ill. This increases the odds that insurers will have to pay claims and so may drive up premiums for healthier people. It should not, however, increase society's total risk.

Moral hazard does. This describes the temptation for a customer, once he has bought insurance, to take greater risks than he otherwise might have done. Moral hazard can take different forms. A customer might, for instance, increase the chances that he will incur a loss; somebody with car insurance may drive more recklessly than he would if he were uninsured. And even though an insured person may try to reduce the odds of a mishap, he may do so in a way that increases the size of the potential loss. A firm that discovers it has a defective product, for example, may withhold its findings to avoid early lawsuits it has to settle itself, while raising the risk of a huge later payout that falls on its insurance company.

Source: The Economist, 29 July 1995

would have nothing to say about it. The *economic aspect* of information pertains to its scarcity and the value that scarce information may have. We illustrate this first for an individual decision-maker who has to choose an action in the face of uncertainty. In the language of game theory (the subject of the next chapter) this is the situation of an individual playing against Nature. In this section we show how the value of information can be determined in such a game.

You are the marketing manager of Standard Breakfast Corporation. A new product has been developed and you have to decide whether or not to introduce it. If the new product is a success you gain 8 (million dollars). If it is a failure you lose 2 (unfortunately also million dollars). Your estimate that the new product will be a success is 0.3, that it will be a failure 0.7. What do you decide? Figure 4.2 summarizes the situation.

If you are risk-neutral, you should simply calculate the expected value of introducing the new product:

$$0.3 \times 8 + 0.7 \times (-2) = 1 \text{ (million dollars)}$$

This is positive, so you should introduce the new product.

STATES OF NATURE

		Success	Failure
ACTS	Introduce	8	−2
	Do not introduce	0	0
Probabilities of states		0.3	0.7

Figure 4.2 An individual decision under uncertainty: whether or not to introduce a new product

Decision tree

Another way of describing this situation is by using a **decision tree** (Figure 4.3). A decision tree may have two kinds of node: nodes where an individual has to choose an act (represented by squares) and nodes where Nature chooses her moves by means of a random process (represented by circles). Working backwards (that is, from right to left), we can calculate the expected value for each node. In Figure 4.3 the expected value for node A is

$$0.3 \times 8 + 0.7(-2) = 1$$

For node B it is zero. Therefore in node C you will choose A rather than B. The expected value for node C is 1 (million dollars). This is the expected value of this game against Nature.

Complete information

Now suppose that you could do test marketing. Suppose, first, that test marketing gives you **complete information**. By complete information we mean information that removes all uncertainty. So by test marketing first, you will know for sure whether or not the new product will be a success. How valuable is complete information in this case? There is a probability of 0.3 that test marketing will tell you that the new product will be a success (see Figure 4.2). Since

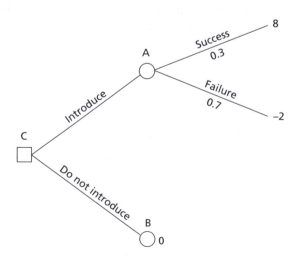

Figure 4.3 Decision tree: introducing a new product

you now know for sure that it will be successful you introduce the new product. Without test marketing, you also introduce the new product. So there is a probability of 0.3 that test marketing will not alter your decision. There is a probability of 0.7 that test marketing will show the product to be a failure. You then decide not to introduce the new product. In this case you save 2 (million dollars). So, by test marketing you have a 0.7 probability of saving 2. The value of the information from test marketing is

$$0.3 \times 0 + 0.7 \times 2 = 1.4 \text{ (million dollars)}$$

If test marketing costs you less than this amount, it is rational to test market your product.

In practice, test marketing seldom gives you complete information. In most cases there will be some uncertainty left. For example, if test marketing is successful, your estimate that the new product will really be a success may be revised to 0.8. If test marketing is a failure, your estimate that the new product will really be a failure may be 0.9. The situation is summarized in Figure 4.4. The information in the figure would be complete if the first and the second row each contained one 1 and one 0. As it is, the information is incomplete.

	THE NEW PRODUCT WILL REALLY BE	
	a success	a failure
TEST MARKETING IS — a success	0.8	0.2
a failure	0.1	0.9

Figure 4.4 **Incomplete information from test marketing**

In order to determine the expected value of this incomplete information, consider Figure 4.5. Working backwards, we calculate the expected value for each node as follows. For node A the expected value is

$$0.8 \times 8 + 0.2 \times (-2) = 6$$

In node C you will choose A, so the expected value for node C is also 6. For node B the expected value is

$$0.1 \times 8 + 0.9 \times (-2) = -1$$

In node D you decide not to introduce, so the expected value for node D is zero. To find the expected value in node E we need the probability, p, that test marketing will be successful. We can calculate p as follows. The probability that the new product will really be a success is equal to

$$p \times 0.8 + (1 - p) \times 0.1$$

This expression must be equal to 0.3, which is the known probability that the new product will be a success.

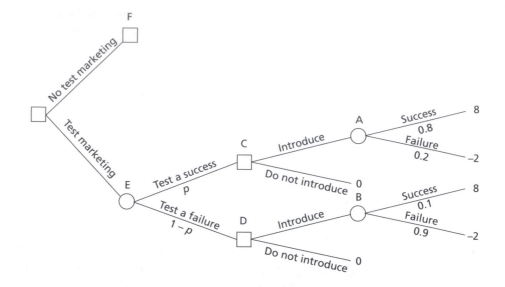

Figure 4.5 Decision tree: introducing a new product with test marketing

So we have

$$p \times 0.8 + (1 - p) \times 0.1 = 0.3$$

Hence

$$p = 2/7$$

The expected value in node E is $2/7 \times 6 = 12/7$.

The value of information from test marketing can now be calculated by comparing the expected value in node E with the expected value in node F, which we know is 1. So the value of the information from test marketing is:

$$12/7 - 1 = 5/7 \text{ (million dollars)}$$

which is about $714,000. Again, if test marketing costs you less than this amount, you should test market your product.

4.5 Summary: information problems for markets and organizations

In this chapter, information has been examined from an economic viewpoint. It has been shown how information can be seen as an economic good, deriving its value from its scarcity. The chapter took an ideal market with perfect competition as its point of departure. Under perfect competition, prices act as sufficient statistics conveying all the necessary information to the market parties. It was shown that perfect competition can work only under conditions of very limited information requirements. If goods are not homogeneous, for instance, it may be necessary to signal a quality dimension to potential buyers. The price mechanism is often an insufficient mechanism to convey such information. Also, under conditions of uncertainty the price mechanism may break down as a co-ordination device. Particular attention has been paid to situations of information asymmetry. In such situations, information is unevenly distributed. This introduces the risk that some economic players will use their informational advantage to gain an economic advantage in executing transactions.

In the economics of information a fundamental distinction is made between *ex ante* and *ex post* information problems. Adverse selection (or hidden information) is an *ex ante* information problem. This problem arises when one party has private information that is relevant to a potential transaction. Private information is unobservable to the other party. In the case of adverse selection this private information already exists *before* parties agree to execute a transaction. We have used the examples of setting up health insurance in Riskaria and of selling used cars to illustrate the concept. Hidden information, or only the suspicion of it, may hinder transactions across markets as well as within organizations. Markets and organizations offer different solutions, however, to the information problems inherent in adverse selection.

Moral hazard (or hidden action) can also develop in both market and organizational settings. This concept refers to an *ex post* information problem. It applies *after* parties have agreed to execute a transaction. Hidden information and hidden action both pertain to private information that one of the parties in a transaction may possess. In the case of hidden action, this information concerns unobservable behaviour of one of the parties in executing the transaction. This information is valuable since it would affect the terms of the trade, if the other party were aware of it. However, the party with private information has no incentive to disclose it. Again, markets and organizations offer different solutions to overcome the problem of hidden action.

Finally, we have illustrated one approach to determining the value of information. It was shown how we should distinguish between decisions where complete information can be obtained (removing all uncertainty) and decisions under conditions of remaining uncertainty (with incomplete information). In both cases we made use of a decision tree to sketch the decision context. This decision tree depicted a game of one individual playing against Nature. In the next chapter we explore more complicated games, involving two or more players.

Questions

1 There are many jokes about the laziness of civil servants. Do you think these jokes contain an element of truth? Let us, for the sake of argument, suppose that government officials are more lazy than employees working for a business firm. Can you explain this phenomenon by using the concepts of hidden information and hidden action?

2 Section 4.2 discusses the market for 'lemons'. The large price difference between new (unregistered) cars and cars that have just left the showroom can be explained by information asymmetry between buyers and sellers of used cars:

the seller knows whether the car is a 'lemon' but the buyer does not. Do you see another explanation for the large price difference between new cars and cars that have just left the showroom?

3 Suppose you are the negotiator for I.G. Metall, an important union in Germany. You expect that in the next four years many companies will have to reduce their labour force substantially. You know that, if a company fires 10 per cent of its employees, there might be a 'lemon effect'. What would you demand from employers in order to eliminate this effect?

4 Mutual insurance companies exist in most European countries together with insurance companies owned by investors. Most mutual insurance companies were founded by farmers, and many today still have close ties with the agricultural sector. In the first decades of the eighteenth century in countries such as Belgium, France, Germany and the Netherlands a class of very small farmers owning the land and the farm they tended emerged (in previous centuries many farms had been owned by the nobility). These farmers were quite poor. They produced their own food and sold the rest in local nearby markets. Their farm houses were usually thatched with straw or hay. Fire brigades did not exist in the countryside. If his farm caught fire the farmer lost everything he owned, including his means of subsistence. Investor-owned insurance companies existed in those days, but most refused to insure these small farms. Can you explain why mutual fire insurance companies arose in those days in the agricultural sector?

Suggested further reading

Arrow, K.J. (1985), 'The economics of agency', in J.W. Pratt and R.J. Zeckhauser (eds), *Principals and Agents: The Structure of Business*, Boston: Harvard Business School Press.

Raifa, H. (1968), *Decision Analysis: Introductory Lectures on Choices under Uncertainty*, Reading, MA: Addison-Wesley.

Notes

1. Samuelson, P., 1976, p.43.
2. Brand names are thus organizational solutions to these information problems. The property rights of a brand name usually belong to organizations. They are sometimes sold on the market, for instance through takeovers, then becoming the property of another organization.
3. Milgrom, P. and J. Roberts, 1987, p.184.
4. An actuary is an expert in the determination of insurance risks. A well-known alternative description of an actuary is 'someone who found life as an accountant too exciting'.
5. A sociologist would rightly point to the importance of norms regulating this behaviour. Of course, the fact that such coverage used to be possible, and now no longer is, has to do with a deterioration of norms regarding use of insurance. All economic transactions are embedded in a set of norms regulating behaviour, as already discussed in Chapter 3.
6. In the longer term he may, of course, bear the risk of getting fired. For the time being, we consider transactions one at a time.

7. Of course, we could conclude this example by pointing toward the insurance implications again, certainly in the context of the 'litigation culture' in the USA. However,
there are huge international differences in dealing with potential medical malpractice
through the legal system. These differences point towards the importance of the
social embeddedness of such transactions (Granovetter, 1985).

5 Game theory

5.1 Introduction

In the previous chapter we discussed the value of information. As an example we used the decision whether or not to introduce a new product. As we saw in section 4.4, that situation can be modelled as a game against Nature. We saw how an individual can make up his mind what to do in the face of uncertainty. In this chapter we introduce game theory. Game theory is concerned with situations in which there are two or more players. Moreover, these players have to make interdependent decisions. By this we mean that any player in the game is affected by what the others do. Each player in making his decision has to take into account the other players' decisions. We assume throughout this chapter that players are rational decision-makers who act only in their own interest. Moreover, we assume that each player knows that other players are rational.[1]

There are several types of game. Two important characteristics of games are:

- the number of players involved;
- the number of stages of the game.

Combining these two characteristics in Figure 5.1, we can distinguish the types of game we discuss in this chapter.

The purpose of this chapter is to acquaint you with some important insights from game theory. Game theory has become an increasingly important tool in a number of sciences, including economics. By introducing game theory we

	2 players	N players (N > 2)
1 stage	Co-ordination game (section 5.2)	Auctions (section 5.4)
M stages (M > 1)	Entry game (section 5.3)	Iterated prisoner's dilemma for many players (section 5.5.2)

Figure 5.1 **Four types of game in this chapter**

hope to give you a feel for the different types of setting in which economic decisions can be made. An important message of this chapter is that different settings (i.e. different structures of games) provide different incentives for players and allow different strategies of play. It is therefore important to discern the basic features of any economic game in theory or in practice.

5.2 The co-ordination game

Co-ordination game

Simultaneous and sequential games

We start with an example of a game between two players. The game is played in one stage. The main question in this game is how players can co-ordinate their actions. Therefore we call it the **co-ordination game**. The co-ordination game introduces the important distinction between **simultaneous and sequential games**.

There are many situations in which two or more players have to co-ordinate their decisions in order to reach the outcome that is best for all of them. An example is the standardization of a new technology. Suppose that Philips and Sony have to decide on the standard specifications of a new piece of electronic technology, say a combination of video and compact disc technology called VIDISC (see also Box 5.1). Both have been working on this breakthrough. There are two types of system both can choose. If they choose the same type of system, the individual payoffs will be larger for both than when they choose different systems. The reason is that with different systems they have to compete not only for brand choices by the consumer, but for system choices as well.[2] The VI technology (video technology with added CD facilities) promises larger payoffs for both than the DISC technology (CD technology with added video facilities). VI is twice as attractive for both players as DISC. Figure 5.2 gives a handy summary of the main game theoretic features of this story.

The numbers in Figure 5.2 indicate the payoffs to both players. The first number always gives the payoff to the row player (Philips in this example) and the second the payoff to the column player. The payoff is the reward enjoyed by a player at the end of the game. For example, if Philips and Sony both choose VI, they will both gain $400 million.[3] If both choose DISC they will both gain $200 million. The worst situation is when one company chooses VI while the other chooses DISC. In that case both incur a loss of $200 million. Which of these results will come about?

SONY

		VI	DISC
PHILIPS	VI	4,4	–2,–2
	DISC	–2,–2	2,2

Figure 5.2 **Philips and Sony with the VIDISC technology**

Box 5.1 ■ Philips, Sony, and video disc in the real world

The example on VIDISC technology was included in the first edition of this book, which appeared in 1991. Meanwhile, it has become clear that the 'game' of video disc technology is played out in the real world as well. Some features of this real world game are:

- More players are involved. At least ten electronics firms have an interest in setting the standard for digital video disc (DVD). DVD has a much higher data storage capacity than current compact discs and is expected to replace them in the future.
- Initially, there were two camps of players, Philips/Sony versus Toshiba/Matsushita/Time Warner. Both camps tried to set the standard for DVD on their own, thus risking a 'standards war', as observed for videos but not for CDs.
- In September 1995 the two camps reached an agreement to form one consortium in order to set a joint technology standard.
- However, within that consortium the haggling over each other's contribution continued. This focused on the licence fees that individual players could require for their contributions to the common standard. The lengthy haggling could jeopardize a rapid and successful introduction of the new technology.
- In 1996 Philips and Sony threatened individually to sell their licences to other hardware and software firms interested in DVD. This does not undermine the common standard, but would require other interested firms to obtain the necessary licences from two separate camps again.
- In 1997 Philips, Sony and Pioneer (the three main DVD patent holders) announced their co-operation. Other firms wishing to produce DVDs would be required to pay a 3.5 per cent royalty fee (on the sales price) to these three firms.

The real world 'game' illustrates some features that we introduce in this chapter. We move from two-player to $N(>2)$-player games. We discuss the potential benefits of co-operation, such as in consortia or cartels, as well as some inherent difficulties. In particular, we show that, for individual players, the central question often is whether to co-operate or to defect.

That depends on the way that the game is played. If both players have to choose simultaneously without any information on the other's preferences, no prediction can be made.[4] The reason for this is that it is not clear what each player will assume the other player will do. If Philips, for example, expects Sony to choose DISC, Philips may be tempted to choose DISC too. However, if one player is allowed to move *after* the other, we can predict that both companies will choose the same technology. This is because, for the second player, it is always the most advantageous choice to follow the first player's move. Suppose Philips has to move first and that Sony can observe Philips' move.

Game tree

We can now represent the game by drawing a **game tree** (Figure 5.3). A game tree is similar to a decision tree, as introduced in Chapter 4, except that in a game tree there are two rational players acting in their own interest, while in a decision tree there is only one. At the end nodes of a game tree, two payoffs are given. The first payoff is for the player that moves first, the second payoff is for the other player.

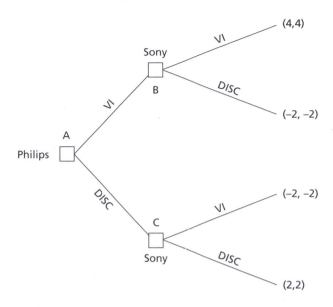

Figure 5.3 **Game tree for the sequential co-ordination game**

Philips has to move first. What should Philips do? Assuming the required information is available, the Philips manager who has to make the decision could look at the game tree of Figure 5.3. The Philips manager will see immediately that Sony will choose VI in node B and DISC in node C. So the Philips manager sees that whatever she chooses Sony will choose too. So Philips chooses VI and Sony follows. Both players receive $400 million.

In this game it is important that one player be allowed to move first. In the sequential game it is easy to co-ordinate the choices by both players. In a simultaneous game it is not at all obvious how co-ordination between the two players' choices can be obtained.

Simultaneous game   When is a game a **simultaneous game**? Is it really necessary that both players make their choices at exactly the same time? No, of course not. Both companies may make their choices at different dates. The point is that when Sony has to make its choice it does not know what Philips has chosen or will choose. This lack of information distinguishes the simultaneous game from the sequential game.

In this game it is in Philips' interest to tell Sony about its choice as soon as it has made a final decision. For Sony there is no reason not to believe the message it receives from Philips. So in this game it is quite likely that reality is represented better by a sequential game than by a simultaneous game.

A sequential game can be represented by a matrix specifying the payoffs or by a game tree. So Figure 5.2 can represent both a simultaneous game and a sequential game. If the matrix represents a sequential game we also need to know who moves first, before we can draw the game tree.

A simultaneous game can be represented by a matrix giving the payoffs and by a game tree. The game tree for the simultaneous co-ordination game is given

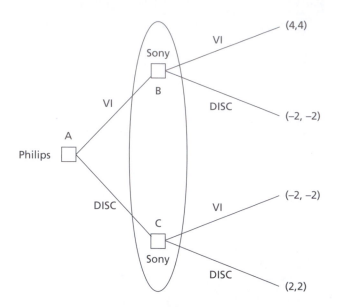

Figure 5.4 **Game tree for the simultaneous co-ordination game**

in Figure 5.4. Figure 5.4 is quite similar to Figure 5.3 except for the oval around Sony's two decision nodes. This oval represents Sony's information set. It indicates the fact that Sony cannot distinguish between these two nodes at the time it has to make its decision. Sony's manager simply does not know whether he is in node B or in node C at the time he has to make his choice. Because of this lack of information, the game has no predictable outcome.

The co-ordination game is a very simple game. If there are only two players, the best solution is reached if the players can communicate (Philips and Sony will simply agree to choose VI). If the number of players is large, it may be necessary to establish a rule. An example is on which side of the road to drive. In a country with only two car-owners government need not establish a rule; the two car-owners can simply agree to drive either on the right or on the left. If the number of car-owners is very large it is difficult and costly for all of them to make an agreement. In this case we see that the government establishes a rule. In a duet for violin and piano the two players must play at the same tempo. The payoff for both of them (in terms of their satisfaction or the number of CDs they sell) is zero if they play at different tempos. However, they can easily agree on the tempo to use. If the number of players becomes large, as in a symphony orchestra, it becomes much more difficult to agree on a tempo (that is one of the reasons why a symphony orchestra needs a conductor). Philips and Sony, the two car-owners, and the two musicians can reach the best solution to the co-ordination game through mutual adjustment (see Chapter 3). A large number of car-owners or the members of a symphony orchestra may need another co-ordination mechanism, such as standardization or direct supervision, to reach the best solution.

This section has illustrated two features of games that are important in the context of economic approaches to organizations:

- The first feature is the distinction between simultaneous and sequential games. It was shown that in sequential games, where the moves of the first player can be observed by the second player, co-ordination is easily achieved. The second player has *information* to base his decision on. In contrast, simultaneous games lack such information and hence have no predictable outcome.
- The second lesson pertains to the observation of how co-ordination between two (or a small number of) players can be achieved through mutual adjustment. Because of the interdependence of the players' decisions, however, this co-ordination mechanism breaks down as the number of players increases. It then has to be replaced by other co-ordination mechanisms (see Chapter 3).

5.3 The entry game

Two-stage games

In this section we move from one-stage games to **two-stage games** by considering the entry game. The entry game is a sequential game between a monopolist and a potential entrant. Suppose, first, that the monopolist restricts output and keeps prices high. This gives a potential entrant the opportunity to enter the industry. We analyze this situation first as a one-stage game and then as a two-stage game.

Suppose that a telecommunications company – let us call this company National Telecom – has a legal monopoly in the market for mobile telecommunications. The incumbent firm, National Telecom, knows, however, that the legal protection it now enjoys will not last for ever, and predicts that within a few years other companies will be allowed to enter this market. Suppose there is a potential entrant, Mobicom, that possesses the know-how and the resources to enter this market. Will Mobicom enter the market? Is there anything National can do to prevent entry by Mobicom? These are the questions considered in the entry game.

In a sequential game like the entry game, it is known which player moves first. Let us suppose that Mobicom moves first. Mobicom has to decide whether or not to enter the market. It knows that National charges relatively high prices. Mobicom knows that it will make a nice profit if National maintains this price level after entry by Mobicom. However, if National lowers its price substantially after entry, Mobicom will not be able to make a profit. What should Mobicom do? We suppose that Mobicom knows exactly what National will earn in each situation. The game tree representing this situation is given in Figure 5.5.

Mobicom's decision depends on the price level that National will choose after entry. Mobicom will have to put itself into National's shoes in order to predict what National will do after entry. It is quite easy to predict what National will do if Mobicom stays out. National's payoff with high prices is 16;

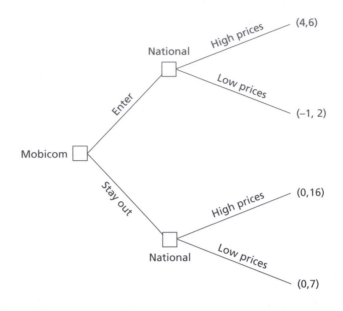

Figure 5.5 **Game tree for an entry game**

with low prices it is only 7. Therefore National will choose high prices if Mobicom stays out. Much more relevant for Mobicom is to predict what National will do after entry. It is easy for Mobicom to see that with high prices National will earn 6 and with low prices only 2. Mobicom knows that National is a rational player acting only in its own interest. Therefore Mobicom predicts that National will choose high prices after entry. Thus Mobicom enters and knows that it will earn a profit of 4. This illustrates an important principle for solving sequential games. This is the **principle of looking ahead and reasoning backwards**. By looking ahead and then reasoning backwards Mobicom is able to predict that entry will be profitable.

| **Principle of looking ahead and reasoning backwards** | (margin term) |

Is there anything that National can do to deter entry? Suppose that, before Mobicom makes its decision, National threatens to choose low prices after entry. If Mobicom believes that National will carry out its threat it will not enter, because with low prices it will incur a loss. It is quite likely, however, that Mobicom will not believe that National will actually carry out its threat. After all, if entry has in fact occurred it is no longer in National's interest to lower its prices. National's threat is not a **credible threat**.

Credible threat (margin term)

Suppose that National already has a large network in place before Mobicom makes its decision. The result of having this large network is that National faces higher fixed costs and thus earns a smaller profit. However, if entry occurs, National already has a large network in place. It can now lower prices and attract many new customers at very low additional costs. Indeed, if entry occurs, National is now better off with low prices than with high prices. Figure 5.6 shows the revised payoffs that result from having this large network. Mobicom will now predict low prices if it enters. Mobicom knows it will incur

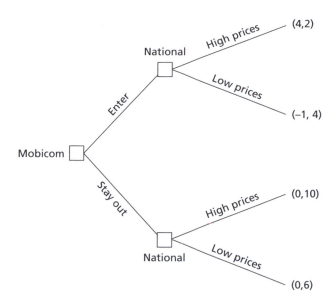

Figure 5.6   Game tree for another entry game

a loss in case of entry and decides not to enter. If National now threatens to lower prices after entry, Mobicom will believe this. National's threat is now a credible threat.

We have seen what happens if National has a small network and what will happen if National has a large network. If National can choose first between a small and a large network, what should it choose? This is a two-stage, sequential game in which National chooses first between a small and a large network, then Mobicom decides whether or not to enter, and finally National chooses between high and low prices. The game tree for this is given in Figure 5.7, which combines the two game trees of Figures 5.5 and 5.6 into one larger tree.

Should National choose a small or a large network? How should Mobicom react to National's choice concerning the size of its network? How should National react to Mobicom's decision? These three questions can be answered by applying the principle of looking ahead and reasoning backwards through the two stages of the game tree. In nodes D and E National will choose high prices. So, in node B Mobicom will decide to enter. In node F National will choose low prices, and in node G it will choose high prices. Mobicom knows this, so in node C it decides to stay out. Now National knows that, with a small network, Mobicom will enter. The result for National is a profit of 6. It also knows that when it decides to build a large network Mobicom will not enter. The result is that it will enjoy a profit of 10. So National decides to build a large network in order to prevent entry.

The point of this example is that, by building a large network, National can commit itself to lower its prices if entry occurs. In the language of game theory, **Commitment**   **commitment** is the process whereby a player irreversibly alters the payoffs

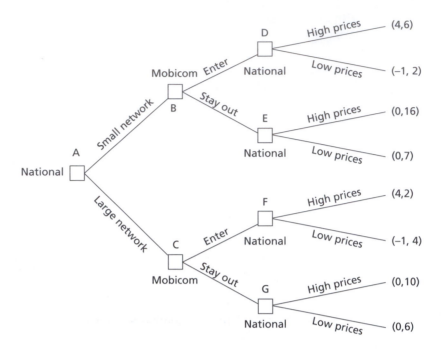

Figure 5.7 **An entry game with commitment**

in advance so that it will be in his own interest to carry out a threat. In this example, by building a large network National alters the payoffs in such a way that after entry it is in National's self-interest to carry out the threat of lowering prices. Hence such commitment makes National's threat credible.

From this section you can infer the following:

- In a sequential game you should *anticipate your rival's response*. You can do so by applying the principle of looking ahead and reasoning backwards through the game tree. If the game tree shows more than one stage, this principle also applies.
- A threat can be made credible by showing commitment. By actions that demonstrate commitment one player can show another that it is in his own interest to carry out the threat. In order to be effective, commitments must be *observable* and *credible*. Box 5.2 illustrates the dangers of making threats that are not credible because they are not backed up by binding commitments.[5]

5.4 Auctions

We now turn to a situation involving more than two players in a single-stage game. A prototypical example is the auction. Auctions come in various shapes

Box 5.2 ■ Commitment in labour negotiations

Labour negotiations can be viewed from the perspective of game theory as well. In any negotiation one party may attempt to formulate a 'take it or leave it' offer at a certain stage of the negotiations. In order for this strategy to be effective, the 'or leave it' part must be credible. If the other party does not believe this to be the final offer, the negotiations may be seriously disturbed, as the following story illustrates.

For a time, General Electric in its labour negotiations used a strategy known as Boulwarism (named after Lemuel R. Boulware, the G.E. vice-president of employee and public relations who introduced it in the 1950s), under which its initial offer, chosen after careful research into wages and working conditions in G.E. and its competitors, was its final offer. Although this take-it-or-leave-it offer was intended to be fair and acceptable to the workers, the union strongly opposed this technique – understandably, given . . . the amount of bargaining power to be gained from commitment. One union response was likewise to present a set of demands and announce they were inflexible. Another was to behave disruptively during negotiations. Another was to strike. Yet another was to complain to the National Labor Relations Board, which found that G.E. was guilty of an unfair labour practice; the adjudicator considered the lack of real concessions by G.E. during negotiations as evidence that G.E. was not bargaining in good faith. By 1970, the union's opposition had induced G.E. to cease using the commitment strategy.

Source: McMillan (1991)

Open auction

Sealed-bid auction

and forms. An important distinction is between the **open auction**, in which the bids of all parties are observable, and the **sealed-bid auction**, in which this is not the case. Again we shall see that the observability of information plays a crucial role.

Imagine that as a manager you are attending the open auction of a piece of land that is adjacent to your factory. Since you are contemplating an expansion that exceeds the boundaries of your current acreage, you are strongly interested in this additional piece of land. You think the land should be worth more to you than to competing bidders, but you are not sure. Several people you do not know are attending the auction. What should your bidding strategy be? How should the seller set up the auction in order to extract the highest possible price from the audience? As we shall see, the answers to these questions are not unrelated.

If the seller sets up the auction as an 'increasing bid' competition, the optimal strategy for you as a potential buyer is straightforward. It is to remain in the bidding competition until the price rises to your own valuation of the land, and to drop out of the competition as soon as the price moves beyond your own valuation. If all bidders are rational and execute this strategy, the land will be transferred to the buyer with the highest private valuation of the land.[6] Note that during the bidding process you will be informed of the other players' private valuation of the land. As the bidding process unfolds, you are able to observe these private valuations by noticing who remains in the competition and who drops out. The bidding process forces the players to reveal their preferences.

Such an increasing bid competition is, however, not entirely optimal from the seller's point of view. In order to grasp this point, imagine that you are among the last two bidders for the property. One of the two must have the highest private valuation: say, it is you. However, the other player will then be the first to drop out of the competition. He drops out as soon as the price rises just beyond his own private valuation. However, this may still be far below your own private valuation. Hence there is good news for you: you acquire the land at a price substantially below the level you were willing to pay. Conversely, this is bad news for the seller: she could have fetched far more for her land.

Dutch auction

There are several strategies the seller may employ to counter this risk. One of the most interesting is to use a '**Dutch auction**' instead of an increasing bid competition. In a Dutch auction the auctioneer starts off from a very high price (that is a price that is, in the auctioneer's opinion, well above the highest private value of all bidders). The auctioneer cries out loudly prices that slowly decrease. This process stops when one of the bidders cries out 'mine'. In a Dutch auction you have to make your bid (that is, you have to cry out 'mine') without knowing what other bidders might be willing to bid. If the piece of land is worth $1 million to you and you estimate that it is worth $700,000 to the second highest bidder, then your best strategy would seem to be to cry out 'mine' when the price is $701,000. This, however, is risky, because your estimate may be too low. If you think that the private value of the second highest bidder is somewhere between $650,000 and $750,000 with an expected value of $700,000 your best strategy is probably to cry out 'mine' at a price level somewhere between $751,000 and $701,000.

In a Dutch auction the seller probably receives at least a part of the difference between the private values of the highest and the second highest bidders. For the seller there is also a risk: in an increasing bid auction the auctioneer can start with a minimum price. In a Dutch auction there is no such minimum. In order to establish a minimum the seller can convert the auction from a one-stage to a two-stage game. In the first stage the game is played as an increasing bid competition. The winner of the first stage gets a financial reward (a fixed fee or a small percentage of his bid), but not the land. The land is subsequently auctioned in a second stage, which takes the form of a Dutch auction. If in the second stage no one cries out 'mine' before the first-stage price is reached, the winner of the first stage has to buy the land for the first-stage price. The bidders in the first stage are usually professional bidders who bid in order to obtain the fee for winning the first stage. They usually do not want the land for themselves.

Notice several interesting features of the open auction game:

■ It is a game with private information: each bidder's private valuation of the land.
■ Most of this private information is revealed as the game is played. However, in the increasing bid case, only the winner's private information can ultimately remain private.
■ The design of the game determines the incentives for players to reveal their

private information. By adding a second-stage Dutch auction, the seller attempts to induce potential buyers above the first-stage price to reveal their private information.

- This private information is valuable – the seller is prepared to pay the first-stage winner a price (the fee or percentage) in order to participate in this design.[7]

Sealed-bid (one stage) auction

In a **sealed-bid (one stage) auction**, all bidders have to submit their bids in a sealed envelope at the same time. The most striking difference from the open auction is that you do not learn about the private information of the other bidders during the auction process. You get only one chance to place your bid under conditions of uncertainty about the other players' private valuations. What is a good strategy for bidders when sellers design the game as a sealed-bid, one-stage auction? To derive the answer, first consider the case where you, as a bidder, have full information on all the other bidders' valuations. If your valuation is the highest, what should you bid? It seems clear that you should bid just above the second highest valuation. If you bid lower than that, you risk losing the competition. However, bidding much higher makes no sense: you would pay more than needed (colloquially, you would leave money on the table).

The full information case gives a clue to how to proceed in the more realistic case in which none of the bidders knows competitors' valuations. Say you are contemplating submitting a bid for a business unit that is divested by its parent company. The parent has solicited the help of an investment banker to set up a one-stage sealed-bid auction. First, you have to determine the likely competition. Which other companies may be interested in acquiring this particular business unit? Which companies are bidding only because they think they can run this business unit better (financial bidders)? Which other companies in addition believe they could realize *synergies* by combining the business unit with their current operations (strategic bidders)? As a potential bidder, you must determine that there is a reasonable chance that your valuation is the highest of all (i.e. that you are the most strategic bidder). If so, the prescription is to estimate what the second highest valuation is most likely to be and to submit a bid slightly above that level. To illustrate, assume that the value of the business unit on sale is €100 million at its current performance level. However, this performance level can already be raised on a standalone basis. If the performance level is raised to 'best practice level', the value increases to €120 million. This means that €120 million represents the maximum amount that the best financial bidder should be willing to submit. However, strategic bidders can go beyond that level if they can also (1) raise the performance level of the unit, and (2) in addition realize synergy benefits. If the combined effects of (1) and (2) are more than €20 million, then strategic bidders can win over financial bidders. If you are the most strategic bidder, the rule is to submit a bid just above the valuation level of your best competitor.

The example above highlights the fact that the value of the bid that you, as the most strategic bidder, submit depends on a number of estimates:

- the performance level to which you can raise the acquired unit as such;
- the synergies to be gained by combination of this unit with your own operations;
- the private valuation of your best competitor in this auction.

It is possible that you make one or more mistakes in these various estimates: it will be highly unlikely that all your estimates are correct. Some will be too pessimistic; some too optimistic. In circumstances of intense competition by many bidders, however, it is quite likely that the winner turns out to have made the most optimistic estimates. If you are the winner, there may therefore be good news as well as bad news in this outcome. The good news is that you have acquired the business unit. The bad news may be that you have based your calculations on the most optimistic calculations of all competitors. This **Winner's curse** phenomenon is called the **winner's curse** in game theory. It refers to situations

Box 5.3 ■ NBC's winner's curse for the Olympics?

Bidding by television networks for the right to broadcast the Summer and Winter Olympics has always been intense. The International Olympic Committee and the local organizing committees play strategically against the networks. The networks play strategically against each other and against the Games organizers. Over the years, the prices paid for broadcasting rights have increased spectacularly. In 1960 CBS acquired the rights to the Summer Games in Rome for $0.4 million; NBC paid $454 million for the Atlanta games in 1996. Similarly, the rights for the Winter Olympics increased from $50,000 for the games in Squaw Valley in 1960 to $300 million for Lillehammer in 1994 (both CBS). This bidding game has led to new creativity in strategic behaviour by one of the players, as the following press release shows:

NBC agreed Monday to pay a stunning $1.27 billion for US television rights to the Sydney Summer Olympic games in 2000 and the 2002 Winter Olympics in Salt Lake City. The deal, put together in under a week as a pre-emptive, take-it-or-lose-it proposition to the International Olympic Committee and the two national organizing groups, shuts out Fox Television and other US networks without hope of a counterbid . . . Network President Robert Wright said his company would not have paid $715 million for the Australian events and $555 million for the US games separately, but believed the two together constituted a profitable package . . . Olympic officials said the $1.27 billion was much higher than either the Sydney or Utah organizers expected from the rights sale . . . G.E. Chairman Jack Welch authorized the $1.27 billion deal after Wright telephoned him with the unprecedented package offer. 'The speed of that decision was inside half an hour', said NBC Sports President Dick Ebersol. An agreement, cobbled together during meetings among Ebersol, other NBC executives and Olympic officials in Sweden and Montreal last week, was reached over the weekend. If agreement had not been struck by Sunday, NBC would have withdrawn its offer with no guarantee it would join an auction among the networks scheduled to start next month.

Source: Reuters, 7 August 1995

where winners obtain the prize not because the true valuation is highest to them, but because of their optimistic expectations.

The main difference between open and sealed-bid auctions pertains to the uncertainty about other players' private valuations. In open auctions most of the players' private valuations become observable as the process unfolds. Only the winner's private valuation may remain unobservable. Sellers who wish to extract more value for their property may therefore wish to design the auction process differently, for instance by adding a second-stage Dutch auction. However, because of the open nature of the auction, a rational winner will never pay more than his private valuation. In sealed-bid auctions, however, the private valuations of all players remain unobservable. In situations of uncertainty regarding the true value of the auctioned object, all private valuations must be based on estimates (in our example of a divested business unit on three estimates). In such situations it is possible that the winner is inflicted with the 'winner's curse', obtaining the prize as a consequence of making the most optimistic estimates – Box 5.3 relates an example.

In concluding this section we want to stress that the way an auction is designed determines the result to a large extent. In this section we have discussed only the most fundamental forms: a single-stage increasing-bid auction, a Dutch auction (which is just one example of a two-stage auction) and a single-stage sealed-bid auction. The outcome of the auction is further determined by the number of bidders, the number of items to be sold, and the rules allowing or forbidding the formation of alliances. All these factors can have important consequences for the outcome of the auction, as is illustrated in Box 5.4.

Box 5.4 ■ The 3G mobile spectrum auctions in Europe

In 2000 many European governments were contemplating how to allocate a new and scarce good: third generation (3G) mobile phone licences. 3G mobile phones would use the Universal Mobile Technology Standard (UMTS), which offers much more bandwidth, allowing applications such as high-speed Internet and video on your mobile phone. The governments owned the rights to the radio spectra necessary for UMTS. How should they allocate these rights among the interested telecom companies?

Some governments (Finland, Poland, Spain, Sweden) chose to distribute the 3G licences on the basis of a 'beauty contest'. In a beauty contest the interested parties compete by demonstrating their qualifications against criteria set by the government. An advantage of a beauty contest may be that governments can set any criteria they deem politically relevant. A disadvantage may be that this invites favouritism by the governments, for instance towards the incumbent national telecom companies.

Economic theory suggests that an *auction* could allocate the new licences efficiently: that is, to those who value them most, not to those whom regulators favour. Governments interested in obtaining the highest prices for the new licences should therefore consider using an auction. In fact, the UK government was the first to use an auction in April 2000. There were nine telecom companies wishing to enter the UK market. These new entrants bid strongly against the four incumbents to obtain one of the five available licences. As a result,

▶

the UK government collected an astonishing £22.5 billion. Finance ministers across Europe started grinning at the prospect of their own auctions.

The next auction was held in the Netherlands. Here there were five incumbents and five new licences available. The Dutch government anticipated that again many new entrants would compete. In fact, many of these potential new entrants formed alliances with the incumbents: BT-Telfort, KPN-NTT Docomo, and Ben–Deutsche Telekom. On the morning before the auction two of the three last new entrants withdrew from the auction, leaving only six players in the auction: the five incumbents and one weak new entrant (Versatel). As a result, the Dutch government collected only €2.7 billion, less than a third of their hopes on the basis of the UK experience.

Revenues from European 3G mobile spectrum auctions in 2000

	Euros per capita
Austria	100
Germany	615
Italy	240
Netherlands	170
Switzerland	20
UK	630

As the table above illustrates, revenues from 3G auctions have varied widely. Revenues were high again in Germany, but very low in Austria and Switzerland. Reasons for these differences include the experience which players acquired over time and the changing market sentiment about the high sums paid initially. But a comparison across the auctions shows that it has also been tremendously important how auctions were designed. Important design features include the following:

- Increasing-bid only or also a Dutch auction second stage?
- Were there incentives for new entrants to compete (such as a special lot reserved for them)?
- What were the rules for forming alliances and for 'collusive behaviour' during the auction?

Many game theorists were employed by governments to advise on optimal auction design and by companies on optimal bidding strategies. They have had a spectacular opportunity to test their theories (see Klemperer, 2001). Moreover, the practical value of a good training in game theory was evident for many in the public sector and the business world. As the *Financial Times* quoted a telecoms analyst: 'All these people who thought that they wasted their first year at university listening to boring game theory lectures are now running around the City feeling really grateful.'

Sources: Klemperer (2001); 'Best bids guaranteed', *Financial Times*, 8 November 2000; 'The price is right', *The Economist*, 29 July 2000

5.5 The prisoner's dilemma: single-stage and iterated

Finally, we introduce a famous class of games: the prisoner's dilemma.[8] We start with the single-stage prisoner's dilemma (for two players) to show its basic structure. We then proceed to play the prisoner's dilemma game repeatedly with two or more players in order to show the difference between single-stage and iterated games.

5.5.1 The single-stage prisoner's dilemma

Two men, Robber and Thief, are being accused of a bank robbery. They are interrogated separately. They know that, if they both confess, each will be sentenced to five years in prison. If neither of them confesses, each will be sentenced to three years for illegal possession of arms. However, if Robber confesses while Thief holds out, Robber will be sentenced for only one year and Thief will receive six years. If Thief confesses, and Robber holds out, the situation will be reversed. The payoffs for this game are given in Figure 5.8.

Robber will now reason as follows. If Thief holds out, then my best choice is to confess (one year in prison is better than three years). If Thief confesses, then my best choice is to also confess (six years in prison is worse than five years). So whatever Thief does, my best choice is to confess. In the language of game theory we say that Robber has a **dominant strategy**: that is, one that is best whatever the other player does. Robber's dominant strategy is to confess.

Dominant strategy

Thief will follow the same line of reasoning, so he will also confess. The result is that both will confess, while both would be better off if they were to hold out.

Suppose that Robber and Thief are allowed to communicate before being interrogated. Perhaps they have been held in the same cell, but they are now interrogated in separate rooms. Suppose Robber and Thief have promised each other not to confess. Will they stick to their promise? If we suppose that each is completely selfish and rational, then we must predict that they will not. It is in Robber's interest to promise Thief that he, Robber, will co-operate (by not confessing) if Thief promises the same. However, having made this promise it is in Robber's interest to break this promise. Whether or not Thief keeps his promise, Robber will always be better off by breaking his promise. The problem is that if each prisoner is dishonest and disloyal (as we would expect bank robbers to be) they cannot make binding commitments. Because they cannot

		THIEF	
		Do not confess	Confess
ROBBER	Do not confess	−3,−3	−6,−1
	Confess	−1,−6	−5,−5

Figure 5.8 The prisoner's dilemma

COLUMN PLAYER

		Co-operate	Defect
ROW PLAYER	Co-operate	R,R	N,T
	Defect	T,N	P,P

Key:
R = reward for co-operation
N = payoff for being naïve
T = temptation to defect
P = penalty for mutual defection

Figure 5.9 **General form of the prisoner's dilemma**

make binding commitments, they have no way to achieve co-operation. However, if they could make binding commitments, co-operation could be achieved.[9] Looking at the dilemma this way, it is logical to relabel the actions that the players can choose 'co-operate' (which for the prisoners is equal to 'do not confess') and 'defect' (which for the prisoners is the same as 'confess'). The general form of a prisoner's dilemma is given in Figure 5.9.

The game represented in Figure 5.9 is a prisoner's dilemma if there are certain relations between the four payoffs that each player can receive. These relations are:

$$N < P < R < T$$

where

$N < P$ means that for the row player it is better to defect if the column player defects;

$P < R$ means that for mutual defection the payoff is less than for mutual co-operation;

$R < T$ means that if the other player co-operates, then it is better to defect (there is a temptation to defect).

Note that the payoffs given in Figure 5.8 for the two prisoners satisfy these inequalities.

The fundamental problem in the prisoner's dilemma is that for each player the dominant strategy is to defect, while they would both be better off by mutual co-operation. There are many situations in which a prisoner's dilemma arises. Consider the following situation. Suppose there are only two oil-producing countries in the world. Let us call these countries Arabia and Russia. Both countries have to choose an output level. If each chooses a low output level, then oil prices will be high and both will make a profit of 3 (billion dollars). If each chooses a high output level, oil prices will be low and each will make a profit of 1 (billion dollars). If Arabia chooses a low output level and Russia a high output level, then oil prices will be moderately high. Now Russia with its high output level will make a large profit of 5 (billion dollars) while Arabia with its low output level will earn nothing. If Russia chooses a low output level and Arabia a high one, then the situation is reversed. The payoffs to each country are given in Figure 5.10.

RUSSIA

	Co-operate	Defect
Co-operate	3,3	0,5
Defect	5,0	1,1

ARABIA (row label)

Figure 5.10 Two oil-producing countries facing a prisoner's dilemma

In this example, to co-operate means to choose a low output level and to defect means to choose a high output level. If oil-producing countries form a cartel, then each country promises to maintain a certain price level and to restrict output. However, having made such a promise it is in each country's interest to produce and sell more oil than its quota, even at a slightly lower price. Since each country will do this, the cartel will break down. In reality we see that OPEC was able to raise oil prices effectively in the 1970s (the oil crises), but has suffered from defection at other times. In particular, certain countries have repeatedly tried to benefit from the lack of observability of actual output levels, as is illustrated in Box 5.5. Furthermore, availability of non-OPEC oil (which increases when oil prices are high) has helped to keep OPEC 'honest'. This shows that our model does not (yet) incorporate all relevant aspects of reality. One important and relevant aspect in many prisoner's dilemmas in the real world is that the game is played many times instead of only once. In the next section we find that this makes a big difference.

5.5.2 The iterated prisoner's dilemma for many players

Suppose that two selfish and rational players play the prisoner's dilemma many times. This is the iterated prisoner's dilemma. In the iterated prisoner's dilemma each player has to choose between co-operate and defect in each round of the game. In making this choice each player can take into account what the other player did in previous rounds. In the repeated game a strategy is defined as a set of rules that specify what action to take given the history of the game so far. To illustrate the concept of a strategy for an iterated game, we give a few examples.

Tit-for-tat

- **Tit-for-tat** is the strategy consisting of the following decision rules: in the first round choose co-operate, in the following rounds choose whatever the other player did in the previous round.
- *Permanent retaliation*: in the first round choose co-operate; if the other player defects in any round, choose defect in all subsequent rounds.
- *All D*: always choose defect no matter what the other player does.
- *All C*: always choose co-operate no matter what the other player does.

Box 5.5 ■ Cheating in OPEC

Cheating has been a persistent problem in the OPEC cartel, regardless of whether the oil price was high or low. After the oil shocks of the 1970s and 1980s, when oil prices reached levels of above $50, the price level had come down again to around $20. However, in the late 1990s the oil price slid towards a level of $10. This caused a lot of turmoil within OPEC, with various members blaming each other:

> After criticizing each other from afar for several weeks, Saudi and Venezuelan oil officials got into the same room and glared at each other: the Venezuelans blinked. As recently as early March, Erwin Jose Arrieta, Venezuela's energy minister, had declared that he was too busy to attend a proposed OPEC meeting and vowed not to cut production 'even by one barrel'. Coming from OPEC's biggest cheater, that attitude was regarded as unhelpful. Oil prices had dropped by 55% since January 1997, to hit a low of $11.27 a barrel, and had been sinking by 50 cents a week for months. Now, under a deal brokered by Mexico, its great non-OPEC rival in the hemisphere, Venezuela has agreed to cheat somewhat less flagrantly, and Saudi Arabia to match cuts by the two big Latin American producers. Ten other producers are having their arms twisted to follow suit. By removing between 1.1m and 2m barrels a day from world markets, the producers hope to 'stabilize' prices.

Oil prices recovered, and by the year 2000 they were above $30 again. High oil prices are a threat to economic growth in many regions. Therefore the OPEC countries have in principle agreed to keep oil prices in a target band of $22–28. If the price remains above $28 for 20 trading days, the cartel is supposed to raise production by 0.5m barrels a day. However, this 'automatic' increase did not happen when in June 2000 the price had sailed past the 20-day upper trigger. This is how *The Economist* analyzed the situation:

> Various confused and contradictory explanations surfaced from ministers, but not the oil. Only at their next officially scheduled meeting did they come up with a meagre quota increase. Even if ministers agree to lift quotas by the magic 500,000 barrels per day (bpd) figure, very little oil may actually reach the markets. That is because this figure does not allow for cheating. At the moment, the cartel's official quotas total about 25.4m bpd, whereas its actual production last month topped 26m bpd. A quota increase of 500,000 bpd will serve merely to legitimize existing cheating. Countries will try to cheat once again on whatever new quotas are agreed.

Sources: The Economist, 28 March 1998 and 9 September 2000

- *Random*: choose randomly (by tossing a coin) between co-operate and defect.
- *Tit-for-tat-plus*: in the first round choose co-operate; in the following rounds, if the other player co-operated in the previous round, choose co-operate with probability $1 - \varepsilon$ and defect with probability ε; if the other player defected in the previous round choose defect.
- *Tit-for-two-tats*: in the first two rounds choose co-operate; in the following rounds choose defect if the other player defected in the last two rounds, otherwise choose co-operate.
- *Uneven*: in the first round and in all subsequent uneven rounds co-operate; in the second and in all subsequent even rounds defect.

Now suppose that you belong to a group of say 10 people. You will successively play the iterated prisoner's dilemma against each of the other members of the group. This is the iterated prisoner's dilemma for many players. What is your best strategy? The answer depends on many factors:

- The payoffs: If T (the temptation to defect in Figure 5.9) is very large, then an occasional unexpected defection could be part of your best strategy.
- The strategies of the other players: tit-for-tat-plus will perform very nicely against tit-for-two-tats but probably not very well against permanent retaliation.
- The way you discount future payoffs.

The iterated prisoner's dilemma has been investigated by Axelrod (1984). Axelrod invited scientists from several disciplines, from mathematics to psychology, to submit strategies for the prisoner's dilemma with payoffs given in Figure 5.10. Note that with these payoffs permanent mutual co-operation is better than taking turns at exploiting each other (permanent mutual co-operation gives each player 3 in each round; taking turns at exploiting each other means receiving 5 and 0 in two consecutive rounds, an average of 2.5). In most real-world situations it is better to co-operate than to take turns at exploiting each other. In the iterated prisoner's dilemma this is equivalent to assuming that $0.5(N + T) < R$.

With the payoffs given in Figure 5.10 and no discounting, Axelrod organized two computer tournaments between the strategies he had received. In each tournament each strategy was paired with each other strategy, with itself and with random. Both tournaments were won by tit-for-tat.

Tit-for-tat has several characteristics that may explain its success. First, tit-for-tat is *nice*. That means that it is never the first to defect. If tit-for-tat is paired with itself, with tit-for-two-tats, with permanent retaliation or with all C then it will receive 3 in each round.

Second, tit-for-tat is *forgiving*. This means that if the other player defects once but then starts to cooperate again, tit-for-tat will punish him only once. Thus, unlike permanent retaliation, tit-for-tat is able to restore co-operation after a single defection.

Third, tit-for-tat is *retaliatory*. If the other player defects, he is punished immediately. For this reason it is difficult to exploit tit-for-tat.

Axelrod's results show quite nicely how two selfish and rational players in the iterated prisoner's dilemma can achieve co-operation even if they cannot make binding commitments (they cannot trust each other not to break promises). This has important consequences for the way that members of an organization co-operate. Suppose the two players are Arabia and Russia and that each country can choose its production level each week. The two countries then play the iterated prisoner's dilemma. Suppose, further, that they agree to have production levels observed. That mutual co-operation can arise in this case is not surprising. Now suppose that the two players are two large firms that have formed a joint venture. To co-operate means giving your partner full access to all relevant know-how; to defect means to give away as little knowledge as possible. If both firms expect to set up similar joint ventures in the

Box 5.6 ■ Reputation as commitment

Dixit and Nalebuff (1991) explain the building of reputation as a form of commitment as follows:

If you try a strategic move in a game and then back off, you may lose your reputation for credibility. In a once-in-a-lifetime situation, reputation may be unimportant and therefore of little commitment value. But, you typically play several games with different rivals at the same time, or the same rivals at different times. Then you have an incentive to establish a reputation, and this serves as a commitment that makes your strategic moves credible.

During the Berlin crisis in 1961, John F. Kennedy explained the importance of the US reputation: 'If we do not meet our commitments in Berlin, where will we later stand? If we are not true to our word there, all that we have achieved in collective security, which relies on these words, will mean nothing.'

Source: Dixit and Nalebuff (1991)

future, co-operation is likely to arise. For these firms it now pays to invest in their *reputation* as a trustworthy partner. Building a reputation is one form of showing a commitment (see Box 5.6). In single-stage games it is not possible to build a reputation: the game is over after your first move. In repeated games, however, players may invest in building reputations. Reputations for trustworthiness and co-operativeness help to establish co-operation, even in the adverse conditions of a prisoner's dilemma.

Similar situations arise when two people have to work together to accomplish a task. They can both choose between a high level of effort (which is equivalent to co-operating) and a low level of effort (defecting). If they have to work together many times, co-operation is more likely to arise than if they work together only once. If the players meet only once, then we predict mutual defection. What happens if they know that they will meet each other 1,000 times? In the last round they will surely both defect, since there is no future from there on in which the other player can punish defection. In round number 999 they will also both defect, since they know they are both going to defect in the last round anyway. This logic taken to the extreme leads inevitably to the conclusion that both players will defect in the first round. Of course, instead of 1,000 any other finite number will yield the same result. Only if both players are to meet an infinite number of times or if they do not know how often they will meet can we expect mutual co-operation.

What is the lesson we can learn from Axelrod's results? Does it mean that, in reality, it is always best to play tit-for-tat? Not necessarily. An important difference between the real world and a computer tournament concerns the possibility of mistakes. In computer tournaments mistakes cannot occur; in reality mistakes are not impossible. Suppose that the heads of two Mafia families, Antara and Brizi, are both tit-for-tat players. Suppose, too, that mistakes are possible. Thus it is possible that while Antara and Brizi both co-operated in a certain round (round *n*), Brizi incorrectly thinks that Antara defected in round

Table 5.1 Two tit-for-tat players with the possibility of making a mistake

Round	Antara	Brizi
1	Co-operate	Co-operate
2	Co-operate	Co-operate
⋮	⋮	⋮
n	Co-operate	Co-operate
$n+1$	Co-operate	Defect
$n+2$	Defect	Co-operate
$n+3$	Co-operate	Defect

n. Brizi will then defect in round $n+1$. Antara will react by defecting in round $n+2$, which means that Brizi will defect in round number $n+3$. This is illustrated in Table 5.1.

One mistake provokes a chain reaction of punishments. Antara and Brizi now take turns at exploiting each other. This is worse than mutual co-operation. When mistakes are possible, tit-for-tat may be too aggressive. If mistakes are possible it may be better to play a strategy such as:

- start co-operating in the first round, and then
- revert to tit-for-tat as soon as you 'observe' two defections in any three consecutive rounds.

5.6 Summary: insights from game theory

In this chapter we have given an introduction to game theory. Game theory is a powerful tool for analyzing situations in which two or more persons have to make interdependent decisions. Four types of game have been discussed. In the one-stage game for two players we distinguished between sequential and simultaneous games. In a sequential game one of the players moves first and the other player can observe this move. In a simultaneous game each player has to make his decision not knowing what the other player has decided or will decide. The difference between a sequential and a simultaneous game has to do with lack of information. Without observable information, co-ordination is difficult to achieve.

The main principle to remember in sequential games is 'look ahead and reason back'. We saw how a potential entrant can use this principle in the entry game. A threat by the incumbent firm to lower prices after entry is an empty threat if, after entry has occurred, it is in the incumbent's own interest not to lower prices. The incumbent can make his threat credible by making a commitment that irreversibly alters the payoffs, so that after entry it is in the incumbent's interest to execute the threat. By applying the principle of looking ahead and reasoning back we saw how the incumbent firm can determine whether it is in its interest to change the payoffs (and thus pose a credible threat). Of course, it is again a necessary condition that the information about the commitment is available to the entrant. If it is, the entrant can apply the same principle of looking ahead and reasoning back to determine whether profitable entry will be possible. By changing the structure of the game the incumbent can thus influence the incentives for the entrant, and thereby the likely outcome of the game.

The role of observable information became even more apparent in the discussion of different types of auction. In open auctions the private information of most bidders is gradually revealed. Only the winner can still possess private information that would have led him to bid substantially higher, if he were forced to. We saw how the seller may therefore consider changing the design of the auction to a two-stage process with a Dutch auction as a second stage. This was another example where one party may change the structure of the game, the incentives for the other party, and thus the likely outcome. In sealed-bid auctions no information about the private valuations of bidders is revealed during the auction. In the face of this uncertainty, winners run the risk of suffering the winner's curse: that is, obtaining the prize as a consequence of making the most optimistic estimates.

For simultaneous games (such as the prisoner's dilemma) we have explained the concept of a dominant strategy. A dominant strategy is a strategy that is best whatever the other player does. In the prisoner's dilemma each player has a dominant strategy. That strategy is to defect. Hence if the game is played only once we would expect both players to defect. Yet mutual co-operation is better for both of them. If they can trust each other – that is, if they can both make binding commitments – then surely they will agree to co-operate. The problem in the prisoner's dilemma is that, after such an agreement has been made, each party has an incentive to cheat. This is the main problem for the stability of cartels: after an agreement has been made to restrict output by cartel members, each member has an incentive to increase output.

Finally, we have explored the consequences of playing a game repeatedly. We saw that co-operation between individual players may then evolve even in the adverse conditions of a prisoner's dilemma. In the iterated prisoner's dilemma a strategy consists of a set of rules that specify what action to take given the history of the game so far. In computer tournaments, tit-for-tat has proven to be a good strategy. This is probably because tit-for-tat is nice (it is never the first to defect), forgiving (it is able to restore co-operation after a defection by the other player), and retaliatory (the other player is punished immediately for defection). However, when mistakes are possible, tit-for-tat may be too aggressive. Since strategy now includes the history of the game so far, players may invest in building reputations. It was shown that reputations can be considered as assets that reflect commitment.

This completes the set of Chapters 2–5 in which we have explained the fundamental concepts and methods underlying the economic approaches to organizations. In Chapters 6–10 we build on this knowledge to introduce five economic approaches to organizations. As you will see, the approaches differ in the problems addressed, in the concepts and language used, and in the modes of analysis. This introduction to game theory will help you discern the basic features of the settings in which the players make their decisions in each of the subsequent chapters. In the final chapter, we return to the common perspective in these approaches and highlight their similarities and differences.

Questions

1 When corporations want to divest individual business units, they often employ the services of an investment banker such as Goldman Sachs or Morgan Stanley. Such investment bankers often use an auction process to find the most suitable buyers for the business. It is customary that these auctions are two-stage and sealed-bid:

- The first stage consists of soliciting non-binding bids from a wide range of potential buyers on the basis of general information distributed in a bid book.
- The second stage consists of a 'due diligence' procedure in which a limited set of potential buyers may investigate the acquisition candidate in depth as a basis for their final (binding) bid.

Discuss the advantages of this procedure for the corporation selling the business unit.

2 Suppose you are a competitor of the business unit to be sold under the conditions sketched in Question 1. You have no interest or not enough money to acquire the divested company. However, you would like to obtain the private information that will be available for inspection in round 2. You contemplate the possibility of making a sufficiently high (non-binding) bid in round 1 to be admitted to round 2, only to decline making a final, binding bid in round 2.

   Apart from legal reasons (you would not be negotiating in good faith), which economic reason could deter you from this course of action?

3 Look at the list of strategies against which tit-for-tat competed in Axelrod's tournament (section 5.5.2). It varies from permanent retaliation to uneven. Against which individual strategies do you expect tit-for-tat to win, tie and lose? Why did tit-for-tat win the tournament?

Suggested further reading

Axelrod, R. (1984), *The Evolution of Cooperation*, New York: Basic Books.
Dixit, A. and B. Nalebuff (1991), *Thinking Strategically*, New York: Norton & Co.
Rasmusen, E. (1989), *Games and Information: An Introduction to the Theory of Games*, Oxford: Basil Blackwell.

Notes

1. By rational we mean that players decide on the basis of their utility functions (or objective functions) only. Game theory usually assumes that players act only in their own interest. This implies that their utility functions include no variables pertaining to the other players' welfare.

2. In fact, with video technology no agreement was reached on standard specifications leading to long and intense competition on system choice. With CD technology such agreement was reached and all parties adhered to the set specifications.

3. This $400 million can be interpreted as the expected net present value from all future cash flows if both companies choose VI.

4. Rasmusen (1989, p.35) concludes a similar example by saying: 'The question is really one of psychology rather than economics.'

5. Credible threats and binding commitments can be made in various ways. Dixit and Nalebuff (1991, ch.6) discuss eight such ways. See also Ghemawat (1991). We return to the subject of commitment in Chapter 9.

6. In economic terms this outcome would be considered efficient since it is Pareto-optimal (see Chapters 1 and 2).

7. In addition, it could be mentioned that different designs allow for different types of strategic behaviour. Consider the use by the seller of a 'straw man' in the bidding or the 'signalling' of a buyer's intentions in the first phase of a two-stage auction.

8. Notationally, there is some confusion in the literature whether to refer to these games as the prisoner's dilemma or the prisoners' dilemma. As will become clear, each prisoner has a dilemma (favouring the singular notation), and all prisoners have the same dilemma (favouring the plural). If you want to identify with more than one prisoner, please feel free to mentally adjust the apostrophe.

9. One way such binding commitments are made in criminal practice is to take hostages. If both prisoners know that their families are threatened if they confess, they will think twice before confessing.

6 Behavioural theory of the firm

6.1 Introduction

How does a business firm make economic decisions? That is the central question of the behavioural theory of the firm developed by March, Simon and Cyert (March and Simon, 1958; Cyert and March, 1963). Examples of economic decisions include decisions on price, output, advertising levels, and investments in machinery.

In standard microeconomics it is assumed that firms are holistic entities that seek to maximize profits. By contrast, the behavioural theory of the firm postulates the firm as a coalition of (groups of) participants, each with their own objectives. Such a coalition of participants need not have maximization of profits as its sole objective. In fact, the process of defining the goals of the organization is the first step in describing actual decision processes within the firm. The second step is to describe how the organization forms expectations upon which the decision processes are based. The third and last step is to describe the process of organizational choice.

6.2 The firm as a coalition of participants

The behavioural theory of the firm postulates the firm as a coalition of participants. Each participant receives from the organization *inducements* in return for which he makes *contributions* to the organization. Each participant will continue his participation only as long as the inducements offered are as great as or greater than (measured in terms of *his* values and in terms of the alternatives open to him) the contributions he is asked to make. Hence the organization will continue to exist only so long as the contributions are sufficient to provide inducements in large enough measure to draw forth these contributions.

Contributions

Inducements

Participants in the firm are employees, investors, suppliers, distributors, consumers and possibly others. **Contributions** made by employees include not only the labour hours they put in but also their ideas for improvements, their intelligence and so on. **Inducements** offered to employees include monetary payments (wages, retirement plans, etc.), but also non-monetary benefits such as self-achievement and job satisfaction. The relationship between the firm and its employees is illustrated in Figure 6.1. A similar figure can be sketched for

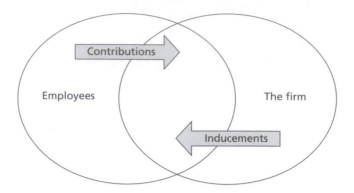

Figure 6.1 **The firm and its employees in behavioural theory**

any other group of participants. The figure suggests that the firm is more than just one group of participants (here the employees). It also suggests that employees have other roles outside the firm (e.g. in their neighbourhood, church, and family).

In order to illustrate the differences between the behavioural theory and standard microeconomics we discuss the decision of an employee to continue participation. In our description of standard microeconomics, employees receive a wage in return for a number of labour hours. In behavioural theory, employees receive several different inducements including monetary and non-monetary payments. In mathematical terms we would say that they receive a vector of inducements (that is, several inducements of different types). They also make a vector of contributions. This, however, is not a fundamental difference since standard microeconomics can also handle a vector of inducements and contributions. The fundamental difference lies in the *information* that employees have concerning alternative job opportunities. In standard microeconomics we assume that each employee knows exactly what she could earn elsewhere. As soon as she sees that she can earn more elsewhere she will take the other job. So for the same work all companies must pay the same wage: in a competitive labour market there can be only one price for labour of a particular type. In the **Aspiration level**   behavioural theory we assume that each employee has an **aspiration level** concerning her wage rate. She is content and will not start looking for another job so long as the wage she receives is greater than or equal to her aspiration level. If the wage she receives continues to be higher than her aspiration level, then her aspiration level is slowly adjusted upwards. Thus it takes some time before the aspiration level reaches the wage she regularly receives. This aspiration level is also adjusted upwards if she hears that another company pays more than her aspiration level for the same work. This adjustment also occurs slowly, so it takes some time before she becomes dissatisfied. If after some time there is a large enough gap between her aspiration level and the wage she receives, she will start looking for another job. If she finds another job that pays significantly more than her current job, she will leave. This process of adjusting one's aspiration level and looking for another job may take a considerable amount of time.

The situation is even more complicated than described above because inducements contain not only monetary payments but also various other benefits. Information about these other benefits may be even harder to obtain than information about wage rates. It is, for example, usually very hard to find out what the atmosphere among colleagues in another organization really is. The harder it is to obtain information about inducements and contributions that other firms make and demand, the slower is the process of adjusting aspiration levels. In behavioural theory the labour market is not a market of perfect competition. Differences between wages and other working conditions can exist for long periods of time because workers cannot compare the inducements offered and the contributions demanded by other firms. They simply lack information.

For other participants we can sketch a similar picture concerning the decision to stay with the coalition or leave. Consider consumers. In the model of perfectly competitive markets, price is all that matters for a consumer (remember that in the model of a perfectly competitive market, products are homogeneous: there are no differences between the products of different producers). Moreover we assume that consumers know exactly what prices quoted by different producers are. Naturally they buy only from the cheapest source. Thus in the model of a competitive market all prices must be equal. If producers quote different prices, only the one with the lowest price will sell anything; all others will cease to exist.

In the behavioural theory we assume that consumers do not know exactly what prices are quoted by other producers. A consumer continues to buy from the same producer so long as the price is less than or equal to his aspiration level. If a consumer gets more information on lower prices quoted by other producers he will slowly adjust his aspiration level downwards. This picture becomes more realistic if we allow quality differences between products from different producers. Then a consumer also has an aspiration level with respect to quality. It seems quite reasonable to assume that a consumer has only vague information about quality levels of products offered by other producers. Thus aspiration levels with respect to quality will be adjusted only slowly.

For every group of participants we can sketch a picture like Figure 6.1. If we do so and combine all those pictures we arrive at a picture like Figure 6.2. Figure 6.2 shows that the firm is a coalition of groups of participants and that each group of participants has other roles and interests outside the firm. The groups of participants in Figure 6.2 are often referred to as *stakeholders* (each group has a 'stake' in the firm). Stakeholders include the investors (the shareholders) as well as employees, suppliers and customers. According to standard microeconomics, managers should serve only the interests of the shareholders. According to behavioural theory, however, a firm can survive only if its managers take care of the interests of all stakeholders, not just the shareholders. (Box 6.1 develops this point further.)

It is clear from this discussion that in behavioural theory there is competition between firms in the labour market, in the market for final products, in the capital market, and so on. However, behavioural theory focuses not on competition between firms but on the process of decision-making within the firm. The competitive context in various markets is further taken as given.

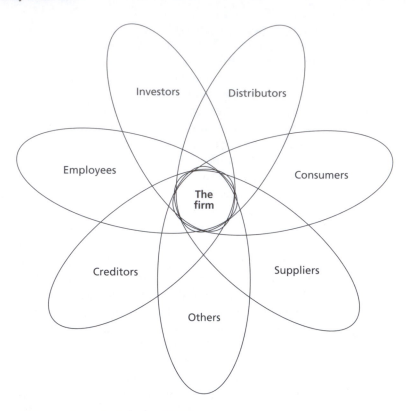

Figure 6.2 **The firm as a coalition of groups of participants**

6.3 Organizational goals

6.3.1 Bargaining and organizational slack

The process of decision-making within the firm starts with the definition of the goals of the firm. In standard microeconomics we assume that the firm has a single goal, usually profit maximization. In the behavioural theory the firm is viewed as a **coalition of participants**. Each participant has his or her own goals. These goals will ordinarily not coincide. In general we expect a conflict of goals from different participants. Consumers cannot be offered lower prices and employees higher wages without lowering profits (the inducements for the providers of equity capital).

In behavioural theory it is postulated that goals of the firm are arrived at through a bargaining process. During this bargaining process both the composition and the general goals of the coalition are established. The **bargaining power** of each potential participant depends on how unique the contribution is that he can offer to the coalition. So an unskilled worker in a country where unskilled labour is plentiful does not have much bargaining power (unless there are strong labour unions). Someone possessing a highly specialized skill that is essential for the success of the coalition has much more bargaining

Coalition of participants

Bargaining power

Box 6.1 ■ Stakeholders and shareholders

One of the liveliest current debates in the management field focuses on the question of which interests the management of a company should serve: those of the shareholders (only) or of the broader set of 'stakeholders' (which includes the employees, customers, suppliers and the community as well as the shareholders)?

Economic theories have different answers to this question. In Chapter 7 we see that agency theory tends to view the shareholders as the owners of the firm. In this view the managers should act as agents of the owners of the firm, maximizing the owner's wealth. In everyday management language this view implies that the management of a company should maximize shareholder value.

The behavioural theory of the firm has a different perspective. It views the firm as a coalition of groups of participants. In this view, management's task is not to maximize the wealth of any particular group of participants, such as shareholders; rather, it is to enhance the firm's wealth by serving all interests of participant (= stakeholder) groups well. (Behavioural theory leaves the question unanswered as to what should happen with any economic surplus (profit) that is left after all participants have received their necessary inducements. In agency theory, this residual value belongs to the shareholders.)

The flavour of this debate can be tasted from the following excerpts of an interview by *Fortune* magazine with the economist John Kay, who is introduced by *Fortune* as 'Britain's leading management thinker'.

FORTUNE: **While the recent trend in the US and elsewhere is to give priority to shareholders' interests, you argue that managers need to balance all stakeholders' interests. Why should managers focus more on the interests of stakeholders like customers, employees, suppliers, and the local community?**

JOHN KAY: Let's turn this around and ask instead: why should managers give priority to shareholders' interests? The most compelling answer I hear is that it's because the shareholders own the business. Now if the business consisted purely of its physical assets, then I would find that fairly persuasive, but I don't think that is true. A company is its history, its structure of relationships, its reputation. These are the things that allow the company to add value, which creates shareholder wealth, and to say that shareholders own these things is kind of bizarre. They don't and they couldn't.

FORTUNE: **Is the primary purpose of management to maximize shareholder wealth?**

JOHN KAY: Economists tend to believe that everyone acts to maximize something. But in our everyday lives, we aren't maximizing any particular thing: rather, we are balancing different and conflicting concerns. I think the same is true of companies, and therefore I don't think companies are there to maximize shareholder value – or social welfare. Managers of companies work to balance several different interests. That is the reality of how companies function.

FORTUNE: **What is a company's purpose, if it is not to maximize shareholder value?**

JOHN KAY: Producing goods and services people want. Business is about providing employment, providing value for customers, for developing skills of employees, for developing capabilities of suppliers – as well as earning money for shareholders.

Source: Fortune, 17 February 1997, p.61

power. For the providers of equity capital, profit maximization or maximization of the value of the firm is an important objective. The extent to which they succeed in realizing their objective depends on the relative bargaining power of the various groups of participants.

The upshot of this discussion is that a real firm ordinarily has no single goal or clearly defined objective function. Only individual participants have goals. These goals are in the form of aspiration levels. The real achievement of the particular goal of a certain participant can be only temporarily below his aspiration level. For all participants achievement levels will be at least equal to their aspiration levels most of the time. For some it will be above their aspiration levels. The difference between total resources and the total payments

Organizational slack   necessary to preserve the coalition is termed **organizational slack**. Participants' aspiration levels adjust to actual payments and to alternatives external to the organization. Hence in the long run we would expect aspiration levels to be equal to actual payments *and* to alternatives external to the organization. If this were the case, there would be no organizational slack. The rate of payments made to coalition members would then be analogous to factor prices in a perfectly competitive market. However, the behavioural theory states that markets are imperfect. The basic reason is that information about levels of goal achievement that participants can realize if they join another organization is difficult to obtain, especially concerning non-monetary payments, so aspiration levels adjust only slowly. In a world without change, aspiration levels would after some time equal actual payments and external alternatives. In a changing world, for example in a world with technological progress, we normally expect organizational slack.

6.3.2   Operational subgoals

In a real firm an overall goal such as profit maximization needs to be translated

Operational subgoals   into several **operational subgoals**. It is often impossible to avoid a conflict between these operational subgoals.

As an example, imagine a firm making soap noodles. Soap noodles are little pieces of soap in the form of noodles. They are made in a chemical plant that uses animal fat as a basic raw material. They are sold to soap manufacturers, who press soap noodles into tablets, and give the soap a colour, an odour, and a brand name. Suppose you are in charge of the soap noodle firm. You have two managers reporting to you – a production manager and a sales manager. You know that the number of soap noodles sold depends on (1) price, (2) the level of effort of your sales manager, and (3) a random factor. You also know that real production cost per unit depends on (1) the number of units sold per year, (2) the number and size of changes in production levels during the year, and (3) the level of effort of your production manager. The sales manager makes decisions on prices quoted to individual customers; the production manager decides how much to produce each week. Assume for the moment that soap noodles can be stored on the factory site at no cost. You want to give each manager an operational subgoal that is consistent with your overall goal of profit maximization. You can do this by specifying the following operational sub-goals. For the sales manager:

Maximize $N \times (P - SC)$

where

N = number of units sold
P = price
SC = standard unit cost

For the production manager you can specify the following goal:

Minimize RC

where

RC = real unit cost

This is equivalent to maximizing $(SC - RC)$ since SC is fixed.

Now assume, for simplicity, that production cost per unit does not depend on the number of units sold (that is, assume there are no scale economies in production). The production manager's goal is then equivalent to

Maximize $N \times (SC - RC)$

We can now combine the goals of the two managers thus:

Maximize $[N \times (P - SC)] + [N \times (SC - RC)]$

This is equivalent to

Maximize $N \times (P - RC)$

Since we assume that inventory costs are zero, this is equivalent to profit max-imization. If inventories can be stored without cost, the sales manager and the production manager can make their decisions independently. In reality, inven-tories cannot be stored without cost. If inventory costs are not negligible, you cannot specify operational subgoals for your two managers without creating a conflict of interests between them. Who should be responsible for inventory costs? The inventory level depends on the decisions made by both the sales manager and the production manager. If you make the production manager responsible for inventory costs, you create a conflict. The production manager will want to keep the inventory levels as low as possible, but this imposes the risk of stock-out on the sales manager. She would rather prefer safe levels of inventory to be able to satisfy customer demand at all times. However, if you make the sales manager responsible for inventory costs, you also create a con-flict. Now the sales manager will want to keep inventory levels as low as possi-ble. She will try to achieve this by frequently ordering very small lot sizes. This means very small lot sizes in manufacturing. The production manager would prefer large lot sizes in order to minimize production cost. If you introduce an inventory manager, what subgoal can you specify for her? You would surely create a conflict between your inventory manager and your sales manager as well as one between your inventory manager and your production manager.

This example demonstrates that it is difficult and often impossible to specify operational subgoals that are consistent with profit maximization and which do not lead to conflicts between managers of functional departments.

In the behavioural theory we assume that operational subgoals are specified and given to managers of functional departments. With each subgoal goes an aspiration level. Managers are rewarded if they at least reach these aspiration levels. This does not eliminate conflict between managers of functional departments — it is *quasi-resolution of conflict* rather than resolution of conflict.

6.4 Organizational expectations

An important assumption of standard microeconomics is symmetric information: everyone has the same information. In the behavioural theory this assumption is relaxed: everyone does not have the same information. In the soap noodle firm you had a production manager and a sales manager reporting to you. The production manager decides how much to produce each week. To make this decision he needs information on future sales. He can make a sales forecast by extrapolating historical data on shipments made. He can also ask the sales manager to make a sales forecast. It is likely that the sales manager can make the better forecast: the sales manager can make the same extrapolation as the production manager, but she can improve upon it by her knowledge of recent changes in market situations.

Suppose the sales manager makes a sales forecast each week. Will the production manager now use this sales forecast only? Empirical evidence shows that many production managers do not. They continue to make their own sales forecast. The reason is that they know that:

- the sales manager is more often than not too optimistic (maybe people with an optimistic nature tend to become sales managers);
- the sales manager has an incentive to make an optimistic sales forecast in order to reduce the probability of a stock-out.

This example demonstrates the use of expectations in decision-making within the firm. Expectations are the result of drawing inferences from available information. Decision-makers within the firm may have different information. In addition, they may draw different inferences from the same set of information. Hence, even if two people within the same firm have the same information, they may still hold different expectations.

6.5 Organizational choice

Another important assumption of standard microeconomics is that behaviour of firms can be adequately described as maximizing behaviour. This makes two assumptions:

- that, at the moment of decision-making, firms know all decision alternatives;

■ that firms are able to compare all alternatives and choose the one that maximizes the objective function.

Behavioural theory rejects both assumptions. In the real world firms have to
make decisions under conditions of partial ignorance. That is, they have to
make a decision on a proposal (e.g. accept or reject a proposal to develop a new
product) without knowing what alternatives will turn up the next day. Of
course, they can also decide to devote resources to search for alternatives before
deciding on the present proposal. In the context of standard microeconomics
we would have to assume that firms are able to calculate the expected marginal
revenue from searching for an alternative and the expected marginal cost of
searching for an alternative. Firms would then, presumably, continue searching
until the marginal cost of additional search equalled the marginal revenue of
additional search. If many alternatives are potentially available, firms would
invest a lot of time (and resources) in searching. So much, in fact, that other
firms could realize significant advantages in deciding more quickly. Moreover,
in the real world, firms cannot possibly hope to evaluate all potential new
products against each other.

In behavioural theory we therefore assume that alternatives are evaluated
one at a time. Firms do not maximize an objective function. Instead they make
a rough estimate of several consequences of a decision alternative. For example, for a proposal to develop a new product they try to estimate:

■ the size of the market;
■ their expected market share;
■ the price and production cost of the new product;
■ the development cost.

There are perhaps other variables as well. They have aspiration levels for all of
these variables. If the market is 'large enough', if their expected market share is
'sufficient', if the margin between price and production cost is 'reasonable' and
if development cost is 'not too high', then they accept the proposal. They do
not maximize in the sense of evaluating all possible proposals for new products

Satisficing   at the same time. Their behaviour is better described as **satisficing**: that is,
searching for a solution that meets aspiration levels and is therefore acceptable.

In behavioural theory, then, we assume that firms satisfice rather than maximize. One reason for this is that decision alternatives come one at a time.
Another reason is that human decision-makers are simply unable to make all
the calculations necessary to compare all alternatives. The calculations often
are too complex. Or, to put it another way, the capacity of the human mind to
make all the necessary calculations is often too small. In behavioural theory we

Bounded rationality   assume **bounded rationality**: that is, we assume that human decision-makers
may try to maximize but are not always able to do so. We return to the notion
of bounded rationality in Chapter 8 on transaction cost economics.

Finally, there is a third reason why firms satisfice rather than maximize. The
firm is seen as a coalition of participants, each having his own objectives. If the
firm has no single objective function, how can it maximize? Instead, organizational choice is described as a process of deciding on alternatives one at a time.

As soon as an alternative is found that meets the aspiration levels of all coalition members, it is accepted. Suppose that a firm wants to buy a new software package for order processing. Suppose further that the sales manager, the production manager and the controller form a three-person committee that has to make the decision. Behavioural theory assumes that each may have a different criterion for choosing the software package. For example, the sales manager wants to buy a package that provides information on inventories available for sale in real time, the production manager wants a package that allows him to make a reliable sales forecast, and the controller one that produces invoices as soon as the order is shipped. The three-person committee cannot maximize, since their three criteria cannot be translated into a single criterion (see Box 6.2). Instead they start looking for a package that meets certain minimum standards (aspiration levels) for each of those three criteria. As soon as they have found a package that is acceptable to all of them, they stop searching for another package.

Box 6.2 ■ Decision-making by a committee

Consider a three-person committee. Suppose each person wants to maximize his or her own objective. Suppose further that all objectives are quantifiable, and denote them as C_1, C_2 and C_3. The three-person committee can maximize only if these three objectives can be combined into a single objective function as follows:

$$C_0 = \alpha C_1 + \beta C_2 + \gamma C_3$$

This requires the three-person committee to

- accept each other's objectives;
- agree on the weights (α, β, γ) assigned to each objective.

Only if the members of the committee are able to meet both conditions, can they jointly maximize an overall objective function (C_0). If either of the two conditions is not met, as will often be the case in real life, satisficing is a ready alternative procedure. Satisficing requires only that each member of the committee is able to specify his or her own aspiration level. If an alternative is found that meets all three aspiration levels, there is a unanimous decision.

6.6 Summary: goals and decision-making within the firm in behavioural theory

In behavioural theory the firm is postulated as a coalition of (groups of) participants, such as shareholders, employees, managers, suppliers, and customers. This is a major difference from standard microeconomic theory, which sees the firm as a holistic entity. Each participant receives inducements from the firm in return for the contributions he makes to the firm. A participant will remain within the coalition if, in his own opinion, the value of the inducements he receives is greater than the value of the contributions he has to make.

In behavioural theory we assume that not all persons have the same information. For example, an employee may not know exactly how much he could earn with another employer or what the atmosphere between colleagues really is in another firm. In behavioural theory we also assume that human beings are boundedly rational. This means that human beings are unable to make all sorts of difficult calculations in a split second, nor can they process all the information they receive. It does not mean that humans do not want to maximize something, only that they are not always able to do so. The behaviour of human beings is better described as satisficing than as maximizing. For example, an employee will have an aspiration level with respect to the wage he wants to receive. As long as the the wage he earns is above this aspiration level, the employee is content. Owing to lack of information he may even be content with a wage lower than what he could earn elsewhere.

In the behavioural theory of the firm, each participant or group of participants has his own goals, usually in the form of aspiration levels. These goals will generally not coincide. The result is that the firm will generally have several goals, which are arrived at through a bargaining process between the (groups of) participants.

The overall goals of the firm need to be translated into operational subgoals in order to be of practical value. This is usually quite complicated even if the firm has only one goal such as profit maximization. Consider a firm owned and managed by one person, the entrepreneur. Why is it impossible for the entrepreneur to hire only people who just do as they are told? In a very small firm this may be possible. Direct supervision is often the most important co-ordinating mechanism in a very small firm, as we saw in Chapter 3. In a larger firm, however, the decisions that have to be made become so numerous that the entrepreneur has to delegate some decisions. For example, one person cannot make all decisions concerning marketing, production and inventory management. It is simply inefficient to transmit all information to a single person so that he or she can make all the decisions. So we have a decision-making process in which two or more people participate. These people bring their own goals to the organization.

Suppose the goal of the entrepreneur is profit maximization. If he appoints functional managers it is impossible to specify operational subgoals without creating a conflict of interests. So managers of functional departments are given an operational subgoal with a target level. Their task is to reach their target level, not to maximize or minimize something. By giving managers of functional departments a target level the entrepreneur leaves some room for mutual adjustment. Mutual adjustment is then used in conjunction with direct supervision as a co-ordinating mechanism (see Chapter 3).

There are four fundamental differences between behavioural theory and standard microeconomic theory:

- Behavioural theory postulates the firm as a coalition of participants.
- Behavioural theory does not assume that the firm has a single objective.
- Behavioural theory assumes that information cannot be transmitted without cost.

■ Behavioural theory assumes that human decision-makers are boundedly rational.

As we shall see in the following chapters, several of these characteristics of decision-making within firms have been incorporated in various economic approaches to organizations, which were developed later. This was recognized by Cyert and March when they wrote a preface to the second edition of their classical *A Behavioral Theory of the Firm* in 1992:

> We had an agenda in 1963. We thought that research on economics and research on organizations should have something to say to each other. We thought that the theory of the firm should be connected to empirical observations of firms. We thought that empirical observations of what happens in firms should be connected to interesting theoretical ideas . . . The agenda and the first steps we proposed were somewhat deviant from dominant ideas in both economics and organization theory when the book first appeared. In the years since 1963 . . . a number of the ideas discussed in the book have become part of the received doctrine. In particular, a perspective that sees firms as coalitions of multiple, conflicting interests using standard rules and procedures to operate under conditions of bounded rationality is now rather widely adopted in descriptions and theories of the firm.

Questions

1 In a period of an economic recession most companies are able to increase production efficiency by reducing their workforce without any decrease in the level of output. Apparently, firms take action to reduce costs only when profit rates are declining. Many firms seem to be able to restore previous profit levels by taking this kind of action. Why do firms not minimize production cost in the first place, before the recession sets in?

2 Reread Box 6.1. We assume that you agree with John Kay that managers should serve the interests of all stakeholders in the firm, not just the interests of the shareholders. Somehow it seems morally right to do so. Now suppose that you meet a proponent of standard microeconomic theory who tells you: 'Yes, I do agree with you that the interests of the employees are very important. That is exactly why managers should take into account only the interests of the shareholders. If they do just that, the result will be a Pareto-optimal allocation of resources in the economy. This is the major result of standard microeconomic theory, and there can be no doubt with respect to the correctness of this statement. The result is that the employees will be better off when the managers do not take into account the interests of their employees explicitly than when they do. If they do take into account the interests of their employees explicitly, they will make decisions that result in an allocation of resources in the economy that is not Pareto-optimal. For example, managers may be tempted to postpone a plant closure because by closing that plant employees would lose their jobs. The result will be that employees will have to continue working in their present job,

while if managers constantly close inefficient plants, people will always work in the most modern plants where they can earn the most.'

Suppose that you are invited to debate with this proponent of standard microeconomics. What would your main arguments be?

3 In the behavioural theory of the firm management's task is not to maximize shareholder value but to achieve a balanced satisfaction of all the firm's stake-holders, including employees, customers, suppliers and shareholders. In the real world a firm's top management team has a choice: it can (a) emphasize share-holder value in its policy statements and use shareholder value as the main objective in strategic decision-making, or it can (b) emphasize stakeholder inter-ests in its policy statements and use a variety of objectives including satisfaction of major stakeholders in strategic decision-making. Can you give arguments why firms choosing (b) might end up creating more shareholder value than firms choosing (a)?

4 Goliath Ltd is a company manufacturing bicycles. It is located in Hemel Hempstead, England. The Goliath product offering includes 20 different models with names such as Goliath-Sport, Goliath-Tourist, Goliath-City and so on. Each type comes in a version for men and one for women, and is available in several colours and sizes. In total, Goliath's product range consists of about 600 differ-ent bicycles. It is quite difficult to make reliable demand forecasts for each of these 600 types.

Goliath sells its bicycles mainly through servicing retailers. These are quite small outlets. On average these outlets have no more than 30 bicycles in store. Very often a potential buyer will choose a bicycle of a certain model, but with a colour or size that is not directly available in the store. In such a case the retailer can check on-line whether the desired bicycle is available in Goliath's central warehouse in Hemel Hempstead. If this is so, the retailer can order the desired bicycle with one mouse click and the bicycle will be delivered within 72 hours to any retailer in England. If the desired bicycle is not available, Goliath is likely to lose the sale.

Mrs Prime is Goliath's sales manager. As such she is responsible for making a new sales forecast every four weeks. She has considerable freedom in setting prices and in spending money on promotions and campaigns. A substantial part of her compensation is tied to the results of her sales department. These results are defined as sales minus cost of sales (at standard cost prices) minus selling costs (such as advertising).

Mr Griffin is production manager at Goliath. As such he is responsible for plan-ning and scheduling production runs. A large part of his compensation is formed by a bonus, which is determined by manufacturing cost per bicycle. Small pro-duction runs are extremely expensive, and Mr Griffin is very reluctant to plan small production runs.

Mr Robbins has been recently appointed as managing director. He soon finds out that Mrs Prime and Mr Griffin have many conflicts. Very often certain bicy-cles are out of stock, so Mrs Prime complains bitterly to Mr Robbins about Mr Griffin's refusal to adjust to what the market demands. And Mr Griffin complains to Mr Robbins that Mrs Prime's sales forecasts are very unreliable.

What do you think Mr Robbins should do in order to improve co-operation between Mrs Prime and Mr Griffin? Discuss.

Suggested further reading

Cyert, R.M. and J.G. March (1963), *A Behavioral Theory of the Firm*, Englewood Cliffs, NJ: Prentice Hall. Second edition 1992.

March, J.G. (1994), *A Primer on Decision Making: How Decisions Happen*, New York: Free Press.

March, J.G. and H.A. Simon (1958), *Organizations*, New York: John Wiley.

7 Agency theory

7.1 Introduction

Agency theory in its simplest form discusses the relationship between two people: a principal, and an agent who makes decisions on behalf of the principal. Here are a few examples of agency relations:

- the owner of a firm (principal) and the manager of a firm (agent), who makes decisions affecting the owner's wealth;
- the owner of an estate (principal) and his steward (agent) who makes decisions affecting the owner's wealth;
- a manager (principal) and his subordinate, who makes decisions affecting the manager's reputation;
- a patient (principal) and his physician (agent), who makes decisions affecting the patient's health;
- an insurance company (principal) and a person holding a fire insurance policy (agent), who makes decisions affecting the insurance company's cash flows;
- a lessor (principal) and a lessee (agent), who makes decisions affecting the lessor's property.

Agency relations can be found both within firms (manager and subordinate) and between firms (for example, licensing and franchising). In this chapter we shall take the agency relation between the shareholder(s) and the manager of a firm as our main example.

Within agency theory two streams of literature can be distinguished: the positive theory of agency and the theory of principal and agent. First, in the **positive theory of agency** the firm is viewed as a nexus of contracts. The main research questions in the positive theory of agency are: how do contracts affect the behaviour of participants, and why do we observe certain organizational forms in the real world? In general it is assumed in the positive theory of agency that existing organizational forms are efficient. If they were not, they would not continue to exist. The positive theory of agency thus sets out to explain why organizational forms are as they are. The theory is not (yet) expressed in the form of mathematical models.

Second, in the **theory of principal and agent** the central question is how the principal should design the agent's reward structure. This question is dealt

Positive theory of agency

Theory of principal and agent

with in formal mathematical models. Both streams of literature (positive agency theory and theory of principal and agent) have their antecedents in the literature on the separation of ownership and control (section 7.2).

The remainder of this chapter is organized as follows. Sections 7.3 to 7.5 discuss three different but strongly related contributions to the positive theory of agency. Two important organizational forms in Western societies are the entrepreneurial firm and the public corporation. The entrepreneurial firm is a firm owned and managed by the same person. The public corporation is a corporation with publicly traded shares and widely dispersed ownership. In the entrepreneurial firm there is no separation of ownership and control, while in the public corporation there is. How ownership structure affects managerial behaviour is discussed in section 7.3. Then, in section 7.4, we explain how team production might explain the existence of entrepreneurial firms. In section 7.5 the existence of both entrepreneurial firms and public corporations is explained by focusing on decision processes in conjunction with residual claims. The theory of principal and agent is then discussed in section 7.6. Section 7.7 looks at corporate governance systems. A summary is provided in section 7.8.

7.2 Separation of ownership and control

Adam Smith recognized the problem resulting from the separation of ownership and control: 'Negligence and profusion . . . must always prevail, more or less, in such a company' (see quote from *The Wealth of Nations* in Box 7.1).

The issue of separation of ownership and control did not receive much attention from other early economic writers. The situation changed when, in 1932, Adolf Berle and Gardiner C. Means published *The Modern Corporation and Private Property*. In this book Berle and Means describe the **separation of ownership and control** in the typical twentieth-century corporation. The large corporation, they say, is owned by so many shareholders that no single shareholder owns a significant fraction of the outstanding stock. Therefore no single shareholder has the power really to control the actions of the officers of the corporation.

Separation of ownership and control

Corporate officers themselves in general also own a very small part of the stock of their corporations. Hence the situation may be characterized as follows:

- The bulk of the dividends goes to the outside shareholders.
- All the major decisions are taken by the corporate officers.
- The outside shareholders are unable to control the corporate officers.

In this situation, Berle and Means say, the interests of corporate officers and shareholders diverge widely. The officers are in search of power, prestige, and money for themselves; the shareholders are interested only in profits. Senior managers, in the view of Berle and Means, are in a position to enrich themselves at the expense of the shareholders, and, they fear, sometimes engage in corporate plundering.

Box 7.1 ■ The joint stock company

A quotation from Adam Smith, *The Wealth of Nations*, Book V, Chapter 1:

The trade of a joint stock company is always managed by a court of directors. The court, indeed, is frequently subject, in many respects, to the control of a general court of proprietors. But the greater part of those proprietors seldom pretend to understand any thing of the business of the company; and when the spirit of faction happens not to prevail among them, give themselves no trouble about it, but receive contentedly such half yearly or yearly dividend, as the directors think proper to make to them. This total exemption from trouble and from risk, beyond a limited sum, encouraged many people to become adventurers in joint stock companies, who would, upon no account, hazard their fortunes in any private copartnery. Such companies, therefore, commonly draw to themselves much greater stocks than any private copartnery can boast of . . . The directors of such companies, however, being the managers rather of other people's money than of their own, it cannot well be expected, that they should watch over it with the same anxious vigilance with which the partners in a private copartnery frequently watch over their own. Like the stewards of a rich man, they are apt to consider attention to small matters as not for their master's honour, and very easily give themselves a dispensation from having it. Negligence and profusion, therefore, must always prevail, more or less, in the management of the affairs of such a company. It is upon this account that joint stock companies for foreign trade have seldom been able to maintain the competition against private adventurers. They have, accordingly, very seldom succeeded without an exclusive privilege; and frequently have not succeeded with one.

In most but not all large corporations the officers own only a very small percentage of all shares. In some large corporations the officers' portion is significant. These corporations might be called owner-controlled and the corporations with widely dispersed shareholding manager-controlled. If the argument of Berle and Means is true, we expect a significant difference in profitability between owner-controlled and manager-controlled companies. Owner-controlled companies should be much more profitable than manager-controlled companies. This is a direct implication of the work by Berle and Means. In empirical work little or no support for this implication has been found. Why do managers of manager-controlled corporations perform as well as managers of owner-controlled corporations? If they have the opportunity to enrich themselves at the expense of shareholders, why do they not do so? It might be that managers refrain from doing so because of ethical considerations, but there can also be mechanisms that prevent these managers from doing so. Let us examine some of these potential mechanisms.

First, there is the stock market. If a corporation performs badly because the managers of that corporation are incompetent, lazy, or not really interested in running that corporation as well as they can, the market price of that company's stock will decline. If, moreover, it becomes clear why the market price of that company's stock is so low, a determined outsider can try to acquire a majority of the shares at a low price. He can then oust the managers, install new managers and control them more tightly. Therefore managers who perform poorly must always fear that their company can be taken over. There is a market not only for individual shares, but also for whole corporations. To put it differently, there is a market for the rights to manage corporations. This market is usually called the **market for corporate control**. Competition between management teams in the market for corporate control increases the pressure on managers to perform well.

Market for corporate control

In the USA there is an active market for corporate control. Managers who do not deliver results can always be ousted by shareholders. Quite often outsiders buy shares of a company that does not perform well with the aim of changing the management of that company. Box 7.2 gives an illustration. In Europe there are large differences, the UK having the most active market for corporate control. In most countries of continental Europe corporations have been able

Box 7.2 ■ ISP versus Hercules: a proxy fight for corporate control

Hercules is an American chemicals company that ran into trouble in the late 1990s. A number of its businesses started underperforming. It then went on to make a very expensive acquisition, buying BetzDearborn, a producer of water treatment chemicals, for $3.1bn. When that acquisition also failed to bring the anticipated results, trouble started brewing. It intensified when the overall results of Hercules became outright disappointing and its stock price declined month after month. In 2000, Hercules started a process of divestment of parts of the company (BetzDearborn first, if possible) or perhaps even the total sale of the company. . .

International Specialty Products (ISP) is also an American chemicals company. For a small part, it produces similar or related 'specialty chemicals' as Hercules, for the major part both companies are in different lines of business. Samuel J. Heyman is chairman of ISP. He has a reputation for taking stakes in companies that are 'in play' (or can be made so). ISP had, for instance, acquired stakes in Dexter Corp. and Life Technologies Inc., and was instrumental in the subsequent sale of the companies. The deals grossed ISP a total profit of $150 million in 1999 and 2000. In July 2000, ISP revealed it had acquired a 9.9 per cent stake in Hercules (10.7 million shares) for a total of $153.2 million, representing an average cost of around $14.29 per share.

The divestment process of Hercules did not progress well. In March 2001, ISP took the initiative to launch a 'proxy fight', soliciting the shareholders of Hercules to vote for four ISP-backed members of the Hercules board instead of the nominees put forward by Hercules itself:

International Specialty Products (ISP) describes the last five years as 'disastrous' for shareholders of Hercules and urges them to place four ISP nominees on the Hercules board. . . ISP hopes to place its chairman, Sam Heyman, on the Hercules board together with three others. In a proxy report filed with the US Securities and Exchange Commission (SEC), ISP said its nominees will commit to completing a sale or merger of Hercules 'in the most timely, effective and efficient manner possible'.

ISP cited declines in the Hercules stock price during the last five years in urging votes for the ISP candidates, noting that Hercules shares have lost nearly 80% of their value since reaching a high of $66.25 on 19 March 1996. In addition, ISP also criticized what it called 'the revolving door' of four chief executives during the last 22 months at Hercules. In particular, ISP also attacked the $14.25m severance package given to R. Keith Elliott when he left the company in May 1999. ISP also chided Hercules for boosting its debt load 11-fold in the last five years to $3.2bn by the end of last year. ISP blamed a lot of the problems on the $3.1bn acquisition of BetzDearborn in 1998, calling it a 'disaster' for the company.

Hercules countered by appointing the well-respected Bill Joyce, former CEO of Union Carbide, as new CEO working together with chairman Tom Gossage:

Analysts of Merrill Lynch said that they remained unclear about the impact of adding Heyman to the board since he agrees with chairman Tom Gossage about the best goal for the future: a sale of the whole company. Moreover, they note that the company's new chief executive – Union Carbide's Bill Joyce – also has 'significant incentive to sell or merge the company' given the particulars of his compensation package. At the same time, they also note a chilling effect for a company bidding on Hercules with Heyman on the board. ML analysts said: 'Should Hercules consider a merger or stock-based transaction, a potential suitor might be reluctant to share information about itself with Heyman'.

All four ISP-backed candidates – Sam Heyman, Sunil Kumar, Raymond Troubh, and Gloria Schaffer – were elected to the Hercules board by the shareholders:

Although they won't hold enough seats to control Hercules (which elected a 14-person board), the ISP candidates have said that they will use their positions to lobby for sale of the company or other improvements as best they can.

Sources: CNI News, 26 March, 24 May, 28 May, 6 June 2001

to shield themselves against unfriendly takeover threats. Within the European Union there is a lively debate on the need to harmonize the legal framework concerning takeovers. A proposal made by the European Commission has been rejected by the European Parliament, meaning that differences between the UK and other European countries are likely to persist (see also Box 7.3).

Does this mean that the managers of companies in continenetal Europe need not worry about the valuation of their company's stock on the stock market? Not necessarily. So long as the company has to issue new shares from time to time, it has an interest in the valuation of its shares on the stock market.

Second, there is a *market for managerial labour*. The top position in a large company usually gives a manager more power, more prestige, more money, and more job satisfaction than the top position in a smaller company. Hence we expect some competition between managers to obtain those few top positions in the largest firms. Therefore every manager has to worry about his reputation. If he acquires a reputation for pursuing his personal interests instead of actively pursuing profit opportunities, it is likely that his chances to get a better position are small.

Third, there are *markets for the company's products*. The more intense the competition in those markets, the less opportunity there is for managers to pursue their own interests. If they do so, the company will have higher unit costs than its competitors, or it will turn out products of a lower quality than that of its

Box 7.3 ■ The European market for corporatism or corporate control?

In Europe the notion of a 'market for corporate control' has always been more controversial. It is quite readily accepted in the UK. However, on the Continent the idea generally prevails that corporations lead a life of their own, aimed at continuity and serving all stakeholders equally – not primarily the shareholders. It actively seeks the dialogue with its various stakeholder groups in order to optimally balance their competing claims on the corporation. This idea is alternatively referred to as the **stakeholder model** (see also Box 6.1), the Rhineland model, or corporatism. The European Commission worked for 12 years to harmonize takeover codes in Europe in a European Directive that would regulate the European market for corporate control. In 2001 it came to the vote:

It could not have been closer. On July 4th the European Parliament split 273–273 on plans to push through a new directive establishing a cross-border code for company takeovers in Europe. For a brief, confusing moment Nicole Fontaine, the parliament's president, declared that this meant the vote had passed, but she had got her procedure muddled. . . After 12 years of work, it looks as if it is back to the drawing board for the takeover directive.

The failure is a blow for economic liberalizers, who saw it as a key part of their strategy for sharpening economic competition within the European Union. The thrust of the directive was to make it harder for European corporate bosses to ward off a hostile bid without first consulting shareholders. The idea was that shareholder rights would be strengthened, and managers forced to become more efficient. A mere 2% of takeovers in Europe are hostile. Such bids are not by nature good in themselves, but as Chris Huhne, a British Euro-MP, says, the possibility of them exerts a welcome pressure on managers. Frits Bolkestein, the commissioner in charge of the internal market, called the rejection of the code a setback to having an integrated capital market in Europe by 2005 and to 'making Europe the most competitive economy in the world by 2010'. Both these goals were endorsed by the leaders of the 15 members of the European Union at a summit in Lisbon over a year ago.

The directive's defeat will not prevent hostile takeovers across European frontiers. After all, Vodafone managed to acquire Mannesmann under the old rules. But it will certainly slow corporate restructuring across Europe, particularly in Germany. It will also make it harder to establish a genuine European single market. The free flow of goods and a common currency are one thing, but if companies have to deal with 15 different takeover codes when making cross-border acquisitions, a true single market is still an illusion.

Source: The Economist, 7 July 2001

competitors. It will lose market share and, ultimately, cease to exist. Therefore competition in product markets also restricts managers from pursuing their own interests.

Finally, even if the corporate officers of a company do not own shares in their company, their pay package may still include a bonus related to annual profits, an option to buy stock at a later date, etc. This can also bring the interests of top managers more in line with those of the shareholders. The role of reward structures is the key issue in the theory of principal and agent. This theory is discussed extensively in section 7.6.

7.3 Managerial behaviour and ownership structure in a world with certainty and symmetric information

The preceding section discussed the separation of ownership and control in quite general terms. Here we discuss this issue in more precise terms. How does the ownership structure of the firm affect behaviour of the manager of that firm? To answer this question, Jensen and Meckling in 1976 developed a theory that is explained in this section.

Consider, first, a manager who owns all the shares of the company he manages. This owner-manager has two conflicting objectives. He is interested in maximizing both the value of the firm and **on-the-job consumption**. The latter may take various forms, such as buying a company jet, furnishing the office in a luxurious way, or spending fewer hours on the job. This is not to say that buying a company jet is always a matter of on-the-job consumption. In order to make this clear, consider what a manager interested only in maximizing the value of his company would do. Such a manager would first calculate the following:

On-the-job consumption

- the present value of the managerial time saved by buying a company jet (a);
- the present value of buying tickets for regular airlines (b);
- the present value of the cash outflows from buying and operating a company jet (c).

A manager interested in maximizing the value of his firm would buy a company jet if and only if

$$c - a < b$$

Now define d as $d = c - a - b$ and suppose that d is greater than zero. A manager interested not only in maximizing the value of his firm but also in prestige and personal comfort might still buy a company jet. If he does so, d is the amount he spends as on-the-job consumption.

From this example it is clear that if a manager engages in consumption on-the-job he is not maximizing the value of his firm. The more spent as consumption on-the-job, the lower the value of the firm. If he spends $1 million as consumption on-the-job (in our example, $d = \$1$ million), he lowers the value of the firm by $1 million. In Figure 7.1 the present value of on-the-job consumption, C, is plotted against the value of the firm, V. It is now clear that the sum of the two variables, value of the firm and present value of on-the-job consumption, is constant. If the manager decides to consume C_4, the value of the firm will be V_4. If he decides to consume C_5 the value of the firm will be V_5. The line V_0C_0 represents all possible combinations of V and C. This line gives the set of combinations of V and C that the manager can choose from and is called the **budget constraint**. In Figure 7.1 the budget constraint V_0C_0 has slope -1. Note that a manager who is interested only in maximizing the value of the firm, not in any form of on-the-job consumption, would not consume anything on the job. The value of the firm then would be V_0.

Budget constraint

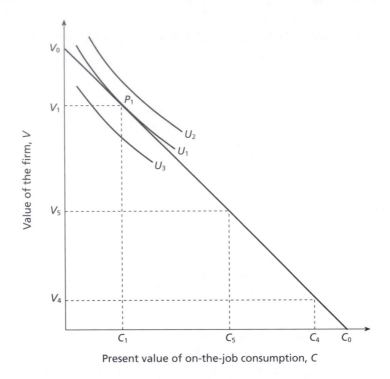

Figure 7.1 Value of the firm (_V_) and present value of on-the-job consumption (_C_). The manager owns all the shares of his firm

The values of C and V chosen by the manager depend on his utility function. In Figure 7.1 all points on curve U_3 represent points of equal utility to the manager. All points on curve U_1 also represent points of equal utility to the manager. Points on curve U_1, however, represent a higher level of utility than points on curve U_3. Points on curve U_2 represent a still higher level of utility, but there is no way the manager can reach this level. The manager maximizes his utility by choosing point P_1 where his consumption is C_1 and the value of the firm is V_1. At this point the marginal utility of an additional dollar of consumption on-the-job is equal to the marginal utility of an additional dollar of wealth.

The curves U_1, U_2 and U_3 in Figure 7.1 are called _indifference curves_, because these curves represent points of equal utility to the manager.[1] Thus the manager is indifferent among the points lying on the same indifference curve. Since we are still dealing with a manager who owns all the shares in the firm, we need only the information in Figure 7.1 to determine his trade-off between the value of his firm and his on-the-job consumption.

Now suppose that the manager sells a fraction $(1-\alpha)$ of his shares to outsiders. The manager then owns a fraction α of the shares himself. For example, α could be equal to 0.7; this would mean that the manager sells 30 per cent of the shares to outsiders and retains 70 per cent himself. If he decides to spend an additional €1 on on-the-job consumption, the value of the firm will be reduced by €1. Now, however, the personal wealth of the manager will be reduced by only 70 cents and the wealth of the outside shareholders by 30 cents. The manager will now spend an amount on consumption such that the marginal utility of an additional €1 of on-the-job consumption is equal to the marginal utility of an additional 70 cents of personal wealth. So we know that he will now spend more money on consumption on-the-job.

How much more the manager will spend on on-the-job consumption depends on the set of possible combinations of personal wealth and on-the-job consumption he can choose from. This set depends on the price he can make for the shares he sells to the outsiders, and this price depends on whether or not the outsiders know beforehand that the manager will spend more on on-the-job consumption after he has sold the shares. Suppose they do *not* know that the manager will spend more after he has sold the shares. Such naïve outsiders will be willing to pay 30 per cent of V_1 for 30 per cent of the shares. The budget constraint now facing the manager must have a slope of -0.7, since the manager can trade \$1 of consumption for 70 cents of personal wealth. The budget constraint must also pass through point P_1. At this point the manager consumes C_1 and his personal wealth is V_1 (he will have 30 per cent of V_1 in cash and the other 70 per cent of V_1 in shares). So the budget constraint now facing the manager must be line L in Figure 7.2. Line L passes through point P_1 and has slope -0.7.

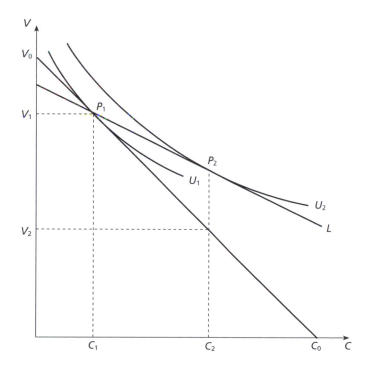

Figure 7.2 **Value of the firm (V) and present value of on-the-job consumption (C). The manager owns a fraction α of the shares. The outsiders expect no increase in on-the-job consumption after the manager has sold a fraction $(1 - \alpha)$ of the shares**

At point P_2 there is an indifference curve (U_2 in Figure 7.2) tangential to the budget constraint L. At this point the manager consumes C_2. The value of the firm is reduced to V_2. Thus the outside shareholders, who paid 30 per cent of V_1 for their shares, now find that their shares have a value of 30 per cent of V_2 only.

Suppose now that the outsiders are not so naïve as to assume that the manager will not increase his on-the-job consumption. Suppose, instead, that the outsiders expect the manager to increase his consumption as soon as he has sold the shares. Suppose, moreover, that the outsiders know the exact shape of the manager's indifference curves. They will have a look at Figure 7.3 and try to find a point P_3 such that P_3 lies on V_0C_0 and the indifference curve passing through P_3 has at point P_3 a slope of $-\alpha$: that is, this indifference curve is tangential at P_3 to a line through P_3 with slope $-\alpha$.

The outsiders will soon find out that there is one and only one such point P_3. Thus they will know that at P_3 the marginal utility for the manager of spending an additional \$1 on on-the-job consumption is equal to the marginal utility of 70 cents of personal wealth. Therefore they are willing to pay only 30 per cent of V_3 for the shares, not 30 per cent of V_1. If they pay 30 per cent of $V3$, the manager's budget constraint becomes line M with slope -0.7. The manager will then decide to consume C_3. The value of the firm will be V_3 and the outsiders will neither gain nor lose on buying the shares.

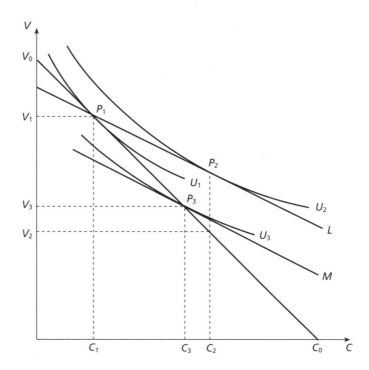

Figure 7.3 **Value of the firm (V) and present value of on-the-job consumption (C). The manager owns a fraction α of the shares. The outsiders know the exact shape of the indifference curves of the manager and adjust the price they are willing to pay accordingly**

The personal wealth of the manager is now V_3. Of this amount he has a fraction $(1 - \alpha)$ in cash and a fraction α in shares. His wealth is reduced by $V_1 - V_3$ and the present value of his on-the-job consumption is increased by $C_3 - C_1$. The result is a decrease in his level of utility: he is now on indifference curve U_3, while he started on indifference curve U_1. So it is clear that no manager would ever sell a fraction of the shares of his company unless there is something else, not included in the analysis presented above, that makes him do so. Two such possibilities are:

- the manager prefers to have a portion of his wealth in cash instead of in shares, because he can then use the cash for other things;
- the manager sees an opportunity for investment that he cannot finance out of his own personal wealth.

7.3.1   Monitoring and bonding

Monitoring

In the above analysis we have ignored the potential for the outsiders to **monitor** the behaviour of the manager. In practice it is usually possible for the outsiders to observe the behaviour of the manager to a certain extent. This can be done, for example, by having the books audited by an external auditor, or by installing a board of directors. Monitoring the behaviour of the manager is not without cost. By spending money on monitoring the outsiders can reduce on-the-job consumption by the manager. The more they spend on monitoring, the better they can observe the manager's behaviour and the more they can reduce on-the-job consumption.

We know from the analysis of Figure 7.3 that the manager bears the full cost of his increase in on-the-job consumption. If the manager can convince the outsiders before selling the shares that he will consume less than C_3, he will be able to sell the shares for an amount greater than 30 per cent of V_3. If he consumes less, the value of the firm increases and it is the manager who captures this increase, not the outsiders. Hence, it is in the interest of the manager to

Bonding

bind himself. This is called bonding. **Bonding** and monitoring are almost the same thing. *Bonding* means that the manager takes the initiative to bind himself and to be monitored; *monitoring* means that the outsiders take the initiative.

Like monitoring, bonding is not without cost. It involves the same kinds of activity as monitoring: the manager takes the initiative to have the books audited or to install a board of directors. Monitoring costs and bonding costs are borne by the manager. By consuming less than C_3 he increases his level of utility. By spending money on monitoring and bonding he decreases the value of the firm. For this reason his budget constraint is no longer given by the line $V_0 C_0$. His budget constraint now is curve S in Figure 7.4. Somewhere there is an optimal amount of money to spend on monitoring and bonding. This is indicated in Figure 7.4 by point P_4. At this point the manager spends an amount MB (equal to the distance $P_5 P_4$) on monitoring and bonding costs. His level of utility is U_4, higher than U_3 but still lower than U_1.

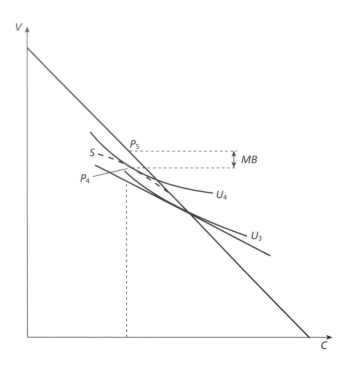

Figure 7.4   **Value of the firm (*V*) and present value of on-the-job consumption (*C*) with monitoring and bonding costs**

7.4 Entrepreneurial firms and team production

Entrepreneurial firm   Why do entrepreneurial firms exist? By an **entrepreneurial firm** we mean a firm owned and managed by the same person. This person (the entrepreneur) co-ordinates and monitors the work of several others (the employees) and receives the residual after fixed contractual payments (such as wages and interest payments) have been paid. Direct supervision is the most important co-ordination mechanism in such a firm. An alternative organizational form is a workers' co-operative in which workers co-operate as peers. In a workers' co-operative, mutual adjustment is the prime co-ordination mechanism. In manufacturing industries, few workers' co-operatives exist. Alchian and Demsetz
Team production   (1972) explain this by using the concept of **team production**.

Team production is a situation in which two or more people can produce more when they are working together than when they are working separately. The classical example is two people loading heavy cargoes into a truck. Suppose two people have to load heavy cargoes into two trucks. They can organize their work in either of two ways: each person can load one truck, working on his own, or they can work together, first loading one truck and then the other. If the second arrangement is more efficient, then there is team production. Some goods or services cannot be produced by one person working alone. Examples are the music made by a symphony orchestra and open heart surgery. These are also examples of team production.

In mathematical terms we can express this as follows. Let $q(x_1, x_2)$ be a production function: q is the quantity produced; it is a function of two different inputs x_1 and x_2. There is team production if and only if:

$$\frac{\partial^2 q}{\partial x_1 \, \partial x_2} \neq 0$$

The production function $q = 3x_1^2 + 7x_2 + x_2^2$ does not represent team production; the production function $q = 3x_1^2 + 5x_1 x_2 + 2x_2^2$ does. The first example of a production function is *separable*; that is, it can be written as a sum of terms such that some terms contain only x_1 and the other terms only x_2. The second production function is not separable. To say that a production function is separable is equivalent to saying that the second partial derivative with respect to x_1 and x_2 is unequal to zero, as in the second case.

A self-employed person receives the fruits of his efforts alone. If he puts in more effort, he produces more and earns more money. How much effort he puts in depends on his utility function. In equilibrium the marginal utility of having an additional unit of leisure is equal to the marginal utility of earning an additional unit of money as income. Now suppose that n people form a team and share the earnings from their production activities. Then each person knows that if he puts in an extra unit of effort, he will receive only $1/n$th part of the additional earnings generated by his additional effort. For this reason he is strongly tempted to put in a much lower level of effort.

We know, then, that people working in a team and sharing the proceeds of their work will put in a lower level of effort than persons who are self-employed. This phenomenon is called **shirking**. Every team member will be tempted to engage in shirking. With everybody shirking the total output of the team will be much lower than if there were no shirking. Every member of the team is willing to put in more effort, provided that everybody else also puts in more effort. The members of a team can discuss this issue. Suppose that the result of this discussion is that everyone promises not to shirk. If shirking by one of the team members is easily detected by the other team members, such mutual promises can work. A team member who shirks could then be expelled. If, however, it is difficult to detect shirking, such mutual promises will not be effective. Here again we see that the unobservability of the effort put in by the team members causes an information problem.

Shirking

Suppose that it is difficult for other team members to detect shirking but not very difficult for someone whose only task is to detect shirking. Let us call this person a **monitor**. A team with a monitor would then produce more than a team without a monitor. If the value of the additional output from having a monitor is sufficiently high, it is in the interest of all team members to have a monitor.

Monitor

How should the monitor be rewarded for his effort? Suppose that the monitor just shares in the proceeds on an equal basis with the other team members. The monitor then has an incentive to shirk himself. So the question becomes, who monitors the monitor? If there is a second monitor to monitor the first monitor, who will monitor this second monitor? There is only one solution: give the monitor title to the residual after the other team members have been paid a fixed wage. If the monitor receives the residual, he will have no incentive to shirk as a monitor.

If the monitor is to be effective, he must have the power to revise the contract terms of individual team members, without having to negotiate with all the other team members. He must have the right to terminate contracts, to attract new members and to adjust the wage rate of every team member to the marginal productivity of that person. Finally, the monitor must also have the right to sell his rights as monitor. Some of his activities, for example his actions to alter the composition of the team, will pay off only after a certain period of time. He will have no incentive to engage in these kinds of activity unless he sooner or later receives the rewards from these activities. If the monitor has the right to sell his rights as monitor, he will have a strong incentive to build an effective team.

Thus we have the entrepreneurial firm. The monitor is the owner of the firm: he receives the residual, has the right to sell his firm, has the right to hire and fire team members, and to adjust their wages individually. The monitor is the entrepreneur: the other team members are his employees.

The classical entrepreneur emerges in this theory as the solution to the problem of shirking within teams. This theory rests on two vital assumptions:

- There is team production.
- Monitoring by someone specializing in that function can reduce shirking.

The second assumption really means that for the other team members it is more difficult or costly to monitor other team members than for someone specializing as monitor. If the team members can see quite easily who is shirking and who is not, they can adjust team membership without having a monitor. Therefore the monitor must be able to detect shirking more easily than the other team members.

7.5 The firm as a nexus of contracts

In sections 7.3 and 7.4, ownership of the firm is a concept of vital importance: ownership restricts consumption on-the-job and shirking by managers. How, then, can we explain the existence of large corporations whose shares are publicly traded and in which managers do not own (a significant portion of) the shares? The answer is that separation of security ownership and control can be an efficient form of economic organization. Note that here we introduce separation of *security* ownership and control. In the theory explained here, ownership of the firm is an irrelevant concept. A shareholder in a large public corporation owns just a number of shares. With ownership of the shares go certain well-defined rights, but this does not mean that a shareholder (or all shareholders jointly) own the corporation in any meaningful sense. They just contract to receive the residual, just as workers contract to receive a fixed wage. Shareholders are just one party in a group of many parties bound together in a nexus of contracts.

Fama and Jensen (1983a, b) use this perspective to explain the existence of both entrepreneurial firms and public corporations. They see the organization as a nexus of contracts, written and unwritten, among owners of factors of production and customers. The most important contracts specify the nature of residual claims and the allocation of steps in the decision process among agents. Most agents receive a fixed promised payment or an incentive payment based on a specific measure of performance. The residual risk is the risk of the difference between stochastic inflows of cash and promised payments. It is borne by the residual claimants or residual risk bearers.

The decision process has four steps:

Initiation

- **Initiation**: generation of proposals for resource utilization and structuring of contracts.

Ratification

- **Ratification**: choice of the decision initiatives to be implemented.

Implementation

- **Implementation**: execution of ratified decisions.

Monitoring

- **Monitoring**: measurement of performance of decision agents and implementation of rewards.

Decision management

Decision control

Initiation and implementation are usually allocated to the same agents. These two functions are combined under the term **decision management**. Likewise, **decision control** includes ratification and monitoring.

Fama and Jensen now posit two complementary hypotheses about the relations between risk-bearing and decision processes of organizations:

- Separation of residual risk-bearing from decision management leads to decision systems that separate decision management from decision control.
- Combination of decision management and decision control in a few agents leads to residual claims that are largely restricted to these agents.

Fama and Jensen call an organization *non-complex* if specific information relevant to decisions is concentrated in one or a few agents. Specific information is detailed information that is costly to transfer among agents. Most small organizations tend to be non-complex, and most large organizations tend to be complex, but the correspondence is not perfect.

In small, non-complex organizations it is efficient to allocate both decision management and decision control to those agents who have the specific information. When decision management and decision control are combined, residual claimants have no protection against opportunistic actions of decision agents. Hence in small, non-complex organizations residual claims are also allocated to the important decision agents. An example is the small entrepreneurial firm, owned and managed by the same person. This example conforms to the second hypothesis.

Now suppose that the small entrepreneurial firm (call this firm company E) is acquired by a larger firm (company L). The manager(s) of company E are now no longer the residual claimants of company E. It is likely, however, that they still possess the specific knowledge relevant to making decisions for company E. It is now efficient to delegate decision management to the managers of company E. Decision control, however, is exercised by the manager(s) and corporate staff of company L. Separation of residual risk-bearing from decision management makes it necessary to separate decision management from decision control. This conforms to the first hypothesis.

In the large public corporation there are many shareholders. Having many shareholders has advantages because the total risk to be shared is large and there are large demands for capital in order to be able to make fixed promises to other agents. It is very costly for all of the shareholders to be involved in decision control. So they delegate decision control to the board. While decision management is diffused within a large public corporation, decision control is exercised by the board on behalf of the shareholders.

7.6 Theory of principal and agent

In section 7.3 the agency relation between the outside shareholder and the manager was analyzed in a deterministic way: risk did not play a role in the analysis. Moreover, neither principal (outside shareholder) nor agent (manager) had private information. In the theory of principal and agent, risk is introduced into the analysis. In addition, we relax the condition of symmetric information for our discussion in this section.

The theory of principal and agent is developed in mathematical models that even in their simplest form are already quite complicated. The essentials of these types of model can be explained by giving an example.

Take the relationship between the owner of a piece of land and someone who is willing to use this land for growing strawberries. The owner is the principal, the other person the agent. The principal is willing to give the agent the right to use his land for growing strawberries for one summer. The principal's problem is to design the agent's reward structure. The quantity and the quality of strawberries that are available for sale at the end of the summer depend on two factors: how well the agent cares for the strawberries, and the weather. In the language of the theory of principal and agent, the payoff (this is the amount of money from the sale of the strawberries) depends on two variables: the level of effort chosen by the agent and a random variable (the weather).

A crucial question in the theory of principal and agent is how well the principal can observe the agent's behaviour. In this respect, three cases will be discussed:

■ Case 1: the principal can observe the agent's behaviour.
■ Case 2: the principal has no information about the agent's behaviour.
■ Case 3: the principal cannot observe the agent's behaviour directly, but he can obtain a signal concerning the level of effort by the agent.

In case 1 there is symmetric information; in cases 2 and 3 there is asymmetric information. In cases 2 and 3 the agent knows his level of effort but the principal does not. It is the agent who has *private information* (about his level of effort).[2]

7.6.1 Principal can observe agent's behaviour (symmetric information)

Assume that the principal can observe the level of effort by the agent. What is the optimal reward structure from the principal's point of view? The agent's compensation can be based on the agent's level of effort. We know that the agent does not like effort. He is willing to put in more effort only if his compensation is also higher. In Figure 7.5, curve I represents one of the agent's indifference curves. The graph plots the agent's level of effort against his income. The higher his level of effort the more additional income he demands for an additional unit of effort. Curve I is really one of a set of indifference curves. Assume, however, that the agent cannot obtain a contract anywhere that gives him a positive income if his level of effort is zero. Curve I then represents the minimum level of utility that the agent is willing to accept. He need not accept a contract giving him a lower level of utility, since he is free not to work. So he can always choose the point at the origin, which puts him at the utility level given by curve I.

The higher the agent's level of effort, the higher the expected payoff. This relation is given by line m in Figure 7.5 (for simplicity we assume that this relation is given by a straight line). The principal now must choose a reward structure for the agent. Before dealing with this, let us try to find out what, from the principal's point of view, is the optimal level of the agent's effort. For the principal, the optimal level of the agent's effort is e_0. At this point the expected

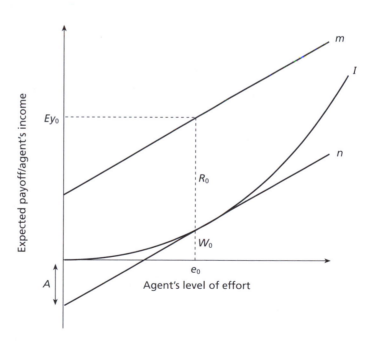

Figure 7.5 The optimal level of the agent's effort from the principal's point of view

payoff is Ey_0; the agent must receive an amount W_0 and the principal receives the difference

$$Ey_0 - W_0 = R_0$$

At any other point the vertical distance between line m and curve I is smaller than R_0. So the principal wants to select a reward structure that induces the agent to choose a level of effort e_0 and which also gives him a payment of W_0 if he chooses e_0. A very simple contract that solves the principal's problem is a **forcing contract**. Under a forcing contract the principal promises to pay an amount e_0 if the agent's level of effort is at least e_0 and to pay nothing if the agent's level of effort is smaller than e_0. Under such a contract the agent is forced to bring his level of effort up to e_0, otherwise he will not be paid. He will not increase his level of effort any further, however, since he receives no extra reward for doing so. Hence the agent is forced to work at level e_0.

Forcing contract

Another solution would be to give the agent the reward structure represented by line n in Figure 7.5. Under this reward structure the agent would have to pay an amount A to the principal if his level of effort is zero. For every additional unit of effort, the agent receives an amount given by the slope of line n. In order to obtain the highest utility level achievable under this reward structure, the agent will again choose effort level e_0.

The point of this whole discussion is this: if the principal can observe the agent's level of effort, the principal can (1) determine which level of effort from his own point of view is optimal and (2) give the agent a forcing contract that obliges the agent to choose this level of effort. Since the principal can observe the actual level of effort chosen by the agent, he will pay W_0 only if the agent works at level e_0.

The set of Pareto-optimal solutions

In the discussion above we have assumed that curve I represents the minimum level of utility that the agent is willing to accept. Call this level of (expected) utility EUA_1. EUA_1 represents the expected utility that the agent can obtain elsewhere. The principal maximizes his own expected utility by designing a reward structure given the constraint that the agent will not accept a contract giving him an expected utility lower than EUA_1. Let EUP_1 be the principal's maximum level of utility, given EUA_1.

Now suppose that the agent perceives an opportunity to obtain elsewhere a level of utility $EUA_2 > EUA_1$. Let EUP_2 be the principal's maximum level of utility, given EUA_2. Since the principal is now faced with a tighter constraint, it follows that $EUP_2 < EUP_1$.

In Figure 7.6 the horizontal axis represents the agent's expected utility, and the vertical level the principal's maximum level of utility. If the minimum level of expected utility that the agent is willing to accept is EUA_1, then the principal's maximum level of utility is EUA_1; this is point 1 in Figure 7.6. If, elsewhere, the agent can obtain EUA_2 then the principal's maximum level of utility is EUP_2. This is point 2 in Figure 7.6. By choosing different values for EUA we can calculate for each value of EUA the principal's maximum level of utility, EUP. All points thus found form the curve cs.

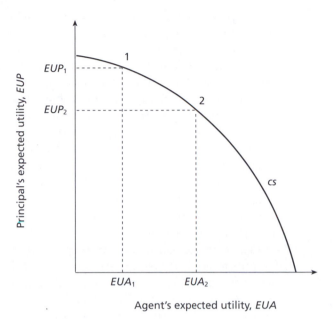

Figure 7.6 The set of Pareto-optimal solutions for the case of symmetric information

Pareto-optimal solution

A **Pareto-optimal solution** of the principal's problem is defined as a solution such that it is impossible to increase one person's expected utility without decreasing the other person's. Point 1 in Figure 7.6 represents a Pareto-optimal solution: the principal can obtain more than EUP_1 only if the agent receives less than EUA_1, and the agent can obtain more than EUA_1 only if the principal receives less than EUP_1. Point 2 is also a Pareto-optimal solution. In fact, curve cs gives the set of Pareto-optimal solutions.

7.6.2 Principal cannot observe agent's level of effort (asymmetric information)

Let us now assume that the principal has no way to observe the level of effort of the agent and that after the summer he also has no information about weather conditions during the summer. All he can observe is the payoff, the amount of money made by selling the strawberries. If the payoff is high, this can be the result of a high level of effort by the agent and average weather conditions or a result of an average level of effort by the agent and good weather conditions.

The principal cannot tell what contributed more to a good result: the effort by the agent or the weather conditions. These are now the conditions under which the principal must specify at the beginning of the summer a reward structure for the agent. How should he do this? There are two extreme solutions.

The first of these is a fixed salary for the agent, independent of the payoff.

Wage contract

This reward structure may be called a **wage contract**. It is like an employment contract with a fixed wage. The problem with this reward structure is that the agent has no incentive whatsoever to do a good job. In the theory of principal and agent it is assumed that the agent likes to receive more money and dislikes delivering more effort,[3] so the agent will choose a level of effort equal to zero if his income does not depend on the payoff.

Rent contract

The second extreme solution is that the agent receives the payoff minus a fixed amount to be agreed at the beginning of the summer. This may be called a **rent contract**. The agent rents the land from the landowner for a fixed amount. The rent is not dependent on the payoff. The agent grows the strawberries and receives whatever he can make for the strawberries after he has paid the rent to the landowner. With this reward structure the agent has a maximum incentive to do his very best.

The wage contract and the rent contract differ not only in the distribution of rewards, but also in the distribution of risks imposed on agent and principal. Under the wage contract the principal bears all the risk. For instance, if weather conditions ruin the strawberry crop, he still has to pay the agent's wage but receives no reward himself. Under the rent contract the situation is reversed. The agent now bears all the risk. He has to pay the rent, whether or not the proceeds from selling strawberries permit him to do so. Hence we can see that the reward structure determines the distribution of risks between principal and agent. What reward structures are acceptable to both parties will also depend on their attitude towards risk. They may be risk-neutral, risk-averse or risk-loving. In most agency models the principal is assumed to be risk-neutral and the agent is assumed to be either risk-neutral or risk-averse.

Compensation for risk-bearing

If both principal and agent are risk-neutral, the best reward structure is a rent contract. This gives the agent maximum incentive. It also imposes all the risk on the agent, but since he is risk-neutral he does not care about risk. To be more precise, a risk-neutral agent does not demand **compensation for risk-bearing** since he does not care about risk. Since risk can be imposed on the agent without cost, a rent contract (giving maximum incentives) is the best reward structure for the agent.

Reservation wage

Suppose that the principal is risk-neutral and the agent is risk-averse. With a rent contract the agent has maximum incentive to put in a high level of effort, but he also has to bear all the risk. Since we now assume that the agent is risk-averse, the agent cares about the amount of risk he has to bear. He is willing to accept more risk only if this is offset by a higher expected income. This is illustrated in Figure 7.7. Curve U is the agent's indifference curve. It is also assumed that the agent has an alternative opportunity to accept another job. This is a job without risk and with an income of W. W is the agent's **reservation wage**. If the principal wants to engage the agent, he can offer a wage contract for an amount W. The principal can also offer a contract where the agent's income depends on the payoff. The agent is willing to accept such a contract provided he remains on the same indifference curve.

The relation between the expected payoff and the amount of risk borne by the agent is illustrated in Figure 7.7 by line I (we assume that this relation can be given by a straight line). The higher the level of risk borne by the agent, the more incentive the agent has to do a good job and the higher the expected

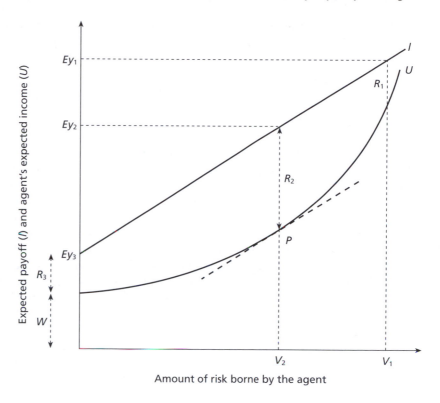

Figure 7.7 **The trade-off between incentives and risk-bearing in the theory of principal and agent**

payoff will be. If the agent bears no risk (a wage contract) the expected payoff is Ey_3. Since the agent will not accept a wage contract if his wage is lower than W, the maximum amount the principal can receive is R_3. If the agent bears all the risk (a rent contract), the expected payoff is Ey_1. The principal can then charge a rent equal to R_1. If the principal charged a higher rent, the agent would not accept the contract. The principal maximizes his expected income by choosing point P on the agent's indifference curve U such that the slope of the indifference curve at point P is equal to the slope of line I. At this point the agent bears some risk (V_2) but not all the risk (V_1).

Figure 7.7 portrays the fundamental trade-off that the principal must make. The principal wants to give the agent incentives in order to make him put in more effort. But in order for this to occur, the agent must also bear risk. The agent is willing to accept risk only if he is compensated in the form of a higher expected income. So the principal must make a trade-off between giving the agent incentives (the more incentives, the higher the expected payoff) and having the agent bear more risk (the higher the level of risk borne by the agent, the more the principal has to pay him in the form of expected income).

As we can see in Figure 7.7, the optimal contract for the principal involves risk-sharing between agent and principal. The agent bears an amount of risk equal to V_2; the principal bears an amount of risk equal to $V_1 - V_2$. This result is true if the principal is risk-neutral and the agent is risk-averse.

Why does the theory of principal and agent assume that the principal is risk-neutral while the agent is risk-averse? If both the principal and the agent are

Box 7.4 ■ Executive compensation

In 1999 Mr Charles Wang, the CEO of Computer Associates (an American company), received $4.6 million in salary plus $650 million in long-term performance-based compensation. Whether Mr Wang really deserved so much money is difficult to say. To some, the amount of compensation paid to American top executives is an indication of corporate plundering. Others may point to the market for managerial labour and argue that managerial compensation is simply the result of supply and demand for managerial talent. Still others argue that one of the ways to motivate middle managers is to let them compete for promotions. To make this competition effective a promotion should be rewarded with a large increase in compensation. That too could explain why the top manager receives such a large amount. Chief executives in the USA receive far more pay relative to factory-floor workers than in other countries. The typical CEO of one of the 500 largest American firms takes home 475 times more than workers. For European CEOs this is 11–24 times as much as the factory-floor worker. In South-East Asia and Latin America the comparable figure is 40–50.

Leaving the amount of compensation aside, we still have the question how to design a pay package for top executives. According to Towers Perrin (a consulting company) there are large differences between countries in this respect. In the USA, for example, long-term performance-based compensation (mainly in the form of stock options) amounts to 111 per cent of base salary. In Europe this percentage is somewhere between 20 and 30 (see the figure below).

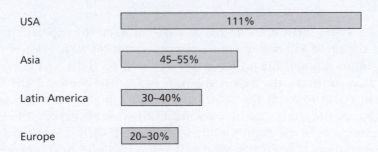

Long-term performance-based compensation as a percentage of base salary for a typical firm with more than $250 million in sales in 2000
Source: Towers Perrin

Whatever the differences between countries, it is clear that a significant part of the total compensation of many top managers is based on performance; quite often managers are given share options. Share options give the manager a right to buy shares in his or her company at a given price. If the share price rises above this level before the option expires, the manager can pocket the difference.

Sources: *The Economist*, 30 September, 2000; Towers Perrin press release 16 October, 2000

Box 7.5 ■ Does it pay to pay CEOs for performance?

On the basis of the analysis in this section we would expect that performance-related pay for CEOs yields the best results for shareholders. Most company boards, especially in the USA, expect this to be true. Yet some doubt remains. In 1997 *Across the Board*, the magazine of the Conference Board, interviewed a number of scholars who had done research on the question whether such performance-related incentives are effective as a component of CEOs' pay packages. Here are some of their opinions:

The issue is largely one of executives' psychological make-up. Sure, some executives' interests lie closer to home than the boardroom. 'But about 70 per cent of executives,' estimates Professor James Davis of the University of Notre Dame, 'are "stewards" rather than "agents", driven by what's good for the company rather than pure self-interest. Stewards treat their company like a football team. If the company wins, they win. The pay just shows that the board appreciates what they've done. Then there are others, agents, who are in this for the perks, for personal gain. They haven't won unless they've piled up money. The achievement they're looking for is personal success, not group success.'

Nearly all modern financial economists believe that 'increased stock-based incentives cause managers to take actions that increase shareholder wealth', says Kevin J. Murphy, professor of finance and business economics at the University of Southern California. However, he notes, there's a scarcity of empirical evidence linking stockholdings to shareholder returns. Murphy's own studies have generally found such a link: 'I found that CEOs with higher pay-performance sensitivities have realized significantly higher shareholder returns over the past one year, five years, and 10 years. The issue is simple and my results are clear', Murphy says.

'There's been a lot of work on whether managers who hold more equity do better; the evidence is really mixed,' says Professor David Larcker of the Wharton School. 'There's a lot of loose talk, but there's no direct relationship between ownership and performance.'

Source: Based on *Across the Board*, The Conference Board Magazine, March 1997

risk-neutral, the optimal contract is a rent contract. The theory then is not very interesting. It also seems reasonable to assume that the principal is risk-neutral and the agent risk-averse if the situation is such that the principal can diversify, while the agent cannot. If, for example, the principal is the landowner and the agent the farmer, the principal may own several pieces of land in countries with different climates. The principal can then make contracts with several agents and thus diversify away most of the risk. The agent, however, can work on one piece of land only and thus cannot diversify his risk. If the principal is the owner of a company and the agent is the manager of that company, we have the same situation: the principal can diversify (by owning shares in several companies) while the agent normally cannot.

In situations in which the model discussed here really represents reality there is no doubt that for the principal it is best to design a reward schedule based in part upon the agent's performance. Since shareholders can be regarded as risk-neutral and the top manager (the CEO) as risk-averse, we would expect to find performance-related pay packages for top managers. This is indeed what

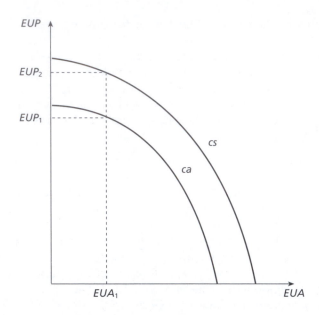

Figure 7.8 **First-best and second-best solutions**

we find in the real world (see Box 7.4 for more details). Moreover we would expect that performance-related pay schemes lead to the best results for shareholders. Although there is wide agreement on this in many boardrooms some doubt remains, as illustrated in Box 7.5.

First-best and second-best solutions

All points on curve U in Figure 7.7 give the agent the same expected utility. Call this level of utility EUA_1. Associated with EUA_1 is EUP_1, the principal's maximum level of utility, given EUA_1. For each level of EUA we can calculate the associated level of EUP. This gives curve ca in Figure 7.8. Curve ca represents the set of Pareto-optimal solutions.

Curve cs in Figure 7.8 is the same curve as curve cs in Figure 7.6. That is, curve cs represents solutions to the principal's problem for the case of symmetric information (the principal can observe the agent's level of effort). Curve ca represents solutions to the principal's problem for the case of asymmetric information (the principal cannot observe the agent's level of effort). The solutions represented by curve cs are called **first-best solutions**; the solutions represented by curve ca are **second-best solutions**. If EUA_1 is the minimum level of utility the agent is willing to accept, then the principal can obtain EUP_1 if he cannot observe the agent's behaviour and EUP_2 if he can. The distance $EUP_2 - EUP_1$ represents the principal's loss of expected utility because of nonobservability. However, moral hazard is also involved. Recall that moral hazard refers to the *ex post* information problem owing to private information

First-best solutions

Second-best solutions

(Chapter 4). In this case the agent has private information on his effort level and may exploit this information asymmetry. To see this, suppose for a moment that the principal cannot observe the agent's level of effort and that the principal can trust the agent on his word. We then have the situation of Figure 7.5. The optimal level of effort from the principal's point of view is e_0. The principal simply asks the agent to deliver this level of effort and the agent promises to do so. There is no need for the principal to observe the agent's level of effort if he can trust him. So the difference between a first-best and a second-best solution is caused by non-observability in the presence of moral hazard.

7.6.3 Principal can observe a signal concerning agent's level of effort

Signal

Now suppose that the principal cannot observe the agent's level of effort directly but that, instead, the principal can observe a **signal** concerning the agent's level of effort. For example, the principal can observe how many hours the agent spends on his job. The number of hours worked by the agent gives the principal an indication about the agent's level of effort. The true level of effort, however, remains unobservable for the principal. This may be the case, for instance, if the agent is required to clock in when he begins to work and to clock out when he stops. His real level of effort, however, remains unobservable.

In formal agency models, one can show that the agent's reward structure should be based on this signal if and only if the agent is risk-averse. To make this result intuitively clear, assume first that the agent is risk-neutral. The agent then does not care about risk-bearing, so he does not demand compensation in the form of a higher expected income if more risk is imposed upon him. Therefore, there is no cost to the principal from imposing risk upon the agent, if the agent is risk-neutral. In this case it is better for the principal to give the agent incentives by letting him bear all the risk (through a rent contract), than by giving him a reward structure based on an imperfect signal concerning his level of effort.

Suppose now that the agent is risk-averse. In this case there is a cost to the principal of letting the agent bear more risk. In this situation a reward structure based both on the signal concerning the agent's level of effort and on the pay-off is better from the principal's point of view than a reward structure based only on the payoff.

Hence the information contained in the signal concerning the agent's level of effort is valuable to the principal if and only if the agent is risk-averse.

7.6.4 Extending the model

In this section we have given an introduction to the theory of principal and agent. In its simplest form this theory concerns the relationship between one principal and one agent. Moreover, this relationship is analyzed in a one-period model. What happens to our conclusions when we examine the relationships between one principal and several agents? And what happens if we analyze the relationship between one principal and one agent in a model with more than one period?

One principal and several agents

Consider first one principal with several agents. As an example, think of a landowner who divides his land into several plots. Now there are several agents who want to grow strawberries on adjacent plots. The weather conditions are the same for all plots. The principal does not know weather conditions either before or after the summer, but he does know that weather conditions are the same for each plot. This gives the principal the opportunity to make comparisons between the payoffs of the agents.

Assume that the principal is risk-neutral and that some agents are risk-averse and the others risk-neutral. Consider, first, agents who are risk-neutral. These agents do not demand compensation for bearing risk, so it is best to give them a rent contract. The principal can now give the other agents a forcing contract: 'If your payoff is not lower than the payoff of the risk-neutral agents, who have a rent contract, your compensation will be the same as theirs; if, however, your payoff is lower, then you will get nothing.'

Assume now that all agents are risk-averse. In this case it is still possible to make comparisons between agents, by making a comparison between the payoff of a certain agent with the average of all agents. The difference between the payoff of a particular agent and the average payoff of all other agents can be due only to that agent's level of effort. For the principal this is a signal concerning that agent's level of effort. From the principal's point of view, an optimal reward structure should be based both on the payoff and on the average payoff of all agents.

Several periods

Consider now one principal and one agent in a setting with several periods. Assume further that the principal cannot observe the agent's behaviour and that the agent is risk-averse (if the agent is risk-neutral, the best contract is again a rent contract). The principal can now base the agent's reward structure on the payoff of the present period and on that of all previous periods. From the principal's point of view such a reward structure is better than a reward structure based only on the payoff of the present period.

7.6.5   Applying agency theory

In the previous sections various agency models have been described. We, the authors, hope that you have enjoyed reading about this fascinating field. In this final section on agency theory we want to stress that extreme care should be taken in applying agency theory in practical situations.

As an example consider a corporation with several business units. This is a situation with one principal and several agents: the CEO is the principal, the managers of the business units are the agents. Suppose this CEO engages you as a consultant to devise incentive contracts for the business unit managers.

How useful is the theory explained in previous sections to you in this situation? If you do not fully understand the theory's limitations, there is a real danger that the theory will be misapplied. There are several reasons for this.

First, the models we have discussed in sections 7.6.1, 7.6.2 and 7.6.3 are one-period models. That is why we have used the example of growing strawberries during one summer. However, you are asked to advise in a situation where the business unit managers will be reviewed periodically by the CEO. This requires a multiple-period model. Multiple-period models have been described only very briefly in section 7.6.4.

Second, you are being asked to advise on a situation with one principal and several agents. In section 7.6.4 we have briefly discussed a situation with one principal and several agents. In this model several agents grow strawberries on adjacent plots. This means that the weather conditions are the same for each plot. So we can assume that each agent faces the same random factor (the same weather conditions). In a setting with several business unit managers each business unit may be affected differently by such random factors as the euro exchange rate or the fortunes of important customers.

Finally, and most important, the CEO will probably be able to collect several signals concerning the effort levels of business unit managers. Since monitoring reduces the information asymmetry problem, it is quite likely that it will reduce the principal's loss of expected utility (see Figure 7.8). But monitoring is costly, so the real issue is not whether to monitor but how and how much to monitor. This is a very complicated issue with no easy solutions. Most CEOs will evaluate the performance of a business unit manager on several financial and non-financial indicators and compare a business unit manager's performance on these indicators with his previous performance on those indicators and the performance of his colleagues on those indicators. These quantitative evaluations may be used to determine bonus payments. When it comes to promoting a business unit manager to a position of more responsibility most CEOs will be reluctant to rely exclusively on these quantitative evaluations. Instead they will tend to supplement these quantitative measures with a qualitative judgement of a business unit manager's qualifications and performance.

7.7 Corporate governance systems

In public corporations there is a separation of management and control. In such firms the firm's top managers may or may not own a substantial part of the shares of the company they run, but in either case there are outside shareholders. This is the agency problem that has been described in section 7.3: the outside shareholders act as principal and the firm's top management team as agent. In different parts of the world different ways to reduce this agency problem have emerged. This has resulted in two rather different corporate governance systems. Roughly speaking, there is a difference between the corporate governance system of Anglo-Saxon countries (the USA, the UK, Canada, Australia, New Zealand) and the corporate governance system in other parts of the developed world (the countries of continental Europe and Japan). In Anglo-Saxon countries **market-oriented systems of corporate governance** prevail, while in other parts of the world **network-oriented systems of corporate governance** have evolved. In market-oriented systems of corporate governance shares are widely dispersed, while in network-oriented systems shareholding is much more concentrated. This has important consequences for the role of the board of directors and for the importance of the market for corporate control.

This section first describes ownership structures in market-oriented and network-oriented systems of corporate governance. Then the role of the board of directors and the importance of the market for corporate control in both systems of corporate governance is discussed.

Market-oriented systems of corporate governance

Network-oriented systems of corporate governance

7.7.1   Market-oriented systems of corporate governance

In the USA almost all large companies are listed on a stock exchange. More than 50 per cent of the shares of these companies are owned by households. The other shares are owned by financial institutions (pension funds, insurance companies, mutual investment companies and commercial banks) and by the firm's managers. In most cases, however, the firm's managers together own only a small portion, usually less than 10 per cent of the shares. Because most of the shares are owned by investors who individually hold only a very small proportion of the shares, no single investor has a strong incentive to evaluate the performance of the firm's managers. Suppose that the largest investor in a certain firm is a Mrs Navratilova and that she owns 6 per cent of the shares of that firm. This means that if Mrs Navratilova incurs costs for monitoring the firm's managers, only 6 per cent of the benefits, in the form of better performance of the firm's managers, accrue to her. The other 94 per cent of the benefits of her monitoring efforts accrue to the other shareholders. Thus there is a *free rider problem*: the other shareholders benefit but they do not share the costs of the monitoring efforts. Since no single shareholder has a strong incentive to monitor the managers there is a severe agency problem. This can lead to excessive remuneration and on-the-job-consumption, or 'corporate plundering', a term used already in 1932 by Berle and Means (see section 7.2).

7.7.2   Network-oriented systems of corporate governance

In countries such as Germany, France, Italy, Spain and Japan shares in large corporations are not as widely distributed as in the USA and the UK. In the UK, for example, more than 60 of that country's 100 largest firms are listed on the stock exchange, while in Italy, a country with roughly the same gross national product, that figure is less than 30. Moreover, for those companies that do have a listing on a stock exchange, shareholding is much more concentrated.

In Germany the so-called universal banks (banks such as Deutsche Bank, Commerzbank and Dresdner bank) do not only provide debt capital to large industrial enterprises, they also provide equity capital. These universal banks are very important shareholders for most of the large corporations in Germany,

Box 7.6 ■ DaimlerChrysler AG and its main shareholder

On Monday 26 February 2001 Juergen Schrempp, chief executive of DaimlerChrysler AG, the German-American auto giant, had some bad news for investors. Chrysler, acquired by Daimler-Benz in 1998, was in deep trouble and had to close six factories in Detroit, cutting 26,000 jobs. Mitsubishi Motors Corporation, of which DaimlerChrysler owned 34 per cent, also announced plans to cut 9,500 jobs in Japan. A final piece of bad news was that two leading rating agencies downgraded DaimlerChrysler's credit standing after the plans to restructure Chrysler and Mitsubishi were announced.

When asked by journalists about the consequences for his own position, Schrempp said 'There is no bigger pressure than the one I put on myself.' However, Deutsche Bank, with 12 per cent DaimlerChrysler's largest shareholder, issued a statement supporting Mr Schrempp but also making clear it expected a turnaround within 12 months. A Deutsche Bank spokesman declined to specify what would constitute a sufficient 12-month turnaround in the bank's eyes. Chairman of the supervisory board of DaimlerChrysler AG was Hilmar Kopper, a retired executive of Deutsche Bank. There were rumours that Deutsche Bank planned to introduce statutory and legal changes in order to prevent competitors acquiring DaimlerChrysler cheaply.

Source: The Wall Street Journal Europe, 27 February 2001

as is illustrated by Box 7.6. These universal banks can also exercise the voting rights of the shares deposited with them by their clients. This, together with the shares they own, gives these banks considerable voting power.

In France, Italy and Spain many large companies, even those listed on the stock exchange, have one or a few owners of large blocks of shares. Examples of such large block owners are financial holding companies (the Société Générale in France), a rich family (Agnelli in Italy), the state, a bank or another industrial corporation.

Keiretsus

In Japan there are many large industrial groups, the so-called **keiretsus**, such as Mitsubishi and Mitsui. These groups are centred around a bank and/or an insurance company that provides the companies belonging to the group with debt capital as well as equity capital. The companies belonging to the group often hold shares in other companies belonging to the same group. Thus a large part of the shares of a company belonging to a keiretsu is concentrated within the group.

In summary, while there are important differences between Germany, France, Italy, Spain and Japan, there is also a common feature. This is that many large companies have one or a few owners of large blocks of shares. Companies having the same person or institution as owner of a large block of shares may be seen as forming a network. For this reason, the term network-oriented systems of corporate governance has been coined (Moerland, 1995).

7.7.3   The role of the board of directors

Inside directors

In the USA and the UK companies are controlled by a board of directors that consists of inside directors and outside directors. The **inside directors**, also called executive officers, are full-time managers of the company. The firm's top manager is always a member of the board. In the USA he or she has the title of chief executive officer or CEO. The **outside directors**, also called non-executive directors or non-executive officers, are mostly senior managers of other large firms. The chairperson of the board may be one of the outside directors or one of the inside directors. Thus one person can combine the functions of CEO and chair of the board.

Outside directors

In certain countries in continental Europe (Germany, Switzerland, the Netherlands) all large companies are controlled by two boards: the **executive board**, which is simply the firm's top management team, and the supervisory board. The **supervisory board** consists of outside members only. This system of corporate governance is called a **two-tier board system**. By contrast the system used in the USA and the UK, in which there is only one board, is called a **one-tier board system**. In a two-tier system there are two boards with a complete separation of executive and supervisory duties. In a two-tier board system decision management (as defined in section 7.5) is the responsibility of the executive board, while decision control is the main role of the supervisory board. In a one-tier board system the board is responsible for decision management as well as decision control.

Executive board

Supervisory board

Two-tier board system

One-tier board system

In Germany 50 per cent of the members of the supervisory board are designated by the employees, the other 50 per cent by the shareholders. The members elected by the employees are often union leaders; the members elected by the shareholders are often bankers (who in Germany are often important shareholders) or executives of other large corporations. The members elected by the shareholders elect the chair of the supervisory board. In the case of a tie in the supervisory board the chair may cast the decisive vote.

In the Netherlands members of the supervisory board are selected and designated by the supervisory board itself. Of course this is possible only if a supervisory board already exists. For new companies the shareholders elect the members of the supervisory board. Once this board is in place vacancies in the board are filled by the board itself. Members of the supervisory board do not represent shareholders or employees.

In France, Italy and Spain almost all companies use a one-tier board system, although in France companies may also choose a two-tier system. Owners of large blocks of shares are usually represented on the board.

Japan has a very complicated system that, nevertheless, comes quite close to the one-tier system used in the USA and UK. For companies belonging to a keiretsu the board contains usually one or more employees of the 'central bank' (the bank around which the group is centred) and/or managers of affiliated companies.

In summary, Germany (and countries such as the Netherlands and Switzerland) uses a two-tier board system, which allows a complete separation of decision management and decision control, while in other countries a one-tier system is dominant. There is, however, an important difference between the USA and UK on the one hand and Germany, France, Italy, Spain and Japan on the other hand: in the latter countries large block holders have a representative on the board of directors, while in the USA and the UK this is not common practice, simply because in many companies there is no large block holder. The owner of a large block of shares has a strong incentive to monitor the managers. As a member of the board (or supervisory board in Germany) the owner of a large block of shares can ask for all the information he or she needs for this monitoring task. Moreover, as a member of the board, this shareholder is paid by the company to perform the task of monitoring the firm's managers. Thus the free rider problem that was discussed earlier in this section is not a severe problem in this case. It is quite likely that in the USA and the UK the outside board members, if they do not own a substantial block of shares, have much weaker incentives to perform their duties as monitors. In those cases where the CEO is also chair of the board, it may also be difficult for the outside members of the board to perform their duties as monitors effectively, since in his role as chair of the board, the CEO controls to a large extent the agenda and the flow of information to the outside members of the board.

7.7.4   The importance of the market for corporate control

As has been explained in section 7.2 managers who perform poorly, perhaps because they do act too much in their own interests as opposed to the interests of the shareholders, must always fear that they may lose their job after the company has been acquired by another firm. Thus every management team

Hostile takeover

risks being ousted after a **hostile takeover** or, to put it differently, faces the discipline of the market for corporate control.

However, in Germany and Japan there are virtually no hostile takeovers. In France, Italy and Spain hostile takeovers are also very rare. The main reason for this is that a hostile bidder has to convince owners of large blocks of shares, who are also board members or are represented on the board, that selling their shares to the bidder is in their best interests. It may be quite difficult for General Motors to convince Mr Agnelli that selling his shares in Fiat to General Motors is in his own best interest!

In the USA and UK, by contrast, there are many examples of hostile takeover bids that have succeeded.

7.7.5   A comparison of the two corporate governance systems

In market-oriented systems of corporate governance severe underperformance by managers is restricted mainly by the fear of a hostile takeover. The board of directors is probably less important in this respect because outside directors may lack the incentive to perform their functions as monitors well. This may be true especially when the CEO is also chair of the board. Thus the market for corporate control is the most important mechanism to reduce on-the-job consumption. Incumbent managers may spend large amounts of money in the form of fees for lawyers and investment bankers in order to resist a hostile takeover bid. This is a waste of money for the shareholders of the target firm. Or to put it differently: transaction costs on the market for corporate control may be very high indeed. As a consequence incumbent managers have some leeway to consume on-the-job. The market for corporate control is far from frictionless, and this is the major disadvantage of market-oriented systems of corporate governance.

In network-oriented systems of corporate governance monitoring of top managers by outside board members is probably the most important mechanism for reducing on-the-job consumption. In network-oriented systems of corporate governance owners of large blocks of shares have the incentives to perform their monitoring role in an effective way. The market for corporate control is of little importance in restraining managers from on-the-job consumption. A disadvantage of network-oriented systems is that markets for equity capital, including venture capital, are less well developed. This may hinder the optimal allocation of equity capital in countries in which network-oriented systems prevail. Another disadvantage may arise when the main private shareholders in a company would not act in the best corporate interest for private reasons, such as retaining family influence or prestige.

7.8 Summary: agency relations between owners, managers and employees

Within agency theory we distinguish between the positive theory of agency and the theory of principal and agent. The positive theory of agency views the organization as a nexus of contracts. It tries to explain why organizational forms are as they are. Two important questions in this respect are: how does the ownership structure of a firm affect managerial behaviour, and why do we observe certain organizational forms in the real world?

In order to explain how the ownership structure of a firm can affect managerial behaviour, let us consider first an entrepreneurial firm. An entrepreneurial firm is a firm owned and managed by the same person. In such a firm there is no conflict of interest between owner(s) and manager(s). A public corporation is a corporation with shares that are traded on a stock market. In a public corporation there may be a real conflict of interest between the (outside) shareholders and the manager(s). Usually, shareholders are interested in a high return on their investment (in the form of dividends and appreciation of the share price on the stock market), so shareholders would like to see managers that maximize the value of the firm on the stock market. Managers, however, may have other interests. Some of them like to have a luxury car, or to travel and to stay in expensive hotels as long as the bill is paid by the company. In other words, managers may engage in on-the-job consumption that decreases the value of the firm. Even in an entrepreneurial firm the manager will engage in consumption on the job. If he sells (part of) his shares to outsiders, he will increase his on-the-job consumption, thus reducing the value of the firm. The outsiders expect this type of behaviour, and this is reflected in the price they are willing to pay for the shares.

In most manufacturing industries there are entrepreneurial firms and public corporations but very few co-operative firms (a co-operative firm is a firm owned by the workers). Why do we observe so many entrepreneurial firms and so few co-operative firms in the real world? The answer may have to do with the existence of team production. Team production is a situation in which two or more persons can produce more when they are working together than when they are working separately. A problem with team production is that it leads to shirking: a member of a team who receives only a portion of the team's output will work less hard than a person working alone. The result is that the output of the team is greatly reduced. Thus team members want to reduce shirking. One solution may be to have a monitor who specializes in observing shirking. In a co-operative firm the monitor would share in the proceeds with other team members. This would give the monitor an incentive to shirk as a monitor. However, if the monitor is the owner of the firm, he has no incentive to shirk. This may explain why entrepreneurial firms are more efficient than co-operative firms. Since we would expect the most efficient organizational forms to survive, we are not surprised to see many small manufacturing firms organized as entrepreneurial firms and very few as co-operatives.

The theory of principal and agent forms the core of modern agency theory. In this theory risk is introduced into the analysis. In its simplest form the theory focuses on the relationship between one principal and one agent. The agent performs a task and in so doing has to choose a level of effort. The output is determined by the level of effort but also by a random factor such as the weather. The problem for the principal is to determine a reward structure for the agent. If the principal can observe the level of effort chosen by the agent, he can specify a minimum level of effort. The agent will receive nothing if he does not meet this minimum level of effort. If his level of effort exceeds the minimum, he will receive a fixed wage.

The principal's problem is much more interesting if the principal cannot observe the agent's behaviour. In that case the agent's attitude toward risk becomes important. If the agent is risk-neutral he is willing to take on risk without asking compensation for risk-bearing. The best solution then is simply to give the agent a rent contract. This allocates all risk to the agent but also gives the agent a very strong incentive to increase his level of effort. If the agent is risk-averse and the principal risk-neutral, the principal has to make a trade-off between giving the agent incentives and having the agent bear more risk. The best solution in this case is to give the agent a reward structure that depends to some extent on the payoff but also contains a fixed element independent of the payoff. Such a contract involves risk-sharing between principal and agent.

Questions

1 Your car has been making a strange noise lately. You don't know what it is but you don't feel comfortable with it, so you bring your car to the garage. You bring your car in the morning and you return in the evening to collect it. Is the relationship you have with your garage an example of an agency relation? Who is the principal and who is the agent? Which kind of action is taken by the agent? Can the principal observe the actual action taken by the agent? Why do the agent's decisions or actions affect the principal's assets broadly defined?

2 Consider, in the theory of principal and agent, the case in which the principal can observe the agent's behaviour. Does the optimal reward structure from the principal's point of view depend on the agent's attitude towards risk? Explain your answer.

3 Fama and Jensen (1983a, b) describe decision processes as consisting of four steps: initiation, ratification, implementation, and monitoring. Further, they introduce the terms decision management and decision control. Consider a small company (S) operating as a subsidiary of a larger company (L). Suppose that the managers of S are contemplating a major investment. Who will exercise decision management and who will exercise decision control? Why? Does this conform to one of Fama and Jensen's hypotheses? If yes, how did Fama and Jensen phrase this hypothesis?

4 Consider, in the theory of principal and agent, the situation in which the principal cannot observe the agent's behaviour and in which both principal and agent are risk-neutral. What is the optimal contract from the principal's point of view?

5 A definition of team production has been given on pages 120–1. Which of the following situations represents team production? Explain your answer.

(a) A violin quartet playing Mozart.
(b) Eighteen persons working in a factory that produces grandfather clocks (see Box 8.1 in the next chapter).
(c) Twenty engineers working on the design for a new car.

6 Ummels Services BV is a Dutch company with limited liability offering maintenance services for chemical processing plants. Ummels Services BV was founded in 1984 by Mr Stef Ummels. The company was owned and managed by Mr Ummels until he died in 1995. Since then 50 per cent of the shares of Ummels Services BV have been owned by his son, Paul Ummels, while the other 50 per cent are owned by his daughter, Lara Ummels. Since his father's death Paul Ummels has managed the company. Lara Ummels is a medical student and intends to become a urologist.

In March 2002 Paul and Lara talk about Lara selling her shares in the company to her brother. Lara would like to cash them in because she has little affinity with the company. Paul is interested in buying because he likes the idea of becoming sole owner. Paul is sure he can borrow the money he needs to buy Lara's shares. Paul and Lara engage Mr Schlösser, an independent financial consultant, to estimate the value of Lara's shares.

Mr. Schlösser calculates the present value of all future cash flows of the company. In estimating future cash flows he uses historical cash flows of the last five years. This results in a value of €4.6 million for the company. He recommends that Lara sell her shares to Paul for €2.3 million.

Lara is now asking you for a second opinion on Mr Schlösser's calculation. Do you see anything that Mr Schlösser may have neglected? How can Lara justify a price higher than €2.3 million? Do you think Paul will be interested in buying at a price higher than €2.3 million? Why?

7 Mr Howard Rothey owns an icecream bar at the beach in Bournemouth, England. He has been running this icecream bar for several years. Icecream sales

at the beach are highly seasonal: almost all sales take place in the period May to September. For this reason Mr Rothey has never taken a holiday during this peak season. Now, however, he wants to visit his son and daughter-in-law in Alaska in July. For this reason he wants to engage someone to run his icecream business during a period of three weeks in July. Alex Waterman, a 22-year-old student from Bath University, is looking for a summer job. Mr Rothey is contemplating the kind of contract he should offer. Mr Rothey is well aware of the fact that ice-cream sales depend to a large extent on the way Alex will treat customers (in the language of the theory of principal and agent we would say that icecream sales depend on Alex's level of effort). And, of course, the weather is quite important. For the English south coast the weather in July can be very nice with lots of sun, but it can also be rainy and cold for several weeks.

(a) Should Mr Rothey offer Alex a forcing contract?

(b) Should Mr Rothey offer Alex a wage contract? If he does and Alex accepts, what will be Alex's level of effort?

(c) What other types of contract can Mr Rothey offer?

(d) What is the best contract for Mr Rothey if Mr Rothey and Alex Waterman are both risk-neutral?

(e) Now suppose that Mr Rothey is risk-neutral and Alex Waterman is risk-averse. Figure 7.9 gives the trade-off between providing incentives and the cost of risk-bearing for this situation.

■ Which variable is indicated on the horizontal axis?

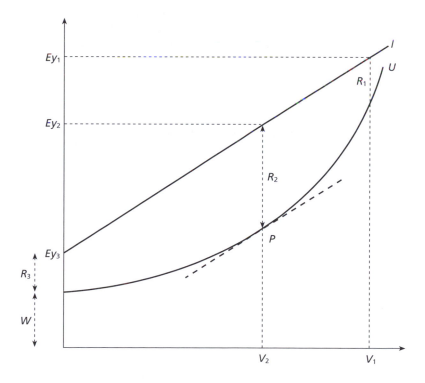

Figure 7.9 **The trade-off between incentives and risk-bearing in the theory of principal and agent**

- What does line *I* stand for?
- What does curve *U* in this figure stand for?

(f) Figure 7.9 also indicates the optimal solution for Mr Rothey. Indicate in Figure 7.9 how much money Alex Waterman receives in the optimal solution.

8 Large multinational companies have many foreign subsidiaries. The relationship between the manager of one of those foreign subsidiaries with company headquarters is an agency relation, with the manager of the foreign subsidiary as agent and headquarters as principal. Managers of the foreign subsidiaries can receive a bonus payment related to the financial results of their subsidiary. There is considerable variation, however, with respect to the relative importance of such financial incentives.

One factor that might explain part of this variation is industry volatility (this refers to the degree to which conditions in the foreign subsidiary's industry fluctuate: some industries are relatively stable, others show large fluctuations in levels of demand and customer preferences). How would you expect industry volatility to influence the use of financial incentives?

Which other factors could possibly explain the variation in the use of financial incentives?

Suggested further reading

Holmstrom, B.R. and J. Tirole (1989), 'The theory of the firm', in: R. Schmalensee and R. Willig (eds), *Handbook of Industrial Organization*, vol. 1, Amsterdam: North Holland.

Jensen, M.C. (1998), *Foundations of Organizational Strategy*, Cambridge, MA: Harvard University Press.

Notes

1. The concept of indifference curve is explained in section 2.3.
2. See Chapter 4 for the concepts of asymmetric and private information.
3. To be more precise, the utility function of the agent is such that the first partial derivative with respect to income is positive and the first partial derivative with respect to effort is negative.

8 Transaction cost economics

8.1 Introduction

In Chapter 1 we laid the framework for this book. This framework was summarized in Figure 1.1. Basically, the argument is that division of labour creates opportunities for specialization. This necessitates co-ordination of economic decisions. There are two ideal types of co-ordination mechanism: markets and organizations.

In transaction cost economics the fundamental unit of analysis is the transaction. Transactions can take place across markets or within organizations. Whether a particular transaction is allocated to the market or to an organization is a matter of cost minimization. Transaction cost economics emphasizes that transaction costs as well as traditional production costs should be taken into account. The term transaction costs includes both costs of market transactions and costs of internal transactions.

According to the argument we have developed so far, firms exist because in some cases the costs of internal co-ordination are lower than the costs of market transactions (see Box 8.1). This is almost a tautology. If we see a firm, then apparently the costs of internal co-ordination are lower than the costs of market transactions. That is not much of a theory. Such a 'theory' can never be empirically tested. If we really want to develop a theory, then we should specify beforehand in which cases we expect the costs of market transactions to be high in comparison with the costs of internal co-ordination. If we can do that, we can hope to derive hypotheses that are suitable for empirical testing. Oliver Williamson has almost single-handedly developed such a theory in numerous publications. This chapter is based primarily on Williamson's work, and especially on his two books *Markets and Hierarchies* (1975) and *The Economic Institutions of Capitalism* (1985).

Transaction cost economics as developed by Williamson is based on the assumption that human beings are *boundedly rational* and sometimes display *opportunistic behaviour*. These two behavioural assumptions are discussed in section 8.2. Whether transaction costs for a particular transaction will be high or low depends on the *critical dimensions* of that transaction. Critical dimensions of transactions are discussed in section 8.3. With these two sections the basic foundations for transaction cost economics have been laid. In the subsequent sections we apply transaction cost reasoning. First we discuss several

Box 8.1 ■ A factory making grandfather clocks

Why do firms exist? Why is not everyone self-employed?

Consider a factory employing 18 people making grandfather clocks. Five of the employees specialize in sawing the wooden parts that together form the clockcases. Two of them assemble the wooden parts to form cases. Another two spray the cases with paint. Two paint faces. Four assemble cases, faces and movements to form complete clocks. There are two salesmen and one general manager. The general manager is also the owner of the company. Why are the first 17 people working as employees? Why is not everyone self-employed? The answer is transaction costs. Consider the following three situations:

- Situation 1: 17 self-employed people working at geographically dispersed locations.
- Situation 2: 17 self-employed people all working under the same roof.
- Situation 3: 17 people employed by the owner of the factory.

Compare, first, situations 1 and 2. In situation 1, the costs of transporting semi-finished goods is high compared with 2. In situation 2 the costs of market transactions between the 17 self-employed people may be high because of small numbers bargaining. For example, if the two persons spraying cases with paint collude, they can try to lower prices of unpainted cases and raise prices of painted cases. This may result in frequent interruptions of the workflow. In situation 1 the two sprayers may have to compete with numerous other sprayers, which would restrict their bargaining power.

Compare now situations 2 and 3. In situation 3 there is no costly haggling over prices of semi-finished goods (no interruptions of the workflow because parties cannot reach agreement over prices of semi-finished goods). Quantities of semi-finished goods that each must produce are determined by the general manager, not by negotiation between self-employed persons. The general manager must also evaluate each person's level of effort. The three situations can be summarized in a table (see below):

	(1) *Self-employed persons working in geographically dispersed locations*	(2) *Self-employed people working under the same roof*	(3) *Employeees working for an employer*
Transportation costs	High	Low	Low
Costs of market transactions	Low	High	Low
Costs of internal co-ordination	Low	Low	High

In a market economy only the most efficient organizational form can survive in the long run. Therefore if we observe in reality grandfather clockmaking factories of type 3 only, then apparently that is the most efficient organization.

organizational forms: peer groups, single-stage hierarchies, and multistage hierarchies. Then we discuss internal markets within firms.

8.2 Behavioural assumptions: bounded rationality and opportunism

8.2.1 Bounded rationality

Bounded rationality

The concept of bounded rationality was introduced in Chapter 6 on behavioural theory. **Bounded rationality** means that the capacity of human beings to formulate and solve complex problems is limited. A good example is the game of chess. A chess player has all the information she needs for her decisions: the positions of the white and black pieces at the moment that she is contemplating a move are all the information she needs. In order to evaluate a certain move she needs only to analyze what moves her opponent can possibly make and evaluate all possible moves that she could make in answer to each possible countermove. The problem in chess is simply that the number of alternative sequences of moves and countermoves is too great even for the world's best chess players. It is not that a chess player does not want to make fully rational decisions. She does want to make fully rational decisions, but her capacity to evaluate fully the consequences of all possible decisions is limited. So bounded rationality refers to human behaviour that is 'intendedly rational, but only limitedly so' (Simon, 1961).

From this discussion it is clear that bounded rationality poses a problem in chess because chess is a complex game. A game such as bridge is characterized both by complexity and uncertainty. In bridge the players do not know the hands of their opponents. If they did, then the game would be much less interesting. In bridge, bounded rationality is a problem because of the combination of uncertainty and complexity.

Now let us return to transactions. Bounded rationality will pose a problem only in environments that are characterized by *uncertainty/complexity*. When you buy gasoline for your car, there is not much complexity or uncertainty. You know the product quite well, you do not have to worry about aftersales service, and the seller does not need any information about you provided you pay directly. To buy gasoline you do not need to write and sign a contract.

Now consider the case of a government that wants to buy a new weapon system. In this case it is necessary to write and sign a contract. Such a contract is very complicated. Product specifications should be clearly defined in such a contract, but this can be quite difficult because of uncertainty about the technology. Is it feasible to develop a new weapon system that meets some clearly defined specifications? How much will it cost to develop such a system? How much will it cost to manufacture these systems? These are elements of uncertainty/complexity in the case of buying new and complex weaponry. It is likely that bounded rationality in conjunction with uncertainty/complexity makes it costly to write a contract for buying a new weapon system.

8.2.2 Opportunism

Opportunism

In Williamson's view, human beings are not only boundedly rational, they also sometimes display opportunistic behaviour. Williamson describes **opportunism** as 'self interest seeking with guile' and as making 'self disbelieved statements'. In plain English, this is trying to exploit a situation to your own advantage.

Williamson does not assume that everybody behaves opportunistically. He assumes only that some people might display opportunistic behaviour *and* that it is difficult or impossible to distinguish *ex ante* (that is, before you make a deal) honest people from dishonest people. Even those who behave opportunistically need not do so all the time. Williamson assumes only that those who might display opportunistic behaviour do so *sometimes* and that it is difficult or costly to tell *ex ante* when they do or do not. Sometimes people blame Williamson for too pessimistic a view of human nature. It somehow does not seem right to build a theory on such a gloomy assumption. If this is your first reaction too, consider the following examples.

Suppose you would like to spend your summer holiday in Greece. You go to a travel agency and you find out that almost everyone wants to go to Greece this year. You have to decide on the spot, and you book a holiday that is a little bit too expensive and not exactly what you want. The next day you see the perfect holiday at another travel agency: exactly what you want and in addition much cheaper. Would you not be tempted to cancel the first reservation if you could? Suppose travel agencies did not make their customers sign a contract that is legally binding, would you not agree that sometimes some customers would deny they had already booked the first expensive holiday? Apparently, travel agencies think so – that is why they have their customers sign a contract.

Consider also the following example. Suppose you want to buy a secondhand car from someone you do not know. The seller tells you that the car has no defects. Do you believe him? Suppose you can have the car inspected by an independent expert. Would you pay the cost of inspection before you buy? If you are prepared to pay the inspection cost, it means that you do not believe everyone. Suppose you can choose between two secondhand cars (A and B) from two different sellers (A and B). You can detect no difference between the two cars. There is only one difference: car A has been inspected by an independent expert, who tells you the car has no defects. Car B has not been inspected. In this case, seller B tells you the car has no defects. Would you prefer car A? That means that you do not rule out the possibility of opportunistic behaviour by seller B.

From these two examples it is clear that travel agencies and buyers of secondhand cars must spend a little amount of money (for drawing up a contract or for having the car inspected), not because they expect all their trading partners to behave opportunistically all the time, but because *some people* might display opportunistic behaviour *sometimes*.

From these two examples it is also clear that opportunistic behaviour can occur *ex ante* (a seller might not tell you about defects before you buy) or *ex post* (after you booked a holiday you might want to back out of it). *Ex ante* opportunistic behaviour leads to adverse selection, a concept that was introduced in section 4.2. *Ex ante* opportunistic behaviour can occur only when there is asymmetric information: the seller of a used car has information that potential buyers do not have.

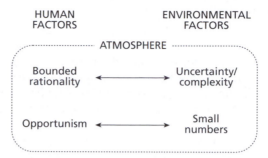

Figure 8.1 **The transaction cost framework**

Now suppose that there are large numbers of sellers and buyers who trade with each other on a regular basis. Suppose that in a certain town there are 10 dealers in secondhand cars. Suppose you buy a secondhand car. If you have a negative experience with one of the dealers you do not want to buy from him a second time. A dealer who behaves opportunistically will damage his reputation. The dealers know this and you know that the dealers know this, so you tend to believe a dealer when he says that a car has no defects. In this case the problem of opportunism is attenuated, because there are many sellers and because reputations matter.[1] You can save the inspection costs. (Note that you can save the inspection costs only if reputations are important and information about reputations is freely available.[2]) There is a problem only if opportunism occurs in conjunction with small numbers of trading partners. This is termed **small numbers exchange**. If there is only one seller, he does not have to worry over his reputation because you do not have an alternative. In this case you want to have the car inspected, so you have to pay transaction costs.

Small numbers exchange

The argument so far is illustrated in Figure 8.1. There are two human factors and two environmental factors. Bounded rationality in conjunction with uncertainty/complexity and opportunism in conjunction with small numbers exchange lead to transaction costs.

8.2.3 Atmosphere

The mode of a transaction (that is, whether a transaction is governed by the market or by an organization) is determined by minimization of the sum of production and transaction costs.[3] However, there is another factor that also determines the mode of a transaction. This factor is called **atmosphere** (see Figure 8.1).

Atmosphere

The factor atmosphere refers to the fact that participants in a transaction may value the mode of the transaction. Consider, for example, the workers making grandfather clocks from Box 8.1. Maybe they derive satisfaction from being self-employed. If this is true, they would be willing to work as an employee only if higher income compensated for loss of atmosphere. For this reason an employer with 17 employees might not be able to compete against a

Box 8.2 ■ Blood donorship

As described in Box 4.1 there is a serious shortage of good-quality blood that can be used for blood-transfusion purposes. Clearly there is a demand for blood. Good-quality blood should command a high price. Yet we observe that blood collection is still organized on a voluntary basis. Blood donors give their blood for free. Why are blood donors not paid?

One reason, explained in Box 4.1, is adverse selection. However, there is a second reason: if blood donors were to receive payment, then that would fundamentally change the nature of the transaction. As it is, blood donors derive satisfaction from the idea that they give their blood for the common good. They voluntarily give to those who are so unfortunate as to need a transfusion. To pay blood donors would transform the act of giving blood into an ordinary commercial transaction. It is quite likely that the result would be fewer (good-quality) donors instead of more.

group of 18 self-employed people even if the transaction costs of the former arrangement were lower than those of the latter.

Sometimes people prefer to give away something for free. In that case they derive more satisfaction from the act of giving than from the money they could receive. This indicates that most people value the nature of a transaction. As an example, read Box 8.2 about blood donorship.

8.2.4 The fundamental transformation

Suppose that an automobile company invites bids from a large number of potential suppliers for a certain part for a new automobile. Suppose the automobile company signs a contract with one of the original bidders for a five-year period. During this five-year period the supplier learns how to produce that component efficiently. After five years, when the contract must be renewed, the original winner of the contract has a significant advantage over other potential suppliers. Through learning by doing, the original situation involving a large number of bidders is transformed into a situation of monopoly: the experience gained by the supplier puts him in the position of a monopolist. However, the supplier can use this experience only in the manufacturing of a part for which there is only one buyer. So the situation is again one of bilateral monopoly.

Fundamental transformation

When learning by doing occurs, an original situation of large numbers exchange is transformed into a situation of small numbers exchange. This is termed the **fundamental transformation**.

8.3 Dimensions of transactions

Critical dimensions of transactions

Transaction costs for a particular transaction depend on the critical dimensions of that transaction. There are three **critical dimensions of transactions**: asset specificity, uncertainty/complexity, and frequency.

8.3.1 Asset specificity

Asset specificity

Transaction-specific assets

The **asset specificity** of a transaction refers to the degree to which the transaction needs to be supported by **transaction-specific assets**. An asset is transaction-specific if it cannot be redeployed to an alternative use without a significant reduction in the value of the asset. Asset specificity may refer to physical or to human assets. To illustrate the concept consider the following example, which refers to physical assets.[4]

Imagine a town located in the centre of a very thinly populated area. Let us call the town Appropria. At present there is no local newspaper in Appropria, but there is a publisher, Mr P, who wants to start a local newspaper. The new newspaper must be printed locally in Appropria because of transportation costs. Mr P does not have printing know-how, so he must rely on the know-how of one of the local printers. There are several printers in Appropria but none of them has a press suitable for printing newspapers. One of the printers in Appropria, Mrs Q, considers buying a press for printing newspapers. If she buys such a press it will be a transaction-specific asset: she can use the press only for the transaction with Mr P since there is no other newspaper in Appropria and since it is very costly to transport newspapers to other towns. To put it in the language of transaction cost economics, the transaction between Mr P and Mrs Q is characterized by asset specificity.

For transactions with high asset specificity the costs of market transactions are high. To see why this is true, let us return to Appropria. Suppose that the new press has an economic life of five years, so Mrs Q wants a five-year contract with Mr P before she buys the press. At first glance it may not seem very difficult or costly to write and sign a five-year contract. To illustrate the difficulties in writing such a contract we use a numerical example.

Assume fixed costs are $3,500 per day, if the new press is depreciated over five years. Assume further that variable costs for operating the new press are $1,500 per day. Mrs Q cannot sell the services of the press to another publisher and she cannot sell the press either. Suppose Mrs Q obtains a five-year contract from Mr P for $5,000 per day and on this basis orders the new press. As soon as Mrs Q has committed herself Mr P has an incentive for opportunistic behaviour. Even though Mrs Q has a legally binding contract with Mr P, Mr P can come back to her. Suppose he tells her: 'Look, this new newspaper is not really the success I expected it to become. With a contract for $5,000 a day I will go bankrupt and then your press will have no value at all. If you can help me a little by agreeing to lower the price to $4,000 a day, I will be able to manage. I am very sorry I have to say this, but really I see no other solution.' If Mrs Q believes this story, she has no other choice than to accept the lower price. In fact she must accept any price higher than $1,500 a day. In business language we would say that for a price higher than $1,500 there is still a positive contribution margin. In the language of economics we would say

Quasi-rent

that for a price higher than $1,500 there is still a positive **quasi-rent**. By making self-disbelieved statements, Mr P tries to appropriate (a part of) this quasi-rent. In Appropria trying to appropriate someone else's quasi-rent is a great sport.

If Mr P cannot go bankrupt under any circumstances, there is no problem. In that case a legally binding contract protects Mrs Q against post-contractual opportunistic behaviour by Mr P. If, however, Mr P can go bankrupt, Mrs Q will not buy the press on the basis of a simple five-year contract. What she needs is a guarantee by Mr P's bank that, in the event of bankruptcy, the bank will pay her the fixed costs ($3,500 a day, assuming no salvage value) for the rest of the five-year period. Now, though, the bank will be vulnerable to Mr P's post-contractual opportunistic behaviour. Now Mr P can go to his banker and say: 'Look, if you pay me $1,000 a day, I will not go bankrupt and you can save your contractual obligation to pay Mrs Q $3,500 a day.' So this does not solve the problem, but transfers it to someone else. In reality, Mrs Q might be willing to sign a contract with Mr P, but before doing so she needs much more information about Mr P's business plan, about his character, about his personal wealth, etc. To acquire this information is costly. In addition she will demand the right to have Mr P's books inspected by an independent auditor, and this is costly too. Finally, since her money will still be at risk, she will demand compensation for risk-bearing. This compensation may come in the form of a price higher than $5,000 a day or in the form of a share in Mr P's profits.

Another solution to these contractual difficulties is a merger between the firms of Mr P and Mrs Q. Then the transaction between publisher and printer would be taken out of the market and allocated to an organization. After a merger, Mr P and Mrs Q jointly own the assets and share the profits, so Mr P no longer has an incentive to behave opportunistically toward his partner.

In this example the degree of asset specificity is so high that a series of sequential spot contracts (say contracts for one day only and daily negotiations on the price for the next day) is not feasible (Mrs Q can never accept this, so she will not buy the press). So there are only two options left: a merger between Mr P and Mrs Q or a five-year contract specifying in detail Mrs Q's right to inspect Mr P's business. Such a long-term contract is an intermediate form between market and organization. In the language of transaction cost eco-

Relational contracting nomics it is termed **relational contracting**.

By the way, there may be another asset that is highly transaction-specific in the example above. A new newspaper normally suffers start-up losses during the first few years. By financing these start-up losses, Mr P invests in an intangible asset. Let us call this intangible asset goodwill. This goodwill is also a transaction-specific asset. Mrs Q now also has an incentive for post-contractual opportunistic behaviour. For example, she might say: 'Look, I made a mistake in calculating the price of $5,000 a day. You really must pay me $5,700 a day. If you don't, I will go bankrupt and the value of your investment in goodwill will be zero.' This story will pose a problem for Mr P if other printers will need at least a few months before they can start printing newspapers. So Mr P and Mrs Q both have to invest in a transaction-specific asset. That means that after they have invested they will be locked into a bilateral monopoly: they both have a monopoly position towards the other with respect to certain assets.

In the introduction to this section we have already distinguished between physical and human asset specificity. Box 8.3 gives a somewhat finer distinction.

Box 8.3 ■ Different types of asset specificity

Transaction cost economics has filtered through to the managerial literature. Consider the following discussion of several types of asset specificity from the *McKinsey Quarterly*:

There are three principal types of asset specificity . . . *Site specificity* occurs when buyers and sellers locate fixed assets, such as a coal mine and power station, in close proximity to minimize transport and inventory costs. *Technical specificity* occurs when one or both parties to a transaction invest in equipment that can only be used by one or both parties and that has low value in alternative uses. *Human capital specificity* occurs when employees develop skills that are specific to a particular buyer or customer relationship.

The upstream aluminum industry has high asset specificity. The industry has two principal stages of production: bauxite mining and aluminum refining. Mines and refineries are usually located close together (site specificity) because of the high cost of transporting bauxite, relative to its value, and the 60 to 70 percent volume reduction typically achieved during refining. Refineries are tailored to process their own bauxite, with its unique chemical and physical properties; switching suppliers or customers is either impossible or prohibitively expensive (technical specificity). Consequently, mine-refinery pairs are locked together economically.

Source: Stuckey and White (1993)

8.3.2 Uncertainty/complexity

The second dimension of transactions, uncertainty/complexity, needs no further explanation: we already know that bounded rationality is a problem only for transactions with a high degree of uncertainty/complexity (remember the examples of buying gasoline and of ordering a new weapon system).

8.3.3 Frequency

When asset specificity is high we expect transactions to be carried out within organizations rather than across markets. However, to set up a specialized governance structure (such as a vertically integrated firm) involves certain fixed costs. Whether the volume of transactions conducted through such a specialized governance structure utilizes it to capacity is then the remaining issue. The costs of a specialized governance structure are more easily recovered for high frequency transactions. Hence frequency is the third relevant dimension of transactions.

8.3.4 Competition between organizational forms

Transaction costs for a particular transaction depend on the critical dimensions of that transaction. For transactions with a high degree of asset specificity, a high degree of uncertainty/complexity and a high frequency the costs of market transactions are extremely high, much higher than the costs of internal transactions. Such transactions tend to be carried out within organizations, at

Box 8.4 ■ Why are dairy firms organized as farmers' co-operatives?

Dairy firms are often, though not always, organized as farmers' co-operatives. Why is this? Before trying to answer this question let us give you some details about the emergence of the first dairy co-operatives in the Netherlands, or more specifically in two provinces of the Netherlands: Friesland and North-Holland.

In the middle of the eighteenth century there were only three dairy products: cheese, butter and fresh milk. In those days farmers made cheese and butter at the farm (this was usually done by women). In 1878 a centrifuge for separating cream from milk was developed. This invention provided economies of scale and led to the emergence of dairy factories. In Friesland the first dairy factory was established in 1879 by a private entrepreneur. Seven years later, in 1886, Friesland had seven dairy firms owned and operated by entrepreneurs. In that same year a dairy factory was established by a group of farmers as a co-operative firm. A dairy firm organized as a farmers' co-operative does not have shareholders; consequently profit maximizing is not its main goal. A farmers' co-operative has members and tries to pay its members as high a price as possible for the milk its members supply. In Friesland the number of dairy factories set up by farmers' co-operatives grew rapidly, but so did the number of dairy firms run by entrepreneurs. In 1898 Friesland had 46 dairy factories run by entrepreneurs and 66 dairy firms run by farmers' co-operatives. In the first 25 years of the next century, however, dairy firms run by farmers' co-operatives grew faster in size and number, while some of the entrepreneurial dairy firms failed. As a result the farmers' co-operative has been the dominant organizational form of dairy firms in Friesland from 1925 onwards.

In the northern part of North-Holland dairy firms developed in the same way as in Friesland: around 1900 there were entrepreneurial as well as co-operative dairy firms, but the co-operatives grew faster. As a result co-operatives came to dominate this region as well. In the southern part of North-Holland there were no farmers' co-operatives around 1900. This area is close to the cities of Amsterdam, Haarlem, Leiden and Utrecht. Milk from this area was sold primarily as fresh milk to consumers in those cities by distributors. These distributors were private entrepreneurs.

Why did the co-operative dairy firm overtake entrepreneurial dairy firms in Friesland and the northern part of North-Holland? And why did co-operative dairy firms not emerge in the southern part of North-Holland?

The answer has much to do with the fact that milk is a perishable product. In the eighteenth century milk could not be stored for more than a day (cooling was not available) and transporting milk over long distances was not feasible. Milk had to be processed into cheese and butter within a short time and not far from the farm. As a result farmers who sold their milk to an entrepreneurial dairy firm were in a situation where they had only one customer. Their investment in cattle is a transaction-specific investment. These farmers had no alternative for their milk but to resume the old way of processing milk at the farm. In the early days of the dairy factories this was probably a feasible alternative, because farmers still had the equipment and the know-how for making butter and cheese. However, as economies of scale became more pronounced and farmers' equipment for making butter and cheese was no longer in a good condition, making butter and cheese at the farm ceased to be a realistic alternative. Farmers were powerless against opportunistic behaviour from entrepreneurial dairy firms, especially since butter and cheese are much less perishable than fresh milk. This prompted more and more farmers who initially sold their milk to entrepreneurial firms to become members of the nearest farmers' co-operative. This

▶

explains the development in Friesland and the northern part of North-Holland, where almost all milk was used for making butter and cheese.

In the southern part of North-Holland the situation was different: here the distributors of fresh milk were as dependent on the farmers as the farmers were dependent on them. The investment by the farmers in cattle is transaction-specific, but so is the investment by the distributors in their customer base and their means of distribution: since fresh milk could not be stored for more than a day, the distributors needed a daily supply of fresh milk. This made opportunistic behaviour of a distributor towards his suppliers unlikely. The main difference between a distributor of fresh milk and an entrepreneurial dairy firm making butter and cheese seems to be that the former needed a daily supply of fresh milk while the latter did not. This explains why co-operative dairy firms did not emerge in the southern part of North-Holland.

least in the long run. In the real world we might see certain market transactions while at the same time similar transactions take place within organizations. This can indicate that the costs of transacting under the two modes are about equal. If the costs of transacting under the two modes differ significantly, then the most efficient form will ultimately prevail. This might take quite a long time, however, as is illustrated in Box 8.4.

The example in Box 8.4 also illustrates how organizational forms compete. In Box 8.4 this concerns competition between co-operative dairy firms and entrepreneurial dairy firms. This is a fundamental assumption in transaction cost economics: there is always competition between organizational forms and in the long run only the most efficient organizational form will survive.

8.4 Peer groups

In sections 8.2 and 8.3 we have laid the foundations for transaction cost reasoning. In the next sections we apply transaction cost reasoning to explain the existence of different organizational forms. The first organizational form to be discussed is the peer group. A **peer group** is simply a group of people working together without hierarchy. In a peer group the most important co-ordinating mechanism is mutual adjustment. There is no boss, so there can be no direct supervision. The peer group sells its output, the proceeds of which are shared among the members of the peer group according to some sharing rule. Examples of peer groups are small partnerships (lawyers, auditors, doctors).

Peer group

8.4.1 Advantages of peer groups

Why do peer groups arise? For example, why do most management consultants work as partners in a partnership instead of working independently? What are the advantages of a peer group over a group of independent self-employed persons?

First, *economies of scale* may be obtained. Suppose two dentists form a partnership. The partnership may then buy equipment for X-ray photography that each dentist uses for perhaps not more than half an hour per day. However, an alternative arrangement would be two dentists working independently (without pooling of revenues) in the same building. They could still jointly own or lease the X-ray equipment. In this example, economies of scale arise because a worker (the dentist) needs the services of expensive equipment on a part-time basis only. Joint ownership (as farmers sometimes have with harvesting machines) is then a viable arrangement for obtaining such economies. It may also be possible to obtain the services of such indivisible specialized physical assets by renting (harvesting equipment that can be moved easily from one farmer to the next provides an example).

Economies of scale may also arise in *information-gathering*. Imagine two consultants who specialize in marketing studies for pharmaceutical companies. Both need background information on developments in the pharmaceutical industry on a continuous basis. Suppose they both employ a young economist for desk research. By forming a partnership they can economize on desk research. Suppose those two consultants decide to remain independent but still want to economize on desk research. Could one of them stop doing desk research and buy the information he needed from his competitor/colleague? Without going into details now, it seems plausible that this would be more difficult than buying the services of specialized equipment. In general it is difficult to trade information because of the fundamental paradox of information (see Chapter 4, section 4.1). So economies of scale in information-gathering are difficult to obtain for two independent consultants.

Second, a peer group may have *risk-bearing advantages* over a group of independent persons. Consider a group of 10 independent marketing consultants. A major risk for each of them is to have no assignments for an extended period. Forming a partnership is one way to obtain pooling of this risk. Again it is useful to ask whether such risk-pooling could be obtained through a market, in this case the insurance market. It may be possible but difficult to obtain insurance for the risk of having no assignments. Those consultants who are weak in selling their services will be especially eager to take such an insurance policy. Also, after having obtained such an insurance policy, it may be quite difficult for the insurance company to check whether or not the consultant really tried hard enough to get assignments. Thus adverse selection and moral hazard would be severe problems for the insurance company. The partners forming a peer group may be able to mitigate adverse selection if they can screen potential partners better than an insurance company can. It also seems plausible that a partnership can mitigate the problem of moral hazard: observability of effort is less a problem for colleagues than for an insurance company.

Third, a peer group may offer *associational gains*. That is, consultants may be more productive when working as member of a partnership than when working independently. If they belong to a partnership, they may feel a responsibility to do their fair share, but working alone they may slack off. Also they may value being a partner and working among peers. This is an example of atmosphere: people may simply prefer one organizational form over another.

8.4.2 Limitations of peer groups

In a small peer group (for example, two authors writing a book on economic theories of organization), shirking may not be a problem at all. On the contrary, each may take pride in doing more than his fair share. However, in a large peer group, shirking often becomes a severe problem. Very large partnerships (in auditing and/or consulting) do exist. However, in these partnerships some of the partners are elected managing partners. It is their duty to restrict shirking by evaluating the performance of other partners and to adjust income-sharing rules accordingly. These large partnerships are, therefore, more accurately described as simple hierarchies than as peer groups.

8.5 Simple hierarchies

Simple hierarchy A **simple hierarchy** is a group of workers with a boss. The boss has the right to adjust wage rates, to alter the composition of the group, and to tell the workers of the group what to do. Most small manufacturing firms (like the factory making grandfather clocks) are organized as simple hierarchies, not as peer groups. In a peer group all members are equal: they receive the same income and have the same decision rights. In a hierarchy some people can tell other people what to do, so direct supervision is an important co-ordinating mechanism. Also in a hierarchy a person's income usually has a relationship to his or her performance, either past performance or expected future performance.

Why do we observe so few peer groups, especially in manufacturing industries? What advantages do simple hierarchies have over peer groups?

8.5.1 Team production

In section 7.4 we have explained how, in the view of Alchian and Demsetz (1972), team production leads to the emergence of a simple hierarchy. Team production, they say, will induce people to shirk. A monitor has to be brought in to reduce shirking. To avoid shirking by the monitor, the monitor must be the residual claimant. Williamson (1975, chapter 3) disagrees with this view. Most production processes consist of several stages, he says, which are technologically separable. As an example, consider again the factory for making grandfather clocks. There are several stages of production, such as sawing, assembling, and painting. These stages can be separated by intermediate products inventories, so the work of the sawyers and assemblers can be separated. There is no team production in this example, yet we see most such firms organized as simple hierarchies rather than as peer groups.

8.5.2 Economies of communication and decision-making

In a peer group, every member participates in decision-making. In a simple hierarchy decisions are taken by the boss. Now suppose that information relevant for decision-making originates with each member. In a peer group each

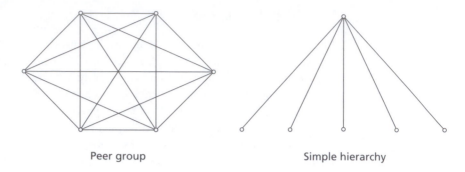

Peer group   Simple hierarchy

Figure 8.2 **Number of communication channels in a peer group and in a simple hierarchy**

member must communicate with all other members. In a simple hierarchy he needs only to communicate with the boss. In a peer group the number of communication channels is $\frac{1}{2}n(n-1)$; in a simple hierarchy it is $n-1$, where n is the number of individuals in the group (Figure 8.2). Transfer of information is costly because of bounded rationality (it takes time to explain things to other team members; information may become distorted when transferred). Thus for

Economies of communication

$n > 2$ a simple hierarchy can realize **economies of communication** over a peer group.

Economies in decision-making

A simple hierarchy can also realize **economies in decision-making**. Where, in a peer group, decisions are reached after discussions in the whole group, in a simple hierarchy the boss alone makes decisions, so less time is needed for decision-making.

8.5.3 Monitoring

As indicated in section 8.4, shirking becomes a severe problem in a large peer group. Thus in a large peer group it is not uncommon to see one or a few members designated to perform productivity audits and given the power to adjust compensation of group members accordingly. This, however, violates the essence of the peer group. Whatever its legal form (partnership or mutual corporation), it is now transformed into a simple hierarchy. For the reasons explained above, we observe relatively few peer groups in the economy. Williamson stresses hierarchy as the alternative to mutual adjustment within peer groups. Most organizations are of a more complex type involving more coordination mechanisms than mutual adjustment and direct supervision (see Chapter 3).

8.6 Multistage hierarchies: U-form and M-form enterprises

In a simple hierarchy there is only one manager who co-ordinates the work of the other team members. Suppose that economies of scale are such that the size of the group is large. Then, because of bounded rationality, a single manager can no longer co-ordinate the work of all team members. Several managers are now needed. This creates an opportunity for division of managerial work so that each manager can specialize. One manager, for example, may specialize in managing the factory, another in managing the marketing and sales people, etc. Thus, within the firm, departments along functional lines are created, and each functional department has a manager. The work of these functional managers is co-ordinated by a general manager. This organization form is used widely by medium-sized firms. Williamson calls this the *unitary form* or *U-form*

U-form enterprise

Multistage hierarchy

enterprise. Within a **U-form enterprise** there are at least two layers of managers. It is a **multistage hierarchy** as opposed to a single-stage or simple hierarchy.

Now suppose that a U-form firm expands by adding several new products. Alfred D. Chandler (1966) studied the history of several large American companies and found that, in the late nineteenth century, most of them were involved in a single activity (for example steel, meatpacking, tobacco, oil) and were organized along functional lines. In the early twentieth century, however, many of these large companies diversified into new products. At first, most of these companies continued as U-form enterprises, but after some time they found out that for the large, multiproduct firm the U-form has severe disadvantages. These disadvantages are of two kinds. First, in a large U-form firm there are several layers of management. Co-ordination of two functional departments (say marketing and production) occurs mainly at the top level. Thus information has to be transmitted across several layers before it is used for decision-making. As information is transmitted, there is usually a loss of information. Data are summarized and interpreted as they move upwards and

Cumulative control loss

instructions are operationalized as they move downwards. This leads to **cumulative control loss**: the corporate board loses control of day-to-day operations as the number of management layers increases. This cumulative control loss is a result of bounded rationality. Only because of bounded rationality do data have to be summarized and interpreted before they reach the top manager, and only because of bounded rationality is the top manager unable himself to give detailed, operationalized instructions.

Second, as the U-form firm grows, the character of the strategic decision-making process alters. The top manager is involved in day-to-day operational co-ordination to such an extent that long-run, strategic decisions receive little attention. This is another manifestation of bounded rationality. Suppose that a management committee is formed that consists of the general manager and the top managers of the functional departments. In a large U-form firm the top manager of a functional department may be interested more in furthering the local interests of his department than of the overall goals for the enterprise. As explained in section 6.3, it is very difficult to translate an overall goal such as profit maximization into operational subgoals for functional departments. A conflict of interest between functional departments cannot be avoided. In a small U-form firm this conflict of interest is mitigated because the general manager is still in a position to judge how much functional managers care for and contribute to overall goals. In a large U-form firm the top manager may find herself to be the only person to attend to overall company-wide goals. The tendency to pursue operational subgoals simply becomes too strong. Departmental interests voiced by functional managers enter the strategic decision-making process.

To summarize: the large, multiproduct U-form firm faces two problems: cumulative control loss and corruption of the strategic decision-making process. The solution to these two problems is to introduce the *multidivisional* or **M-form enterprise**. In the 1920s the multidivisional structure was a major organizational innovation that occurred first in the USA. Most large American multiproduct firms adopted this structure before the Second World War. Most large European multiproduct firms followed in the 1950s and 1960s.

M-form enterprise

The M-form firm is divided at the top level into several quasi-autonomous operating divisions, usually along product lines. Top management is assisted by a general office (corporate staff). The main characteristics and advantages of the M-form are as follows:[5]

- The responsibility for operating decisions is assigned to more-or-less self-contained operating divisions. The divisions operate as quasi-firms.
- The corporate staff attached to the general office performs both advisory and auditing functions. Both have the effect of securing greater control over operating division behaviour.
- The general office is principally concerned with strategic decisions including the allocation of resources among the operating divisions.
- The separation of the general office from operations provides general office executives with the psychological commitment to be concerned with the overall performance of the organization rather than becoming absorbed in the affairs and subgoals of functional departments.

Compared with the U-form organization of the same activities, the M-form serves to economize both on bounded rationality and on opportunism. Bounded rationality is less a problem in the M-form than in the U-form firm because information need be transferred less often. Opportunism is attenuated in the M-form firm because goal congruence is easier to obtain: it is easier to translate an overall company goal (e.g. profit maximization) into operational subgoals per division (e.g. profit maximization for each division).

8.7 Organizational markets

8.7.1 Markets for intermediate goods and services

Within M-form enterprises, division managers are evaluated primarily on the basis of indicators of financial performance such as return on sales, return on assets, etc. Between divisions, numerous transactions of intermediate goods and services take place. There are internal markets within the M-form enterprise for intermediate goods and services. The financial results of each division are affected by the prices (usually called transfer prices) at which these internal transactions take place. Transfer prices may be either set by corporate headquarters or negotiated between divisions. If divisions are left free to negotiate transfer prices for internal transactions, then one advantage of organizations over markets (reduction of transaction costs due to costly haggling and work-flow interruptions) is seriously impaired.

Transactions can also occur between corporate headquarters and an operating division. As an example, consider a group of internal management consultants belonging to the corporate staff. Suppose the internal management consultants do not have to charge the operating divisions for their services but are paid out of corporate funds. In this case the marginal cost to operating divisions of an additional consulting hour is zero, so the operating divisions will demand more services until the marginal revenue to the division of an additional consulting hour is zero. The result is an oversized group of internal management consultants at the corporate level. Now suppose that the management consultants do have to charge the operating divisions for the full cost of their services. If operating divisions are not allowed to hire external consultants, the internal consultants have a monopoly for consulting services. The result will be monopoly pricing and shirking by the internal consultants. This can be avoided by giving the operating divisions freedom to engage external consultants. The internal consultants now have to compete with external consultants, and an internal market for consulting services with several suppliers has been created. When, in addition, the internal consultants are allowed to offer their services on the external market, the difference between the internal and external market virtually disappears. There is simply one market for consulting services with several suppliers (one of which is the group of internal consultants) and several customers (operating divisions and numerous other companies).

8.7.2 Internal labour markets

Internal markets also exist for human resources. Two ways of organizing the internal managerial labour market will be considered. First, managers may be rotated among divisions according to a plan made by a corporate personnel department. Operating divisions notify the corporate personnel department if there is a vacancy, and the corporate personnel department then selects a person to fill this vacancy. Second, operating divisions may simply compete for the best managers on the internal managerial labour market. If there is a vacancy, they advertise in a corporate newsletter or on the intranet. Managers from other divisions who are interested may apply. If they have to compete with candidates from outside companies, there is really no difference between the internal managerial labour market and the external one.

8.7.3 Internal capital market

Finally there is an internal capital market. Three ways to organize the internal capital market will be discussed:

- Case 1: the operating divisions are not allowed to reinvest automatically the cash flow they generate. Instead, the general office reallocates the entire corporate cash flow among divisions. Moreover, operating divisions are not allowed to raise equity capital or debt capital on the external capital market.

■ Case 2: the operating divisions are allowed to reinvest the cash flow they generate. Moreover, operating divisions are free to raise debt capital on the external capital market but not equity capital.

■ Case 3: the operating divisions are allowed to reinvest the cash flow they generate. Moreover, they are allowed to raise both equity capital and debt capital on the external capital market.

Case 1 is the normal situation in most M-form enterprises. The general office reallocates cash flows among divisions to high-yield uses. This is a fundamental attribute of the M-form firm. Williamson argues that the general office in an M-form enterprise is in a better position to allocate capital to the highest-yield uses than is the external capital market. His argument is as follows. Compare an M-form enterprise with, say, five operating divisions with a set of five independent comparable companies. The general office has an advantage over the external capital market in monitoring the performance of the division managers: it has an internal relationship to the division and thus better access to information than external investors have to independent companies. Also, the general office is in a better position to evaluate investment proposals. The manager of an operating division can provide sensitive internal information to the general office, while the disclosure of such information to outsiders (including competitors) might jeopardize the project.

In case 2 the general office is in essence reduced to a clerical agency for the preparation of financial reports. The role of the general office is simply that of a large shareholder: as long as financial results of an operating division are satisfactory the general office does not interfere. Only when results of an operating division are deteriorating may the general office take steps to replace the division manager or to sell the division. Williamson calls this organization

Holding company   form a **holding company** (**H-form**).

In case 3 the operating divisions are really autonomous companies forming a loose federation. An example is the Belgian Société Générale. There is a central holding company, holding majority as well as minority interests in numerous operating companies. Also, between operating companies there are several interlocking shareholdings. Other examples are venture capital companies that also have majority as well as minority shareholdings in several operating companies.

8.8 Markets and organizations: are these all there is?

In the conceptual framework of this book (Figure 1.1) markets and organizations are seen as two alternative ways of co-ordinating economic decisions. Markets are co-ordinated by means of the price mechanism; organizations by any (combination) of the six mechanisms we introduced in Chapter 3. To refresh your memory, these organizational mechanisms are repeated in Figure 8.3 together with the organizational configurations they are associated with. In

PRIME CO-ORDINATING MECHANISM	CONFIGURATION
Direct supervision	Entrepreneurial organization
Standardization of work processes	Machine organization
Standardization of skills	Professional organization
Standardization of outputs	Diversified organization
Mutual adjustment	Innovative organization
Standardization of norms	Missionary organization

Figure 8.3 **The six organizational co-ordination mechanisms**

Chapter 3 we also argued that, in practice, these organizational co-ordinating mechanisms will often be combined. While we can distinguish the six pure types of organizational configuration that are mentioned in Figure 8.3, in practice we often observe that bundles of co-ordination mechanisms will govern specific transactions. Moreover, we showed in Chapter 3 that market co-ordination and organizational co-ordination often operate in conjunction: within organizations markets exist and markets are always more or less organized.

So far in this chapter organizations have been analyzed from a narrower perspective. Williamson's transaction cost economics is also called the '**markets and hierarchies**' paradigm. In this view markets are replaced by hierarchies when price co-ordination breaks down. In this sense, Williamson is a direct descendant from Coase, who also argued that organizations are characterized primarily by 'authority' (in our terminology: direct supervision). However, within organizations there are other co-ordinating mechanisms, such as mutual adjustment and standardization of norms. Mutual adjustment is the main co-ordinating mechanism in a small peer group (for example a partnership of a few consultants). Mutual adjustment is also very important in larger organizations, and occurs between departments (such as marketing and product development) in a U-form firm and between divisions in an M-form firm. Mutual adjustment can also occur between two organizations, for example between a supplier and a buyer. It is hard to see how mutual adjustment can work smoothly between parties who display opportunistic behaviour. For this reason it is not surprising that Williamson's version of transaction cost economics has evoked several critical comments.

These critical comments pertain to two points:

- Transaction cost economics relies too much on the assumption of opportunistic behaviour. In the real world people often co-operate because they trust one another. Many commercial transactions cannot occur without a certain level of trust between the parties to that transaction. This is especially true for transactions that are conducted over a period of time.
- Markets and hierarchies should not be viewed as two mutually exclusive governance structures. In the real world we also see organizational forms such as long-term relationships between buyers and suppliers, joint ventures, and various forms of network organizations. These are examples of

Markets and hierarchies

Hybrid organizational forms

intermediate or **hybrid organizational forms**. By this we mean that these organizational forms fall somewhere between markets and hierarchies.

That hybrid organizational forms exist has also been recognized by Williamson. For him these hybrid forms occur for intermediate levels of asset specificity. Other scholars have argued that some hybrid forms can be understood only if the assumption of opportunism is relaxed. For these scholars these two critical comments are very much related.

We shall first discuss an approach in which the assumption of opportunism is partly replaced by allowing for trust. In this approach clans are defined as organizations that rely to a great extent on mutual trust. This approach makes a distinction between markets, bureaucracies and clans as three alternative ways to co-ordinate economic decisions and is explained in section 8.8.1. In section 8.8.2 we explain in more general terms the role of trust. After these critical comments on the assumption of opportunism, we discuss various hybrid organizational forms (in section 8.9).

8.8.1   Markets, bureaucracies and clans

One of the earliest extensions of the markets and hierarchies framework was provided by William G. Ouchi. This professor of management drew on organizational theory to suggest that a more appropriate framework would encompass markets, bureaucracies and clans (Ouchi, 1980; Ouchi and Williamson, 1981). In this extension, hierarchies were substituted by bureaucracies and clans were added as a third way of co-ordinating economic transactions. The substitution of hierarchies by bureaucracies is in accordance with mainstream organizational sociology. It was the German sociologist Max Weber (1925) who proposed that in modern organizations personal authority had been replaced by organizational authority. While older organizations had relied on the personal authority of the ruler, modern organizations had acquired the legitimacy to substitute organizational rules for personal authority. Such modern organizations were described by Weber as bureaucracies.[6] Ouchi therefore argued that in organizational co-ordination prices were replaced by rules. The rules contained the information necessary for co-ordination. The essence of this type of co-ordination was therefore not its hierarchical but its bureaucratic nature.

Moreover, Ouchi argued that there was a third way of co-ordinating transactions. This third way relies on the socialization of individuals, which ensures that they have common values and beliefs. Individuals who have been socialized in the same way have common norms for behaviour. Such norms can also contain the information necessary for transactions. By way of example, Ouchi (1980) pointed to Japanese firms that rely to a great extent upon socializing their workers to accept the company's goals as their own and compensating them according to length of service and other non-performance criteria. For these firms it is not necessary to measure performance of their employees, since the employees' natural inclination (thanks to socialization) is to do what is best for the firm.

Thus Ouchi basically argued that Williamson's framework did not acknowledge the richness of organizational co-ordination, as summarized in Figure 8.3. The markets and hierarchies paradigm pays too little attention to the role of rules and norms. However, Ouchi's proposal of markets, bureaucracies and clans does not capture the full richness either. In our view Ouchi's proposal is subsumed in Mintzberg's typology, displayed in Figure 8.3: Ouchi's emphasis on the importance of rules corresponds with standardization of work processes, standardization of skills and standardization of output, while socialization is equivalent to standardization of norms. For this reason, in this book we have not adopted Ouchi's proposal to distinguish between three governance structures. Rather, we argue that markets are replaced neither by hierarchies nor by bureaucracies but by *organizations* when the price mechanism starts to fail. Organizations do not rely on authority (direct supervision) only but employ the full set of six co-ordination mechanisms identified by Mintzberg.

8.8.2   The role of trust

Williamson's version of transaction cost economics is built on the assumption of opportunism. As we have explained in section 8.2.2 Williamson does not assume that everyone behaves opportunistically all the time. Rather he assumes that some people might behave opportunistically sometimes *and* that it is difficult to tell *ex ante* (that is, before you enter into a transaction) whether your partner will behave opportunistically. This means that you don't know up front who you can trust (especially if you haven't dealt with the person before). Several scholars have attacked this assumption. It has been argued[7] that the tendency of a certain person to behave in an opportunistic way depends on two things: the immediate net benefits of such behaviour and 'disposition toward the transaction partner'. This recognizes that many people will not cheat their partner in a transaction, simply because they would not have a good feeling doing so. If you like your trading partner and you feel that he trusts you, you will probably not cheat on him even if that would bring you some financial gain. And if you trust your trading partner and he trusts you, you can develop a long-time mutually profitable relationship.

Thus many economists now recognize that trust is an important concept, and several have tried to investigate under which circumstances trust is likely to develop. Box 8.5 presents some of the results.

Trust

Trust plays a role both *between* and *within* organizations. Between organizations very often long-term trading relations develop. These long-term relations are to a large extent based on mutual trust. Such long-term relations are often of crucial importance for the organization's success. Within organizations it is very important that employers place a certain level of trust in their employees. Employees who feel that they are being trusted by their employer will be more inclined to 'act in good faith' than employees who feel they are not. Employees might see very close monitoring by their boss as a sign they are not being trusted. This will have a negative effect on their 'disposition' towards their firm and thus increase rather than attenuate opportunistic behaviour. An employer who installs close monitoring on the assumption that his employees will

Box 8.5 ■ Economic research on trust

Economists have begun to measure trust in order to establish when it is present and to explore the circumstances in which it is increased or decreased over time. Some of the early research outcomes indicate that:

■ *different people behave differently*. This has been established in experimental games such as 'iterated prisoner's dilemmas' (see Chapter 5) in which they have to decide whether to co-operate or defect during several rounds of play. For instance, in a game set up by Clark and Sefton (2001) the first mover began by trusting 57 per cent of the time, and in 35 per cent of those cases the second mover reciprocated by trusting also. In the other instances the players decided to defect, thus undermining the best (trusting) outcome.

■ *to a certain extent, these differences can be traced to their personality traits*. For instance, people differ in their attribution of causes for their success or failure. Some people tend to point towards external, environmental causes. Others attribute their successes and failures more to their own choices and behaviour. The former tend to prefer co-operative strategies while the latter favour competitive strategies. Other personality traits, such as sensation seeking, also help to explain individual variations in players' behaviour (Boone, de Brabander and van Witteloostuijn, 1996, 1999).

■ *culture matters too*. A striking example is in the study of Henrich (2000), who showed that the Machiguenga Indians of the Peruvian Amazon strongly deviate from Western game-theoretic predictions in a bargaining game.

■ *over time, levels of trust can increase or decrease*. In the game of Clark and Sefton (2001) the percentage of first movers trusting their counterparts went down from 57 per cent in the initial rounds to 32 per cent in the tenth round. Trust is fragile, and prone to break down altogether in the event of negative experiences.

■ *incentives matter*. If for instance the rewards for solitary confessors are increased in the prisoner's dilemma game, defections tend to increase.

■ *already knowing each other helps*. Glaeser *et al.* (2000) designed a game in which the first player received $15, of which he could give any part to a second player. The amount sent to the second player was then doubled by the researchers, and the second player could decide how much to send back to the first player. The trusting outcome is that the first player sends all of the $15 to the second, and the second sends half of the doubled sum back. This allows both players to walk away with $15. In this game, however, the first players sent an average of $12.41 to their partners, who returned an average of 45 per cent of the doubled sum. The existence of a previous acquaintance helped, however: both the amount initially sent, and the percentage returned by the second player, rose in proportion to the length of time the players had known each other.

■ *belonging to the same 'group' helps*. In the game of Glaeser *et al.* (2000) the ratio of money returned was much lower when players were of different races or nationalities. Alesina and La Ferrara (2001) found that members of racially mixed communities were less likely to trust each other than members of racially homogeneous communities.

■ *seemingly unrelated, personal experiences play a role too*. Alesina and La Ferrara (2002) report that respondents who had recently suffered a personal setback – for instance, serious illness or financial problems – also reported lower levels of trust.

Overall, these first studies show that trust is prevalent in many situations and can then help towards achieving the best collective outcome. However, trust cannot be taken for granted, and people differ in the trust they have in dealing with others. Moreover, trust is fragile, and it can be destroyed more easily than built. Economic research thus supports both the view that trust is an important foundation for many economic transactions and Williamson's admonition that opportunism cannot be excluded from the outset.

behave opportunistically will indeed find that his employees behave opportunistically. Opportunistic behaviour thus becomes a self-fulfilling prophecy!

Summing up: in this book we have adopted the perspective that all non-price co-ordination is organizational in nature. We have adopted Mintzberg's rich description of six such organizational mechanisms. As a consequence, all non-market co-ordination is organizational by definition in our framework. We have thus maintained Williamson's bipolar distinction between markets and 'something else'. For Williamson this 'something else' consisted of *hierarchies* (= vertical co-ordination based on authority); for us it is *organizations* in all their possible variations. Organizational theorists were right to argue that Williamson took too narrow a view on opportunism as a basic assumption of human behaviour. As a consequence Williamson could see only one form of non-market co-ordination: hierarchy. By allowing for rules (standardization) or trust to develop between parties to a transaction we can adopt the full set of six organizational mechanisms proposed by Mintzberg. Our bipolar distinction in this book is between markets and organizations. As repeatedly stressed, this bipolar distinction refers to ideal types of co-ordination. In practice we shall encounter many mixed cases or hybrid forms. The next section discusses several examples of hybrid forms.

8.9 Hybrid forms

In the previous section we have argued that markets and organizations should not be viewed as two mutually exclusive governance structures. In the real world we see many organizational forms that fall somewhere between markets and organizations. In this section we discuss several examples of such hybrid forms.

That hybrid organizational forms exist has also been recognized by Williamson. For him these hybrid forms occur for intermediate levels of asset specificity. In our discussion we shall stress that trust plays a vital role in explaining some of these hybrid forms.

In this section we discuss five examples of hybrid forms: long-term relations between buyers and suppliers, joint ventures, business groups, informal networks and franchising.

8.9.1 Long-term relations between buyers and suppliers

Companies offering tangible products often buy materials, parts or components from suppliers. For example an automobile manufacturer buys tyres, window panes, electrical systems, sparks, steel and many other items on a regular basis. Some of these intermediate products (dashboards for example) are designed for a particular car model; other parts or components are not specific to one car model. A company making a part specifically designed for the Audi A4 Avant has only one customer for this part. Its investment in tooling and design for this part are transaction-specific. Because of this high level of asset specificity, transaction cost economics predicts organizational co-ordination, which means that the part in question will be manufactured by Audi itself. In the real world, however, we also see that such parts are manufactured by outside suppliers. The suppliers are independent (in the sense that they are not owned by the automobile company) and usually have long-term relationships, supported by long-term contracts with one or more automobile companies.

Why would an outside supplier place itself in a position where it is vulnerable to opportunistic behaviour by its customer(s)? There are several answers to this question:

■ A long-term contract may offer some legal protection against opportunistic behaviour by the buyer.
■ The buyer expects benefits from future co-operation with the supplier that far outweigh any short-term financial gain from opportunistic behaviour.
■ The buyer knows that opportunistic behaviour towards one supplier will affect his reputation *vis-à-vis* other suppliers as a dependable trading partner: thus opportunistic behaviour towards one supplier will negatively affect the value of past investments in reputation.
■ The buyer may pay for and own the design and tooling for the specific part: this reduces the level of asset specificity.
■ Both parties know that the benefits of co-operation are maximized when both of them 'act in good faith'. This could mean that the buyer transfers technological know-how to the supplier, that the buyer visits the factory of the supplier on a regular basis, that the supplier is eager to improve efficiency although he knows this will result in a lower price for the part, and that the buyer shares his business plan with the supplier. All this is much more easy when buyer and supplier trust each other.

The first four answers are perfectly consistent with the assumption of opportunism. The fifth answer, which stresses the importance of both parties acting in good faith, is not.

8.9.2 Joint ventures

Joint venture

Box 8.6 gives an example of two established companies deciding to set up a new business in a newly formed company. This is an example of a **joint venture** – in this case an international joint venture because it is a joint venture between companies from two different countries. A joint venture is another example of a hybrid organizational form. Why do joint ventures exist?

In order to answer this question let us have a closer look at the example of Box 8.6. Apparently there is a business opportunity to set up a third mobile network in Turkey. Telecom Italia and Is-Bank have formed a joint venture to bid for a licence. Telecom Italia did not bid for a licence alone, probably because it knew that operating in a foreign country in which it had no practical experience would not be easy. To set up a new company from scratch can be quite difficult if you are not familiar with local 'ways of doing things', including labour relations, management practices and ways to deal with local authorities. This can be quite important since a new mobile operator needs all sorts of licences from local authorities (for permission to install transmitters). So

Box 8.6 ■ A joint venture between Telecom Italia Mobile SpA and Is-Bank AS

In March 2001 IS-TIM Telekomunikasyon Hizmetleri AS started its operations as the third mobile operator in Turkey. IS-TIM is a joint venture between Telecom Italia Mobile SpA and Is-Bank AS, a major Turkish bank. At that time Turkey already had two mobile operators, but a penetration of only 25 per cent. Prepaid customers account for almost 40 per cent of the market. According to the *Wall Street Journal Europe* IS-TIM hoped to benefit from Telecom Italia's experience in entering a market that already had established competitors. IS-TIM said it did not intend to discriminate in pricing between subscribers and prepaid customers. Prepaid customers can use Is-Bank automated teller machines to recharge their cards.

Source: *Wall Street Journal Europe*, 22 March 2001

Telecom Italia needed the experience, know-how and relations of a local partner. Then why did Is-Bank not bid alone for a licence? Probably because it lacked the know-how on how to set up a mobile operator. So in order to exploit this business opportunity one needs both technological and managerial know-how (how to run a mobile operator) and local contacts. These are examples of intangible assets. It is quite difficult to buy these intangible assets in the marketplace. One way to combine these intangible assets is to set up a joint venture. The new joint venture benefits from Telecom Italia's know-how in setting up a mobile operator and its experience in entering a market with established competitors, and also benefits from Is-Bank's knowledge of local circumstances. Another way to combine these intangible assets would be a merger between the two companies or one company acquiring the other company. For example, Telecom Italia could have acquired Is-Bank. That however would have given Telecom Italia many assets (such as a network of bank branch offices) that it does not need.[8]

To put it in more general terms: a joint venture will be the preferred mode of organizing when the following conditions are met:

1 There is a business opportunity that requires resources from two existing companies, A and B.
2 It is difficult or even impossible to trade these resources. This is often the case with intangible assets (such as know-how in entering a mobile telecom market with established competitors, or contacts with local authorities): *both* the resource needed from company A and that from company B are difficult to trade (if the resource needed from A can be easily bought and sold, B can simply buy the resource from A and set up a wholly owned subsidiary).
3 If company A buys company B (or if B buys A) it acquires a lot of resources it does not need.

If all three conditions are met a joint venture will be the preferred organizational form. If conditions 1 and 2 are met but the third is not, a merger or acquisition is an alternative solution.

Intangible assets such as managerial know-how or local contacts are difficult to trade because of opportunism. It is very difficult to specify in a contract what you buy when you buy 'access to local contacts'. To put it differently: very high transaction costs in the markets for these intangible assets lead to the formation of joint ventures. We want to note that after the joint venture has been formed it is still very difficult for one partner to assess whether the other partner really contributes the intangible assets expected from him. A certain level of mutual trust is necessary for the joint venture's success.

If IS-TIM, the mobile telecom company set up in Turkey by Telecom Italia and Is-Bank, is successful, it is quite likely that after a few years IS-TIM itself will have know-how of local circumstances and access to local authorities as well as the technological and managerial know-how required to run a mobile telecom company. If this is true IS-TIM may be able to function as an independent company or as a subsidiary of one of its founders. For example, Telecom Italia could buy the shares of Is-Bank in IS-TIM. IS-TIM would then continue as a subsidiary of Italia Telecom. There may be some benefit in doing this if technological know-how continues to evolve.

8.9.3 Business groups

A business group is a group of legally independent firms, which are nevertheless bound together by one or more formal or informal ties. Formal ties include reciprocal shareholding between members of the group, interlocking directorates, companies owned in part by the same (group of) individual shareholders, cross-guarantees of bank loans, and trading of parts and supplies between group companies. Informal ties include family ties between managers of group companies, and managers of group companies belonging to the same social or ethnic group. Business groups play an important role in many developing countries such as India (where they are called business houses) and South Korea (where they are called *chaebol*) and many other countries in South-East Asia and Latin America.

Business groups may share a brand name, raise capital jointly, lobby together for political support, recruit managers as a group, rotate managers among group companies, and pool resources to invest in new ventures. The main reason why business groups play such an important role in developing countries is probably the fact that transaction costs in several markets are much higher than in developed countries. Group companies may pool resources to set up a new venture, for example, because the market for venture capital is not well developed and consequently transaction costs for obtaining venture capital from financial institutions or private investors are extremely high. Transaction costs in the markets for intermediate goods may be high because the system of civil law and courts enforcing the law are less well developed. This may induce group companies to trade within the group, where conflicts can be settled without using the courts. Transaction costs in the market for managerial talent may also be very high in developing countries, largely because reliable information about a manager's abilities is hard to come by in these countries. Samsung, a leading chaebol in South Korea, and the Tata Group, one of India's leading business houses, recruit talented managers as a group and rotate them among group companies.

8.9.4 Informal networks

A network may be thought of as a rather 'flat' organizational form in contrast with vertically organized hierarchical firms. It consists of essentially equal members that have informal relationships with one another. The basis of these relationships is trust. A network is characterized more by co-operation than by competition:[9]

> If it is price competition that is the central co-ordinating mechanisms of the market and administrative orders that of hierarchy, then it is trust and co-operation that centrally articulates networks.[10]

Networks exist within organizations as well as between organizations. Within organizations networks may exist between people who come from the same region, who went to the same university, or who know each other well from 'the old days'. Such common backgrounds may provide a basis for trust for dealing with each other. An example of a network between organizations may be *interlocking directorates*: members of a relatively small number of organizations serving on each others' boards as outside directors. Again, such contacts may build an atmosphere of mutual trust and co-operation. Another example is the informal networks that exist in Italy between small and medium-sized firms, which work together in a subcontracting mode.

It is difficult to explain the existence of networks within the over-narrow perspective of the original markets and hierarchies framework. This framework suggests that the only choice is between market co-ordination and hierarchical (vertical) co-ordination. As the examples above suggest, however, there are also forms of 'horizontal', non-market co-ordination. These can be seen as alternative 'third ways' of co-ordination. We would submit, however, that they can also be seen as organizational forms with a bundle of (two) organizational co-ordination mechanisms. In Mintzberg's typology the mechanism of *mutual adjustment* refers to the co-ordination achieved by informal (horizontal) communication. As discussed above, the trust underlying the operation of networks can be understood as evolving from the *standardization of norms* (through socialization or selection).[11] In the organizational perspective we have adopted from Mintzberg, networks can therefore be seen as organizational forms co-ordinating mainly by the devices of mutual adjustment and standardization of norms. For instance, our first example above of the 'old boys' network' in organizations operates through standardization of norms (members self-select, are selected and are socialized) and through mutual adjustment (mainly through informal communication). These organizational mechanisms are so strong that outsiders find it very difficult to penetrate into such a network. Where such 'old boys' networks' exist and are literally made up of men only, women will find it very hard to become members. In our second example, of Italian networks of small and medium-sized firms, the mechanisms of mutual adjustment and standardization of norms operate as well, in this case probably combined with some market co-ordination (prices do play a role in subcontracting). So, in our framework the first example of an 'old boys' network' refers to organizational co-ordination, while the second example pertains to a hybrid form

Box 8.7 ■ *Guanxi*, transaction costs and rules

Many countries in Eastern Europe and Asia are making a difficult transition to more market-based economies. In Eastern Europe these are mostly replacing former (communist) planning-based systems. In Asia the economies have often been characterized as more network- or relations-based. Economists around the world have been impressed by the difficulties that such a transition encounters. In particular, the extent to which market-based economies rely on clear and transparent rules, as well as on institutions that safeguard and enforce these rules, has become evident. One particular analysis by Professors Li Shuhe and Li Shaomin of the City University of Hong Kong was summarized as follows in an *Economist* survey of Asian business:

> The familiar word used to describe the old (Chinese) system is *guanxi*. Usually translated as 'connections', *guanxi* conjures up images of karaoke outings with officials, nods of understanding in smoke-filled rooms, and the invisible hand not of the market, but of influence. *Guanxi* is a cliché, but is only too real.
>
> Western investors tend to assume that Asian tycoons turn to *guanxi* for deep-seated cultural reasons, but in fact they do so out of necessity. Both a rules-based and a *guanxi*-based system of governance incur expenses. For both, these are made up of the fixed costs of keeping the system running – say, training and paying judges, regulators and auditors – and incremental costs, such as the effort and expense of signing one more contract, sealing one more transaction, and so on.
>
> Developed economies have rules-based governance systems that incur enormous fixed, but negligible incremental, costs. The fixed costs, however, are spread over huge numbers of transactions and business relationships, so that the average cost of any single deal is quite low. By contrast, the poor countries of Asia so far have not been able to afford the investment in the high fixed costs of such a system, and have therefore settled on the large incremental costs of a *guanxi*-based system. As long as the number of transactions and business relationships remained comparatively small, the average cost of transactions was bearable.
>
> As *guanxi* economies grow and become more complex, however, the incremental costs of doing business shoot up. What worked with a hundred clients, a dozen suppliers, two creditors and one shareholder no longer works with thousands of all of these. So there comes a point, Messrs Li reckon, when the average cost of doing business in a *guanxi*-based system of governance exceeds that in rules-based systems. When this happens, companies and countries that rely on *guanxi* can no longer compete. Market forces initiate a transition to a rules-based system. This is probably the largest and riskiest step that countries and companies ever have to take.

Source: 'In praise of rules: a survey of Asian business', *The Economist*, 7 April 2001

between organizations and markets. Transactions in the Italian network will be governed by a bundle of market and organizational co-ordination mechanisms.

Networks also play an important role in some developing countries, such as China. In China the rules and institutions that are used in the West to settle disputes are less well developed. This may explain to some extent why networks based on personal relations play a larger role, as suggested by the text in Box 8.7.

8.9.5   Franchising

In this section we discuss franchising as an example of a hybrid form. In order to explain what franchising is, consider McDonald's. In 2001 there were more than 29,000 McDonald's restaurants in more than 120 countries. McDonald's is a good example of franchising. Some 8,000 restaurants are owned and operated by McDonald's Corporation, but the rest (around 21,000) are owned and operated by local entrepreneurs. These entrepreneurs have a contract with McDonald's Corporation giving them the right to operate under the name McDonald's. Such a contract is called a **franchise contract**. The two parties to such a contract are the franchisor (McDonald's Corporation) and the franchisee (the local entrepreneur owning and operating a McDonald's restaurant). McDonald's Corporation has developed a formula for operating fast-food restaurants. This formula consists of a range of products (including the way these products have to be prepared), a house style (this refers to things such as the furnishing of the restaurant, the clothing of personnel, and the way customers are treated), and a brand name. Under the franchise contract the franchisees are allowed to use this formula in return for a fee (usually a fixed amount plus a percentage of sales).

Franchise contract

Franchising is a hybrid organizational form. It is not a hierarchy (we would have a hierarchy if all restaurants were owned and operated by McDonald's Corporation). It is not a market either (we would have a market if the 21,000 local entrepreneurs were to operate independently, without organizational ties with McDonald's Corporation).

Franchising is typically found in industries such as fast-food restaurants (McDonald's, Kentucky Fried Chicken), hotels (Hilton, Sheraton, Holiday Inn) and retailing. These industries have two characteristics in common:

- They provide services that have to be 'produced' locally while the customer is present.
- There are large advantages in developing and maintaining a 'business formula' and a brand name.

Why does franchising exist?

Why does franchising exist? There are two answers to this question. The first answer is called the *resource scarcity thesis*. According to this thesis, a firm that has developed a highly successful formula is faced with resource constraints (scarcity of capital and talented managers) if it wants to expand rapidly. Franchising is seen as a means to overcome these constraints. The second answer is the *administrative efficiency thesis*. In this thesis franchising is analyzed from an agency theory and transaction cost perspective. According to this view franchising is, in certain industries, a more efficient governance structure than either a pure hierarchy or a pure market.

Resource scarcity thesis

Suppose that the owner of a restaurant develops a highly successful formula, and that he sees an opportunity to open many other restaurants operating under the same formula. If he wants to do so through full ownership, he has to set up and subsequently manage many local units. This requires large amounts of capital and many motivated and capable managers. If he lacks these resources, he is faced with the problem of resource scarcities. This problem can be overcome, it is argued, through franchising. The franchisee invests in his own local unit, which means that the level of investment by the franchisor is greatly reduced. The franchisee also manages his own local unit. If we suppose that talented managers are eager to work as franchisees but unwilling to work as salaried managers, then franchising also solves the problem of finding capable managers.

The resource scarcity thesis can explain why a small company that happens to find a successful formula in the service sector has little choice but to grow through franchising. It may be very important to grow quickly, and a small company may face serious difficulties in attracting large amounts of capital and many talented managers for new local units.

The resource scarcity thesis cannot explain, however, why a company such as McDonald's Corporation continues to use franchising when it expands still further. Consider first the problem of obtaining additional capital. McDonald's Corporation is a large and highly profitable company. Its shares are listed on the New York Stock Exchange and on many other foreign stock exchanges. Such a company is surely not faced with the problem of scarce financial resources. On the contrary, it is quite likely that McDonald's Corporation can acquire additional capital (in the form of both equity and debt) on better conditions than local entrepreneurs.

Let us now consider the problem of hiring talented young managers. It is hard to see why a company like McDonald's Corporation could not attract talented managers working for a salary, while other large multinational companies, such as Unilever and Nestlé, are able to recruit hundreds of talented young managers every year.

To summarize: the resource scarcity thesis can explain why small companies that have found a highly successful formula start to grow through franchising, but it cannot explain why large, established companies continue to use franchising when they expand still further. This brings us to the second view of franchising: the administrative efficiency thesis.

Administrative efficiency thesis

According to the administrative efficiency thesis, franchising exists because in certain industries it is a very efficient organizational form. Recall that franchising is found primarily in service industries where production occurs in many local units and where there are significant advantages from operating many local units under the same formula and brand name.

There are, in principle, three organizational arrangements that could be used in this type of industry:

- one company owning and operating all units (a hierarchy);
- franchising;
- a set of independent companies using a common brand name.

In a large company with many dispersed units the main problem is shirking by local managers. Suppose, first, that local managers receive a fixed wage (not related to sales or profit of the unit they manage). In the language of the theory of principal and agent this is a wage contract. This theory then predicts that the agent will choose a low level of effort. One way to reduce shirking by local managers is through monitoring. This requires frequent visits by the district manager to the local units in her district. Another way is to give a local manager a share in the profits of the unit he manages, or to offer local managers career prospects within the company.

In a franchising arrangement the franchisor usually receives a franchise fee consisting of a percentage of the sales of a local unit plus a fixed annual payment. The profits of the individual unit after payment of the franchise fee are for the franchisee. Thus, although the franchise fee is not a fixed payment (it depends on sales), the risk of variations in profitability is borne by the franchisee. This comes very close to a rent contract. The franchisee has strong incentives to run his unit efficiently. Shirking by the local manager (the main problem in a hierarchy) is not at all a problem here. There are, however, three other problems.

Inefficient risk-bearing   First there is the problem of **inefficient risk-bearing**. Since there are so many restaurants, McDonald's shareholders do not worry about the risk of an individual restaurant. In the agency relationship between franchisor and franchisee the principal is (almost) risk-neutral and the agent probably risk-averse. We know from section 7.6.2 that in this case the agent should not bear all risk. Yet it seems that in most franchising contracts almost all risk is borne by the agent (the franchisee).

Free riding by a franchisee   The second problem is **free riding by a franchisee** on the common brand name. The franchisee may be tempted to use cheaper inputs for his products. This lowers the quality level. If there are very few repeat customers anyway, perhaps because the restaurant is located at an airport, this can increase local profits. The result, however, is that the value of the general brand name deteriorates. The point is that the decrease in the value of the brand name is borne by the franchisor and all franchisees together. If all other franchisees continue to deliver high quality, then one individual franchisee can deliver a low quality and free ride on the common brand name. In order to reduce this problem the franchisor usually monitors quality very closely. Monitoring quality only is much cheaper than monitoring all aspects of a local operation.

Appropriability of quasi-rents   The third problem concerns **appropriability of quasi-rents**. Suppose that the franchisee has to invest in a building that is designed as a McDonald's restaurant and that the resale value of that building, should the franchisee's contract with McDonald's Corporation be terminated, is much lower than the original investment. The building then is a transaction-specific investment for the franchisee. The difference between original investment and resale value is a quasi-rent that could be appropriated by the franchisor. This problem vanishes if the franchisor owns the building and lets it to the franchisee (as does McDonald's Corporation in many cases).

Consider, finally, an arrangement between, say, 100 hamburger restaurants that have decided to use a common brand name. The main problem in this

Table 8.1 **Problems associated with three types of organization arrangement**

Problem	Hierarchy	Franchising	Independent companies with common brand name
Shirking	yes	no	no
Inefficient risk-bearing	no	yes	yes
Free riding on brand name	no	no	yes
Quasi-rent appropriation	no	no	no

case is free riding on the brand name. Such an arrangement can work only if there is a central party to the contract who closely monitors quality levels. This central party should have the right to terminate the contract with an individual company if quality levels are consistently below standard. Then we have not a contract between 100 hamburger restaurants, but 100 contracts between a central party and 100 hamburger restaurants. This is an arrangement very much like a franchise arrangement.

The discussion is summarized in Table 8.1. We have looked at three organizational arrangements (one large company, franchising, and a set of independent units) and we have identified four problems: shirking by the local manager, inefficient risk-bearing, free riding on the brand name, and appropriation of quasi-rents. The table indicates whether a particular problem is really an important issue in a particular organizational arrangement.

In Table 8.1 we have indicated that free riding is not a severe problem in the case of franchising. This is because in a franchising contract the franchisor normally has the right to monitor quality levels and to terminate the contract if quality is below standard. We have also indicated that appropriation of quasi-rents is not a severe problem in the case of franchising. This is because this problem is solved if the franchisor owns the building.

By way of summary we can conclude that a set of independent companies using a common brand name is not a feasible arrangement: the problem of free riding on the brand name cannot be solved in this case. When comparing franchising with one large company, it seems that franchising is the preferred solution if shirking is a severe problem.

Finally we want to note that McDonald's Corporation uses a bundle of co-ordinating mechanisms to co-ordinate the actions of the managers of the restaurants it owns: direct supervision, standardization of outputs (products in this case), standardization of work processes and probably also standardization of norms. In its role as franchisor, McDonald's Corporation uses exactly the same bundle of co-ordinating mechanisms to co-ordinate the actions of its franchisees. The main difference is that, with respect to its franchisees, direct supervision focuses on quality levels, whereas with respect to the managers of its own restaurants, direct supervision includes all aspects of the local manager's job. Another important difference between 'owning' and 'franchising' is the market relation between McDonald's Corporation and its franchisees: McDonald's Corporation sells the right to use its business formula at a price (the franchise fee). In addition, the franchisee can buy ingredients and equipment from the franchisor.

8.10 Summary: effect of transaction costs on the choice between markets and organizations and among organizational forms

Transaction cost economics attempts to explain which transactions will be executed across markets and which transactions will take place within organizations. Transaction cost economics is based on two assumptions with respect to human behaviour: (1) that human beings are boundedly rational, and (2) that human beings are opportunistic. In comparison, behavioural theory also assumes bounded rationality but not opportunism, while the theory of principal and agent assumes full rationality and opportunism.

The choice between markets and organizations depends on three critical dimensions of transactions: asset specificity, uncertainty/complexity, and frequency. Transactions are said to have a high level of asset specificity when these transactions need to be supported by assets that can be used only in those specific transactions. The higher the levels of asset specificity, uncertainty/complexity and frequency, the higher the costs for executing the transaction across a market. Thus transactions with high levels of asset specificity, uncertainty/complexity and frequency tend to take place within organizations rather than across markets.

Transaction cost economics can also be used to explain why we observe different organizational forms, such as peer groups, simple hierarchies, U-form firms and M-form firms in different circumstances.

Providers of professional services, such as management consultants, accountants, lawyers and doctors, frequently form partnerships. They do so because forming a partnership offers advantages (economies of scale in information-gathering, pooling of risk) that are difficult to obtain through market transactions between independent professionals. A small partnership can function as a peer group – that is, a group of equals co-operating without hierarchy. In a large peer group, communication and decision-making become quite complicated and time-consuming. That is why large partnerships usually have a managing board and thus a form of hierarchy. Hierarchy in a large partnership also helps to reduce shirking.

Small manufacturing firms are usually organized as a simple hierarchy: a group of workers with a boss. This occurs mainly because a simple hierarchy offers advantages in communication and decision-making. If there is team production, these benefits can explain why a simple hierarchy is an efficient form of organization.

Suppose that because of economies of scale an efficient firm needs to employ 100 workers. Such a firm needs at least two levels of managers because one manager cannot direct the work of so many workers. In a firm of this size it is usually efficient for the workers to specialize in one type of activity such as manufacturing, sales, or billing. This leads to the formation of functional departments, with managers also specializing in the functional activities of those departments. This is the unitary or U-form firm.

Now suppose that the firm grows by adding more and more product lines. If the firm continues to use the U-form, its top managers will experience cumulative loss of control. This firm may also face a corruption of the strategic decision-making process because functional top managers may display too much loyalty to their department. The solution to these problems is to create a multidivisional (M-form) firm in which the divisions are responsible for manufacturing and marketing of a more limited product range. The divisions operate as quasi-autonomous firms, responsible for all day-to-day decisions. In an M-form firm there is a general office responsible for strategic decisions and for allocating cash flows among divisions.

A major criticism of transaction cost economics is that it ignores the role of social relations and culture. Many relations between human beings are built on trust. Without trust it is difficult to understand how people can co-operate within a firm or build lasting commercial relations. That is why clans have been proposed as a third governance structure besides markets and hierarchies. A clan corresponds closely to an organization that relies heavily on standardization of norms as its main co-ordinating mechanism. That is why we argue that markets are replaced not by hierarchies but by organizations. In practice there are many hybrid forms (one example is franchising) that combine market relations with co-ordinating mechanisms used within organizations.

Another criticism is that transaction cost economics is static: in comparing different organizational forms it simply assumes that the most efficient forms have survived. This ignores the dynamic process of competition between different organizational forms. This process takes centre stage in the next chapter.

Questions

1   Suppose you are Spanish and living in Sevilla. You have bought a car from a garage in Sevilla and you bring it regularly to this garage for ordinary maintenance. Now you are on holiday in the Netherlands. Your car has been making a strange noise lately, so you decide to go to a local garage. You bring your car in the morning and you return in the evening to collect it. There is, of course, the problem of opportunistic behaviour by the garage: the garage can misrepresent the amount of time spent in fixing your car. Do you expect that this problem will be more severe or less severe than when you take your car to the garage in Sevilla? Why?

2   Mayer GmbH is a small German company involved in car body repair. Mayer GmbH employs 10 people: Gert Mayer, who owns all the shares in Mayer GmbH, and nine other people working as employees. The production process involves three stages: parts repair, painting, and assembly. Four people are working in parts repair, two in painting, and three in assembly. Mr Mayer takes care of marketing, sales, bookkeeping, and general management.

Autofix is one of Mayer's competitors. Autofix is a workers' co-operative and has recently been set up by 10 people. Four people are working in parts repair, two in painting, three in assembly, and one in marketing, sales, and bookkeeping. All decisions within Autofix are being taken by the general assembly consisting of all 10 worker-members. The general assembly is chaired each week by a different worker-member.

(a) How would you characterize Mayer GmbH in Mintzberg's typology of organizational configurations? What is the main co-ordinating mechanism in this configuration? Now answer the same questions for Autofix.

(b) How would you characterize Mayer GmbH in the language of transaction cost economics? And Autofix? Compare, using transaction cost economics, the organizational form of Mayer GmbH with the organizational form of Autofix in terms of efficiency advantages and disadvantages.

(c) Suppose that competition in the car body repair industry becomes very intense. Which of the two companies is more likely to survive this competitive battle? Why?

3 In some industries private firms compete with non-profit organizations. An example is the hospital industry in the USA, where hospitals owned and run by private companies compete with hospitals owned by foundations, charities and local governments. Private hospitals and public hospitals face the same make-or-buy decisions: services such as laundry, maintenance, restaurant, physical therapy, laboratory and pharmacy can be bought from outside suppliers or supplied in-house. Transaction cost economics predicts that transactions with high levels of asset specificity, uncertainty/complexity and frequency will be supplied in-house, while transactions with low levels of asset specificity, uncertainty/complexity and frequency will be bought from outside suppliers. A recent study examined whether this was really the case. The study also examined whether the prediction from transaction cost economics was true for both private and non-profit hospitals. Do you expect this prediction to be equally true for private and non-profit hospitals? Why?

4 Rock bands emerged in the late 1950s and early 1960s in coastal areas of the UK (Liverpool, for example) as very informal partnerships of young males. Originally bands performed in dance venues, did not produce their own songs, and did not make much money. This changed with the meteoric rise of the Beatles, which was built on original songs written by band members. The example of the Beatles was soon followed by other bands who also integrated writer and performer functions. This created income disparities between band members according to their writing royalties.

   Most rock bands were organized as partnerships. However, some rock bands were organized as hierarchies with one band member acting as entrepreneur and the other members receiving wages as workers. What do you think are the advantages and disadvantages of partnerships versus hierarchies in the case of rock bands?

5 Renata Girndt holds a degree in business administration from a well-known Swiss university. She has three years' experience in working for a major Swiss pharmaceutical firm. Her main task for this firm has been to investigate ways to enter eastern European markets. Annamaria Schalke holds a degree from the same university as Renata and has five years of experience in working for a major international consulting firm based in Frankfurt, Germany. Her main experience

is in designing joint ventures between German and eastern European firms. Renata has been considering starting her own business as a self-employed consultant. So has Annamaria. When they meet during an alumni day, a plan to form a partnership begins to form. In this partnership they will share all revenues and expenses. The partnership will focus on German companies willing to enter eastern European markets through strategic alliances.

For Renata one of the main risks of starting to work as a self-employed consultant is the risk of having no consulting assignments during a certain period of time. As she sees it, one of the advantages of forming a partnership with Annamaria is to share this risk. Do you think Renata would be able to buy an insurance policy for this risk from an insurance company? What kind of problem(s) might occur for an insurance company offering such a policy? Do these same problems occur when Renata and Annamaria share this risk by forming a partnership? Do you see other advantages of forming a partnership instead of Renata and Annamaria each setting up their own business independently?

6 Telecom Italia entered Turkey by forming a joint venture with a local partner (see Box 8.6). In this way Telecom Italia acquires knowledge of local circumstances it initially lacks. After a couple of years Telecom Italia may feel that it is now sufficiently familiar with local circumstances and therefore no longer needs its local partner. It can then offer to buy the shares of its local partner. The joint venture will then continue as a subsidiary of Telecom Italia.

What could be the most important benefits for Telecom Italia of buying out its local partner? Do you expect firms in a high-technology industry to benefit more from buying out their local joint venture partners than firms in industries with a mature technology?

Suggested further reading

Thompson, G., J. Frances, R. Levacic and J. Mitchell (1991), *Markets, Hierarchies and Networks*, London: Sage.

Williamson, O.E. (1975), *Markets and Hierarchies: Analysis and Antitrust Implications*, New York: Free Press.

Williamson, O.E. (1985), *The Economic Institutions of Capitalism*, New York: Free Press.

Williamson, O.E. (1996), 'Economics and organization: a primer', *California Management Review*, vol. 38, 131—46.

Notes

1. As discussed in Chapter 5, reputations matter in multiperiod games.
2. In section 4.2 we discussed the used-car market as an example of a market with adverse selection. As a solution to the problem of adverse selection we suggested relocation of the risk that a car is a lemon from the buyer to the seller through a warranty. The problem for the seller is to make a credible promise to the potential buyer. For a qualified dealer this is easier than for a junkyard garage. The main reason is that a qualified dealer risks losing more (his qualification) if he does not provide the services specified in the warranty.

3. We do not mean to say that human beings always make explicit comparisons of the production and transaction costs of alternative governance structures. They probably cannot do so because of bounded rationality and complexity. However, in a world with competition between governance structures, it is likely that the most efficient governance structures will survive in the long run. Thus the governance structures we observe in the real world are probably close to the cost-minimizing solution.

4. We have borrowed the idea for this example from Klein *et al.* (1978).

5. Williamson (1975), p.137.

6. For Weber the bureaucracy was a modern phenomenon enabling stable and efficient organizational arrangements. He emphasized the improvements that bureaucracies brought over the more traditional forms of organization. It was only later that 'bureaucracy' also acquired more pejorative meanings, related to the stifling of individual freedom and initiative by excessive rules.

7. Goshal and Moran (1996).

8. To give prepaid customers access to the branch offices of a bank you do not need to own that bank. A long-term contract will do.

9. The literature on networks is quite diverse. We rely for this discussion on Thompson *et al.* (1991). On social systems of trust see Coleman (1990). On sociological analyses of networks see, for example, Burt (1992).

10. Frances et al. (1991) p.15.

11. While Ouchi stressed socialization as the mechanism by which standardization of norms is achieved, we should like to point out that selection plays a role as well. Selection may take place in the form of self-selection (only persons with specific values and norms apply for membership of certain organizations) and/or in the form of organizational selection (at entry or later). Indeed, in an analysis of the culture of accounting firms, selection and self-selection effects were found to be stronger than socialization effects (Soeters and Schreuder, 1988).

9 Economic contributions to strategic management

9.1 Introduction

In Chapters 6–8 three different but closely related economic theories of organization (behavioural theory, agency theory and transaction cost economics) have been discussed. This chapter focuses on economic contributions to the field of strategic management. As you will see, these contributions do not (yet) form one integrated theory, although they have much in common.

There are two levels of strategy in a multibusiness firm: competitive strategy (also termed business strategy) and corporate strategy. A **competitive strategy** is a strategy for a single business unit: it specifies *how* the business unit's managers compete in a given industry.[1] A **corporate strategy** is a strategy for a portfolio of business units: it specifies *where* (that is, in which industries and in which countries) a multibusiness firm competes.

The field of strategic management has a normative and a descriptive part (as do many other empirical fields). Normative questions deal with what firms *should* do. Descriptive questions deal with what firms *actually* do. The literature on strategic management may be further divided into contributions that focus on the *process* and on the *content* of strategic management (see Table 9.1). Economics attempts to analyze the content of firms' strategies. To see whether the analysis has explanatory power, it is compared with the actual behaviour of firms. If the analysis does correspond to real firms' behaviour and, furthermore, if it indicates which choices are best, then we have a basis for normative recommendations. That is why it is hard to divide economic contributions to the content of strategic management into normative and descriptive contributions.

The early literature on strategic management (for example, Ansoff, 1965) emerged out of a need to help the practitioner with the process of strategic

Table 9.1 The literature on strategic management

	Process	Content
Normative	Normative models of strategic management processes	Economic contributions to strategic management
Descriptive	Description of actual strategic management processes	

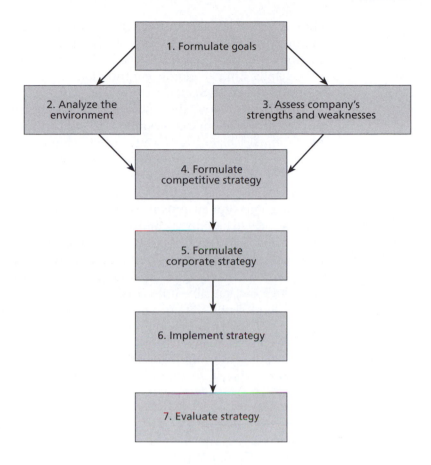

Figure 9.1 **The process of strategic planning in a multibusiness firm**

Strategic planning   planning. **Strategic planning** is the component of strategic management that aims at the formulation of a firm's strategy.[2] An important issue in this literature is how the process of strategic planning should be structured. It is argued that the process of strategic planning should consist of a logical sequence of steps, such as the seven steps indicated in Figure 9.1. This figure is an example of a normative model of strategic planning. You might wonder why this sequence of steps is the most logical one or whether it leads to the best results. Economics has little to say on this question. Since we want to focus on economic contributions to strategic management, we shall not try to answer it.

You may also wonder whether in real firms the process of strategic planning is always as neatly structured as Figure 9.1. Descriptions of actual strategic planning processes show that it is usually not, but again this issue falls outside the scope of this chapter.

The economic contributions to strategic planning and strategic management focus on issues of content, not of process. Economics deals with the actual information that firms need and the actual choices they have to make in formulating their strategy, not with the process they may use to arrive at these choices and to implement their chosen strategy.[3] Important economic contributions have been made to the content of steps 2–5 in the diagram; very few economic contributions have been made to the other three. Since the focus of this chapter is on economic contributions to strategic management, we concentrate on steps 2–5 only.

This chapter follows the sequence of steps outlined in Figure 9.1. Section 9.2 discusses the economic contributions to industry analysis. This concerns step 2 of the strategic planning process, since the industry in which a firm operates is an important part of its environment. Section 9.3 discusses the economic contributions to competitor analysis. This is a way to assess a company's strengths and weaknesses relative to its competitors' (step 3). The economic contributions to competitor analysis also come from the field of industrial organization. Another way to describe a company's strengths comes from the resource-based view of the firm. This is the subject of section 9.4, which discusses the formulation of competitive strategy in a static context and relies again on industrial organization. According to the resource-based view of the firm, a competitive advantage is sustainable if it is based on the possession of resources that other firms cannot easily obtain. This is explained in section 9.5. Section 9.6 discusses the formulation of competitive strategy in a dynamic context, drawing on concepts from game theory. Sections 9.7–9.9 discuss vertical integration, diversification and multinationalization. These three issues form the core of corporate strategy formulation (step 5 in Figure 9.1). A summary is provided in section 9.10.

9.2 Industry analysis

Structure–conduct–performance paradigm

The economic contributions to industry analysis stem from the field of industrial organization. Industrial organization emerged as an academic discipline in the 1950s and 1960s. Its main paradigm was the **structure–conduct–performance** (or S-C-P) **paradigm**. Structure refers to characteristics of the industry, such as the number and size distribution of firms in that industry and the barriers that impede other firms entering the industry. Other examples of characteristics that determine industry structure are given in Figure 9.2. Conduct refers to the behaviour (or the strategies) of firms in the industry. Aspects of firm conduct are collusion (that is, the extent to which firms co-operate), pricing strategy of firms in the industry, and product strategy. Performance refers to performance of the industry in such terms as profitability, growth in output and employment.

According to the S-C-P paradigm the structure of an industry determines the conduct of the firms in that industry, and conduct in turn determines industry performance (see Figure 9.2). As an example of how structure determines conduct and conduct determines performance consider the US automobile industry during the 1960s. There were only four firms: General Motors (GM), Ford, Chrysler and American Motors (AM). General Motors and Ford were much bigger than Chrysler or American Motors. There were many buyers (dealers), so

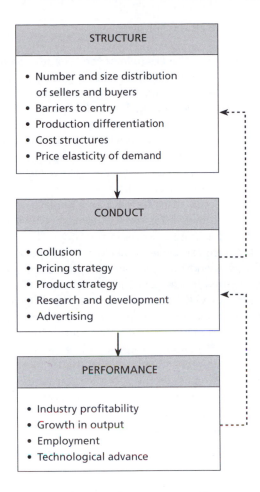

Figure 9.2 **The structure–conduct–performance paradigm**

sellers were few and unequal in size, while buyers were numerous. Moreover, barriers to entry into the automobile industry were high. In this industry economies of scale are very important: you can produce cars efficiently only if you produce on a large scale. If a new competitor were to consider entering the industry it would have to enter on a large scale. This would create overcapacity in the industry, prices would fall, and no one would make a profit. Hence, in the automobile industry, economies of scale constitute a barrier to entry. Another barrier to entry is the technological know-how required to develop a new car. In the US automobile industry during the 1960s GM and Ford were the most efficient producers, so GM and Ford could set prices, while Chrysler and AM followed GM's and Ford's pricing strategy. Although the four firms probably never co-ordinated their pricing strategy, the result was co-ordination on prices. Such *tacit collusion* is greatly facilitated if there are only a few sellers of unequal size and if there are significant barriers to entry. In the Internet era tacit collusion may be facilitated by the way web sites, such as business-to-business (B2B) marketplaces are designed (Box 9.1 gives an example).

Box 9.1 ■ Collusion on B2B exchanges?

In the main text we use the example of the US automobile industry in the 1960s to explain the risk of (tacit) collusion in a concentrated industry. At the beginning of this millennium the industry had become even more concentrated: General Motors, Ford and Daimler Chrysler formed the surviving Big Three. The risk of collusion had not become less in the Internet age. To illustrate this point we use a report of JP Morgan on business-to-business (B2B) exchanges: marketplaces where business suppliers sell to business customers. The first wave of such B2B marketplaces consisted of independent companies that saw an opportunity to broker between buyers and sellers. However, in many industries, large companies buying many components from a large number of suppliers soon struck back by creating their own marketplaces, often forming an alliance to do so. An example is Covisint, a B2B marketplace created by the Big Three automakers, which collectively represent about 85% of their industry's purchasing power in the USA.

A B2B marketplace can come quite close to the pure or ideal market we have described in Chapter 1 if two conditions are met. First, there are many buyers and sellers, and second, there are no information asymmetries. However, if there are only a few buyers B2B marketplaces can form a vehicle to aggregate demand from those few buyers, thus enhancing their purchasing power even further. And if those few buyers design the web site, they have an opportunity to create information asymmetries that work to their advantage.

Covisint is a very ambitious enterprise. It has the potential to shift tens of billions of dollars in annual procurement transactions to the Internet. Its development has been slowed, however, because it has been the subject of an inquiry by the Federal Trade Commission (FTC), the antitrust authority in the USA. Moreover, the FTC will monitor the structure and procedures of such Internet sites for evidence of collusion, just as it evaluates other business alliances and arrangements.

Source: JP Morgan, *B2B Marketplaces: The Third Wave*, New York, 5 September 2000

Therefore structure (number and size distribution of sellers and buyers, barriers to entry) determined conduct (pricing strategy). Pricing strategy, of course, directly affects profitability. Thus an element of conduct (pricing strategy) affects performance (profitability). These relationships are indicated by the solid arrows flowing from the top to the bottom of Figure 9.2.

In the S-C-P paradigm the direction of causation runs, therefore, from structure to conduct and from conduct to performance. However, it is now increasingly recognized that conduct of firms can also affect industry structure and that performance of the industry can also affect the conduct of firms in that industry. For example, firms can try to erect barriers to entry. They may, for instance, protect their product and process innovations through patents. If such patents are awarded, the firm can prevent competitors from using the latest technology. Patents are an example of strategic barriers to entry. The conduct of firms (their patenting behaviour) thus affects industry structure. In addition, performance may affect conduct, as when industry profitability affects the amount of R&D carried out. These relationships are indicated by the dotted 'feedback' arrows in Figure 9.2.

A crucial view in many early empirical studies was that since structure determined conduct and conduct determined performance, one could ignore conduct and look directly at industry structure in trying to explain performance. Thus many studies sought to explain an indicator of industry performance (such as industry profitability) by using elements of structure as determinants. By comparing several industries in the same time period it became clear that (1) not all industries are equal in terms of profitability, and (2) differences in profitability between industries can be explained in large measure by the elements of structure indicated in Figure 9.2. As a result, the profitability of a multibusiness firm is determined to a certain extent by the choice of which industries to compete in.

Forces driving industry competition

These findings from industrial organization inspired Michael Porter's well-known model of **forces driving industry competition** (Figure 9.3). Intensity of rivalry among existing firms depends *inter alia* on number and size distribution of firms, level of product differentiation, and cost structures. The threat of new entrants depends on barriers to entry. Bargaining power of buyers depends *inter alia* on number and size distribution of buyers and level of product differentiation. A similar statement can be made for bargaining power of suppliers. Therefore, in Porter's five-forces model, industry structure determines intensity of competition and thus industry profitability.[4]

Five-forces model

Porter's **five-forces model** has proved to be a valuable tool for analyzing present and future levels of an industry's level of competition and profitability. Box 9.2 provides an illustration.

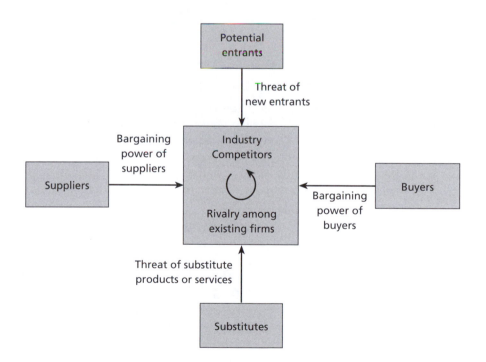

Figure 9.3 **Forces driving industry competition**
Source: Porter (1980), p.4

Box 9.2 ■ Porter's five-forces analysis applied to the pharmaceutical industry

In the pharmaceutical industry patents play an important role. Proprietary drugs are drugs that are protected by patents. Patents offer protection for a limited number of years only. After expiry of a patent other companies are free to offer low-cost copies (generic drugs).

Application of Porter's five-forces model to the pharmaceutical industry in 1997 shows that competition comes mainly from rivalry between industry competitors. This may change, however, as biotechnology companies enter the industry or as buyers organize themselves into more powerful purchasing groups.

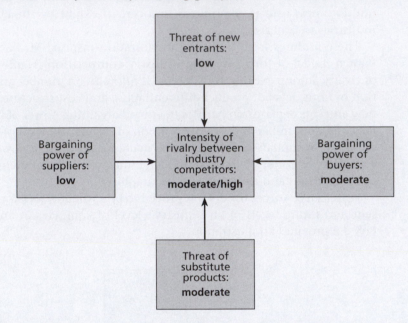

Intensity of rivalry between industry competitors is characterized by several factors:

■ Global competition is concentrated among a limited number of very large companies.
■ Competition is based mainly on product differentiation.
■ Patent protection limits competition among incumbent firms.
■ Most companies focus on particular types of disease therapy.
■ Government intervention increases and puts pressure on prices.
■ Rivalry focuses on developing blockbuster drugs and on decreasing time-to-market, resulting in sharply rising R&D costs.

The threat of new entry is low because there are large economies of scale in R&D and high risks inherent in developing new drugs. However, biotechnology firms could enter the industry in the near future.

The threat of substitutes comes mainly from generic drugs. As buyers become more cost-conscious, consumption of generic drugs is growing.

Bargaining power of suppliers to the pharmaceutical industry is low.

Bargaining power of buyers is moderate but growing, as buyers tend to aggregate demand (that is, hospitals forming alliances, concentration among drug distributors, rise of managed care organizations).

Source: The Corporate Strategy Board, *Changes in the Pharmaceuticals Delivery Chain*, Washington DC, December 1997

9.3 Competitor analysis

In the S-C-P paradigm discussed in section 9.2 the unit of analysis is the industry. In this paradigm, industry structure determines firm conduct, which in turn determines industry performance. If industry structure were to completely determine firm conduct, there could be no differences between the conduct of firms in the same industry. For example, if industry structure determines a firm's pricing strategy, all firms in the industry should follow the same pricing strategy. If, moreover, all firms in the industry have the same unit cost (they employ the same technology, are of the same size, etc.), profitability differences between firms in the same industry can be attributed only to random disturbances. However, the firms in an industry are clearly not all alike. The result is that there are usually differences in profitability between firms in the same industry. How important are differences between industries relative to differences between firms in the same industry? This important question has been examined by Rumelt (1991). He studied a large sample of business units from large (*Fortune* 500) firms over a period of four years and found that differences between firms in the same industry are far more important than differences between industries.

Firms belonging to the same industry can differ in many respects. They differ along dimensions such as pricing strategy, advertising levels, R&D levels, degree of vertical integration, breadth of product line, cost position, and so on. Such disparities may be due to differences in information: firms may perceive different profit opportunities when they enter an industry. For example, firm A may decide to heavily advertise a high-quality product and firm B to pursue a high-volume line because they do not have the same information. Once firms A and B have made these decisions, they become committed to a strategy. Firm A invests in building a brand name; should firm A decide to change its strategy, then its past advertising expenditures lose most of their value. As long as it sticks to its present strategy, these past expenditures constitute an intangible asset. Similarly, firm B has to invest in facilities for high-volume production. If firm B changes its competitive strategy, its high-volume production facilities are likely to decline in value. So both firms A and B have to invest in assets that probably decline in value if the firm changes its strategy. This is one reason why firms' strategies are likely to be 'sticky' and difficult to alter radically. Another explanation is that firms use organizational routines in making strategic decisions: as long as profit performance is satisfactory, firms tend to follow the same rules of thumb (in setting advertising levels, R&D levels, etc.) that they used in the past.[5] Firms do not maximize but satisfice, as explained in Chapter 6. That is to say, as long as their routines lead to satisfactory results, firms have few incentives to search for better routines. In some industries (for example, industries with many small firms and very low entry barriers), rivalry may be so intense that only one strategy can survive. In other industries (for example those with a few large firms and high entry barriers), two or more different strategies may turn out to be sufficiently profitable to allow survival.

Strategic dimensions

It seems likely, then, that firms in the same industry differ along certain key variables. These key variables are the **strategic dimensions** of that industry. In addition, it seems likely that these differences persist for several years. If both propositions are true, then an industry can be viewed as composed of groups of firms where each group consists of firms following similar competitive strategies. The competitive strategy of a firm is that firm's choice with regard to the strategic dimensions of that particular industry. Strategic dimensions can vary with the industry studied. Examples of strategic dimensions are advertising levels, R&D levels, cost position, product differentiation, breadth of product line, and degree of vertical integration. Groups of firms following similar competitive strategies are called **strategic groups**. Firms within a strategic group closely resemble one another. Profitability differences between firms in the same strategic group are likely to be small. However, profitability differences between firms in different groups (firms pursuing different strategies) may be large.

Strategic groups

Following this line of reasoning, two empirical questions have to be answered:

- Do differences in strategies persist over time? (If they do not, the concept of strategic groups has little meaning.)
- Are profitability differences between strategic groups significant?

Several studies have examined these questions. Most have come to the conclusion that strategic groups can be identified in many industries. Moreover, strategic groups tend to be stable over time. Significant profitability differences between strategic groups are found less often. Hence in many industries there appear to be several roads to (roughly the same kind of) success. Strategic planners can use the concept of strategic groups to construct a map showing the competitive strategies of their own company and of their competitors. As an example, consider Box 9.3, which shows a **strategic map** of the European brewing industry in 2001.

Strategic map

The strategic map shown in Figure 9.4 uses brand strategy (one local brand, several local brands, several local brands plus at least one international brand, one international brand only) and market share as strategic dimensions. Other strategic dimensions that may be important in the brewing industry (such as level of diversification, level of advertising or level of vertical integration), cannot be shown in the same map.

9.4 Competitive strategy

Generic competitive strategies

A competitive strategy reflects the firm's choices concerning the strategic dimensions of its industry. Since there are many strategic dimensions, and different industries may have different strategic dimensions, many competitive strategies are possible. In many industries, however, two successful competitive strategies can be identified: cost leadership and product differentiation. Both strategies can be applied industry-wide or to a few segments only. These so-called **generic competitive strategies** have been discussed extensively by

Box 9.3 ■ The European beer industry

The European beer industry consists of a large number of companies. In Germany there are many (several hundred) small breweries, each serving a small regional market. Small breweries with only one brand serving a local or national market can be found in many other European countries. Heineken sells beer under a variety of brand names: Heineken, Amstel and Murphy's (which are sold in almost all countries in Europe) and a large number of national brands (for example Moretti and Dreher in Italy). Interbrew also uses a variety of brand names: Stella (its most international brand) and a large number of local or regional brands. SAB (South African Breweries) has acquired several European breweries, each with its own brand name, but SAB does not have a pan-European brand. Finally, the American brewers Anheuser-Bush and Miller are active in Europe with their flagship brands (Budweiser and Miller respectively). Thus, on the basis of brand strategy and market share, four strategic groups emerge (Figure 9.4).

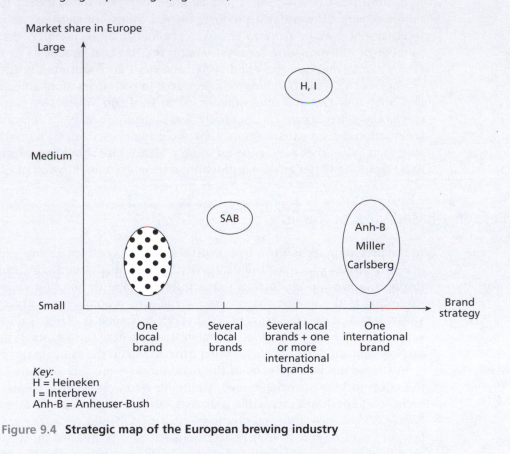

Figure 9.4 **Strategic map of the European brewing industry**

| Strategy of cost leadership | Michael Porter.[6] Under a **strategy of cost leadership** the firm tries to manufacture and distribute products at the lowest possible unit cost. Quite often, cost leadership can be attained only through large-scale production (economies of scale) or through experience. Both economies of scale and experience are |

Strategy of product differentiation

easier to obtain if the firm has a large market share. Under a **strategy of product differentiation**, the firm competes by offering a product that the customers perceive as more valuable than the competitors' products. It can do so by offering a product that differs from other products in quality, safety, design, reliability, ease of repair, durability, taste, or whatever. If buyers recognize the additional value, the firm can charge a higher price. For a strategy of product differentiation, brand name recognition is usually very important. Thus advertising levels tend to be high for firms using this strategy.

As discussed above, firms' strategies are likely to be sticky as a result of the necessary commitment to a chosen strategy and also because of the development of successful routines. Once a firm has chosen to pursue one of Porter's generic strategies, it is likely to continue along that path for quite some time. This may be dangerous, however. A firm committed to a strategy of cost leadership must be aware that its customers compare the standard low-cost products with differentiated products offered by its competitors. As income levels rise or demand patterns change, customers may increasingly demand a number of differentiating features, forcing the low-cost producers to incorporate these in their product offerings. The Model T Ford and the VW Beetle are examples of very successful low-cost products; in both cases more differentiated cars offered by GM and others finally forced Ford and Volkswagen to develop new, more differentiated cars. Similarly, firms pursuing a strategy of product differentiation cannot remain complacent about their costs. Buyers do not simply seek high value; they seek value for money. Hence care should be taken not to overemphasize Porter's useful distinction in generic competitive strategies.

9.5 Resource-based view of the firm

In the preceding section two competitive strategies – cost leadership and product differentiation – have been discussed. A firm may attain cost leadership through large-scale production (economies of scale) or through experience. According to the resource-based view of the firm, a competitive advantage is always based on the possession of certain resources, such as a large-scale plant or experience. The extent to which a competitive advantage is sustainable depends on how difficult or costly it is for other firms to obtain the same resources.

Resource-based view of the firm

In the **resource-based view of the firm** resources are defined quite broadly. Resources include financial resources, tangible resources (such as plants, equipment, buildings) and intangible resources (such as patents, know-how, brand names, experience and organizational routines). Some resources are easily bought and sold on (nearly) perfect markets. This is true for most financial assets such as marketable securities. Other assets are much more difficult to buy and sell. For example, there are active markets for new and secondhand cars and trucks, but there is no market for 'organizational routines' (the concept of organizational routines is explained in section 10.5).

According to the resource-based theory of the firm, a resource can be the basis of a competitive advantage only if that resource has certain properties. First, it must be difficult to buy and sell the resource. In order to understand this, consider a market with five firms of equal size, each having a market share of 20 per cent. Suppose that firm A has more modern equipment than the other firms and thus enjoys a cost advantage. If the other firms can easily buy the same equipment, then firm A's advantage will be short-lived. However, if firm A has developed its own equipment, and the development of this type of equipment demands special skills or experience that only firm A's employees possess, then firm A's competitive advantage is sustainable. In the latter case, firm A's competitive advantage is, in the final analysis, based on an intangible resource (the skills and experience of its employees) rather than on a tangible asset (the equipment itself). It is, generally speaking, much more difficult to 'buy' intangible resources such as skills or experience than it is to buy tangible assets such as equipment.

For intangible resources it is useful to make a distinction between resources for which property rights are well defined (such as patents, brand names and copyrights) and intangible resources for which property rights are ill defined (such as technological know-how not protected by patents, organizational routines, and the know-how and experience of the top management team). It is quite difficult to trade in know-how that is not protected by patents because of the fundamental paradox of information (see section 4.1). This type of know-how can be the basis of a sustainable competitive advantage. If several competing firms obtain a licence to use the same patented know-how in return for a royalty payment, the use of this know-how is unlikely to be the source of a competitive advantage.

Second, the resource must be difficult to replicate. Some resources, such as point-of-sale systems in retailing, can be replicated fairly easily by competitors. By contrast, highly complex organizational routines are much more difficult to replicate.

Third, it must be difficult to substitute the resource by another resource. For example, pipelines and tankers are substitutes for shipping oil. The possession of a pipeline will give a firm a competitive advantage only if it is more costly or impossible to use tankers.

Finally, the advantage that the resource may yield must not be competed away by *ex-ante* competition. Suppose that the government announces that it will allow only one firm to use a radio frequency for mobile telecom services. Surely the concession to use this frequency has a value. If, however, the government organizes an auction to sell this frequency to the highest bidder, a (large) part of this value will be cashed by the government. If all bidders make the same estimates concerning future sales and costs, and if these estimates are correct, then each bidder will bid the same: the winner will have to be chosen at random but will not make any economic profit (this is the paradox of profits described in section 2.4.3). However, if the winner obtains the concession based on overly optimistic expectations, this is an example of the winner's curse (see section 5.4)

9.6 Move and countermove

In the discussion in the preceding section we have ignored the fact that in the real world companies choosing a competitive strategy usually take into account how competitors are likely to react. When a firm chooses a competitive strategy, it chooses values for the strategic dimensions of its industry. For example, it chooses its level of advertising expenditures, R&D expenditures, etc. When a firm makes these choices, it should (and usually does) take into account how competitors will react. If it does not, it is like a chess player who, when considering a move, does not analyze possible countermoves by his opponent. If you have ever played chess, you will know that you will probably lose the game if you play that way.

In this section we want to show how a company, when considering a strategic move, can take into account possible countermoves by a competitor. We shall do this by discussing how a monopolist can impede entry into its industry by a potential entrant. This is a complicated subject since many moves and countermoves are possible. To make things as simple as possible we shall use a particular industry to illustrate moves by the monopolist and countermoves by the potential entrant: the icecream-selling business. After our analysis of the icecream-selling industry we shall translate our main findings to other industries.

9.6.1 The icecream-selling industry

Imagine a beach with a length of 480 metres. Potential customers are evenly distributed along this beach. There are two companies that consider setting up icecream stands on this beach. Let us call them Mr Sun and Mrs Orange. There is another company, Rent-a-Stand, that specializes in letting icecream stands. Rent-a-Stand itself is not interested in selling icecream. Icecream stands can be rented for $140 a day. Both Mr Sun and Mrs Orange can rent as many icecream stands as they want.

The price of an icecream is $1.00. This price has been determined by the municipality, and neither Mr Sun nor Mrs Orange is allowed to sell icecreams at any other price. Mr Sun and Mrs Orange both have to buy icecreams from a distributor at $0.90 a piece, so on each icecream they sell, they make a gross margin of $0.10.

The number of icecreams that are sold by an icecream stand depends on its location and on the location of other icecream stands. This is illustrated in Figure 9.5.

In diagram (a), for example, there is only one icecream stand located in the middle of the beach. The stand is indicated by the small black box; the distances from the corners of the beach (240 m) are also indicated. We assume that, per metre of beach, a maximum of 10 icecreams per day, generating sales of $10.00, can be sold. As you can see in diagram (a), sales decrease linearly with distance: no potential customer is prepared to walk more than 240 m for an icecream. That is why in (b) sales are only half as much as in diagram (a). Total icecream sales for (a) can be calculated as follows: if no potential customer should have to walk a single step in order to reach an icecream stand then total sales would be 480 × $10.00 = $4,800.[7] This amount ($4,800) corresponds to the area of the rectangle. If there is one icecream stand in the middle of the beach (diagram (a)) sales are half as much, $2,400 (this is the shaded area in (a)).

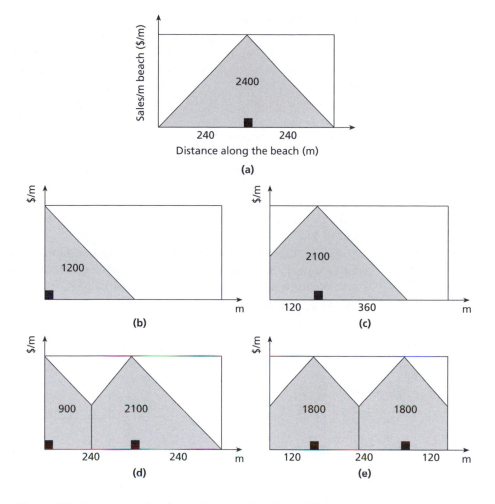

Figure 9.5 **Icecream sales dependent on location of the icecream stands**

Following the same logic one can calculate sales in the other diagrams. In (d) and (e) there are two icecream stands with a distance of less than 480 m between them. In this case all customers walk to the nearest icecream stand.

9.6.2 Number of icecream stands

Mr Sun arrives at the beach one day. He has to decide how many icecream stands to place on the beach and also where to locate these stands. As soon as Mr Sun has placed his stands, Mrs Orange arrives. Then Mrs Orange has to decide whether and where to place icecream stands on the beach. This, of course, is an entry game (see section 5.3 for another example of an entry game).

Let us return to Mr Sun deciding how many stands to place on the beach. Suppose first that Mr Sun chooses only one stand. By looking at the diagrams of Figure 9.5 it is clear that he should locate this stand at the middle of the beach. If Mrs Orange decides to stay out of the icecream-selling business, then his sales are $2,400, his gross margin is $240 and his net profit $240 – $140 = $100. Will Mrs Orange enter if Mr Sun locates one stand at the middle of the beach? Suppose first that Mrs Orange locates one stand to the left of Mr Sun's stand.

Diagrams (a), (b) and (c) in Figure 9.6 show her sales for three different locations: (a) at the corner of the beach, (b) at the middle of the beach just left of Mr Sun's stand, and (c) 96 m to the left of Mr Sun's stand (a little calculation shows that this is the optimal location given Mr Sun's location).[8] In diagram (a), Mrs Orange's gross margin is only $90; this is not enough to cover the rent of $140. In (b), Mrs Orange's gross margin is $120; again not enough to cover the rent. In (c), Mrs Orange generates a gross margin of $144; after paying the rent, her net profit is $4. So Mrs Orange enters by placing a stand 96 m to the left of Mr Sun's stand.

Mrs Orange can, of course, also place a new stand 96 m to the right of Mr Sun's stand. There Mrs Orange will also make a net profit of $4 a day. Mr Sun's gross margin will then drop to only $86.40 a day. As a result his net profit will be negative ($86.40 – $140.00 = –$53.60).

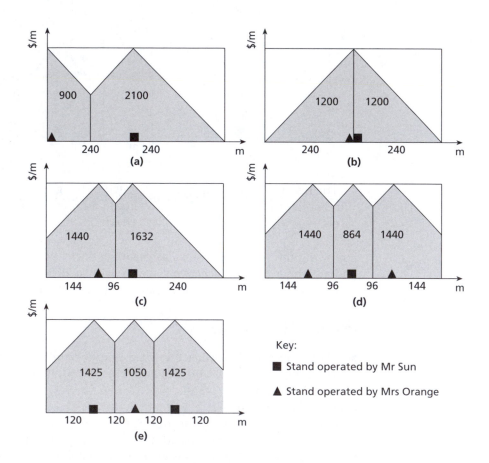

Figure 9.6 Icecream sales by Mr Sun and Mrs Orange

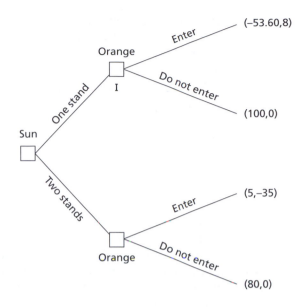

Figure 9.7   Game tree for the icecream-selling game. Mr Sun can move first to determine the number and location of his stands

Now suppose that Mr Sun decides to place two stands on the beach ((e) in Figure 9.5). If Mrs Orange stays out, Mr Sun's sales will be $3,600, his gross margin $360 and his net profit $360 − $280 = $80. Will Mrs Orange enter after Mr Sun has placed two stands on the beach? If she decides to enter, the best place she can choose is the middle of the beach ((e) in Figure 9.6). She will then generate sales of $1,050, a gross margin of $105. This is not enough to cover the rent of $140, so she will not enter.

The results of this analysis are indicated in the game tree of Figure 9.7. If Mr Sun applies the principle of looking ahead and reasoning back, he will decide to choose two stands. Note that Mr Sun would choose only one stand if he had a legal monopoly. By choosing two stands instead of one he can effectively deter entry. The essence of this strategy is to 'blanket' potential demand for icecream, leaving no room for Mrs Orange to enter.

9.6.3   Commitment

In section 5.3 we introduced the idea of commitment. There we discussed a situation in which the incumbent firm can commit itself to lower prices after entry has occurred. The icecream example offers an opportunity to illustrate another form of commitment. Suppose that there are now two types of icecream stand: movable stands (on wheels) and immobile stands (on legs). Movable stands can be moved along the beach without cost. Both types of stand can be rented from Rent-a-Stand for $150 a day. Mr Sun has to decide how many stands to place on the beach, whether to choose stands on legs or stands on wheels, and where to locate these stands on the beach. Then Mrs Orange has to decide whether to enter, how many and what type of stands to choose, and where to locate the stands on the beach. Finally, if Mr Sun has one or more stands on wheels, he has to decide whether he wants to move those stands along the beach.

Suppose, first, that Mr Sun locates one stand on legs in the middle of the beach. If Mrs Orange does not enter he makes a profit of

$$\$240 - \$150 = \$90$$

If Mrs Orange decides to enter, the best she can do is to place a stand 96 m to the left (or right) of Mr Sun's stand. At that location Mrs Orange will generate sales of $1,440 ((c) in Figure 9.6); Mrs Orange will then realize a gross margin of $144. This is not enough to cover the rent of $150, so she will make a loss of $6.

Now suppose that Mr Sun employs a stand on wheels at the middle of the beach. Mrs Orange can now place a stand on legs next to Mr Sun's stand. Now Mr Sun has to decide whether or not to move his stand along the beach (he can move his stand without cost). Given that he now has a stand on legs next to his own stand, the best he can do is to move 96 m to the right or to the left. By doing so he increases his sales from $1,200 to $1,440 and his gross margin from $120 to $144. The result is a loss of $6 if he moves and a loss of $30 if he does not move. If Mr Sun moves 96 m away, Mrs Orange's sales increase from $1,200 to $1,632. If Mr Sun does not move, she makes a loss of $30, but if Mr Sun does move, she makes a profit of $13.20.

This results in the game tree of Figure 9.8. If Mrs Orange applies the principle of looking ahead and reasoning back, she will not enter if Mr Sun employs a stand on legs. However, she will decide to enter if Mr Sun employs a stand on wheels. After all, she knows that if she locates next to him, Mr Sun will move away because it is in his own interest to do so. Now Mr Sun knows that he must choose a stand on legs. From looking ahead and reasoning back he sees that with a stand on legs he will make a profit of $90, with a stand on wheels he will lose $6.

In this example one stand on legs is enough to deter entry. One stand on wheels will not deter entry. If Mr Sun uses a stand on legs, he cannot move. Mrs Orange then sees that Mr Sun cannot move, so Mrs Orange will not enter. By using a stand on legs rather than a stand on wheels, Mr Sun can deter entry. This is another example of an entry-deterring strategy. Mr Sun shows he is committed to his place on the beach. This *spatial commitment* deters Mrs Orange from entering.

Thus far we have ignored the time dimension. We have assumed that the future consists of only one day. Suppose now that both Mr Sun and Mrs Orange have a time horizon of one week rather than one day. Suppose that Mr Sun can choose between two types of rental contract: a fixed contract and a flexible contract. A fixed contract is a contract for one week that cannot be cancelled by Mr Sun. If Mr Sun chooses a fixed contract, he has to pay the rent ($150 a day) for seven days even if he does not sell a single icecream. A flexible contract is a contract that gives Mr Sun the option to cancel the contract after one day. After Mr Sun has signed a rental contract with Rent-a-Stand, Mrs Orange has to decide whether she wants to rent a stand. For simplicity we assume that Mrs Orange can choose only a fixed contract.

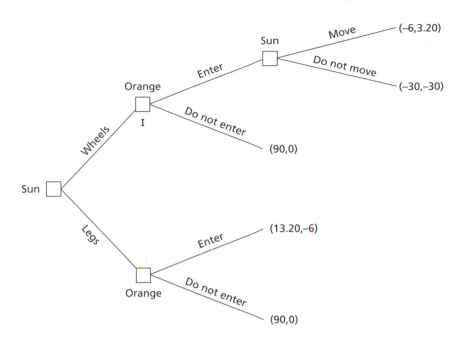

Figure 9.8 **Game tree for the icecream-selling game. Mr Sun can move first to choose between a stand on wheels and a stand on legs**

To analyze this situation, suppose first that Mr Sun decides to choose a flexible contract. He rents one stand and places it on the middle of the beach. Suppose Mrs Orange decides to enter and to place also one stand at the middle of the beach. Then both will make a loss of $30 during the first day. After the first day Mr Sun will have to decide whether to cancel the rental contract with Rent-a-Stand. If he does not cancel the contract, he will make a loss of $30 during each of the remaining six days, or $210 for the whole week. If he cancels the contract, his loss during the whole week will be only $30. Mrs Orange will then make a profit of $90 during each of the remaining six days, or a profit of $510 for the whole week. This results in the game tree of Figure 9.9 (we have explained how the payoffs are calculated if Mr Sun chooses a fixed contract; you should be able to do these calculations yourself now). Assuming that both Mrs Orange and Mr Sun apply the principle of looking ahead and reasoning back, it is easy to see that Mr Sun should choose a fixed contract. In that case Mrs Orange will not enter. This is an example of *temporal commitment*. By signing a contract for a week rather than for a day Mr Sun commits himself to the icecream-selling business and so deters entry.

9.6.4 Lessons from the icecream example

Two important lessons emerge from the icecream example. First, from section 9.6.2 we see that Mr Sun can block entry by employing two stands rather than

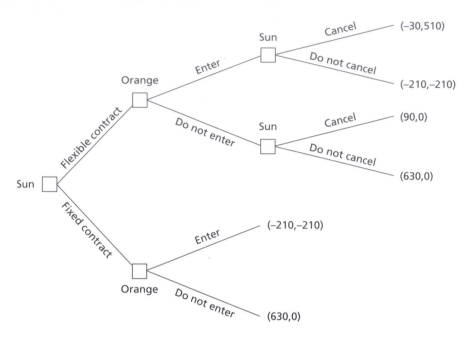

Figure 9.9 **Game tree for the icecream-selling game. Mr Sun can move first to choose between a fixed and a flexible contract**

one. This finding has an important analogy in product competition, as we shall explain below (in section 9.6.6).

Second, from section 9.6.3 we know that Mr Sun can deter entry by making **Credible commitment** a **credible commitment**. If Mr Sun has to choose between a stand on wheels and a stand on legs, he can deter entry by using a stand on legs. Suppose Mr Sun uses a stand on wheels and then simply tells Mrs Orange that he will not move if Mrs Orange locates next to him. Mrs Orange, however, may not believe him. The problem for Mr Sun is to convince Mrs Orange that he will not move. Mr Sun must make a credible threat not to move and can do so by using a stand on legs.

If Mr Sun has to choose between a contract for a day and a contract for a week, he can make a credible commitment by signing a contract for a week with Rent-a-Stand. Suppose Mr Sun does not make a long-term contract with Rent-a-Stand but instead simply tells Mrs Orange that he will not leave the ice-cream business. Again Mrs Orange may just not believe him. Mr Sun must make a credible threat not to leave the icecream business. By binding himself to a long-term contract and by making this known to Mrs Orange, he makes such a credible threat.

The lesson from the games in Figures 9.8 and 9.9 is that Mr Sun must make a credible threat. The simple but important point is that it is easier to convince someone of something that is true than of something that might not be true. By using a stand on legs or by signing a long-term contract Mr Sun cannot move along the beach or leave the icecream business. Mr Sun's threat is credible because he has committed himself.

It is often thought that strategic flexibility is always an advantage. In section 9.6.3 we analyzed situations where flexibility (the ability to move the stand along the beach or to leave the industry) is a disadvantage rather than an advantage. Flexibility is always an advantage when you play against Nature. Nature's moves are determined by a random process: they are not determined by whether or not you are committed to a certain strategy. If, however, you play against a human opponent, it may be better to commit yourself rather than to retain flexibility. To use a military analogy: burning the bridges behind you signals a credible commitment that you are willing to fight.[9]

9.6.5 Spatial competition

Spatial competition

Selecting locations for icecream stands on a beach is an example of spatial competition.[10] A clearer example of **spatial competition** is the competition between supermarket chains for new locations. This would differ from our icecream example in the following respects:

- It is spatial competition in two dimensions instead of one (our beach could be represented by a line and thus had only one dimension; an area has two dimensions: north/south and east/west).
- Zoning regulations and existing buildings exclude a part of the total area as possible sites for a new supermarket.
- Customers tend to shop at the nearest supermarket, but not everyone always shops at the nearest supermarket.
- Population, and thus demand, need not be evenly distributed over the area.
- Population shifts may occur. To be able to forecast population shifts correctly is an important competitive weapon.

9.6.6 Product competition

Spatial competition has an important analogy in product competition. Imagine two companies selling different brands of cola drink, which differ along one dimension (for example, sweetness). If sweetness can be expressed in a number, the position of a brand can be given by a number. To introduce a new product is then the equivalent of opening an icecream stand on our beach. Potential customers have different tastes. The distribution of tastes is the parallel of the distribution of potential customers along the beach. Each customer will buy the brand that comes closest to his or her taste. Of course, products can differ in more than one dimension and consumer preferences may change over time. Under these conditions the game of introducing new brands is analogous to the game of selecting new supermarket sites.

In most real-life cases, firms compete on several dimensions. For example, soft drinks companies compete not only on the sweetness of their products but also on other product characteristics, on choice of distribution channels, price, etc. This adds further complexity to the competitive game of move and countermove. However, the basics of competitive interaction have now been illustrated.

The main lessons from this section can be summarized as follows:

- Given a (potential) demand for a certain product, firms may deter entry by 'blanketing' this demand: that is, leaving no room for other firms to enter profitably. If, however, they leave certain niches open for potential entrants, these may be profitably exploited. Niches may be of a geographical or a product differentiation nature.
- Incumbents may also deter entry by showing that they are committed to their (place in the) industry. In order to be an effective deterrent, the commitment needs to be observable by and credible to the potential entrant.
- As a corollary: flexibility is not always the strategic advantage it is usually assumed to be. If potential entrants interpret an incumbent's flexibility as the likelihood that it will accommodate new entries, entry may in fact be encouraged.

9.7 Vertical integration

Sections 9.2–9.6 discussed competitive strategy. Now we shift our focus to corporate strategy. As indicated in section 9.1, the main question in formulating a corporate strategy is *where* (that is, in which industries and in which countries) to compete. The profitability of a multibusiness firm depends to a certain extent on the set of industries in which it operates. There are three ways in which a company can extend its portfolio of business units: through vertical integration, through diversification, and through multinationalization. This section deals with vertical integration. Diversification and multinationalization are discussed in the next two sections.

Every production process consists of several technologically separable stages. The production of automobiles, for example, consists of assembling an automobile from components such as the body, engine, gearbox, wheels, etc. Each
Vertical integration   of these components consists of several other components. **Vertical integration** means moving into the production of previous stages (backward integration) or subsequent stages (forward integration). It is easy to see that no firm can be *fully* integrated. For example, for a textbook publisher to be *fully* integrated would mean not only printing, bookbinding and operating bookstores, but also producing paper, ink, computers, printing presses, bookbinding equipment and all inputs for producing paper, ink, computers, etc. So the question is not whether or not to be fully integrated, but rather in *which stages* of the production process you want to be involved. For example, an automobile company may or may not produce its own gearboxes or ignition systems; it is unlikely, however, to consider producing tyres or light bulbs.

In order to analyze vertical integration we can directly apply transaction cost economics, discussed in Chapter 8. An automobile company making its own seats and a small building contractor buying nails from a hardware store rely on different governance structures: the first uses a managerial hierarchy while the latter relies on the market. Between these two extremes are long-term contracts such as a five-year contract between an automobile company and a seat manufacturer. Such long-term contracts are sometimes called *quasi-vertical integration*. Other examples of quasi-vertical integration involving long-term contracts between firms are franchising and licensing contracts.

9.7.1 Technological interdependence

It is sometimes thought that technological factors determine whether two subsequent stages in a production process will be vertically integrated. As an example, consider steelmaking.

Steelmaking consists of two stages: iron is produced out of iron ore in a blast furnace and then this iron is used to produce steel in a rolling mill. Significant energy savings are realized when these two stages are located next to each other: molten iron need not cool and be reheated but is used directly as input for the rolling mill. Thus it is sometimes argued that the production of iron and steel should be vertically integrated because of technological interdependence. Williamson argues that technological interdependence alone does not necessarily lead to vertical integration.[11] The blast furnace and the rolling mill could be owned and operated by two independent firms. Of course, they should still be located next to each other in order to capture the energy savings.

9.7.2 Critical dimensions of transactions

In order to explain why, in practice, we observe integrated iron and steelworks instead of two separate firms, we need a transaction cost argument in addition to the technological factors.

What factors determine the choice between vertical integration, quasi-vertical integration through long-term contracts or a series of spot contracts? As discussed in Chapter 8, three dimensions of transactions are important:

- asset specificity;
- uncertainty/complexity;
- frequency.

Asset specificity and uncertainty/complexity are more important than frequency, so, for simplicity, we shall ignore frequency for the moment.

Asset specificity can be low for both parties to a transaction, it can be high for one party and low for the other party, or it can be high for both parties. If asset specificity is high for one party but low for the other, the party with highly transaction-specific assets is vulnerable to opportunistic behaviour by the other party. If, however, asset specificity is high for both parties to a transaction, they are in the same position as two enemies holding hostages. If one party hurts the hostages it holds, the other party can retaliate. Such a situation encourages both parties to be careful. In military terms, there will be an incentive to aim for a truce. In economic terms, two parties with mutually high asset specificity may aim for a long-term contract. If either party violates the contract, both will be

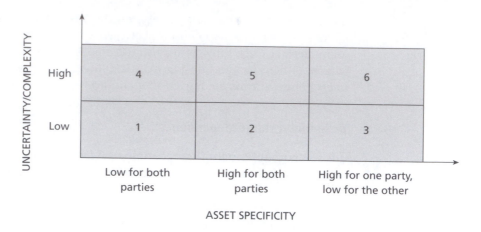

Figure 9.10   Six different cases with regard to asset specificity and uncertainty/complexity

hurt. Under such conditions a long-term contract may work quite well, provided that not too many contingencies need to be included in it.

If we say that asset specificity can be low for both parties, high for one party and low for the other, or high for both parties, and that uncertainty/complexity can be low or high, we have six different situations (see Figure 9.10).

We discuss each of these six situations below and analyze which governance structures are efficient in each case.

Case 1: Asset specificity low on both sides, uncertainty/complexity low

An example of such a situation is a building contractor buying nails. Spot contracts are very efficient in this case.

Case 2: Asset specificity high on both sides, uncertainty/complexity low

As an example of this situation, consider again the relationship between a newspaper publisher and a printer in an isolated town discussed in section 8.3. For the printer the press is transaction-specific since there is only one newspaper publisher in that town. The printer cannot sell the services of the press to newspaper publishers in other towns because of transportation costs. For the publisher, his investment in goodwill with subscribers and advertisers is transaction-specific because there is only one printer. Hence asset specificity is high for both parties: they are dependent upon each other for a transaction to occur.

The major source of uncertainty/complexity would seem to be whether the publisher will be able to pay. If the printer has no doubts concerning the publisher's ability to pay (either because she knows that the publisher has ample financial resources or because she knows the newspaper will generate enough cash flow), a long-term contract will work quite well.

Case 3: Asset specificity high on one side, uncertainty/complexity low

As an example consider the relationship between an auto component manufacturer and an automobile company. If the component manufacturer has to invest in specialized tooling for components that can be sold to one automobile company only, asset specificity is high for the component manufacturer but not for the automobile company. The component manufacturer would be vulnerable to opportunistic behaviour by the automobile company. Even if uncertainty/complexity is low, vertical integration will probably be the preferred solution.[12]

Case 4: Asset specificity low on both sides, uncertainty/complexity high

As an example of this situation, consider the relationship between an oil company and a management consulting firm. The potential transaction might be advice about the oil company's organizational policies. Asset specificity is low on both sides: the oil company can turn to many other consulting firms for advice; the management consulting firm has many other potential clients. It may be quite difficult, however, to specify in a contract the services of the management consulting firm. Often, the specific problems that have to be dealt with only become clear as the consultancy work progresses, so uncertainty/complexity may be quite high. Now frequency may become an important dimension.

If frequency is very low (if the oil company seeks this type of advice only very rarely), vertical integration cannot be the solution. Somehow the two parties must agree on a contract, even in the face of high uncertainty/complexity. Perhaps the consultancy work will be split into phases, with the oil company retaining the right to reconsider the transaction after a pilot study by the consulting firm. If, however, frequency is high (if the oil company needs this type of advice regularly), vertical integration might be a good solution. The oil company then builds an internal group of management consultants. This solution becomes even more efficient when asset specificity is not totally absent. This may be the case if some organization-specific knowledge is necessary. In this case, then, we would say the preferred solution depends primarily on frequency.

Case 5: Asset specificity high on both sides, uncertainty/complexity high

Consider again steelmaking. Suppose the two stages in steelmaking (blast furnace and rolling mill) were organized in two separate firms. In order to realize energy savings, the blast furnace and the rolling mill should be located next to each other. The blast furnace would have only one customer for its molten iron and the rolling mill would have only one supplier of molten iron. This implies that for both the blast furnace and the rolling mill most of the physical assets would be transaction-specific.

Uncertainty/complexity is also high. One source of complexity may be the fact that the quality of the different grades of steel depends to a large extent on the quality of the molten iron, while the quality of molten iron is hard to measure. Since the quality of the molten iron depends on the quality of the iron

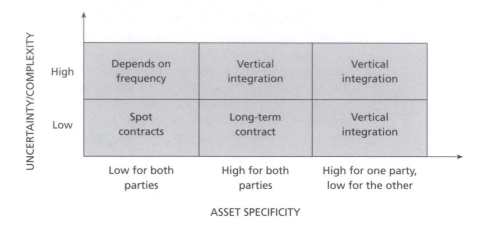

Figure 9.11 **How asset specificity and uncertainty/complexity determine governance structure**

ore used by the blast furnace, and grades of iron ore differ in quality and in price, the owner of the blast furnace has an opportunity to behave opportunistically. Under these circumstances it is very difficult to write and enforce a contingent claims contract.[13] In this case, vertical integration is the most efficient solution.

Case 6: Asset specificity high for one party and low for the other, uncertainty/complexity high

Consider a component manufacturer who has to invest a large sum in the development of a component for which there will be only one customer. The investment in development is then highly transaction-specific. Uncertainty/complexity may come from two sources: the development costs may be uncertain and/or demand for the final product (and thus for the component) may be uncertain. If uncertainty from either source is high, it is very difficult to write and enforce a contingent claims contract. Vertical integration is the most efficient solution.

The six cases discussed above are summarized in Figure 9.11.

9.8 Diversification

A firm can also extend its portfolio of businesses through diversification. It will be useful to make a distinction between *related* and *unrelated diversification*. **Related diversification** occurs when the new business is in some way related to the firm's existing business. Examples of related diversification are a coffee firm diversifying into coffee creamer (market-related), a dairy firm currently producing only cheese, butter and fresh milk products that diversifies into cof-

Related diversification

fee creamer (input-related), and a commercial aircraft company diversifying into military aircraft (technology-related).

9.8.1 Related diversification

Economies of scope An important reason for related diversification is the existence of **economies of scope**. Economies of scope exist when the joint production of two goods is less costly than the cost of producing those two goods separately.[14] As an example, consider the joint production of fruit and sheep.[15] A fruitgrower must have space between fruit trees in order to facilitate adequate growth of the trees and the movement of farm machinery between the trees. This land can be used as pasture, where sheep can graze. Since land can be used as a common input, the joint production of fruit and sheep on one piece of land is less costly than the production of fruit and sheep separately on two different pieces of land. A more industrial example is the joint use of a physical distribution system for beer and soft drinks.

The existence of economies of scope does not imply that both goods should be produced by the same firm, as has been pointed out by Teece (1980). The fruitgrower can diversify into sheep and thus realize economies of scope. As an alternative, however, he may lease the land to a sheepfarmer. In the latter case, a market transaction in the common input factor (land) occurs. The fruitgrower can choose between two governance structures: the firm (if he diversifies) or the market (if he leases his land to a sheepfarmer). Teece's argument here is analogous to Williamson's discussion of vertical integration of iron and steel production (see section 9.7). In both cases a market arrangement can be used to capture the economies of scope or the energy savings. The actual choice between these two arrangements will thus be driven by the transaction costs involved.

Economies of scope can always be traced to a common production factor. If market transactions in this common production factor are relatively costly, joint production of the two products in one firm may be the least cost solution. Common production factors leading to economies of scope are:

- specialized indivisible physical assets;
- technological know-how;
- organizational know-how;
- brand names.

Specialized indivisible physical assets The services of **specialized indivisible physical assets** may be difficult to sell (exactly because the assets are specialized). As an example, consider once again a newspaper publisher in an isolated town. Suppose this publisher prints his own newspaper. For this purpose the press is used six days a week. One day a week the press is idle. Suppose this idle capacity can be used to print a Sunday paper. The newspaper publisher can start a Sunday paper or he can write a contract for printing a Sunday paper with someone else who wants to start such a paper. Both solutions would seem feasible (see our earlier discussion in section 9.7).

Technological know-how **Technological know-how** may also lead to economies of scope. Technological know-how may be difficult to trade across markets for two reasons:

- Property rights may be ill defined.
- Transfer of know-how within a firm may be easier than across markets.

Not all technological know-how is patentable. Also, firms often choose not to patent technological findings, even if patents could be obtained. One reason is that they have to register their findings at the patent office. By registering, they reveal their knowledge. This is not always strategically advantageous. It is usually difficult to sell technological know-how if property rights are not protected by patent law. A seller must try to convince a potential buyer of its value and in doing so must reveal some of his know-how. A potential buyer can assess the real value of the know-how only after he has received it – but then he already possesses the know-how and will refuse to pay for it. This is the fundamental paradox of information, as described in section 4.1: its value can only be revealed to another party by disclosing the information, while such disclosure destroys its value. The paradox emerges because potential buyers may behave opportunistically. Suppose that a buyer agrees to pay in advance for technological know-how. Now the seller may behave opportunistically by transferring only a minor part of the know-how. Thus the possibility of opportunistic behaviour by both buyers and sellers leads to the fundamental paradox of information.

Suppose now that property rights to know-how are protected by patent law. Now a potential buyer knows what he buys. Opportunistic behaviour by buyer and seller is less of a problem. Transfer of know-how within a firm may still be easier (and thus cheaper) than between firms. If a recipe or a blueprint is all that needs to be transferred, it is easy to realize the transfer both between firms and within a firm. Frequently, however, more than a recipe or blueprint needs to be transferred: if the know-how contains an element of learning by doing, then training and consulting are part of the transfer. If engineers working for the same firm have received a similar training, the transfer between engineers working for the same firm may be easier than between engineers working for different firms. In such a case, related diversification may again be efficient.

Organizational know-how is the third production factor giving rise to economies of scope. Organizational know-how refers to the fact that organizations 'know' how to respond to external events. Organizations use *routines* to respond to external events. An important characteristic of routines is that they are to a large extent *tacit*: each organization member finds it difficult to articulate why she responds to a stimulus in a particular way. Yet organizations seem to 'remember by doing'. The concept of organizational routines (developed by Nelson and Winter, 1982) is discussed more fully in section 10.5. Here we want to state that organizational know-how is often *fungible*: that is, organizational know-how often has several kinds of application (Teece, 1982). For example, automobile companies can use their organizational know-how also for making tanks (as they did during the Second World War), breweries can use their organizational know-how to produce soft drinks, etc.

It is nearly impossible to trade organizational know-how across a market. If one manager is transferred from one firm to another, he must learn the organizational routines of his new firm. Organizational routines are more difficult

Organizational know-how

Box 9.4 ■ Retailing versus e-tailing

With the advent of the Internet many companies ('dotcoms') were set up to challenge incumbents in various industries. One example is from retailing. Here the idea was that many consumers would eventually rather order their groceries over the Net and have them delivered at home (or at a convenient place such as the office) than do their laborious shopping in their sparse time off. This idea was the basis of new business models in 'e-tailing', pursued by start-up companies such as Kozmo, Streamline, Peapod and Webvan. Webvan, for instance, collected $1.2 bn of financing in 1999 and built 26 enormous distribution centres with the latest web-enabled inventory management systems and a huge fleet of delivery vans. Nevertheless, it went bankrupt in mid 2001. Similarly, many other e-tailers did not survive: they also folded or were taken over.

The incumbent retailers were at first rather slow to react. However, in the endgame they may be the eventual survivors in e-tailing by blending it with their conventional 'bricks-and-mortar' approach (sometimes the blend is referred to as 'clicks-and-mortar'). Ahold, the Dutch retailer, has taken over Peapod and is now keen on acquiring the employees and customers of Webvan. On 25 June 2001 Tesco, Britain's biggest grocer, announced a deal with Safeway, California's biggest food retailer, to bring its successful Internet shopping service to the USA. Tesco has worked hard to perfect its so-called 'store-picking' system, under which orders placed online are plucked from the shelves of existing stores. It is now the world's biggest Internet grocer with a turnover of over $420 million.

Sources: *The Economist*, 30 June 2001; *Het Financieele Dagblad*, 11 July 2001

to transfer. Through diversification organizational know-how can be exploited across different applications. Thus organizational know-how is a fundamental reason to diversify.

Brand names

Brand names can also lead to economies of scope. This is because it is usually cheaper to introduce a new product under an established brand name than under a new one (suppose Daimler-Benz were to diversify into motorcycles; it would then be cheaper to use the Mercedes brand name than to use a new name). Brand names can also be traded across markets. We shall say more on this subject in section 9.9.

Sometimes economies of scope can be quite important. In food retailing, for example, there seem to be important economies of scope between traditional supermarkets and 'e-tailing' (food retailing using the Internet), as is illustrated in Box 9.4.

The argument so far can be summarized as follows. An important reason for related diversification is the existence of economies of scope. Economies of scope always rest on use of a common production factor. Four such factors have been identified: specialized indivisible physical assets, technological know-how, organizational know-how, and brand names. Economies of scope can be exploited through market arrangements or through organizational arrangements. The actual choice between the two, and thus the choice for related diversification, depends on the transaction costs involved.

9.8.2   Unrelated diversification

Unrelated diversification

As we have argued above, related diversification may be the most efficient way to realize economies of scope. In the case of **unrelated diversification**, economies of scope cannot arise in R&D, production, marketing or distribution. However, as Williamson has submitted, a firm with several unrelated business units (a conglomerate firm) may still have an advantage: it may be more efficient in allocating cash flow to high-yield uses than is the external capital market. If a conglomerate firm adopts an M-form structure, it can realize all the advantages of the M-form (see section 8.6). The general office of such a conglomerate evaluates investment proposals from the business units and allocates cash flow to the most profitable proposals. Thus the general office performs the task of the capital market. In comparison with the capital market, the general office of a conglomerate has two advantages. First, business unit managers are subordinates. The general office can demand much more information than can outside investors. Second, business unit managers will be prepared to share with the general office confidential information that they would not like to give to a large number of external investors. Hence, again, the conglomerate organization arises as a solution to an *information problem*.

The benefits of unrelated diversification must be balanced against the costs. As conglomerates grow larger and older, the general office tends to grow and

Box 9.5 ■ Gillette's product portfolio

Gillette, an American company based in Boston, Massachusetts, has three major product divisions: grooming, portable power and oral care. Grooming includes products for male shaving, such as razors, both manual and electrical, razor blades, shaving preparations and after-shaves. Gillette's grooming business also includes hair removal products for women. Gillette's portable power business consists mainly of Duracell, a company offering alkaline batteries for use in a wide variety of consumer products. Duracell was acquired by Gillette in 1996.

Gillette's oral care products include manual toothbrushes and a variety of oral care appliances sold under the Braun brand name.

At first glance there appears to be little possibility for economies of scope between Gillette's three divisions. If one division, say the grooming business division, has unused manufacturing capacity then it is highly unlikely that this capacity can be used by another division, simply because razor blades, batteries and toothbrushes require highly different manufacturing facilities. Thus specialized indivisible physical assets cannot be the source of economies of scope. The same is true for technological know-how (batteries are quite different from razor blades and toothbrushes), for brand names (batteries are sold under the Duracell brand name, oral appliances under the Braun brand name). It is possible, however, that economies of scope may be obtained by using one sales organization for the products of all three divisions, especially in certain developing countries (Gillette's products are sold in over 200 countries). In this case economies of scope would be based on organizational know-how (local marketing know-how in countries such as China and India).

Gillette's product portfolio may be classified as related (economies of scope from the joint use of marketing and sales operations in certain countries), but then only distantly related.

corporate overhead costs tend to rise. Thus, without substantial economies of scope, the financial performance of conglomerates is, on average, not impressive.[16]

It is not always easy to classify a firm's portfolio as either related or unrelated. Perhaps it is better to speak about the degree of relatedness. As an example consider Gillette's product portfolio described in Box 9.5.

9.9 Horizontal multinationalization

Horizontal
multinationalization

In sections 9.7 and 9.8 we discussed why a firm may extend its portfolio of business units through vertical integration and diversification. A firm can also extend its portfolio through horizontal multinationalization. By **horizontal multinationalization** we mean becoming involved in the same activities in another country. An example is the acquisition of an American truck company by a German truck company.

Consider a firm operating two different plants in two different countries (say the USA and Germany). Suppose, further, that both plants produce the same product (trucks) and that there are no shipments of intermediate goods between the two plants (if there were, we would have the case of vertical integration, which was discussed in section 9.7). Suppose, further, that transportation costs or import duties make it efficient to operate two plants (in the USA and Germany) instead of one. What advantage can be realized by bringing the US plant and the German plant under one managerial hierarchy? Since there are no shipments of intermediate goods or finished products, the reason must be the realization of economies of scale through the joint use of intangible assets. Three types of asset are relevant here:

- technological know-how;
- organizational know-how;
- brand names.

These three types of asset have also been mentioned in the preceding section. There we discussed economies of scope, now we discuss economies of scale. There is a strong similarity between related diversification (which is one way to exploit economies of scope) and horizontal multinationalization (which is one way to exploit economies of scale). For this reason the discussion here resembles closely that of the preceding section.

- *Technological know-how*. As an example suppose that the German firm has an excellent capability for design of aerodynamic trucks. There are two ways in which it can exploit its technological know-how in the USA. It can try to sell this capability to US truck manufacturers or it can acquire a US truck manufacturer and transfer the know-how to the new subsidiary. Hence, again, a market arrangement or an organizational arrangement can be used to exploit the economies of scale from technological know-how. The difficulties involved in trading technological know-how have already been discussed in section 9.8.

- *Organizational know-how*. Suppose a Dutch brewery, such as Heineken, has expert knowledge in the marketing of premium beers. Through horizontal multinationalization this know-how may be applied in other countries. See also section 9.8 for the difficulties involved in selling organizational know-how across markets.
- *Brand names*. Suppose an American hotel chain (Hilton or Sheraton) has invested heavily in developing a brand name. Suppose, further, that the hotel appeals especially to business people who also travel a great deal abroad. Clearly a hotel in Beijing, or New Delhi, or Amsterdam would be in a better position to attract American business people if it can use the Hilton brand name. Hilton now has three alternatives: it can start its own hotels in other countries (or buy existing ones), it can sell the Hilton brand name once and for all, or it can use franchising.

  Suppose Hilton wants to continue to use the Hilton name in the USA but decides to sell the right to use the Hilton brand name in the Netherlands once and for all to a Dutch firm. For Hilton this would entail a big risk: the Dutch firm may, after the sale, behave opportunistically by charging high prices (customers would book because of the Hilton name) and not delivering quality. The American Hilton hotels would in time be hurt because the value of the brand name would decline owing to the opportunistic behaviour of the Dutch firm. Franchising, however, is a feasible alternative. Through franchising, the Dutch firm acquires the right to use the Hilton name for a limited period of time only. The franchisor (the American Hilton) has the right to inspect the franchisee's (the Dutch) hotel during this period. If the franchisee does not comply with specified quality standards, he loses the right to use the Hilton name in the next period. Of course, instead of franchising, horizontal multinationalization is a feasible alternative for Hilton.

By way of summary we may state that three types of intangible asset (technological know-how, organizational know-how, and brand names) may lead to economies of scale when used outside the firm's home country. In principle, both market arrangements and organizational arrangements may be used to realize these benefits. The actual choice depends on the transaction costs of these arrangements.

9.10 Summary: how economic analysis can contribute to the formulation of competitive and corporate strategies

In a multibusiness firm there are two levels of strategy: at the business and at the corporate levels. Each business unit needs to have a competitive strategy that specifies how that business intends to compete in its given industry. At the corporate level there is a need for a strategy that specifies where – that is, in which industries and in which countries – the company intends to compete.

If a firm or a business unit wants to formulate a competitive strategy it should first analyze its environment and assess its strengths and weaknesses. Porter's five-forces model, which is based on the results of several studies in the tradition of the structure–conduct–performance paradigm, has proved to be a useful tool for assessing the attractiveness of the industry in which the firm operates. The concept of strategic groups provides a foundation for analyzing differences in performance between companies (or business units) belonging to the same industry. This gives the strategic planner a tool with which to assess a business unit's strengths and weaknesses.

In formulating a competitive strategy the firm has many options. The options that are available depend on the industry and on the firm's position within that industry. However, two successful strategies – those of cost leadership and of product differentiation – have been identified in many industries. Any firm should at least consider these so-called generic competitive strategies.

In formulating a competitive strategy a firm should take into account how its competitors will react. This is true especially in an oligopolistic industry – that is, an industry consisting of a few large companies. For example, when Philips decides to develop a new product standard for a digital videodisc it has to take into account how its competitors (Sony and Matsushita, among others) will react. Game theory, discussed in Chapter 5, can help in this respect. The game of selling icecream on a beach shows (1) how companies can try to prevent entry by other firms by offering several competing brands, and (2) that by making a credible commitment to an industry a company can discourage other firms from entering that industry.

At the corporate level, the firm needs to decide in which industries and in which countries it wants to operate. There are three ways in which a firm can extend its scope: vertical integration, diversification, and horizontal expansion.

Vertical integration means that the firm moves into activities that were previously performed by its suppliers or its customers. Transaction cost economics, discussed in Chapter 8, can usefully be employed to analyze when it will pay to integrate vertically. The important dimensions of transactions to be included in the analysis are asset specificity and uncertainty/complexity. Two polar cases stand out: if asset specificity is low and uncertainty/complexity is also low, then spot contracts are efficient. Vertical integration is not warranted in this case. If asset specificity is high and uncertainty/complexity is also high, then vertical integration is desirable.

Diversification means that the firm enters another industry. Diversification may be related or unrelated. Related diversification occurs when the new business is related to the firm's existing business. Through related diversification the firm may realize economies of scope. Economies of scope arise when the joint production of two products is less costly than the production of each product separately. This may occur when the firm can use one input factor in producing two different products. When it is difficult or impossible to sell the services of those input factors on the market for input factors, related diversification is an efficient way to realize the economies of scope. Examples of input factors that may lead to economies of scope and that are also difficult to trade are specialized machinery, technological know-how, organizational know-how, and brand names. A firm that has these types of input factor and that sees an opportunity to employ them in another industry may be well advised to take this opportunity. This will then lead to related diversification.

Unrelated diversification occurs when there is no relation between the new business and the firm's existing business(es). A firm engaging in unrelated diversification cannot hope to realize economies of scope. However, it may reap the benefits of an internal capital market. An internal capital market can be more efficient than the external capital market in allocating cash flows. This advantage should be weighed against the costs of corporate overhead.

Horizontal expansion occurs when the firm extends its activities within the same industry. When in doing so it crosses national borders, it engages in horizontal multinationalization. A firm operating plants that produce the same products in different countries may realize economies of scale if those plants share the use of intangible assets such as technological know-how, organizational know-how, and brand names. Since these intangible assets are generally difficult to sell across markets, horizontal multinationalization may be the only way to capture these benefits.

Questions

1 Consider an industry that you know well, for example the industry consisting of the bars in the town where you live. Use Porter's model of the forces driving industry competition to describe the intensity of competition in that industry.

2 You are managing director of a small, young electronics firm. One of your engineers has developed a specialized kind of memory chip. This new chip can be manufactured in either of two ways: by buying highly specialized equipment or by buying less specialized equipment. The specialized equipment can be used only to produce the new chip. The less specialized equipment can be used to produce the new chip but could, with a minor additional investment, also be used to produce a variety of other chips. Demand for the new chip is highly uncertain. The new chip could turn out to be a bestseller or a complete failure in the market. Also uncertain is whether other firms are already working on the development of a similar chip. You know that it is impossible to protect the new chip by patents.

Do you see an advantage in buying the specialized equipment? Assume that the amount to be invested and unit cost for the specialized equipment are the same as for the less specialized equipment.

3 Electricité de France (EDF) is the French state-owned power utility. Although its main source of energy is nuclear power, it also generates electricity from coal. For this purpose it has several riverside-based power plants fuelled by coal. Most plants use coal from France, delivered by rail, but also coal imported from overseas. Demand for coal for each power plant is very stable. Imported coal is delivered to these power plants by barges. In France there are three rivers that can be used by these barges: Loire, Seine and Rhône. These rivers differ considerably in depth and sluice size. Two types of barge can be used to transport coal on

these rivers: general-purpose barges that can be used to transport a variety of goods and can be used on all rivers, and special barges that can be used to transport coal only and can be used on one river only. These special barges are adapted to the circumstances of one particular river. Moreover these special barges require special unloading facilities that have been built by EDF. These special barges are much more efficient than general-purpose barges as they use the depth and sluice size of each river to the maximum.

Coal is imported into France by independent suppliers. On each river there is only one supplier. Although EDF is state-owned it is driven very much by efficiency considerations.

(a) Do you think that general-purpose barges will be used to a great extent or that most of the coal will be transported by special barges?

(b) Suppose first that general-purpose barges are used: do you think it is important who owns the barges? Suppose the supplier owns the barges: do you expect long-term contracts or short-term contracts between EDF and the supplier in question?

(c) Now suppose that special barges are used, do you think it is important who owns the barges? Suppose the supplier owns the barges: do you expect long-term contracts or short-term contracts between EDF and the supplier in question?

4 Norwegian salmon is farmed all along the Norwegian coast by fish farmers. They sell their fish mainly to exporters, who sell the fish fresh to importers in the UK, Germany, France, Spain, the USA and Japan. Because of the cold and pure water along the Norwegian coast, and strict quality standards at all levels of the industry, Norwegian salmon is a high-quality product. Given its high quality, most of the fresh salmon ends up in gourmet restaurants. The duration of the relationship between the Norwegian exporters and the importers varies from one occasional transaction to several years. In your opinion, which factors determine the duration of these relationships?

5 Box 9.4 describes how Tesco, Britain's largest food retailer, successfully entered the Internet-based food retailing business, while companies such as Webvan failed. What explains the superiority of Tesco's business model? Do you see potential economies of scope between traditional food retailing and Internet-based food retailing? Which production factors will probably lead to economies of scope in this case?

6 During the last two decades the big global auditing firms (firms such as KPMG, PricewaterhouseCoopers, and Ernst&Young) have diversified into areas such as consulting, IT services, legal advice and headhunting (also called executive recruiting). The reasons for this were discussed in an article in *The Economist* (7 July 2001). According to *The Economist* the auditing firms themselves see two reasons for transforming into professional-service conglomerates.

The first reason is risk reduction. The risk that auditors worry most about today is the risk of being sued. Expensive settlements of shareholder lawsuits are increasing. According to *The Economist* the best way to reduce this risk is not to offer more services, but to seek incorporation as a limited liability company.

The second reason given by professional service firms, according to *The Economist,* is that their corporate clients want it. Again *The Economist* is sceptical: many large global businesses use several different consulting firms.

The Economist suggests a third reason: networking: 'In professional-service conglomerates, old-fashioned networking is a powerful influence on business. The addition of legal (and other) services to the big firms' menu of offerings will expand their networking potential considerably. At a time when there is downward pressure on fees for professional services of all kinds, that could help explain their enthusiasm for diversification.'

Compare these three reasons with the logic underlying related and unrelated diversification as given in the text. On the basis of this, can you come up with a list of other possible reasons? In order to be able to get an idea of the relevance of those reasons, what kind of additional information would you need?

Suggested further reading

Barney, J.B. (1997), *Gaining and Sustaining Competitive Advantage*, Reading, MA: Addison-Wesley.

Hill, C.W. and G.R. Jones (1995), *Strategic Management Theory, An Integrated Approach*, Boston: Houghton Mifflin.

Kay, J. (1993), *Foundations for Corporate Success: How Business Strategies Add Value*, Oxford: Oxford University Press.

Porter, M.E. (1980), *Competitive Strategy: Techniques for Analyzing Industries and Competitors*, New York: Free Press.

Porter, M.E. (1985), *Competitive Advantage: Creating and Sustaining Superior Performance*, New York: Free Press.

Notes

1. The term 'strategy' may be used in a normative or in a descriptive sense. If we say that a competitive strategy specifies how the business unit's managers should compete in a given industry, we use the term in a normative sense. We can also say that a competitive strategy specifies how the business unit's managers actually compete in a given industry. We then use the term in a descriptive sense.
2. In terms used by Mintzberg, strategic planning is directed towards the formulation of a *deliberate* strategy that the firm intends to pursue and implement. In addition, firms have *emergent* strategies: patterns of strategic behaviour that develop over time in the absence of, or even in spite of, deliberate intentions. See Mintzberg and Quinn (1991).
3. If you are interested in this issue, see, for example, Mintzberg and Quinn (1991).
4. For a detailed discussion of Porter's five-forces model see Porter (1985), chapter 1.
5. The concept of organizational routines has been introduced by Nelson and Winter (1982). See section 10.5 for an exposition of this concept.
6. Porter (1980), chapter 2, and Porter (1985), chapters 3 and 4.
7. This, however, would leave hardly any room on the beach for customers, so this does not seem a very practical strategy.

8. If Mrs Orange's stand is x metres to the left of Mr Sun's stand, then Mrs Orange's gross margin (the shaded area around her stand in Figure 9.6 (c)) is

$$120 + \frac{1}{2}x - \frac{5}{8} \times \frac{x^2}{240}$$

This expression reaches its maximum value for $x = 96$. Its value is then 144.

9. For a further discussion of strategic commitment, see Ghemawat (1991).

10. Our model of icecream stands on a beach is a very simple model of spatial competition. In our model price is not a decision variable, since we assumed that price was determined by the municipality. In more general models, demand depends both on distance and on price. Firms then have two decision variables: location and price. See, for example, Rasmusen (1989, pp. 269–73), Hotelling (1929), or d'Aspremont *et al.* (1979).

11. Williamson, (1975), section 5.1.1. See also Box 8.3 in Chapter 8.

12. Another solution may be to have the automobile company own the specialized tooling. Then, however, the automobile company has to invest in transaction-specific assets, which makes it vulnerable to opportunistic behaviour by the component manufacturer. This problem may be mitigated, however, if the automobile company can transfer the assets to another component manufacturer. For a further discussion of this issue see Masten *et al.* (1989).

13. The term contingent claims contract was introduced in section 4.1.

14. This can be expressed more accurately in a mathematical formula. Let $c(x_1, x_2)$ be the cost of producing x_1 units of good 1 and x_2 units of good 2. Economies of scope exist if and only if

$$c(x_1, x_2) < c(x_1, 0) + c(0, x_2) \text{ for all positive } x_1 \text{ and } x_2$$

15. We have borrowed this example from Teece (1980).

16. See, for example, Rumelt (1974, p.94) and Goold *et al.* (1994).

10 Evolutionary approaches to organizations

10.1 Introduction

While the preceding chapters dealt mainly with the explanation of current organizational forms, the perspective now shifts to the *development* of organizational forms over time. In economic terms we shift from a static to a dynamic perspective. In organization theory such dynamic, developmental perspectives are usually called *evolutionary*. A biological example (the long necks of giraffes) introduces the perspective in the next section. Then we move on to consider the usefulness of evolutionary ideas in explaining organizational phenomena. Two examples of evolutionary approaches represent the core of the chapter. One of these approaches is decidedly economic in nature; the other is presented as sociological. This demonstrates that the evolutionary perspective transcends the boundaries of several scientific disciplines, and it has the potential to integrate the contributions of various disciplines to the study of particular organizational phenomena. This potential is outlined in the final section.

10.2 Giraffes

Our biological example is a famous one: why do giraffes have such long necks? This simple question allows us to separate evolutionary and creationist arguments and, within the evolutionary strand, Darwinist and Lamarckian arguments.

The creationist answer to the question of why giraffes have such long necks is quite straightforward: because they were made that way. *Creationist* arguments involve deliberate design. Giraffes were designed with long necks. This characteristic allowed them to survive among other species. Only giraffes could reach for the leaves at the top of trees. This monopoly among the leaf-eating species guaranteed them a continuing food supply. Evolutionary arguments, on the other hand, emphasize **cumulative adaptation**. Giraffes were not designed with long necks, but gradually acquired them. This was a process involving many generations of giraffes. The evolutionary process consists in small steps that over time may make a large difference. Moreover, evolutionists argue that the cumulative effect of these changes over time amounts to adaptation of the species to its environment. It is a particular type of adaptation to its environ-

Cumulative adaptation

ment that allows a species to survive in the competition with other species. Giraffes can survive because they occupy the 'niche' of 'high leaf eaters'. In this niche there is hardly any competition from other species.

Within the evolutionary perspective, there are several explanations that account for the process of cumulative adaptation. One explanation can be traced to Lamarck, another to Darwin.[1] The **Lamarckian explanation** is based on two principles: the inheritance of acquired characteristics, and the principle of use and disuse. The **principle of use and disuse** states that those parts of an organism's body that are used grow larger. Those parts that are not used tend to wither away. For individual giraffes, this principle would translate into a lengthening of the neck through continuous striving for higher leaves. However, the second Lamarckian principle takes care of the intergenerational effect. Characteristics acquired by individuals can be inherited by future generations. The longer necks acquired by father and mother giraffes can be passed on to their offspring. Each generation thus ends up with a slightly longer neck than its predecessor, and passes this on to the next generation. This evolutionary advancement continues until giraffes can reach the highest leaves.

Lamarckian explanation

Principle of use and disuse

The **Darwinian explanation**, on the other hand, emphasizes the role of cumulative **natural selection**. A Darwinist explains the giraffe's long neck as the result of the cumulative selection, step by step, over many generations, of small mutations (or variations) in giraffe genes. Consider a stage in the development where giraffes have medium/long necks. They can reach halfway up the tallest trees. At that stage, all kinds of small mutations in the genes of that generation of giraffes occur. Only one or a few of these mutations cause longer necks. The giraffes that embody this mutation have better survival chances in the environment (other things being equal) – they can reach just a bit higher for their food. Put differently, given competition for food resources, the environment will tend to select giraffes with longer necks. The reason is that the selected animals are better adapted to their environment. Over time, mutations that cause longer necks will be increasingly passed on in the gene pool of the giraffe species. Hence, while the individual mutation is a chance process, the cumulative selection is not. Over generations of giraffes, natural selection will favour the growth of necks and will cause a better adaptation of the species to its environment. Individual (chance) **variations**, natural **selection** as a result of environmental conditions, and **retention** (in the gene pool) of the adaptive characteristics thus form the causal chain of the Darwinist explanation.

Darwinian explanation

Natural selection

Variation

Selection

Retention

Why bother with giraffes in a book on organizations? The reason is that such a biological example serves as a useful analogy for contemplating possible explanations for the evolution of organizational forms. In the next section we consider to what extent biological explanations can be transposed to the organizational field. To conclude this section it should be emphasized that, while the analogy is useful, there is no reason to expect that it is perfect. In biology, the Darwinist explanation appears to have the best scientific credentials (although not everyone is convinced – see Box 10.1).[2] However, organizations are different beasts from the species examined by biologists. Perhaps creationist or Lamarckian arguments (or still other explanations) should carry

Box 10.1 ■ Darwin in Germany

Darwin published his evolution theory in *On the Origin of Species* in 1859. One of its implications is that humans descended from apes. This implication has been hard to accept by people all over the world, and some incredulity remains even today:

In spite of the theory of evolution set out by Charles Darwin nearly 150 years ago, one in five Germans remains unconvinced that humans descended from apes. At least, that was the finding of the Allensbach Institute for Opinion Research, which surveyed a test group of 1,112 Germans earlier this year: 62 per cent of the group said that they believed that apes and humans shared common ancestors, while 21 per cent said that they did not believe this; 17 per cent did not know.

Age seems to affect whether or not people believe in evolution: 29 per cent of Germans over 45 do not accept Darwin's ideas, compared with 14 per cent of the under-45s. Overall, however, the percentage of those believing in evolution is increasing: a similar survey made in 1970 found that 40 per cent disagreed with Darwin.

Source: Holland Herald, August 1996

greater weight in the organizational field. Indeed, we shall see that competing explanations currently run neck and neck.

10.3 Organizations and giraffes

First of all, let us repeat that we are now dealing with a different set of questions from those in the previous chapters. We are now interested in explanations of the development of organizational forms over time. Of course, we may take as a starting point the question of why we observe so many different organizational forms in the present.[3] However, the explanation of current forms will necessarily involve arguments that address their development over time, if we are to regard them as dynamic or evolutionary. Second, the analysis now explicitly deals with populations of organizational forms (our equivalent of biological species). It is not the individual organization in which we are interested, it is the class of similar organizational forms. Third, the development of organizational forms is not analyzed in isolation from the environments in which the organizations operate. Environmental selection plays a prominent role in both of the evolutionary approaches outlined in the following sections.

What use can we make of our biological analogies? What are some obvious differences and similarities between organizational forms and biological species? We briefly discuss one cluster of differences and one cluster of similarities. The

Human constructs   differences relate to the fact that organizations are **human constructs**. To denote organizations as human constructs has two kinds of implication. The first is that organizations are created and constructed by human actors. Entrepreneurs create small firms; governments create their agencies; managements regularly redesign the organization; and human decision-makers are similarly involved in the merger or discontinuance of organizations. Giraffes cannot (re)design themselves. Organizations are, to some extent at least, purposively created and designed. Of course, they often turn out different from how they were originally intended – organizations can lead a life of their own, to continue the biological analogy – but the element of purposive human behaviour and of rational construction is always there (Scott, 1992). This means that creationist arguments, emphasizing purposive design, will probably play a greater role in the organizational field.

The second implication follows from the term 'construct'. Organizations are not only constructed in the real sense of deliberate design, they are also constructs in the more philosophical sense that they are products of human mental activity. This can perhaps be best illustrated with the anecdote of the three baseball umpires being interviewed on how they call balls and strikes. They answered as follows:

- The first: I call them as they are.
- The second: I call them as I see them.
- The third: They are nothing until I call them.

The first umpire assumes that there are balls and strikes 'out there' and that he sorts them out correctly. The second acknowledges that there may be a difference between reality and his perception or his judgement. The third shows that it is nothing but his judgement that makes them into balls and strikes. The third is right, of course, in the sense that baseball rules dictate that it is only his judgement that counts. In philosophical terms the first umpire is a realist, the third an idealist or constructionist. In the constructionist view, reality has to be constructed through human mental activity.

What about organizations and giraffes? Without delving too much into philosophical issues it may be said that many organizational theorists would regard organizations as much more constructional in nature than giraffes. Consider the questions:

- What do organizations/giraffes consist of?
- What are the boundaries of organizations/giraffes?

There is more room for differences in judgement about organizations than about giraffes. Organizations are much less 'out there': we have first to construct them in our minds before we find them. This delicate philosophical point has important consequences. One of those consequences is that it is harder to agree on the delineation of organizational forms than of biological species. Another consequence is that it is much less clear what exactly is being 'selected', 'reproduced' in the next generations, etc. There is room for choice, and the choices made will depend partly on who makes them. The two approaches discussed later in this chapter also take different viewpoints here.

The cluster of similarities evolves from the recognition (1) that organizations, whatever they are, have environments, and (2) that environments will play a role in explaining the development of organizational forms. In some of the previous chapters we examined organizational phenomena without much reference to the environmental context. Agency relationships, for instance, are analyzed rather 'context-free'. In transaction cost analysis the environment is represented in two variables: uncertainty/complexity and small numbers exchange. In industrial economics and strategy, the environment begins to play a more prominent and complex role. This role is extended in the present chapter. It is extended in two ways. First, we explicitly analyze the development of organizational forms, rather than the development of individual firms (as in most of the strategy literature). Second, the concept of the environment is broader. It includes any dimension of the environment that may influence selection processes. These dimensions are not only economic in nature, but may also be social, political, cultural, or institutional. As we shall see, the concept of legitimacy of an organizational form is important in the next section.

By using the biological analogy, our attention is directed towards selection processes rather than adaptation processes. Most organizational theory focuses on the adaptation of individual organizations to environmental circumstances and change. Yet it cannot be denied that selection processes are important too. There is such a thing as organizational mortality. Organizations go bankrupt, are abandoned by their members, or cease to exist in other ways (e.g. prohibition). Organizational forms also have their lifecycles: new forms come into being (often as a result of new technology), old forms die. In many professions and industries the medieval guilds gave way to more modern forms of organization. So there is no question that selection, birth and death, replacement and other such phenomena are important objects of organizational study as well. The approaches to be outlined in the following sections illustrate the usefulness of the biological analogy.

10.4 Organizational ecology

Organizational ecology

The first approach is labelled *population ecology* or, more appropriately, **organizational ecology**. It has been elaborated by a relatively small number of authors over the past decade, foremost among whom are Michael T. Hannan and John Freeman.[4] In the exposition that follows, their work will feature most prominently. Hannan and Freeman present their work as sociological. However, as will become clear, their approach uses economic concepts such as competition, and is often likened to economic analysis.[5] We, too, believe that this approach intersects with economic analysis and can be fruitfully integrated with it (see section 10.6). Hence it is included in this overview of economic approaches to organizations.

Organizational ecology distinguishes between three levels of complexity of the analysis. The first level deals with the *demography* of organizations. At this level, various rates of change in organizational populations are the central interest. Foremost are founding rates and mortality rates. The next level concerns the *population ecology* of organizations, and attempts to link vital rates between populations. How are the founding and mortality rates of organizational populations interlinked? The third level is the *community ecology* of organizations. At this level the central question is how the links between and among populations affect the likelihood of persistence of the community as a whole. It is fair to say that much of the work done so far concerns the first (demographic) level. Some studies are located at the second level, for instance the studies comparing the survival rates of generalist and specialist restaurants in different environmental situations.[6] Hardly any studies could aspire to be located at the third level of analysis.

Ecological studies use data on individual organizations. These data are used, however, to analyze developments at the population level. Ecologists are not so much interested in explaining the founding, growth, decline and death of individual organizations as wanting to find out what the aggregate rates are at the population level. We therefore need a definition of populations and a procedure to separate one population of organizational forms from the other. For biologists the main criterion to distinguish populations of different species is interbreeding. A biological species is a collection of forms that can interbreed – that is, constitute a gene pool. No such operational definition exists for organizational analysis. An analogy to interbreeding is probably not very useful, since we observe mergers and joint ventures between all sorts of firms in the real world. And what should we do, for example, with conglomerate firms? Theoretically, this is a difficult issue.[7] In practice, most ecological studies focus on populations that are readily acceptable as distinct, such as newspapers, restaurants and labour unions. As working definitions (adopted from Carroll and Hannan, 1995) we can say that an **organizational form** summarizes the core properties that make a set of organizations ecologically similar. Thus organizations with the same form depend in a common way on the material and social environment. A set of organizations possesses the same form in this sense if environmental changes affect them similarly. An **organizational population**, then, consists of the set of organizations with a specific form within a particular time and space. A public bureaucracy and an investment bank are examples of organizational forms. The set of public bureaucracies in Japan from 1946 to 1997 and the set of investment banks in the USA during the same period are examples of interesting organizational populations.

An important assumption in organizational ecology is that organizations are characterized by **relative inertia**. They are rather slow to respond to changes in their environment. It is not claimed that organizations never change; rather it is argued that, if radical change is required, organizations are hard pressed to implement it. Such changes are infrequent, subject to serious delays, and often unsuccessful. Therefore organizations tend to be inert, relative to changes in the environment. This is an important assumption since it separates organizational ecology from many other organizational approaches that emphasize adaptability. Below we explore the assumptions that form the basis of organizational ecology and indicate how the assumption of relative inertia fits into this foundation.

Why are organizations assumed to be inert? In most of the approaches discussed so far, efficiency arguments are used. Efficiency drives organizations to change or else they are replaced by more efficient organizations. Hannan and Freeman take a different route. They argue that organizations have different competences. The first of these is **reliability**. Theoretically, organizational products and services could often be produced by *ad hoc* groups of skilled work-

Organizational form

Organizational population

Relative inertia

Reliability

ers just as well. Compared with such *ad hoc* groups, however, organizations will tend to produce more reliably: that is to say, with less variance in the quality of performance, including its timeliness. Given uncertainty about the future, potential members, investors and clients might value reliability more than efficiency. That is, they may be willing to pay a relatively high price for the certainty that a product or service of a minimum quality will be available when needed. Therefore they transact with organizations. Within organizations, **Routines**   **routines** develop that direct the activities. Such routines can be retained within organizations, but not in *ad hoc* groups of varying composition. The routines play an important role in ensuring the reliability of performance.[8] To empathize with this argument, imagine yourself as a businessperson travelling to an unfamiliar country and needing a rented car. Would you book your car with an international chain (such as Avis or Hertz) or with a local individual who makes you an offer through the mail? Indeed, international hotel chains, car rental agencies and financial services may thrive more as a result of our need for reliable services than as a result of their being the low-cost alternative in any specific case.[9]

Accountability   Organizations are not only more reliable than *ad hoc* groups, but they can also be held accountable more easily. **Accountability** is an important property in the modern world. Sociologists argue that norms of (procedural) rationality are pervasive. Decisions and actions must be explained in rational terms. For instance, investors expect reasonable and consistent accounts of the allocation of resources. The profession of accountants arose in response to such desires. Employees demand rational explanations of hiring and firing practices, and will evaluate these explanations against widely held social standards (such as equal opportunity). Consumers demand rational justifications of product performance. This can be most clearly seen in the case of litigation: if taken to court on product liability, producers must be able to argue their case convincingly based on full documentation of procedures, decisions, and actions. Hannan and Freeman argue that organizations can produce such rational accounts of their decisions and actions more readily than can *ad hoc* groups. An important factor is the existence of appropriate rules and procedures within organizations. Just like the production routines, such rules and procedures are also more easily developed and retained within organizations than within other collectives (such as *ad hoc* groups). The plethora of information that they collect and file means that they can document how resources have been used and can reconstruct the sequences of decisions, rules and actions that produced an outcome. In a world that increasingly demands procedural rationality, this accountability gives organizations an advantage over *ad hoc* groups.

Hannan and Freeman summarize the present stage of the argument as follows:[10]

> The modern world favors collective actors that can demonstrate or at least reasonably claim a capacity for reliable performance and can account rationally for their actions. So it favors organizations over other kinds of collectives and favors certain kinds of organizations over others, since not all organizations have these properties in equal measure. Selection within organizational populations tends

Box 10.2 ■ Reproducibility in the ING Group

The ING Group is a large banking and insurance group with its roots in the Netherlands. It was one of the first corporations to combine banking and insurance (*bancassurance*) in one group on a large scale. It globally employs more than 100,000 people. It is well known for its Internet daughter ING Direct. Below are excerpts from an interview with one of its board members, Alexander Rinnooy Kan:

Our activities are characterized by very high process requirements in terms of reproducibility and documentation. That is true globally, across all distribution channels and across the full range of financial products. Regulatory bodies also require this, both on the banking and on the insurance side. Those tight process requirements are a necessary condition to be active in this sector. They are not easily compatible with an environment that is primarily focused on creativity, flexibility, and improvization. In the financial world, today's whim is not tomorrow's product.

We may not lose sight of which products the ING Group offers. Concepts such as trust, predictability and solidity are crucial. Particularly in the current hectic environment, people need dependability of financial services. Look what happens when electronic banking [*initially*[11]] turns out to be less reliable than everybody thought. We therefore have the task to retain that trust, also in times of turbulent change. It is an important part of the value we can add. That is only possible by meticulously safeguarding the quality of all processes enabling our services. This requires a tight organization.

Source: *Management Scope*, October 2000 (translated by authors)

---

to eliminate organizations with low reliability and accountability . . . Thus we assume that selection in populations of organizations in modern societies favors forms with high reliability of performance and high levels of accountability.

From this summary to the conclusion that organizations exhibit high levels of inertia requires one more step. That step is the recognition that organizational reliability and accountability require that organizational structures are highly **reproducible**. The routines, rules and procedures that determine reliability and accountability must stay in place. The organizational structure – the structure of roles, authority, and communication – must therefore be very much the same today as it was yesterday. That is to say, it must be reproducible from day to day. Indeed, it will be (very nearly) reproduced from day to day to ensure reliability and accountability. As one executive of a large financial services company put it (Box 10.2), this requires a tight organization.

Reproducible

Selection pressures will work in this direction. The conclusion that organizational structures will be (very nearly) reproduced is equivalent to saying that they will be (relatively) highly *inert*. Selection pressures will thus favour organizations whose structures have high inertia. Structural inertia, according to Hannan and Freeman's argument, is a *consequence* of selection rather than a precondition.

The preceding argument can be represented diagrammatically to show the interrelationships between the various basic assumptions (Figure 10.1).

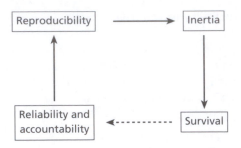

Figure 10.1   **Interrelationships between the four basic assumptions**
Source: derived from Young (1988)

We shall not attempt to spell out the entire theoretical structure that is built on these basic assumptions of organizational ecology. Rather, we shall move on to some of the more solid empirical results. These apply to the founding and death rates within organizational populations. Specifically, the ecological perspective has convincingly shown that these vital rates are dependent on the density of the population. Below, we first focus on the theoretical reasoning underlying the empirical work, and then summarize some results.

What determines the size of an organizational population? In other words, how many individual organizations do we expect to find within a certain population? The answer depends on various factors. First of all, we have to know **Niche** in what environmental **niche** the population resides. A niche expresses the population's way of earning a living, its role and function in a community.[12] **Carrying capacity** The niche is assumed to have a particular **carrying capacity**. There are social and material limits to the extent to which we need particular roles and functions to be performed in society. There is only so much 'written news' we can absorb, for instance. As a consequence, the environment will allow only a certain volume of newspapers. This volume can, however, be filled by a few large newspapers or by many small ones. The carrying capacity of an environmental niche thus only represents an upper bound on the aggregate levels of activity performed by a certain organizational form.

The actual number of organizations inhabiting a certain niche will then depend on the founding rate, the mortality rate, and the merger rate over time. Assume, for instance, that we observe a particular population that remains constant in number over a certain period of time (Figure 10.2). How can this phenomenon be explained? If we were dealing with biological populations, there would be two answers:

- Over that period of time, the population consisted of exactly the same individuals.
- The birth rate equalled the death rate.

For organizational populations the second explanation would remain valid in the absence of mergers. Otherwise, it should be amended to read:

- The birth rate equalled the death rate + merger rate.

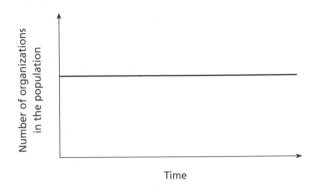

Figure 10.2   **A hypothetical population over time**

In addition, the interpretation of the term 'birth rate' has to be slightly changed for organizations. It includes not only new foundings but also migrations of organizations into the population. Animals cannot change population, but organizations can. For example, the 3M Corporation was originally called the Minnesota Mining and Manufacturing Company. Whereas mining was its initial activity, now it is strong in the bonding and coating business. By changing its major activities, it can be said to have migrated to a new population.

How do *actual* organizational populations develop over time? Hannan and Freeman argue that two forces mainly account for actual developments: *competition* and *legitimation*. These two forces will both affect the **density of the population** (the number of organizations in the population), but they have opposite effects. The force of competition is, of course, familiar to economists. If resources within the niche are scarce, there will be competition within the population for these resources. Moreover, there may be competition between populations. Think of the competition between all sorts of shops and stores for the best locations in shopping areas.

Density of the population

The force of **legitimation** is less familiar to economists; it is a sociological concept. Basically, it refers to the social 'acceptance' of the organizational form. New forms have a low legitimacy. As they perform reliably and accountably over time, they may acquire a higher legitimacy. However, if they do not conform to social norms over time, they may not acquire the legitimacy that is necessary to survive.

Legitimation

Roughly, organizational ecology assumes that both legitimacy and competition increase with the age of the organizational form. As stated above, a new form has a low legitimacy. It has to acquire it over time. As the form acquires legitimacy, it becomes easier to found organizations of that form. In addition to increasing legitimacy, a variety of other factors may contribute to the self-reinforcement (or positive feedback) of the early growth of an industry.[13] These factors include changes in consumer tastes and habits, the development of markets, collective gains in efficiency from learning-by-doing, and the emergence of supporting institutions. Hence we expect the founding rates to increase with the age of the form (at least initially). On the other hand, competition will increase too. As more organizations come to inhabit the niche, competition within the population will increase. Competition will have a negative effect on founding rates. It will be harder to found a new organization or to migrate into a more competitive environment.

In the language of organizational ecology the vital rates of an organizational population – the rates of founding and mortality – are *density dependent*. Legitimacy processes produce positive density dependence in *founding rates* and competition produces negative density dependence. By similar reasoning it is assumed that the *mortality rate* is high at first (owing to insufficient legitimacy, **Liability of newness** there is a '**liability of newness**'), then falls with increasing density up to a point (the neighbourhood of the carrying capacity), and then rises with increasing density (owing to competitive effects). All in all, then, organizational ecology expects:

- the relationship between density and mortality rates to have a U-shape;
- the relationship between density and founding rates to have an inverted U-shape.

The empirical work that has been done to date has largely borne out these expectations (see Carroll and Hannan, 1995). The observed densities of organizational populations produce a figure like Figure 10.3. While this charts the number of newspapers in the San Francisco Bay area, such graphs have been produced for other newspaper populations, unions, and restaurants, for example. The organizational ecology approach has given us empirical insight into the density dependence of founding and mortality rates. It has, therefore, also given us an approximation of 'typical' developments of populations over time.

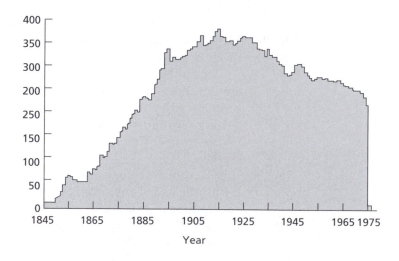

Figure 10.3 **Density of newspaper publishing firms by year (1845–1975) in the San Francisco Bay area**
Source: Hannan and Freeman, 1989a, p.239

These results are encouraging.[14] In the following sections they are compared with another evolutionary approach, developed by the economists Nelson and Winter.

10.5 An evolutionary theory of economic change

In their book *An Evolutionary Theory of Economic Change* (1982) the economists Richard Nelson and Sidney Winter outline another evolutionary perspective. This perspective shares a number of features with organizational ecology, including:

- an emphasis on organizational routines and on limits to organizational adaptability;
- the population or system level of analysis;
- the importance of environmental selection.

Nelson and Winter's theory is different from Hannan and Freeman's in several respects as well. One important difference is that Nelson and Winter attempt to provide an alternative to what they label orthodox economic theory. With this label they refer to standard micro- and macroeconomic theory and, specifically, to the standard concepts of maximizing behaviour by firms and equilibrium outcomes in markets. Instead, their alternative view stresses *routine* behaviour by firms and *development* of economic systems. Nelson and Winter provide an alternative 'microfoundation' of macroeconomics. Their models show, for instance, the effects of technological change on macroeconomic growth. In this section we concentrate on the main features of their microfoundation: their modelling of firm behaviour and of the selection process. This allows us to compare the two evolutionary approaches in section 10.6.

Nelson and Winter conceive of organizations as being typically much better at the tasks of self-maintenance in a constant environment than they are at major change, and much better at changing in the direction of 'more of the same' than they are at any other kind of change. Their primary concept to
Routines   denote organizational functioning is routines. **Routines** refer to all regular and predictable behaviour patterns of firms. There are production routines, advertising routines, hiring and firing routines and strategic routines. Routines rather than deliberate choice determine for a large part how an organization functions. Routines explain why organizations are resistant to change. Routines are the organizational analogue of biological genes. In 'organizational genetics' routines are selected by the environment. Let us examine how these ideas are introduced and developed.

Organizational routines may be understood by comparison to individual
Skills   **skills**, such as riding a bicycle, playing tennis, or operating a computer. Such skills have two features in common. First, they require exercise. It is not enough to read how to ride a bike, it must be practised; learning by doing is involved. At the outset the learning is very conscious. Every detail of the performance is observed. During practice, however, the conscious attention to the

Box 10.3 ■ Tacit knowledge

Michael Polanyi (1962, 1967) developed the concept of 'tacit knowledge'. The importance of tacit knowledge is nowadays widely recognized, as can be seen from the following excerpt from the magazine published by the consultancy company Arthur D. Little:

When Banc One decided to grow through acquisitions, its learning challenge was at the *process* level: how to create a particularly effective process for making many successful acquisitions – identifying, acquiring, and integrating companies that would be a good strategic, operational, and cultural fit.

When Mercedes-Benz opened a new factory to produce its cars in India, the Indian organization needed to learn at the *procedures* level: to acquire and use explicit knowledge from Mercedes to produce Mercedes cars.

The distinction between process and procedure is essential. Procedures contain only *explicit* knowledge. Processes embed procedures in *tacit* knowledge of both the expert and the social kinds. Many of the problems of re-engineering can be traced to the treatment of processes as though they were procedures – i.e. as though people's tacit knowledge didn't matter.

Source: Nayak *et al.* (1995)

performance is gradually transformed into a behaviour programme. Riding a bike becomes a capability that can be exercised automatically. Individual skills, like organizational routines, can be usefully regarded as such automatic behaviour programmes. Second, it is ordinarily very difficult to fully articulate the programme. It is, for example, impossible for most people to express fully in words how to ride a bike. There is **tacit knowledge** involved (see Box 10.3). Similarly, it is often impossible in organizations to explain fully particular behaviour programmes, such as the selection of job candidates. Skills and routines share this tacit component, which may vary in importance. Skills such as computer operation and routines such as production schedules can probably be articulated more fully than the examples given above. However, such articulation is often not necessary for correct execution, is difficult to reproduce when called for, and is almost never complete.

Organizational routines are thus the analogue of individual skills. In executing these automatic behaviour programmes, choice is suppressed. When riding a bike, we normally do not consider all the choice options when we approach a red light. Instead we automatically slow down and come to a halt, if necessary. Similarly, many behaviours in organizations are evoked automatically. The clock tells people when it is time for lunch or the weekly meeting. The calendar marks the time for closing budgets. One activity automatically leads to the next, as when a typist reacts to a draft letter in the in-basket, or when products reach the next stage in the assembly line. Responses to external signals can be nearly automatic, such as the prescription to match price cuts by the competition. Numerous examples can be added. In all cases, behaviour is governed largely by routine-like programmes, and the role of deliberate choice is much less pronounced than 'orthodox' economic theory would have it.

Tacit knowledge

Organizational routines

Routines thus abound in organizational life. Before categorizing organizational routines, it is useful to point out two other aspects. One is that routines serve as organizational *memories*. Organizations remember largely by doing, according to Nelson and Winter. Routines that are not used for some time wither away. The organization loses the capability to perform such routines. Individuals lose the required skills to perform the routines, and to play the organizational role required of them. Routine-like co-ordination is disturbed. Memories are further endangered when there is individual turnover. Turnover is one cause of mutations in routines, as we observe later. The second aspect is that routines also serve as an organizational *truce*. By this metaphor, Nelson and Winter refer to the behavioural foundations of their concept of organizations (see Chapter 6). Satisficing takes the place of maximizing, and the existence of organizational conflict is not assumed away. Routines may be seen as a stabilizing force in organizations: in that sense they represent a truce in intraorganizational conflict. Changes in routines will upset existing political balances:[15]

> The result may be that the routines of the organization as a whole are confined to extremely narrow channels by the dikes of vested interest . . . fear of breaking the truce is, in general, a powerful force tending to hold organizations on the path of relatively inflexible routine.

Three broad classes of organizational routines can be distinguished:

- *operating characteristics*, which relate to what a firm does at any time, given its prevailing stock of plant, equipment, and other factors of production that are not readily augmented in the short run;
- the predictable patterns in the period-by-period changes in the firm's *capital stock* (those factors of production that are fixed in the short run);
- routines that operate to *modify over time* various aspects of the firm's operating characteristics.

The last category represents 'higher-order' routines that may act occasionally to modify lower-order ones. Thus it may be customary in a firm to review the R&D policy from time to time, or to change advertising agencies, or to make a competitive analysis. Nelson and Winter argue that such 'strategic' behaviours are often also subject to quite stringent rules within a firm. Thus the routine-changing processes are themselves routine-guided. In Nelson and Winter's terminology, organizational search is itself routine-like.[16] It may lead to mutations in organizational routines. Just as in biological species the genetic make-up partly determines the potential mutations, so the routine make-up of firms partly determines the outcomes of their search.

Mutations of organizational routines can thus come about by chance or by deliberation. An example of a chance process is the turnover among individuals in the firm. A deliberate mutation may result from organizational search. Deliberate mutations will, however, first be sought in the neighbourhood of existing routines. In this respect, Nelson and Winter again use ideas from the behavioural school ('local search', see Chapter 6). Whatever change takes place, it is expected to follow the path of least resistance. Staying close to prevailing routines minimizes the disturbance of the organizational truce. Moreover, it enhances the probability of success, since firms will be able to draw largely on the (tacit) knowledge and experiences they have collected.

Environmental selection will favour successful routines. For firms, this translates to higher profit levels. If an existing routine is a success, replication of that success is likely to be desired. The point emphasized by evolutionary theory is that the firm that is already successful in a given activity is a particularly good candidate to be successful in an attempt to apply that routine on a larger scale. From one period to another, this implies that successful routines will be increasingly incorporated in the 'routine pool' of the particular industry concerned:[17]

> Search and selection are simultaneous, interacting aspects of the evolutionary process: the same prices that provide selection feedback also influence the directions of search. Through the joint action of search and selection, the firms evolve over time, with the condition of the industry in each period bearing the seeds of its condition in the following period.

In their models, the distribution of routines is carried over from one period to the next by means of a stochastic (Markov) process. While the technicalities of such modelling do not interest us here, the basic idea is clear. It is the basic idea of all evolutionary approaches: *variations* (or mutations) of routines, environmental *selection* (according to the value of the routine for the survival chances of the firms in the population), and cumulative *retention* of successful routines.

The original contribution by Nelson and Winter has given rise to a growing economic literature employing such evolutionary approaches. Surveying this literature, Nelson (1991) remarked that the common element is a focus on firm-specific dynamic capabilities. Comparing *An Evolutionary Theory of Economic Change* (1982) with the current state of the literature, Nelson observes that 'with the vision of hindsight, it is clear that our writing then was handicapped by insufficient study of the writings of Chandler, particularly his *Strategy and Structure* [1966]'. He goes on to point out that there are 'three different if strongly related features of a firm that must be recognized if one is to describe it adequately: its strategy, its structure, and its core capabilities'. The evolving insights about these three features together constitute an 'emerging theory of dynamic firm capabilities'. In this theory, the concept of *strategy* connotes a broad set of commitments made by a firm that define and rationalize its objectives and how it intends to pursue them. Some of the strategy may be formalized and written down, but some may also reside in the organizational culture and the management repertoire. Strategy tends to define a desired firm structure in a general way, but not in its details. *Structure* involves the way a firm is organized and governed, and the way decisions are actually made and carried out. Thus the organization's structure largely determines what it does, given the broad strategy. Changes in strategy may require changes in structure, but the latter are difficult to carry out. The reason is that structure involves not only the organization chart but, much more basically, the routines governing the operating-level decisions. Changing these is time-consuming and costly, so it is a major task to get the new structure into shape and operating smoothly.

The reason for contemplating a change of the organization's structure is to change, possibly to augment, the things that a firm is capable of doing well: its **core capabilities**. Strategy and structure call forth and mould organizational capabilities, but what an organization can do well also has something of a life of its own. Nelson and Winter (1982) had already proposed that firms working well can be understood in terms of a hierarchy of practised organizational routines that define lower-order organizational skills and how these are co-ordinated, as well as higher-order decision procedures for choosing what is to be done at lower levels. This notion of a *hierarchy of organizational routines* is the key building block of Nelson and Winter's concept of core organizational capabilities.

This summary of the developments in the evolutionary approaches in the economic literature illustrates how influential this line of thought has been. While most people would, for instance, believe that the concept of core capabilities or core competences was developed by Prahalad and Hamel and popularized by them in their very successful book *Competing for the Future* (1994), the origins of this line of thought can be traced much further back. Similarly, just as the organizational ecologists provided a fresh, dynamic approach to the organizational literature, so the evolutionary economists have provided a healthy antidote against too much (comparative-)static and equilibrium thinking in economics.

In conclusion, we therefore want to summarize the basic process of economic change that is incorporated in Nelson and Winter's models. This change starts with firms that are characterized with behaviourist notions. They satisfice rather than maximize, they would rather not upset intraorganizational balances, and, if they have to change, they search locally for solutions (that is to say, they start searching as near to their current routines as possible). Search is modelled probabilistically, by assuming that the probability of finding a superior technique – by innovation or by imitation – is a function of the amount invested in the search. Search may be induced by adverse conditions or it may itself be a routine – firms often have routinized R&D and strategic planning. Selection by market forces will favour firms that happen to find better techniques or which happen to use better search rules than the others. Their features – the techniques or search rules that make them successful – will spread in the population of firms, partly by expansion and partly by imitation. In that process, however, new mutations of routines will be generated. Replication of routines by successful firms will often already be less than perfect; imitation by other firms probably involves a higher mutation rate; and innovation will occur. Innovation is modelled by Nelson and Winter as a routinized activity, and it consists, for a large part, of new combinations of existing routines[18] (but discontinuous, radical innovation is not excluded). Through all these sources, the economic system is continually injected with new mutations of routines. It is thus in continuous flux, and equilibrium will be the exception rather than the rule.

Core capabilities

10.6 Comparison

As a starting point for a comparison of the two evolutionary approaches, let us return to the introductory comments we made on the biological strands of arguments. We distinguished between evolutionary and creationist arguments, and within the evolutionary branch between Darwinism and Lamarckianism. How do the approaches discussed in this chapter relate to these distinctions? The answer is quite straightforward: Hannan and Freeman's perspective is Darwinistic, while Nelson and Winter's is Lamarckian. (We would add that both leave room for creationist arguments to play a role.)

Nelson and Winter classify themselves as follows:[19]

> It is neither difficult nor implausible to develop models of firm behavior that interweave 'blind' and 'deliberate' processes. Indeed, in human problem solving itself, both elements are involved and difficult to disentangle. Relatedly, our theory is unabashedly Lamarckian: it contemplates both the 'inheritance' of acquired characteristics and the timely appearance of variation under the stimulus of adversity.

Hannan and Freeman take the following position:[20]

> our work approximates a Malthusian–Darwinian position on the nature of change in organizational populations over time. We think that the current diversity of organizational forms reflects the cumulative effect of a long history of variation and selection, including the consequences of founding processes, mortality processes, and merger processes . . . The line of theory we develop builds on the assumption that change in core features of organizational populations is more Darwinian than Lamarckian. It argues that inertial pressures prevent most organizations from radically changing strategies and structures.

Both approaches leave room not only for organizational members to make rational plans for change but also for the possibility that organizations may be founded with a rational design. In the latter sense, they both allow creationist elements. They further agree that organizations show intrinsic rigidities that hamper change. Finally, both view organizational adaptability not as an all-or-nothing proposition, but in relation to environmental change. That said, Hannan and Freeman subsequently argue that the original organizational 'imprint' will basically remain intact. Inertial pressures will prevent major change and will cause a major gap between individual intentions for change and organizational (inertial) outcomes (see Box 10.4). Ecologists generally regard successful adaptation as unlikely for two reasons (Carroll and Hannan, 1995). First, organizations frequently cannot make good forecasts about future states of the environment. Second, it is uncertain whether designed organizational adaptations will have their intended effects (if not, the cure may be worse than the disease). The ecologists' position, therefore, basically states that adaptation is random with respect to the future.[21] Nelson and Winter, on the other hand, allow for more learning, imitation, and conscious adaptation through search. However, they also argue that prevailing routines will seriously

Box 10.4 ■ Changing Auntie

The launch of digital broadcasting services in Britain by Rupert Murdoch's BskyB is expected to boost the number of TV channels from 30 to 200-plus in 1997. As a result the BBC's fore- casts show that audience share for the four traditional channels – BBC 1, BBC 2, ITV and Channel 4 – may fall from 90 per cent to 65 per cent within 10 years. This has led the BBC's director-general to propose a major reorganization:

It's a tricky business trying to change 'Auntie'. That's the nickname for the 74-year-old British Broadcasting Corp., and it rightly conveys the affection most British have for the publicly funded broadcaster. John Birt, director-general of the BBC, discovered in June how quickly the public would rush to Auntie's aid when he announced dramatic plans to merge the TV and radio operations – including the revered World Service. A roar of protest arose from BBC reporters, ordinary viewers, and government officials, all fearful that the BBC's standards would be hopelessly compromised. One Member of Parliament denounced Birt for acting like some tyrannical czar.

Source: Business Week, 12 August 1996, p.25

constrain such processes and that organizations are therefore much less adapt- able than other organizational theories would have it. Which of these approaches is more accurate in explaining particular organizational and eco- nomic phenomena will remain a question for empirical research for many years to come.

Care should be taken that the biological analogy is not overemphasized. In both approaches the authors are very explicit about this:[22]

We are pleased to exploit any idea from biology that seems helpful in the under- standing of economic problems, but we are equally prepared to pass over any- thing that seems awkward, or to modify accepted biological theories radically in the interest of getting better *economic* theory.

Hannan and Freeman explain in much the same manner:[23]

we did not seek to use biological theory to explain organizational change. Nor did we propose to develop metaphors between biotic populations and organiza- tional populations . . . We relied on models from population ecology because these models appeared to clarify the social processes of interest . . . We have adapted ecological models to sociological uses and have changed them in the process.

Therefore, it is inappropriate to judge these approaches on the basis of the (too) simple question, What does biology have to say about organizational or economic phenomena? The appropriate question is indeed whether the imported and adapted ideas contribute to our understanding of these phenom- ena. To this latter question we would suggest an affirmative answer.

We have already indicated the main similarities between the two approaches, namely (1) the emphasis on organizational routines and on limits to organizational adaptability, (2) the population or system level of analysis, and (3) the importance of environmental selection. It is now useful perhaps to point out some differences. One major difference concerns the question of what it is that is selected by the environment. In organizational ecology this is the 'organizational form'. Although a precise definition of organizational forms is lacking, it is clear that forms are collections of core properties of organizations. It is this entire collection of properties of, say, newspapers or labour unions that is selected. In contrast, Nelson and Winter propose that specific characteristics of organizations (particular routines) are selected: theirs is a 'routines as genes' approach (Winter, 1990).[24] Owing to their Lamarckian perspective, these specific characteristics may change, while the form remains intact in other respects. Furthermore, their approach allows the possibility that particular competences are 'inherited' by other organizations, for example by acquisition or by sharing in an alliance.[25]

A second major difference is closely related. It is the observation that Nelson and Winter have more to say about intraorganizational processes. Both approaches are interested in phenomena at the population level, but only Nelson and Winter provide a microfoundation for changes at the population level. They explicitly incorporate a number of behavioural features in their models of organizations. As a result, we have an idea of the forces at the micro level that contribute to stability and change. In comparison, the organization is a relatively empty box in organizational ecology. The emphasis is more on the external demands on organizations (demands of reliability and reproducibility) than on internal processes. Organizational ecology has relatively little to say about what goes on inside organizations.

A third and final difference pertains to the description of organizations and their relative success. Organizational ecology generally treats all organizations in a particular population as alike: it relies heavily on counting numbers of organizations. This research strategy tends to disregard differences among the members of the population. Evolutionary economics, on the other hand, accords particular significance to the organizations' size and their success. The two are, of course, interrelated: successful organizations are assumed to grow. The economic approaches tend to focus on the *firm* as its particular subject of interest. Hence it can model success with a profit measure and with capital accumulation. Organizational ecology, on the other hand, aspires to be a more general organization theory and empirically examines non-firm types of organization as well (such as labour unions). This makes a general approach to the modelling of success much more difficult.

10.7 Further developments

In conclusion, we should like to observe that there appears to be a great potential for further development and integration of these evolutionary approaches. The evolutionary perspective is still young in our field and has attracted increasing numbers of researchers in recent years. As a result, it is to be expected that the perspective will be developed and refined. In that process, it is to be hoped that a more integrative framework for the evolutionary analysis of organizational phenomena will emerge. Ecological and evolutionary models have a great potential for incorporating insights from various disciplines. For a multidisciplinary field such as organization studies, it is to be hoped that this potential will be realized.

As an illustration of this potential, we can speculatively point to two fields of interest. The first is the further analysis of organizations as 'bundles of routinized competences'. Particularly in the learning perspective of evolutionary economics, the conceptualization of the firm as a bundle of competences may provide a unitary framework for a number of theoretical and empirical observations, including the following:

- The finding that firms that have a head start (or, more formally, a *first mover advantage*) along a competence-building pathway that eventually turns out to be a success, often experience significant *increasing returns* (Arthur, 1994b, 1996). Again, think of Microsoft as an example, or contemplate all the electronic firms competing for dominance in the area of DVDs. The firm that can set the standard for the development of such new environmental niches will reap a disproportionate share of the resources that the niche will provide (see Box 10.5).

- One reason why, for such firms, success breeds success is the early accumulation of resources, which allows them to pursue dominance of the niche more aggressively. Another organizational reason may be that its early start increases the possibility that the firm will also develop the necessary supporting competences earlier. Eventually, it will need to arrive at a 'configuration' of competences that allows it to exploit the possibilities of the niche to the optimum. Think of the various competences that allowed IBM to dominate the niche of mainframe computers for several decades, or, alternatively, of the competences that McDonald's needed to acquire in order

Box 10.5 ■ An example of increasing returns (or positive feedback)

The history of the videocassette recorder furnishes a simple example of positive feedback. The VCR market started out with two competing formats selling at about the same price: VHS and Betamax. Each format could realize increasing returns as its market share increased: large numbers of VHS recorders would encourage video outlets to stock more prerecorded tapes in VHS, thereby enhancing the value of owning a VHS recorder and leading more people to buy one. (The same would, of course, be true for Beta-format players.) In this way, a small gain in market share would improve the competitive position of one system and help it to further increase its lead.

Such a market is initially unstable. Both systems were introduced at about the same time and so began with roughly equal market shares; those shares fluctuated early on because of external circumstance, 'luck', and corporate maneuvering. Increasing returns on early gains eventually tilted the competition toward VHS: it accumulated enough of an advantage to take virtually the entire VCR market. Yet, it would have been impossible at the outset to say which system would win, which of the two possible equilibria would be selected.

Source: Arthur (1994b)

first to dominate the US market in its niche and then to internationalize successfully.

- However, such successful configurations often contain the seeds of their demise. Miller (1990, 1994) has shown how successful corporations can become simple over time, focusing exclusively on the successful repertoire of routines, and becoming intolerant of deviation or variation. It is well documented how IBM underestimated the potential impact of the personal computer and has had great difficulty in catching up. Similarly, former dominant players in their industries such as Steinway pianos or Singer sewing machines have lost their dominance or have even ceased to exist. Large corporations such as ITT and Texas Instruments have floundered. Miller has labelled this phenomenon the *Icarus paradox* after the Greek saga of Icarus, who suffered a fatal fall after achieving a great success.[26]

- On the other hand, many firms do live a long life. Some are able to persist among the industry leaders during decades of economic and social change (e.g. General Motors, Shell). Others are completely transformed along the way, such as STORA, a Swedish company that has gone from copper mining to forestry operations, paper production and power generation in the 700 years of its existence to date (see Box 10.6).

Further development of the evolutionary approaches will, it is hoped, lead to more systematic insights into the organization/environment interplay that gives rise to such pathways and to the triggers of its various episodes. As will be evident from the above, a key theme will be the relative importance of *inertia versus adaptability* in various circumstances. As Boone and van Witteloostuijn (1995) have noted, this theme shows close correspondence to the 'commitment versus flexibility' theme in industrial organization and strategic management, which we encountered in Chapter 9. It is therefore very likely that cross-fertilization of these various approaches offers ample opportunities to increase our understanding of these important phenomena.

A second, related area of interest is *intraorganizational ecology and evolution*. As noted above, organizational ecology is rather silent about what goes on within the organization. Evolutionary economics has more to say about processes within the firm. In particular, the behavioural concept of local search near existing routines is incorporated in this theory. In terms of organizational change, this concept implies that firms will prefer to stay close to current competences. Organizational change, then, will be predominantly *incremental* (see Quinn, 1982). Such incremental organizational change will allow a firm to keep up with slow to moderate environmental change. It does not seem to explain how firms can survive amidst turbulent change, nor does it seem to allow for complete transformations of firms, such as in the example of STORA above. A promising avenue of inquiry that may contribute to our understanding of these phenomena relates to *intra*organizational ecology and evolution. The basic idea here is that selection takes place within the organization as well. Various worldviews may exist among the organization's members; different analyses of the organization's challenges may vie for prominence; too many requests for resource allocations may compete for scarce resources; different

Box 10.6 ■ The history of STORA

STORA is probably the world's oldest company. It was officially founded in 1288, when Bishop Peter signed a deed of exchange. This was the document upon which the 700th anniversary of the founding of STORA was based in 1988. The company brochure *STORA's world* describes its history as follows:

The world's oldest company

STORA's history commences with a copper mine, which in the 14th century produced approximately 200 tons of crude copper per year. Some 300 years later, the mine entered its golden era, producing an ore that was richer in copper content than at any time previously. During the 17th century, the mine was generating about 1,500 tons of crude copper per year. In 1687, the great cave-in occurred, which signalled the end of the golden era. Operations continued after the collapse, however, with the extraction of new products, such as sulphur, vitriol, and pigment for red paint. This latter product continues to be used today to decorate many homes throughout Sweden.

The mining of copper ore based on a 'fire-setting' process required substantial quantities of wood. And to obtain wood, forests were required. Toward the end of the 18th century, the company's operations shifted increasingly toward forestry and the production of iron. In the middle of the 1870s a large iron mill and one of the largest saw mills in Europe were built near the coppermine.

At the end of the 19th century, a sulphate (kraft) and sulphite pulp mill was constructed in Skutskar in central Sweden. Around this time, the first paper mill was also built in Kvarnsveden, not far from Falun. In 1972, Kvarnsveden produced approximately 300,000 tons of newsprint and magazine paper. At the end of the 1970s, the mining and steel operations were gradually phased out.

During the next decade, the Swedish companies Billerud, Papyrus and Swedish Match were acquired and incorporated within the STORA Group. Following the acquisition of Germany's Feldmühle group in 1990, STORA could without doubt be ranked as one of the world's leading forest products companies. In 1998 STORA merged with Enso, a Finnish forest products company, to become STORA Enso.

strategies may be propagated, etc. (see Bettis and Prahalad, 1995). How do the internal selection processes of the organization operate under such circumstances?

Burgelman (1990, 1991) has proposed a distinction in strategic processes that may contribute to an intraorganizational ecology of strategy formation: induced processes versus autonomous processes.[27] *Induced strategic processes* fit with the current strategy, as propagated by top management, and are compatible with current routines and competences. Induced processes serve to ensure that organizational actions will remain consistent with top management preferences as incorporated in the current strategy. In this vein, induced processes are within the current strategic domain and hence also demarcate what the organization will *not* do. Hence Burgelman identifies such processes as variation-reducing.

Autonomous strategic processes, on the other hand, refer to strategic initiatives outside the current strategic domain. They arise 'bottom up' from the managers who are directly in contact with new technological developments and changing market conditions, and who have some budgetary discretion. Such autonomous initiatives are expected to emerge unpredictably, but not completely randomly, since they are rooted in and constrained by the evolving competence set of the organization (including newly acquired and perceived competences at lower levels of the organization). Hence such processes tend to be variation-enhancing rather than variation-reducing.[28] An important task of top management is to nurture such operational-level strategic initiatives, since these spur continuous strategic renewal. All in all, Burgelman's perspective is that the long-run survival of firms is enhanced by the balancing of variation-reducing and variation-enhancing mechanisms. One process leads to relative inertia and incremental adjustments; the other expands the organization's domain and renews its competence base. Likely propositions are that:

■ The appropriate balance of the two will depend upon environmental conditions.
■ The episodes of organizational success and failure, which we observed above, depend on the appropriateness of the actual choices made by firms, given the then prevailing environmental conditions.

In this latter statement, our two 'speculative fields of interest' are coming together. Conceptualizing the firm as a bundle of competences allows us to analyze whether it makes *competent* choices with regard to its environmental challenges. This is no coincidence. We see the evolutionary perspectives as capable of integrating theoretical and empirical contributions from various disciplines.

10.8 Summary: the evolutionary perspective

This chapter has presented two strands of the evolutionary perspective on organizations. We started out by exploring the biological analogy and examining different biological explanations for the long necks of giraffes. This allowed us to distinguish creationist and evolutionary arguments and, within the latter, Lamarckian and Darwinist explanations. These distinctions are also helpful in the organizational field. We were careful, however, to point out that there are both differences and similarities between organizational forms and biological species. The differences imply that successful biological explanations do not necessarily translate to the organizational field. While the Darwinian perspective currently has the strongest scientific credentials in biology, creationist or Lamarckian (or still other) arguments may be much more important for organizational evolution. We saw that Nelson and Winter's evolutionary theory of economic change is decidedly Lamarckian in nature, while Hannan and Freeman's organizational ecology is Darwinist. Both, however, employ the basic environmental mechanism of variation–selection–retention as their main explanatory device.

Evolutionary perspectives direct our attention to the development of organizational forms in the interaction with their environments. These perspectives therefore accord more importance to environmental selection processes than most of the other organizational theories that tend to emphasize organizational adaptability. In organizational ecology it is assumed that organizations are relatively inert. That is to say, they have a hard time responding to changes in their environment. The reasons for this relative inertia are sought in the demands upon organizations for reliability, accountability, and reproducibility. Selection pressures will favour organizations whose structures have high inertia. Therefore organizational ecology sees inertia as a consequence of selection. The empirical work within this approach has tended to concentrate on the vital rates of organizational populations: the rates of founding and mortality. These rates have been found to be density-dependent. More recently, attention is growing for evolutionary processes within organizations. As an example, Burgelman's analysis of autonomous versus induced strategic processes was presented.

Nelson and Winter's evolutionary theory of economic change focuses on organizational routines as the primary concept to describe organizational functioning. Routines refer to all regular and predictable behaviour patterns of firms. They often contain a component of tacit knowledge. Routines explain why organizations are resistant to change and therefore, again, relatively inert. In this approach, routines are the organizational analogue of biological genes. Successful routines are those that have survived environmental selection. They serve as organizational memories. In addition, they may be seen as a stabilizing force in organizations, representing a truce in intraorganizational conflict. Nelson and Winter clearly build on the foundations of the behavioural theory of the firm. Their emphasis on organizational routines has been extended to encompass all firm-specific dynamic capabilities. These define what a firm does well. They are modified over time by a firm's strategy and structure, but a firm's core capabilities also 'lead a life of their own'. This perspective on organizations as a hierarchy of organizational routines or capabilities has been popularized by Prahalad and Hamel.[29]

The evolutionary approaches to organizations shed light on the dynamics of organizational functioning. They also give insights into the long-term organizational evolution. They show that, in the interaction between populations of organizations and their environments, conditions may change over time. Organizational ecology shows how the forces of competition and legitimation develop with the density of the population. This has an effect on the founding and mortality rates. All in all, the conditions for survival change substantially over the lifetime of a population. Similarly, the analysis of firms as bundles of routinized competences sheds light on a number of formerly disparate theoretical and empirical observations. It shows how firms may have initial success by building competences along a new pathway. Success will reinforce the routinization of these competences. As competences become more routinized, the relative inertia of the firm increases. Thus success breeds not only success but also its own demise when environmental conditions change and organizational adaptation is called for. On the other hand, many firms do live a long life and succeed in adapting when necessary. A deeper understanding of the conditions leading to relative inertia on the one hand and relative adaptability on the other is one of the greatest challenges for current organizational theory. We return to this theme in the closing section of the next chapter.

Questions

1 In evolutionary approaches to organizations, biological analogies play an important role. It is argued that populations of organizational forms develop over time as a result of environmental selection, just as populations of giraffes do. Yet a major difference between organizations and giraffes is that organizations are human constructs. This difference has two kinds of implication for the analogy between populations of organizations and populations of giraffes. Explain these two implications.

2 Skills and routines are two important concepts in the evolutionary theory of economic change developed by Nelson and Winter.

   (a) Give an example of a skill.
   (b) Name two characteristic features of skills.
   (c) Give an example of a routine.
   (d) What is the major difference between a skill and a routine? What are the major similarities between skills and routines?

3 In a number of countries there has been experimentation with a new form of pharmacy: mail order pharmacy. This new distribution form would allow patients to receive their regular prescriptions by mail. In the Netherlands the early experiments with this new form of pharmacy were set up by entrepreneurs. These early attempts were not successful: the entrepreneurial firms failed (the experiments continue, but now under the auspices of health insurance companies). What could explain the early failures if you adopt the perspective of organizational ecology?

4 Read Box 10.6 on the 700-year history of STORA again. If you look at this history from the perspective of Nelson and Winter's evolutionary theory of economic change, what may be factors contributing to STORA's remarkably long survival as a company?

5 In 1959 almost all petrol in major North American cities was sold by service stations. Service stations provide simple car repair services, and sell tyres, batteries and car accessories as well as petrol. They also employ 'pump jockeys', who fill up the tank and may provide other services such as washing the windscreen. Thirty years later this situation had changed dramatically. Less than 30 per cent of all petrol sold was sold by traditional service stations and the rest in roughly equal proportions by 'gas bars' (outlets selling petrol only), convenience stores (petrol sales plus convenience retail) and car washes (petrol sales and automated car washes). Table 10.1 provides data on the city of Edmonton in Alberta, Canada.

Table 10.1 **Number of outlets selling petrol in Edmonton, Alberta, Canada**

Year	1959	1988
Service stations	262	104
Gas bars	1	73
Convenience stores	0	73
Car washes	1	84
Other outlets selling petrol	15	40

Source: Usher and Evans, 1996

Using population ecology, how would you explain the transition that occurred in Edmonton between 1959 and 1988? Which information would you need in order to know whether your explanation from the point of view of population ecology is correct?

Suggested further reading

Arthur, W.B. (1996), 'Increasing returns and the new world of business, *Harvard Business Review*, July/August, pp.100–9.

Baum, J.A.C. (1996), 'Organizational ecology', in: Clegg, S.R., C. Hardy and W.R. Nord, *Handbook of Organization Studies*, London: Sage.

Carroll, G.R. and M.T. Hannan (1995), *Organizations in Industry: Strategy, Structure, and Selection*, Oxford: Oxford University Press.

Hannan, M.T. and J. Freeman (1989), *Organizational Ecology*, Cambridge, Mass.: Harvard University Press.

Nelson, R.R. (1991), 'Why do firms differ and how does it matter?, *Strategic Management Journal*, vol.12 (special issue), pp.61–74.

Nelson, R.R. and S.E. Winter (1982), *An Evolutionary Theory of Economic Change*, Cambridge, Mass.: Harvard University Press.

Winter, S.G. (1990), 'Survival, selection, and inheritance in evolutionary theories of organization', in: Singh, J.V., *Organizational Evolution: New Directions*, Newbury Park, CA: Sage.

Notes

1. The following account is based primarily on Dawkins (1986). As is argued in section 10.3, his rejection of Lamarckian explanation for biological evolution does not transfer to the organizational field.
2. See Dawkins (1986) for a popular overview, which also discusses some other strands of evolutionary arguments, such as salutationism and punctuationism. The second author's son advanced a new hypothesis on the long necks of giraffes. According to him, giraffes were created when a baby dromedary had difficulty leaving its egg. This led its parents to pull it out. Since the little dromedary was really stuck in the egg, the parents had to pull so hard that a giraffe with a long neck was born.
3. As, for instance, Hannan and Freeman (1989a) do. Their approach is outlined in the subsequent section.
4. Others are Howard Aldrich (e.g. 1979) and Glenn Carroll (e.g. 1987, 1988).
5. For instance by Pfeffer (1982) and by Young (1988). Hannan and Freeman (1989a, p.10) also recognize the potential fruitfulness of more integration between ecological and economic studies.

6. Some studies are located between these two levels of analysis, for instance the studies that use environmental variables as 'proxies' for competition by other organizational forms.

7. Hannan and Freeman (1989a) attempt to solve it by arguing, first, that there is a fundamental duality between niches and forms – 'niches define forms and forms define niches' (p.50) – and, second, by focusing subsequently on boundaries around populations: 'boundaries should be drawn in organizational space to produce uniformity within populations in terms of observable attributes and relations' (p.53). This still does not give us theoretically satisfactory definitions and procedures. Hannan and Freeman (1989a, p.63) are frank enough to admit that they themselves have relied in large part on 'the conventional wisdom of participants and observers'.

8. In section 10.5 we shall see that Nelson and Winter also stress the role of routines.

9. An economist would probably point out in addition that the choice for international chains economizes on search costs, particularly if the problem occurs frequently (that is, you often have to find car rentals in unfamiliar countries). In this sense, individual routines in decision-making can be efficient, as the behavioural school has argued (cf. Chapter 6).

10. Hannan and Freeman (1989a), p.74.

11. Added by the authors. Rinnooy Kan is referring to some early breaches in security in Internet banking by several suppliers of such services.

12. Ecologists distinguish between the 'fundamental niche' (roughly, the maximum potential space a particular form can occupy in its environment) and the 'realized niche' (the restricted environmental space in which a population can be sustained in the presence of competing populations). Since only the realized niche can be observed, this is the concept used in most studies.

13. Interestingly, these ideas bear close resemblance to the 'increasing returns' argument that has recently received recognition in economics (see Arthur, 1994a, 1994b, 1996). In this strand of the economic literature it is argued that industries can be subject to self-reinforced growth, and that particular firms in the industry can realize substantial 'first-mover advantages' if they set the new standards. Microsoft is often mentioned as a case in point.

14. See Carroll and Hannan (1995) for further elaborations of organizational ecology, including density delay, resource partitioning, and segregation.

15. Nelson and Winter (1982), pp.111–12.

16. Again, this conforms to ideas of the Carnegie school. See Cyert and March (1963, chapter 6).

17. Nelson and Winter (1982), p.19.

18. In this sense, they are decidedly neo-Schumpeterian. Schumpeter (1934) also identified innovation as the 'carrying out of new combinations'.

19. Nelson and Winter (1982), p.11.

20. Hannan and Freeman (1989a), pp.20–2.

21. Again, this corresponds closely to the Darwinian point of view, where mutations are also random. Many organization theorists would, however, regard this as an extreme position.

22. Nelson and Winter (1982), p.11.

23. Hannan and Freeman (1989b), p.428.

24. By analogy to biology, Hannan and Freeman thus represent the original Darwinian position that species (= forms) are selected. Nelson and Winter hold the now common position that selection operates on the gene level. It goes without saying that the analogy to biology represents no arguments for or against particular *organizational* theories.

25. In this respect, of course, organizational theories are decidedly different from biological theories, where only offspring can inherit.

26. In Greek mythology, Icarus found that he could attach wings to his arms with wax and fly. Unfortunately, he was too successful and flew higher and higher towards the sun, thus provoking the gods. This success turned to disaster when the heat from the sun melted the wax, leaving Icarus to plummet back to earth.

27. Note that we are now discussing strategic processes, the left side of Table 9.1 (see p.182), which we could not deal with in the previous chapter.

28. Burgelman's description of strategic processes corresponds closely to Mintzberg's view of intended/deliberate and emerging strategies, where the realized strategy is usually a mix of the two. See Mintzberg and Quinn (1991).

29. Since Prahalad and Hamel are strategists, it is not surprising that they tend to focus much more on the adaptability of a firm's core capabilities (or competences) than evolutionary theorists like Nelson and Winter, who stress relative inertia.

11 All in the family

11.1 Introduction

You have now been introduced to the main economic approaches to that are currently available. You are familiar with the problems addressed by each approach, the basic concepts used, and the particular mode of analysis. Our task in this final chapter is to provide you with an overall perspective on the various approaches included in this book.

First, we return to the basic conceptual framework laid out in Chapter 1. Having thus refreshed your memory, we proceed to discuss in section 11.3 what the similarities are among our family of economic approaches to organizations. In section 11.4 we turn to the family differences. Together, these two sections should provide a balanced view of our family. Do they quarrel a lot? Are there any clear family traits? Do they have the same views or hobbies? Can we discern a family structure? Section 11.5 summarizes our findings and section 11.6 sketches a concluding perspective.

11.2 The basic conceptual framework

In Chapter 1 we developed a basic conceptual framework, which is reproduced in Figure 11.1. The framework took as its starting-point the division of labour in society. This division of labour allows economies of specialization to be gained. This, however, is only one side of the coin. The other side is that co-ordination is necessary in a specialized economy. Without some kind of co-ordination no exchange transaction could take place between specialized economic actors. Specialization and (the need for) co-ordination are thus the inseparable consequences of division of labour.

We argued that markets and organizations offer alternative solutions for the co-ordination of exchange transactions. We characterized markets and organizations by means of the co-ordination mechanisms they employed. Markets use the price mechanism. Organizations use any of six alternative mechanisms. We argued that pure market co-ordination and pure organizational co-ordination are rare. In practice, we often find a mix of co-ordination mechanisms. The actual mix that we find in any situation will depend mainly on the informa-

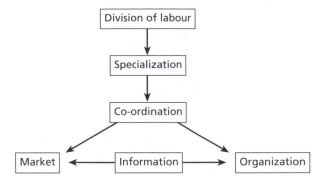

Figure 11.1 **The basic conceptual framework**

tion required to execute the transaction. Thus information was the concluding element of our basic conceptual framework.

In Chapter 1 we showed how the basic economic perspective expressed in Figure 11.1 could be traced to some founding fathers of modern economics. Division of labour and its consequences was a main theme of Adam Smith; the efficiency of market co-ordination by the price system was vigorously expounded by Friedrich Hayek; and the idea that organizational co-ordination could arise as a remedy to flaws in market co-ordination was first systematically addressed by Ronald Coase. Now that we have surveyed more recent economic approaches to organizations, to what extent can we say that this basic conceptual framework underlies the spectrum of approaches that are currently available?

To some extent, would be our answer. If anything has become clear in the preceding chapters, it should be the diversity of the approaches surveyed. In section 11.4 we chart this diversity in more detail. Notwithstanding this diversity, we also see a common foundation to the economic approaches to organizations. Three of the common elements, which are included in our framework, are discussed below.

11.3 Family resemblances

11.3.1 Organizations and markets

The first common element in the economic approaches to organization is indeed that economists always tend to compare organizations with markets. Their background leads economists to think of markets as natural benchmarks for the appraisal of organizations. This is probably most obvious in Chapter 8, where we discussed transaction cost economics. Williamson's initial formulation of this approach in terms of markets and hierarchies brings it out clearly. The leading question in this approach is how to explain the relative occurrence of markets and firms as governance structures for economic transactions. It represents an extension of Coase's fundamental question of why we observe so many firms (with internal governance of transactions) if the market functions so efficiently. Both Coase and Williamson take the market as their point of departure and explain organizations as a result of 'market failure'.

Another, perhaps more implicit, way of comparing markets with organizations is to analyze the boundaries of organizations. Consider the corporate strategies discussed in Chapter 9. Vertical integration, horizontal multinationalization and corporate diversification all extend the boundaries of the organization. Under a vertical integration policy the firm absorbs a supplier or a customer firm. If multinationalization or diversification is effected by mergers and acquisitions, again two firms are integrated into one.[1] In all these cases we now find one firm instead of two. The relevant comparison is between one integrated firm and two firms with a market relation between them. Again, this boils down to a comparative assessment of organizational versus market co-ordination of transactions.

Finally, consider the agency explanation for the existence of firms.[2] As elaborated in Chapter 7, this explanation involves the concept of team production. Team production denotes the situation where two or more people can be more productive when they join forces than when they operate separately. Again, the (implicit) comparison is between an organizational arrangement and a market arrangement. Organizational arrangements come into being when market arrangements would be inferior.

11.3.2 Efficiency

By what standards would the market arrangement be inferior? This question leads us to the second common element in the economic approaches to organization. It is the observation that the primary economic criterion for evaluating market versus organizational co-ordination is efficiency. As broadly defined in Chapter 1, the efficiency criterion refers to the optimal allocation of scarce resources. That is to say, resources are efficiently allocated if they are directed towards their most productive use, or, alternatively, if a given amount of production is achieved with a minimum of resources. If, moreover, all resources can be expressed in money terms, this translates into the 'least cost' condition that most people would intuitively associate with the term 'efficiency'.

Efficiency considerations abound in the preceding chapters. In the behavioural theory, organizational participants weigh the contributions they have to make against the inducements they are offered. They compare this ratio with the alternatives available elsewhere. They strive for the most efficient allocation of their resources. The manager in agency theory wonders about the effects of buying a company jet on the objective of maximizing her utility (her utility depends on the value of the firm and on her on-the-job consumption). Are the company's resources efficiently spent on a jet? The strategist of another firm considers moving from a cost leadership position to a differentiation strategy. He concludes that this is feasible only if the increase in revenues outweighs the increase in costs.

Hence efficiency considerations are in part manifest in the assumed thoughts and behaviour of economic actors. Economists tend to presume that people are not totally unaffected by the expected efficiency of the resources at their disposal. However, efficiency considerations play an additional and more important role in economic analysis. Efficiency is the economic selection mechanism. It is our main criterion to assess which co-ordination arrangements have the highest survival value when selection pressures are operative. Economists usually assume that the least efficient arrangements will tend to be selected out (after some time).

This is evident in Nelson and Winter's evolutionary theory of the firm. Environmental selection favours successful routines. Successful routines are indicated by higher profit levels of the firms incorporating them. Profit is an indicator of efficiency. Hence efficient firms will tend to be selected by the environment and inefficient firms (with less successful routines) will tend to be selected out. Similarly, in transaction cost economics the governance structure that economizes on production and transaction costs (and is thus more efficient) supersedes the less efficient alternative.

Efficiency, therefore, is the second common element that binds the various economic approaches to organization together. It is partly implicit in the basic conceptual framework of Figure 11.1. As discussed above, it is the primary economic criterion that determines the selection of either markets or organizations as co-ordination devices for particular transactions.[3] For another part, however, we have made it explicit by focusing on one specific source of efficiency: informational advantages.

11.3.3 Information

The focus on information is the third and final common element we want to discuss here. An important impetus to both agency theory and transaction cost economics was provided by the development of the 'economics of information'. It was increasingly recognized that information itself was a scarce resource, which could be unevenly distributed. Uneven distributions of information present opportunities for strategic behaviour. Whether the relevant information is observable to all players or not is a prime distinction in the games that people (and organizations) play, as we saw in Chapter 5. There is economic value in the possession of private information. Informational asymmetries can be exploited, whether opportunistically or not.

Agency theory and transaction cost economics share a concern for such situations. Both maintain that such informational problems pervade (economic) life, and both seek efficient contractual arrangements to deal with these problems. Since markets and organizations differ in the types of information problem they can handle (efficiently), a good part of the choice between them will be explained by the information requirements of particular transactions.

Although less clearly at first sight, information is a central concept in most other economic approaches to organizations as well. The behavioural theory of the firm, for instance, departs from standard microeconomics in the assumptions that (1) information is often imperfectly available to economic actors, and (2) these actors are only boundedly rational in processing the information that is available. These behavioural assumptions spurred later developments in organizational economics, as we have seen, and have often been incorporated in later approaches. In the evolutionary approach, much information is stored in the organizational routines. These routines embody tacit knowledge. Tacit knowledge is difficult to articulate and, therefore, to communicate. It is consequently also difficult for third parties to acquire. In this sense, tacit knowledge embodied in organizational routines represents a well-protected form of private information to the organization. A fundamental information asymmetry exists between firms with and without successful routines.

We do not want to overemphasize the commonality between the economic approaches to organizations. Each common element discussed above is probably to some extent debatable.[4] Together, however, they represent the main binding features, as we see them. In the next sections, some important differences among these approaches are discussed and summarized together with the similarities. Taken together, these sections should provide a balanced overall picture.

11.4 Family differences

Let us now turn to the differences among our family members. You will have noticed abundant differences in reading through Chapters 6–10. Our purpose here will not be to enumerate all these differences. Rather, we shall attempt to provide some structure by ordering the various approaches along some dimensions that we believe are particularly instructive. Three such dimensions are discussed below.

11.4.1 Process versus content approaches

The first dimension refers to the subject matter of the various approaches: the problems they deal with. Here we borrow a distinction from the strategy literature in order to classify our approaches. It is the distinction between process theories and content theories of strategy. Process theories deal with the processes by which strategies come into being.[5] Content theories deal with the content of those strategies: the firm's strategic posture and positioning on the market. Similarly, we shall distinguish here between **process and content approaches to organizations**. The former deal with organizational processes but hardly inform us about the likely outcomes of those processes. The latter focus on substantive outcomes without being very informative about the processes leading to these outcomes.

Process and content approaches to organizations

To illustrate this dimension, let us contrast two of our approaches. The behavioural theory of the firm is a process approach. It explains the internal functioning of the firm when seen as a coalition of participant groups. It highlights the potential conflict between these groups as well as the organizational processes that may lead to quasi-resolution of such conflicts: for instance, satisficing and sequential decision-making. It does not tell us, however, what the specific outcome of these processes will be. This is completely dependent upon the detailed decisions and behaviours of the organizational participants involved.

Contrast this with principal/agent theory. How do the principal and the agent arrive at the choice between, say, a wage contract or a rent contract for growing strawberries (section 7.6)? Is this a matter of intense dispute with fierce bargaining from both sides? Or is one party in a better bargaining position, maybe because of a lack of alternatives for the other party? Is it only a bilateral exchange situation or perhaps what Williamson would call a large numbers exchange situation (*ex ante*)? Principal/agent theory is silent on such process and content issues. It presents the expected outcomes, given the variables on which it focuses (utilities, reservation wages, effort levels, etc.) and the efficiency criterion it employs.

Figure 11.2 presents our ordering of the various approaches along this dimension. Behavioural theory and Nelson and Winter's evolutionary theory are fairly pure process theories.[6] Organizational ecology is only somewhat more content oriented. The contents refer to the expected development of the population over time and the density dependence of founding and exit rates.

At the other end of the spectrum, positive agency theory is slightly more process oriented than principal/agent theory because it is occasionally more explicit about the mechanisms that produce particular outcomes, such as the operation of a market for corporate control. It roughly shares this position with transaction cost economics. The latter is explicit about one particular process: the fundamental transformation that may occur as a result of increasing asset specificity (see section 8.3). Transaction cost economics leaves the selection process, which is assumed to lead to efficient outcomes, open, however.

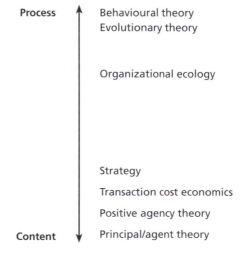

Figure 11.2 **Process and content approaches**

Finally, we turn to the classification of economic approaches to strategy. As explained in Chapter 9, traditional industrial organization is clearly a content theory. It attempts to explain the structure, conduct and performance of (firms within) an industry. In so far as industrial organization is the basis of our approach to strategic management, we are therefore applying a content theory. It informs us about the posture and positioning of firms within and across industries. Our discussion of move and countermove is only partly more process oriented to the extent that the development of strategies over time is considered. The economic contribution to strategic management leaves the internal processes of strategy formation and development undiscussed, however.

Figure 11.2 makes it clear that there is currently a rather wide gap between process- and content-oriented approaches. While this is true of economic theories of organization, it reflects the more general tendencies in the field of organization studies (Mohr, 1982). A fully integrated content and process model of organizational behaviour and development is still beyond our reach.

11.4.2 Static versus dynamic approaches

The second dimension we use to order our economic approaches to organizations is not unrelated to the first one discussed above. It is, however, sufficiently different to merit a separate discussion. It is the distinction between static and dynamic theories. This distinction allows us to make some observations about the various modes of analysis used in our theories. It also allows some remarks on the timeframe that is inherent in each theory.

In Figure 11.3 the vertical axis corresponds to Figure 11.2 and represents the process/content dimension. We have now added the static/dynamic dimension along the horizontal axis. Each axis is divided into three parts, which define regions of the figure. Following the vertical axis, we find that the process approaches are in the top region and the content approaches in the bottom region. The empty middle region illustrates the absence of integrated process/content theories. The horizontal axis is also divided in three parts. The regions defined by the horizontal axis are discussed in turn below.

To the left we find the agency theories. These employ a mode of analysis that is known as *comparative-static* in economics. A comparative-static analysis compares one (static) situation with another. For instance, the principal/agent situation under a wage contract is compared with the situation under a rent contract. The analysis is aimed at discovering whether one of these situations is superior to the other (given the variables included in the analysis and the criterion of efficiency). What the analysis reveals, therefore, is a ranking of alternative situations, given the (efficiency) criterion employed. It will not tell you how the present situation may evolve or how to get from here to there if you are now in an inferior situation.

To the right, we find the ecological and evolutionary theories that are characterized by their long-term perspective. The cumulative selection and adaptation processes, which are required for these theories to work, clearly indicate their long-term dynamic character.

Figure 11.3 **Static and dynamic approaches**

Behavioural theory and strategy occupy a middle position between these two extremes. They usually take the present situation as a starting-point for the analysis and may then ask, what's next? In behavioural theory we might analyze the effects of the rise of aspiration levels. In strategy we may contemplate a strategic move. While, therefore, partly dynamic in character, these approaches certainly do not share the long-term timeframe of their neighbours to the right.

This leaves transaction cost economics to be classified. As is evident from Figure 11.3, this classification is not unambiguously possible in just one of the three boxes along the static/dynamic dimension. The reason is that transaction cost economics employs a mode of analysis that can be characterized as *comparative-institutional*. It compares the functioning of one institution (such as markets) with the functioning of another (such as hierarchies). The criterion for comparison is again efficiency (now including transaction costs, of course). In this respect it is analogous to a comparative-static approach that compares one situation with another. However, it also answers some 'what's next?' questions. The progression of hierarchical forms – from peer groups via simple hierarchies to more complex hierarchies – is one case in point. Another is the fundamental transformation (see section 8.3). These elements of transaction cost theory belong in the middle column. This is why we have placed this approach in both the left and the middle region of the static/dynamic axis.

11.4.3   Levels of analysis

Our third and final dimension refers to the level(s) of analysis to which the theories are addressed. A *level of analysis* denotes the level at which the problems that a theory is attempting to analyze are located. Psychological theories, for example, are directed mainly towards the individual level of analysis: they attempt to explain individual behaviour. To which level(s) of analysis are the economic approaches to organization addressed? To surprisingly many, we submit. We feel obliged to distinguish the following seven levels of analysis:

- *person dyad*: a pair of individuals in an exchange relationship;
- *group*: a (relatively small) number of individuals bound together by a community of purpose, interest, or function;
- *intergroup*: the relations between organizational groups with different purposes, interests, or functions;
- *organization*: the nexus of contracts, the coalition of participant groups and/or the administrative structure that forms a unity and is usually legally recognized as such;[7]
- *organizational dyad*: a pair of organizations in an exchange relationship;
- *population of organizations*: all organizations of a particular type or form;
- *system*: the entire set of organizational populations, environmental characteristics, and their interrelationships, relevant to the analysis of aggregate phenomena.

These seven levels form the vertical axis of Figure 11.4. The figure shows which levels of analysis are covered by the approaches included in this book. The position of each approach is discussed in turn below.

Agency theory spans the person dyad to organizational levels of analysis. *Principal/agent theory* is specifically geared to the person dyad level. It formally examines agency relationships between two persons. Although attempts are made to extend principal/agent theory to multiple agent and/or multiple principal settings, this proves to be very difficult. The formal analysis soon poses intractable problems when heterogeneity among principals or agents is introduced. The insights gained from principal/agent analysis, therefore, strictly apply only to the one principal, one agent level of analysis. Often they are used, however, as a paradigm for analyses at a higher level. It should be clear that considerable caution is in order when such inferences are made.[8] Already at the group level, all kinds of heterogeneities and group interactions may start to play a major role.

Positive agency theory takes the analysis up from the group to the organizational level. An example at the group level might be the analysis of the managerial reward structures. For instance, how should managerial reward packages at the corporate and divisional levels be different? The intergroup level of analysis is reached when potential conflicts between, for instance, shareholders and bondholders in public corporations are analyzed. The organizational level of analysis pertains to, for example, takeovers and the market for corporate control.

Transaction cost economics focuses at the group level when it analyzes peer groups. Most of its attention is directed to the organizational level (e.g. the comparison of U-, M-, and H-forms) and the organizational dyad level (e.g. vertical integration). Interestingly, the intergroup level of potential conflicts between participant groups is hardly analyzed.[9] Transaction cost analysis has a rather holistic view of organizations.

It is, of course, a major characteristic of *behavioural theory* that the theory explicitly deals with intraorganizational processes, particularly intergroup conflict. The organization is analyzed as a coalition of participant groups, and organizational behaviour is explained from that perspective.

The *economics and strategy* literature spans three levels of analysis. It analyzes individual organizations and contemplates their strategic development (e.g. the diversification issue). However, it also studies competition and rivalry both at a dyadic level (the moves and countermoves of two strategic players) and at a population level (rivalry within an industry).

Ecological and *evolutionary theories* are both located at the population level of analysis. They both analyze the population of organizations of a particular type or form. Both also have the potential to extend to the system level. An interesting difference is that Nelson and Winter's evolutionary theory does have some analyses at the organizational level (e.g. the operation of routines), while organizational ecology rather treats organizations as inert 'black boxes' (see also section 10.6). If, however, the few scattered examples of attention for selection processes *within* firms develop into a fully fledged *intraorganizational ecology*, this situation may be remedied (see section 10.7). Therefore, we have included this potential at the appropriate organizational level of Figure 11.4.

We may make three final observations on the levels of analysis addressed by economic approaches to organizations. The first is that they vary widely. This is probably due to the fact that economics has something to contribute as soon as there is an economic aspect involved in the phenomena that interest us (see Chapter 1). At all levels of analysis, from the two-person to the system level, economic aspects are involved.

The second, related, observation is that the various approaches tend to address quite different problems. This is in part due to the different levels of analysis. The evolution of organizational forms over long periods of time is a very different sort of problem from that of the short-term strategic moves that a company may make in a strategic battle. Each level of analysis has its own particular characteristics: groups are more than a collection of dyads; organizations are more than a collection of groups. Care should be taken to specify clearly the level of analysis at which certain findings apply and not to make any undue inferences to other levels.

Third, even if we stay on the same level of analysis, different theories tend to see different problems. Take the organizational level to which nearly all theories apply (not surprisingly in this book). Agency theories tend to see an organization as a nexus of contracts; transaction cost economics as a governance

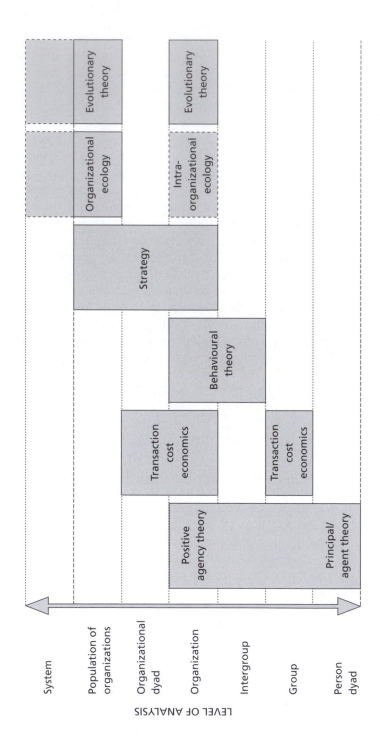

Figure 11.4 **Levels of analysis**

structure of transactions; behavioural theory as a coalition of participant groups; and evolutionary theory as a collection of routines or competences. Different theories look through different lenses at the world. The image of the organization that underlies any particular theory strongly shapes the kinds of problems observed and the importance attached to these.[10]

11.5 All in the family?

We have now discussed the three major similarities we observe among the economic approaches to organizations as well as the three major dimensions of their differences. These are summarized in Table 11.1. The final question remains whether the similarities outweigh the differences or not. Are the approaches included in this book members of a family?

In the final analysis we should like to leave this question for you to decide. We have presented the approaches themselves, as well as our view on their resemblances and differences, in some detail. This should enable you to form a judgement. Obviously, our judgement is that they belong together in this book; and yes, we do regard them as a family. We pursue this metaphor, offering some observations on the structure of the family as we see it.

Agency theory, transaction cost economics, and industrial economics-cum-strategy and game theory are the members of the *nuclear family*. They represent the hard core of the present economic approaches to organizations. These are the fields where most of the current attention is focused and where most of the research work in organizational economics is at present done.

The other approaches belong to the *extended family*. We may think of behavioural theory at the grandparent level. It has generated work in many areas. Within organizational economics its strongest influence has been on transaction cost economics and evolutionary theory. However, there are other siblings too, in microeconomics as well as in theories of organizational behaviour.

Evolutionary theory might be a cousin (perhaps once removed). One familial link is through the behavioural foundations of its concept of organizations. This connects it to organizational theory. On the other hand, it has a clear lineage in economics. Such a family tree leaves no doubt about its inclusion in the family of organizational economics.

Organizational ecology, finally, may be regarded as the 'odd member out' of the family. It is clearly a relative of evolutionary theory, and it is also a member of the family of organizational theories. Its links to the economic family are

Table 11.1 **Family resemblances and differences**

Major similarities	Major differences
Organizations versus markets	Process versus content approaches
Efficiency	Static versus dynamic approaches
Information	Levels of analysis

tenuous, however. Its clearest connection with economics is through the concept of competition, but since that concept is not well developed in organizational ecology, doubts remain. Our reasons for including organizational ecology in this book were twofold: (1) its relation to evolutionary theory, and (2) our expectation that it will develop more links with economics over time (see sections 10.6 and 10.7). In fact, it is already quite attracted to industrial organization, with which it shares some basic interests.[11]

That rounds off our picture of the family structure. For us, the similarities discussed in section 11.3, as well as our perception of the family structure, led us to include these approaches in the book. Some judgement is involved, however. What is more, the family structure is not static; it will develop over time. As with human families, new offspring may be generated, and the family may redefine its structure as its members are perceived to grow either closer or apart. That's all in the family.

11.6 Organizations as complex, adaptive systems

In this final section we want to sketch a theoretical perspective that we expect will have a significant impact on the future development of our family of economic approaches to organizations. It is the perspective of complexity. The **complexity perspective** spans several scientific disciplines, and it is being developed by a truly interdisciplinary set of scholars.[12] In this section we want to focus on potential implications of this perspective for the study of organizations.

Complexity perspective

As a starting-point, look back to Figure 11.4. This figure describes a hierarchy of levels of analysis. Individuals may form dyads, dyads may cluster into groups, various groups may constitute organizations, organizations have relations with other organizations and belong to populations, populations together form a community system. At each level of analysis the phenomena we study are usually complex. At the lowest level of our analysis, the dyad,[13] people may already have complex relationships with one another. Organizations certainly represent complex systems. Complexity in this sense has no generally accepted definition (Gell-Mann, 1994) but usually refers to systems in which numerous agents are interacting with each other in a great many ways:[14]

> Whenever you look at very complicated systems in physics or biology, . . . you generally find that the basic components and the basic laws are quite simple; the complexity arises because you have a great many of these simple components interacting simultaneously. The complexity is actually in the organization – the myriad possible ways that the components of the system can interact.

When scientists from different backgrounds came together to compare notes on such complex systems, they found that:[15]

> every topic of interest had at its heart a system composed of many, many 'agents'. These agents might be molecules or neurons or species or consumers or

even corporations. But whatever their nature, the agents were constantly organizing and reorganizing themselves into larger structures through the clash of
mutual accommodation and mutual rivalry. Thus, molecules would form cells,
neurons would form brains, species would form ecosystems, consumers and corporations would form economies, and so on. At each level, new emergent structures would form and engage in new emergent behaviors.

Emergence

Emergence is thus a central concept in the science of complexity (see Holland,
1998 and Johnson, 2001). It denotes the common finding that the properties,
behaviours and structures of systems cannot simply be deduced from the properties, behaviours and structures of the constituent agents. Complex systems
'lead a life of their own'. Knowledge of their parts is helpful, but knowledge of
the whole requires more than knowledge of all the parts. In other words, applying this to organizations, we cannot hope ever to understand organizations
fully by taking them apart and examining all their parts. The reason is that the
interaction of the parts and the interaction of the organization with the environment co-determine the organizational evolution.[16] In the language of com-

Self-organization

plexity: complex systems self-organize. The exact form of this **self-
organization** emerges from the evolution of the system. Remember Box 10.5
on the evolution of competition on the market of video recorders between Beta
and VHS? As Brian Arthur told the story, the outcome could have gone in either
way. In the language of complexity, the competitive outcome emerged from
the self-organization of the market.

In Chapters 3 and 8 we have argued that within large organizations we often
see markets for intermediate goods and services. Self-organization and decen-
tralized decision-making are often superior to direct supervision and centralized planning in large complex organizations. Recent insights from complexity
theory are usefully applied in this context, as illustrated in Box 11.1. The
examples in Box 11.1 show that in large complex systems detailed top-down
planning may be inferior to self-organization of the system. This insight corresponds well to Mintzberg's (1985) empirical observation that strategies arise
in organizations in (a mix of) two ways: deliberate and emergent. In deliberate
strategies, pre-existing intentions or plans are realized over time. In emergent strategies, a strategic pattern of behaviour develops in the absence of
intentions or plans (and sometimes even in spite of other pre-existing intentions or plans). Emergent strategies are thus one manifestation of self-
organization or organizational systems.

In this self-organization, small factors may make a huge difference. The reason is that complex systems can behave in a way that mathematicians describe
with non-linear dynamics.[17] One of the most striking non-linear phenomena
has come to be known as 'chaos' (Gleick, 1987): under the right circumstances,
tiny perturbations and slight uncertainties may grow until the system's future
becomes utterly unpredictable. Moreover, patterns of regularity and chaos
seem to alternate in the evolution of most complex systems:[18]

> researchers began to realize that even some very simple systems could produce
> astonishingly rich patterns of behavior. All that was required was a little bit of
> nonlinearity. The drip-drip-drip of water from a leaky faucet, for example, could

Box 11.1 ■ Complexity science in business

Complexity science has attracted the interest of the business community in recent years. The Corporate Strategy Board prepared an overview document titled 'Current State of Complexity Science' in 1998. It contains an overview of complexity science from a business perspective as well as a number of illustrative cases. Some of these cases describe how companies have moved away from centralized control of their operations, for instance in their production scheduling. Recognizing that such centralized control is vulnerable to breakdown in circumstances of high uncertainty, companies have been experimenting with models that allow a solution (e.g. to a scheduling problem) to 'emerge' from the interaction of organizational units acting as free agents. Two cases in point are:

General Motors

In 1992 Dick Morley, one of the creators of the floppy disk, developed a factory control system based on complexity theory principles. Morley's computer system was put to the test in the paint shop of a GM assembly plant in Fort Wayne, Indiana. Morley enabled 10 paint booths, previously routed by a centralized controller, to act as free agents with a simple goal: paint as many trucks as possible using as little paint as needed. Each booth electronically 'bids' for the right to paint a certain truck based on color and the queue in front of the booth. A central computer then compares the bids and assigns a 'winner'. This system saved $1 million per year in paint alone. . .

Cemex

The problems Cementos Mexicanos faces in delivering ready-mix concrete to its customers involve many constantly changing variables. A limited window for delivery, congested traffic and work stoppages create an environment that defies linear, command-and-control optimization and is not conducive to top-down scheduling. The complexity approach to this scheduling dilemma included revamping the systems with global positioning satellite equipment to pinpoint the location of every concrete truck at a very low cost and almost real time.

Manipulation of this data and other information about truck cargo, plant conditions and construction allows trucks to become independent agents within a network of plants, rather than appendages of a particular plant held to fragile, centrally controlled schedules. With the help of a complex, adaptive systems approach, Cemex's delivery window dropped from the industry average of approximately within two hours of request to within 30 minutes of request and the company is now moving toward a ten-minute window.

Source: The Corporate Strategy Board, *Current State of Complexity Science*, Washington DC, October 1998

be as maddeningly regular as a metronome – so long as the leak was slow enough. But if you ignored the leak for a while and let the flow rate increase ever so slightly, then the drops would soon start to alternate between large and small: DRIP-drip-DRIP-drip. If you ignored it a while longer and let the flow increase still more, the drops would soon start to come in sequences of 4 – and then 8, 16, and so forth. Eventually, the sequence would become so complex that the drops would seem to come at random – again, chaos. Moreover, this same pattern of ever increasing complexity could be seen in the population swings of fruit flies, or in the turbulent flow of fluids, or in any number of domains.

The non-linear, dynamic behaviour of complex systems implies that their evolution can be very *sensitive on initial conditions*. Small variations in the circumstances at the start of their development may have large consequences for its direction and outcome (see again Box 10.5). An organizational example may be the 'imprint' that founders leave on their companies, even long after they have retired. Sam Walton's impact on Wal-Mart and Walt Disney's lasting influence on the Disney Corporation are cases in point.

Another property of complex systems is that they seek to adapt to their environment. They do so by constantly revising and rearranging their building blocks as they gain experience. The brain will continually strengthen or weaken myriad connections between its neurons as an individual learns from experience with the world. A firm will promote individuals who do well, attempt to transfer best practice across its units, and occasionally reshuffle its organization chart. A particular set of building blocks are the internal models from which complex systems anticipate and predict the future. From bacteria upwards, every living creature has an implicit prediction encoded in its genes. Every creature with a brain has numerous predictions encoded in what it has learned. As we have seen in Chapters 3 and 10, organizations have routines that serve as internal models for prediction. Such organizational routines guide organizational behaviour. In the perspective of complexity, such routines are not passive blueprints, but are subject to continuous testing, refinement and rearranging as the organizational system gains experience. It is through this process of readjustment of its internal models that a complex system learns to adapt its predictions and, consequently, its behaviour.

These ideas correspond closely to insights in organization theory about organizational learning (and unlearning), managerial repertoires, and dominant logics. We want to illustrate this potential of applying 'complexity theory' to organizations with one example, which we borrow from Bettis and Prahalad (1995). We use this because it sheds additional light on the inertia versus adaptability theme that we raised at the end of Chapter 10. As noted in section 10.7, successful firms can become 'simple' over time, focusing exclusively on their successful repertoire of routines and becoming intolerant of deviation or vari-

Dominant logic ation. Bettis and Prahalad refer to the '**dominant logic**' of such a firm. Its dominant logic serves an organization well so long as its predictions about the environment are largely borne out. However, when the environment is turbulent and conditions change rapidly, the organization may need to 'unlearn' its dominant logic. Complexity theorists have shown that complex systems can achieve such unlearning when they move far from (the previous) equilibrium.[19] Bettis and Prahalad visualize these notions with the three graphs in Figures 11.5–11.7. All three figures show organizational stability plotted against a composite environmental variable, which is assumed to be composed of the major environmental variables combined in some fashion. Hence different points on the horizontal axis represent different environmental conditions.

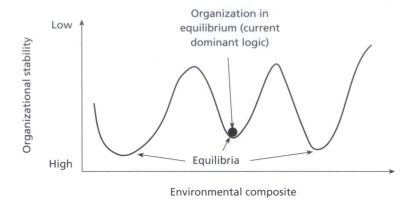

Figure 11.5   **Organizational stability**

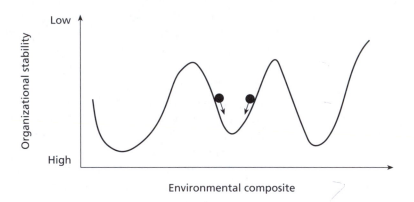

Figure 11.6   **Small fluctuations return to original equilibrium**

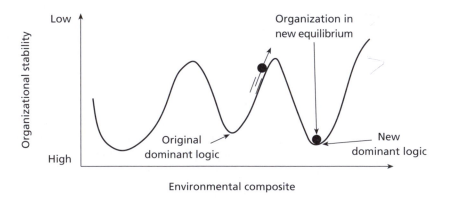

Figure 11.7   **Moving far from equilibrium allows firms to establish new equilibrium**

The organization is shown as a small marble at rest in Figure 11.5 in one of the 'valleys' or equilibria of the stability function. This particular equilibrium corresponds to the current dominant logic that is matched to the environment facing the firm. Figure 11.6 shows how small displacements from equilibrium, corresponding to small changes in the environment, will result in the firm 'rolling back' into its previous repertoire called forth by the dominant logic. This is the situation described by organizational ecology when it argues why organizations tend to be relatively inert. Under such circumstances the match between dominant logic and environment may deteriorate, but because of the

Box 11.2 ■ Punctuated equilibrium and computer technology

The birth of a new species

About 570m years ago, in the ancient oceans of the early earth, something odd happened. In the space of just a few million years, the seas, which had previously held only microscopic organisms, exploded with a huge variety of life, from a metre-long armoured slab of a fish with a mouth like a rubbish disposal chute to a bizarre beast that walked on 14 stilts and had seven mouths on stalks. For the next few hundred million years, evolution progressed at its usual stately pace. Then, 225m years ago, something else odd happened. Perhaps an asteroid hit the planet; scientists cannot agree. Whatever it was, it caused 96% of marine species to disappear and dinosaurs to appear. There followed another uneventful interval, until 65m years ago it was suddenly out with the dinosaurs and in with the large mammals, including, eventually, man.

This sort of progression, described beautifully in Stephen J. Gould's *Wonderful Life*, is called 'punctuated equilibrium'. Over millions of years species adapt to fill every imaginable niche. Then along comes some external force – a volcano, an asteroid, an ice age – that changes all the niches and launches a mad scramble for survival. Evolution favours new forms of life that, through a sort of biological lateral thinking, can find a whole new way to thrive. Wings, legs, lungs: all were revolutionary mutations once. Life down the ages has tended to evolve in sudden great leaps, separated by periods of slow change.

The same is true for technology, though the timescale is a little more compressed. In the past half-century, computer technology has evolved in three large jumps, each one followed by an explosion of new companies, a period of rapid change, and then the gradual emergence of a few dominant species that rule until the next digital disturbance . . . Start around 1950, with the IBM mainframe, when the term 'data processing' entered the language. The next big upheaval came in the mid-1960s, when the minicomputer arrived to open the computing market to a host of upstarts such as Digital Equipment . . . Then, in 1981, IBM introduced the personal computer, causing a market explosion from which emerged some of today's strongest companies: Intel, Microsoft, Compaq.

Now the time has come for another shock, duly delivered in the shape of the Internet, which has emerged practically overnight from 25 years of boffin obscurity into the light of mass-media ubiquity. It was made possible by the serendipitous convergence of three technological developments: the spread of PCs and computer networks in offices; a rapid drop in communication costs; and the appearance of the World Wide Web, a brilliantly simple way of linking multimedia documents around the world over the Internet.

Source: *The Economist*, 25 May 1996

small differences the current dominant logic may continue to be useful. However, if there are large enough changes in the environment (Figure 11.7), organizations may get sufficiently shaken up to roll over an adjacent hill into a new equilibrium, based on a newly developed dominant logic. This proposition corresponds closely with the empirical observation that organizations often develop such new logics only in response to crises – or fail (Schreuder, 1993b). It may also suggest why firms that recognize that they must do something completely different increasingly locate new activities far away from their current activities. When IBM struggled to catch up with developments in the PC field, it established a separate unit that was geographically and managerially insulated from the 'old IBM' with its mainframe mentality. Similarly, when General Motors wanted to build its new Saturn model with innovative production techniques it established a separate organization for this purpose. Finally, this proposition may explain why new competitors often displace experienced incumbents in an industry when major structural change occurs (see Box 11.2 on the software industry). The new entrants are, in essence, starting with a clean sheet and do not have the problem of having to climb up an unlearning curve (the 'hills' in Figures 11.5–11.7) before being able to run down a learning curve. If, finally, the steepness of these hills and/or their height were to depend on the strength of the dominant logic, we would have an explanation of the Icarus paradox discussed in Chapter 10. Continuous success would have the effect of reinforcing the dominant logic of the incumbent firm, deepening the 'valley' of its current position and thus making it harder to migrate over the unlearning curve to a new and more appropriate position when external change would demand so. All in all, such a perspective explains why success carries the seeds of its own demise and why successful companies so often fail after some time.

All in all, complexity theory allows us to see the organization as a complex, adaptive system. This system has several levels of analysis. Each level acts as a building block for the next higher level. At the same time, each level cannot be completely explained by understanding the lower levels. In this sense, each level leads a life of its own. Each level is subject to internal as well as external selection. For instance, in organizations there is internal selection of competing views, routines, proposals, etc., and there is external selection (by the environment) acting upon the resulting organizational configuration of strategy, structure, and capabilities. Organizations can adapt, but this is a process that can lead as often to failure as to success. We are beginning to see some of the mechanisms underlying these processes. A better understanding of these phenomena is of utmost theoretical as well as practical significance.

Questions

1 Which definitions of the firm have been given in this book? Indicate for each definition how co-ordination between several (groups of) persons within the firm is achieved.

2 Consider Box 11.2. What relevance does this extract have for the discussion in the text of Bettis and Prahalad's view on dominant logics and organizational adaptability (through learning)?

Suggested further reading

Gould, S.J. (1989), *Wonderful Life*, New York: Norton

Milgrom, P. and J. Roberts (1992), *Economics, Organization and Management*, Englewood Cliffs, NJ: Prentice Hall

Scott, W.R. (1992), *Organizations: Rational, Natural and Open Systems* (3rd edn), Englewood Cliffs, NJ: Prentice Hall

Stacey, R.D. (1996), *Strategic Management and Organisational Dynamics* (2nd edn), London: Pitman

Notes

1. If the policies are pursued by internal growth (instead of mergers and acquisitions), the analytical benchmark from an economic point of view remains that a separate entity could have been created and a (co-operative or competitive) market relation established.

2. We thus leave behavioural and evolutionary theories out of this discussion. However, we believe that the markets versus organizations perspective applies to both as well, albeit probably to a lesser extent than to the other three approaches (see also section 11.5). Behavioural theories arose in opposition to the view of firms as holistic entities responding automatically to market changes. Evolutionary theories model organizations as subject to environmental selection. To the extent that markets are important elements of the environment (which they often are), a market versus organization perspective can be discerned in the economic strands of this approach too.

3. Observing that efficiency is the primary economic criterion determining selection implies that it is not the only criterion recognized in economics. Monopolistic tendencies, for instance, are recognized as well. Furthermore, it is an empirical question to what extent efficiency explains selection in the real world (and how important the economic aspect of the phenomenon we are studying is). Sociologists may be quite right that, for example, schools or parts of the public sector are not primarily subject to efficiency selection pressures. Most economists, however, would agree that a large part of the world of economic transactions is subject to important efficiency pressures. Exceptions are noted, for instance, in the 'increasing returns' literature (see section 10.7).

4. In particular, our emphasis on the centrality of the information concept may be regarded as too strong by some economists.

5. Strategies may, for instance, be deliberately formulated and subsequently implemented. Alternatively, they may emerge from the firm's current operations and be formulated only afterwards. Recall Burgelman's distinction between autonomous

and induced processes of strategy formation (section 10.7). We discuss this futher in section 11.6.

6. Evolutionary theory is assessed here on its microfoundations. Particular assumptions may be introduced at this level that lead to more substantive outcomes on the macro (or system) level, but that exercise falls outside the scope of this book.

7. It is perhaps ironic to observe that the organizational level of analysis is hardest to define. The reason is that each approach has its own image of the organization: for example, the nexus of contracts view in agency theory versus the hierarchical view in transaction cost economics. Again, this is representative of a more general characteristic of organizational theory (see Morgan, 1997).

8. We saw in Chapter 5 how games with more than two players (and/or more than one stage) differ from two-player, one-stage games.

9. One exception is the analysis of potential interdepartmental conflict within the U-form firm (see Chapter 8, section 8.6).

10. As Weick (1979) has observed, we should be very careful that, as a consequence, 'I believe it when I see it' and 'I see it when I believe it' do not become too intermingled.

11. See, for example, Schreuder and van Witteloostuijn (1990) and Boone and van Witteloostuijn (1995).

12. See, for instance, Waldrop (1992) or Lewin (1995) for popular introductions to complexity.

13. The dyad is not the lowest conceivable level of analysis. Dyads consist of individuals, who in turn represent complex systems with several levels of analysis (down to genetics and biochemistry). These levels fall outside the scope of a book on organizations.

14. Waldrop (1992), p.86.

15. *Ibid.*, p.88.

16. For those with a philosophical bent, this implies that reductionism is not a viable approach to the study of complex systems.

17. Non-linear refers to the fact that if you plot a non-linear equation on a graph paper, it is curvy. This implies that cause and effect are not proportional: a large cause may have a small effect and vice versa. Since systems must be described with various such equations, they can exhibit very unexpected behaviour.

18. *Ibid.*, p.66.

19. See Prigogine and Strengers (1984) or Kauffman (1993, 1995). When systems move 'far from equilibrium', this is identical to 'at the edge of chaos'. The example from Bettis and Prahalad that follows in the main text bears close resemblance to Kauffman's account of how complex, adaptive systems may move through a 'fitness landscape'. For further examples in the fields of strategic management and organizational dynamics see Stacey (1996).

References

Akerlof, G.A. (1970), 'The market for "lemons": qualitative uncertainty and the market mechanism', *Quarterly Journal of Economics*, vol. 84, 488–500.

Alchian, A.A. and H. Demsetz (1972), 'Production, information costs and economic organization', *American Economic Review*, vol. 62, 777–95.

Aldrich, H.E. (1979), *Organizations and Environments*, Englewood Cliffs, NJ: Prentice Hall.

Alesina, A. and E. La Ferrara (2002), 'Who trusts others?', *Journal of Public Economics*, forthcoming.

Alvesson, M. and L. Lindkvist (1993), 'Transaction costs, clans and corporate culture', *Journal of Management Studies*, vol. 30, 427–52.

Amit, R. and P.J.H. Shoemaker (1993), 'Strategic assets and organizational rent', *Strategic Management Journal*, vol. 14, 33–46.

Ansoff, H.I. (1965), *Corporate Strategy*, Harmondsworth: Penguin.

Arrow, K.J. (1963), 'Uncertainty and medical care', *American Economic Review*, vol. 53.

Arrow, K.J. (1973), *Information and Economic Behavior*, Stockholm: Federation of Swedish Industries.

Arrow, K.J. (1985), 'The economics of agency', in: Pratt, J.W. and R.J. Zeckhauser (eds), *Principals and Agents: The Structure of Business*, Boston: Harvard Business School Press.

Arthur, W.B. (1994a), *Increasing Returns and Path Dependence in the Economy*, Ann Arbor: University of Michigan Press.

Arthur, W.B. (1994b), 'Positive feedbacks in the economy', *McKinsey Quarterly*, no. 1.

Arthur, W.B. (1996), 'Increasing returns and the new world of business', *Harvard Business Review*, vol. 74, July/August, 100–9.

Axelrod, R. (1984), *The Evolution of Cooperation*, New York: Basic Books.

Barney, J.B. (1989), 'Asset stocks and sustained competitive advantage: a comment', *Management Science*, vol. 35(12), 1511–13.

Barney, J.B. (1991), 'Firm resources and sustained competitive advantage', *Journal of Management*, vol. 17(1), 99–120.

Barney, J.B. (1997), *Gaining and Sustaining Competitive Advantage*, Reading, Mass.: Prentice Hall.

Barney, J.B. and W. Hesterly (1996), 'Organizational economics: understanding the relationship between organizations and economic analysis', in: Clegg, S.R., C. Hardy and W.R. Nord (eds), *Handbook of Organization Studies*, London: Sage.

Barney, J.B. and W.G. Ouchi (eds) (1986), *Organizational Economics*, San Francisco: Jossey Bass.

Baum, J.A.C. (1996), 'Organizational ecology', in: Clegg, S.R., C. Hardy and W.R. Nord (eds), *Handbook of Organization Studies*, London: Sage.

Berle, A.A. and G.C. Means (1932), *The Modern Corporation and Private Property*, New York: Commerce Clearing House.

Bettis, R.A. and C.K. Prahalad (1995), 'The dominant logic: retrospective and extension', *Strategic Management Journal*, vol.16(1), 5–14.

Boone, Ch. and A. van Witteloostuijn (1995), 'Industrial organization and organizational ecology: the potentials for cross-fertilization', *Organization Studies*, vol.16(2), 265–98.

Boone, Ch., B. de Brabander and A. van Witteloostuijn (1996), 'CEO locus of control and small firm performance: an integrative framework and empirical test', *Journal of Management Studies*, vol. 33, 667–99.

Boone, Ch., B. de Brabander and A. van Witteloostuijn (1999), 'Locus of control and strategic behavior in a prisoner's dilemma game', *Personality and Individual Differences*, vol. 27, 695–706.

Bose, P.P. (1992), 'Commitment: an interview with Pankaj Ghemawat of the Harvard Business School on new directions in strategic thinking', *McKinsey Quarterly*, no. 3, 121–37.

Bowman, E.H. and C.E. Helfat (2001), 'Does corporate strategy matter?', *Strategic Management Journal*, vol. 22 (1), 1–23.

Brandenburger, A.M. and B.J. Nalebuff (1995), 'The right game: use game theory to shape strategy', *Harvard Business Review*, vol. 73, 57–71.

Brickley, J.A. and F.H. Dark (1987), 'The choice of organizational form, the case of franchising', *Journal of Financial Economics*, vol. 18, 401–20.

Burgelman, R.A. (1990), 'Strategy-making and organizational ecology: a conceptual integration', in: Singh, J.V., *Organizational Evolution: New Directions*, Newbury Park, Calif.: Sage.

Burgelman, R.A. (1991), 'Intraorganizational ecology of strategy making and organizational adaptation: theory and field research', *Organization Science*, vol. 2, 239–62.

Burt, R.S. (1992), *Structural Holes: The Social Structure of Competition*, Cambridge, Mass: Harvard University Press.

Cameron, S. and A. Collins (1997), 'Transaction costs and partnerships: the case of rock bands', *Journal of Economic Behavior and Organization*, vol. 32, 171–83.

Carney, M., and E. Gedajlovic (1991), 'Vertical integration in franchise systems: agency theory and resource explanations', *Strategic Management Journal*, vol. 12, 607–29.

Carroll, G.R. (1987), *Publish and Perish: The Organizational Ecology of Newspaper Industries*, Greenwich, Conn.: JAI Press.

Carroll, G.R. (ed.) (1988), *Ecological Models of Organizations*, Cambridge, Mass.: Ballinger.

Carroll, G.R. and M.T. Hannan (1995), *Organizations in Industry: Strategy, Structure, and Selection*, Oxford: Oxford University Press.

Casson, M. (1997), *Information and Organization: A New Perspective on the Theory of the Firm*, Oxford: Oxford University Press.

Caves, R.E. (1992), *Multinational Enterprise and Economic Analysis*, Cambridge: Cambridge University Press.

Chandler, A.D. (1966), *Strategy and Structure*, New York: Doubleday.

Clark, K. and M. Sefton (2001), 'The sequential prisoner's dilemma: evidence on reciprocation', *Economic Journal*, vol. 111, 51–68.

Clarke, R. and T. McGuinness (eds) (1987), *The Economics of the Firm*, Oxford: Basil Blackwell.

Clegg, S.R., C. Hardy and W.R. Nord (eds) (1996), *Handbook of Organization Studies*, London: Sage.

Coase, R.H. (1937), 'The nature of the firm', *Economica*, vol. 4.

Coleman, J.S. (1990), *Foundations of Social Theory*, Cambridge, Mass: Harvard University Press.

Coles, J.W. and W.S. Hesterly (1998), 'The impact of firm specific assets and the interaction of uncertainty: an examination of make or buy decisions in public and private hospitals', *Journal of Economic Behavior and Organization*, vol. 36, 383–409.

Collins, J.C. and J.I. Porras (1998), *Built to Last: Successful Habits of Visionary Companies*, London: Century Business.

Collis, D.J. and C.A. Montgomery (1995), 'Competing on resources: strategy in the 1990s', *Harvard Business Review*, vol. 73, 118–28.

Cyert, R.M. and J.G. March (1963), *A Behavioral Theory of the Firm*, Englewood Cliffs, NJ: Prentice Hall. (Second edition, 1992) d'Aspremont, C., J. Gabszewicz and J.F. Thisse (1979), 'On Hotelling's "stability in competition"', *Econometrica*, vol. 47, 1145–51.

Dawkins, R. (1986), *The Blind Watchmaker*, Harlow: Longman.

Day, J.D. and J.C. Wendler (1998), 'The new economics of organization', *McKinsey Quarterly*, 1998, no. 1, 4–17.

Demsetz, H. (1995), *The Economics of the Business Firm: Seven Critical Commentaries*, Cambridge: Cambridge University Press.

Dharwadkar, R., G. George and P. Brandes (2000), 'Privatization in emerging economies: an agency theory perspective', *Academy of Management Review*, vol. 25(3), 650–69.

Dierickx, I. and K. Cool (1989), 'Asset stock accumulation and sustainability of competitive advantage', *Management Science*, vol. 35(12), 1504–11.

Dixit, A. and B. Nalebuff (1991), *Thinking Strategically*, New York: Norton & Co.

Doeringer, P. and M. Piore (1971), *Internal Labor Markets and Manpower Analysis*, Boston: Heath & Co.

Douma, S.W. (1997), 'The two-tier system of corporate governance', *Long Range Planning*, vol. 30(4), 612–14.

Dyer, J.H. and K. Nobeoka (2000), 'Creating and managing a high-performance knowledge-sharing network: the Toyota case', *Strategic Management Journal*, vol. 21(3), 345–67.

Fama, E.F. (1980), 'Agency problems and the theory of the firm', *Journal of Political Economy*, vol. 88, 288–307.

Fama, E.F. and M.C. Jensen (1983a), 'Separation of ownership and control', *Journal of Law and Economics*, vol. 26, 301–26.

Fama, E.F. and M.C. Jensen (1983b), 'Agency problems and residual claims', *Journal of Law and Economics*, vol. 26, 327–50.

Ferguson, T.D. (2000), 'Do strategic groups differ in reputation?', *Strategic Management Journal*, vol. 21(12), 1195–214.

FitzRoy, F.R., Z.J. Acs and D.A. Gerlowski (1998), *Management and Economics of Organization*, Harlow: Pearson Education.

Frances, J. *et al.* (1991), Introduction, in: Thompson, G., J. Frances, R. Levacic and J. Mitchell, *Markets, Hierarchies and Networks*, London: Sage.

Gell-Mann, M. (1994), *The Quark and the Jaguar: Adventures in the Simple and the Complex*, London: Little Brown.

Ghemawat, P. (1991), *Commitment: The Dynamic of Strategy*, New York: Free Press.

Gibbons, R. and L.F. Katz (1991), 'Layoffs and Lemons', *Journal of Labor Economics*, vol. 9(4), 351–80.

Gilbert, X. and P. Strebel (1988), 'Developing competitive advantage', in: Quinn, J.B., H. Mintzberg and R.M. James (eds), *The Strategy Process*, Englewood Cliffs, NJ: Prentice Hall.

Glaeser, E.L., D.I. Laibson, J.A. Scheinkman and C.L. Soutter (2000), 'Measuring trust', *Quarterly Journal of Economics*, vol. 115(3), 811–46.

Gleick, J. (1987), *Chaos*, New York: Viking.

Goold, M., A. Campbell and M. Alexander (1994), *Corporate-level Strategy*, New York: John Wiley.

Goshal, S. and Moran, P. (1996), 'Bad for practice: a critique of the transaction cost theory', *Academy of Management Review*, vol. 21(1), 13–47.

Gould, S.J. (1989), *Wonderful Life*, New York: Norton.

Granovetter, M. (1985), 'Economic action and social structure: the problem of embeddedness', *American Journal of Sociology*, vol. 91(3).

Grant, R.M. (1991), 'The resource-based theory of competitive advantage: implications for strategy formulation', *California Management Review*, vol. 13, 114–35.

Hall, R. (1992), 'The strategic analysis of intangible resources', *Strategic Management Journal*, vol. 13, 135–44.

Hall, R. (1993), 'A framework linking intangible resources and capabilities to sustainable competitive advantage', *Strategic Management Journal*, vol. 14, 607–18.

Hannan, M.T. and J. Freeman (1989a), *Organizational Ecology*, Cambridge, Mass.: Harvard University Press.

Hannan, M.T. and J. Freeman (1989b), 'Setting the record straight on organizational ecology: rebuttal to Young', *American Journal of Sociology*, vol. 95(2), 425–35.

Hatten, K.J. and M.L. Hatten (1988), *Effective Strategic Management: Analysis and Action*, Englewood Cliffs, NJ: Prentice Hall.

Haugland, S.A. (1999), 'Factors influencing the duration of international buyer–seller relationships', *Journal of Business Research*, vol. 46, 273–80.

Hayek, F.A. (1945), 'The use of knowledge in society', *American Economic Review*, vol. 35(4).

Henrich, J. (2000), 'Does culture matter in economic behavior?: ultimatum game bargaining among the Machiguenga of the Peruvian Amazon', *American Economic Review*, vol. 90, 973–79.

Hennart, J.F. and S. Reddy (1997), 'The choice between mergers/acquisitions and joint ventures: the case of Japanese investors in the United States', *Strategic Management Journal*, vol. 18(1), 1–12.

Hill, C.W. and G.R. Jones (1995), *Strategic Management Theory: An Integrated Approach*, Boston: Houghton Mifflin.

Hillman, A.J. and G.D. Keim (2001), 'Shareholder value, stakeholder management, and social issues: what's the bottom line?', *Strategic Management Journal*, vol. 22(2), 125–39.

Holland, J.H. (1998), *Emergence: from Chaos to Order*, Cambridge, Mass.: Perseus.

Holmstrom, B.R. and J. Tirole (1989), 'The theory of the firm', in: Schmalensee, R. and R. Willig (eds), *Handbook of Industrial Organization*, vol.1, Amsterdam: North Holland.

Hoskisson, R.E. and M.A. Hitt (1990), 'Antecedents and performance outcomes of diversification: a review and critique of theoretical perspectives', *Journal of Management*, vol. 16(2), 461–509.

Hotelling, H. (1929), 'Stability in competition', *Economic Journal*, vol. 39, 41–57.

Hymon, D.N. (1986), *Modern Microeconomics: Analysis and Applications*, St Louis, Miss.: Times Mirror/Mosby College Publishing.

Imai, K. and H. Itami (1984), 'Interpenetration of organization and market', *International Journal of Industrial Organization*, vol. 2, 285–310.

Irvin, R.A. and E.G. Michaels III (1983), 'Core skills: doing the right things right', *McKinsey Quarterly*, summer, 4–19.

Jacobides, M.G. and D.C. Croson (2001), 'Information policy: shaping the value of agency relationships', *Academy of Management Review*, vol. 26(2), 202–23.

Jensen, M.C. (1998), *Foundations of Organizational Strategy*, Cambridge, Mass.: Harvard University Press.

Jensen, M.C. and W.H. Meckling (1976), 'Theory of the firm: managerial behavior, agency costs and ownership structure', *Journal of Financial Economics*, vol. 3, 305–60.

Johnson, G. and K. Scholes (1988), *Exploring Corporate Strategy* (2nd edn), Hemel Hempstead: Prentice Hall.

Jones, G.R. and C.W.L. Hill (1988), 'Transaction cost analysis of strategy–structure choice', *Strategic Management Journal*, vol. 9, 159–72.

Johnson, S. (2001), *Emergence: the Connected Lives of Ants, Brains, Cities and Software*, New York: Scribner.

Katz, M.L. and H.S. Rosen (1998), *Microeconomics*, Boston, Mass.: Irwin/McGraw Hill.

Kauffman, S. (1993), *The Origins of Order: Self-organization and Selection in Evolution*, New York: Oxford University Press.

Kauffman, S. (1995), *At Home in the Universe: The Search for Laws of Complexity*, London: Viking.

Kaufman, A., C.H. Wood and G. Theyel (2000), 'Collaboration and technology linkages: a strategic supplier typology', *Strategic Management Journal*, vol. 21(6), 649–63.

Kay, J. (1993), *Foundations of Corporate Success: How Business Strategies Add Value*, Oxford: Oxford University Press.

Kay, J. (1996), *The Business of Economics*, Oxford: Oxford University Press.

Kessel, R.A. (1974), 'Transfused blood, serum hepatitis, and the Coase theorem', *Journal of Law and Economics*, vol. 17(2), 265–89.

Khanna, T. and J.W. Rivkin (2001), 'Performance effects of business groups in emerging markets', *Strategic Management Journal*, vol. 22(1), 45–74.

Klein, B., R.A. Crawford and A.A. Alchian (1978), 'Vertical integration, appropriable rents and the competitive contracting process', *Journal of Law and Economics*, vol. 21, 297–326.

Klemperer, P. (2001), 'What really matters in auction design', paper downloadable from www.paulklemperer.org

Lafontaine, F. (1992), 'Agency theory and franchising: some empirical results', *RAND Journal of Economics*, vol. 23(2), 263–83.

Lewin, R. (1995), *Complexity: Life on the Edge of Chaos*, London: Phoenix.

Li, Shaomin, Li, Shuhe and Zhang, Weiying (2000), 'The road to capitalism: competition and institutional change in China', *Journal of Comparative Economics*, vol 28(2), 269–92.

Macaulay, S. (1963), 'Non-contractual relations in business: a preliminary study', *American Sociological Review*, vol. 28(1).

McMillan, J. (1991), *Games, Strategies, and Managers*, Oxford: Oxford University Press.

Maher, M.E. (1997), 'Transaction cost economics and contractual relations', *Cambridge Journal of Economics*, Vol. 21, 147–70.

March, J.G. (1994), *A Primer on Decision Making: How Decisions Happen*, New York: Free Press.

March, J.G. and H.A. Simon (1958), *Organizations*, New York: John Wiley.

Marshall, A. (1890), *Principles of Economics*, London: Macmillian. (Reprinted 1949)

Masten, S.E., J.W. Meekan Jr, and E.A. Snyder (1989), 'Vertical integration in the US auto industry: a note on the influence of transaction specific assets', *Journal of Economic Behavior and Organization*, vol. 12, 265–73.

Michael, S.C. (2000), 'Investments to create bargaining power: the case of franchising', *Strategic Management Journal*, vol. 21(4) 497–514.

Milgrom, P. and J. Roberts (1987), 'Informational asymmetry, strategic behavior, and industrial organization', *American Economic Review*, vol. 77, 184–93.

Milgrom, P. and J. Roberts (1992), *Economics, Organization and Management*, Englewood Cliffs, NJ: Prentice Hall.

Miller, D. (1990), *The Icarus Paradox*, New York: Harper.

Miller, D. (1994), 'What happens after success: the perils of excellence', *Journal of Management Studies*, vol. 31(3), 325–58.

Mintzberg, H. (1979), *The Structuring of Organizations*, Englewood Cliffs, NJ: Prentice Hall.

Mintzberg, H. (1983), *Structure in Fives: Designing Effective Organizations*, Englewood Cliffs, NJ: Prentice Hall.

Mintzberg, H. (1985), 'Of Strategies, Deliberate and Emergent', *Strategic Management Journal*, 257–72.

Mintzberg, H. (1989), *Mintzberg on Management*, New York: Free Press.

Mintzberg, H. and J.B. Quinn (1991), *The Strategy Process*: Concepts, Contexts, Cases, Englewood Cliffs, NJ: Prentice Hall.

Moerland, P.W. (1995), 'Alternative disciplinary mechanisms in different corporate systems', *Journal of Economic Behavior and Organization*, vol. 26, 17–34.

Mohr, L.B. (1982), *Explaining Organizational Behavior: The Limits and Possibilities of Theory and Research*, San Francisco: Jossey Bass.

Morgan, G. (1997), *Images of Organization*, London: Sage.

Moschandreas, M. (1997), 'The role of opportunism in transaction cost economics', *Journal of Economic Issues*, vol. 31(1), 39–57.

Nair, A. and S. Kotha (2001), 'Does group membership matter? Evidence from the Japanese steel industry', *Strategic Management Journal*, vol. 22(3), 221–35.

Nayak, P.R. D.A. Garvin, A.N. Maira and J.L. Bragar (1995), 'Creating a learning organization', *Prism*, 3rd quarter.

Nelson, R.R. (1991), 'Why do firms differ and how does it matter?', *Strategic Management Journal*, vol. 12 (special issue), 61–74.

Nelson, R.R. and S.G. Winter (1982), *An Evolutionary Theory of Economic Change*, Cambridge, Mass.: Harvard University Press.

Nickerson, J.A., B.H. Hamilton and T. Wada (2001), 'Market position, resource profile and governance: linking Porter and Williamson in the context of international courier and small package services in Japan', *Strategic Management Journal*, vol. 22(3), 251–73.

Noorderhaven, N.G. (1995), 'Transaction, interaction, institutionalization: toward a dynamic theory of hybrid governance', *Scandinavian Journal of Management*, vol.11(1), 43–55.

O'Donnell, S.W. (2000), 'Managing foreign subsidiaries: agents of headquarters, or an independent network?', *Strategic Management Journal*, vol. 21(5), 525–48.

Oster, S. (1982), 'Intraindustry structure and the ease of strategic change', *Review of Economics and Statistics*, vol. 64(3), 376–83.

Ouchi, W.G. (1980), 'Markets, bureaucracies and clans', *Administrative Science Quarterly*, vol. 25, 129–41.

Ouchi, W.G. and O.E. Williamson (1981), 'The markets and hierarchies perspective: origins, implications, prospects', in: Van de Ven, A. and W.F Joyce (eds), *Assessing Organizational Design and Performance*, New York: John Wiley.

Park, S.H. and Y. Luo (2001), 'Guanxi and organizational dynamics: organizational networking in Chinese firms', *Strategic Management Journal*, vol. 22(5), 455–77.

Parsons, T. (1960), *Structure and Process in Modern Societies*, Glencoe, Ill.: Free Press.

Perloff, J.M. (2001), *Microeconomics*, Boston, Mass.: Addison-Wesley.

Peteraf, M.A. (1993), 'The cornerstones of competitive advantage: a resource-based view', *Strategic Management Journal*, vol. 14, 179–91.

Pfeffer, J. (1982), *Organizations and Organization Theory*, Marshfield, Mass.: Pitman.

Pigou, A.C. (1920), *The Economics of Welfare*, London: Macmillan.

Polanyi, M. (1962), *Personal Knowledge*, New York: Harper.

Polanyi, M. (1967), *The Tacit Dimension*, Garden City: Doubleday.

Porter, M.E. (1980), *Competitive Strategy: Techniques for Analyzing Industries and Competitors*, New York: Free Press.

Porter, M.E. (1985), *Competitive Advantage: Creating and Sustaining Superior Performance*, New York: Free Press.

Prahalad, C.K. and G. Hamel (1994), *Competing for the Future*, Boston, Mass.: Harvard Business School Press.

Prigogine, I. and I. Stengers (1984), *Order out of Chaos*, New York: Bantam.

Putterman, L. (ed.) (1986), *The Economic Nature of the Firm*: *A Reader*, Cambridge: Cambridge University Press.

Quinn, J.B. (1982), *Strategies for Change: Logical Incrementalism*, Homewood, Ill.: Irwin.

Quinn, J.B., H. Mintzberg and R.M. James (eds) (1988), *The Strategy Process*, Englewood Cliffs, NJ: Prentice Hall.

Raiffa, H. (1968), *Decision Analysis: Introductory Lectures on Choices under Uncertainty*, Reading, Mass.: Addison-Wesley.

Rasmusen, E. (1989), *Games and Information*: *An Introduction to the Theory of Games*, Oxford: Basil Blackwell.

Reuer, J.J. (2001), 'From hybrids to hierarchies: shareholder wealth effects of joint venture partner buy-outs', *Strategic Management Journal*, vol. 22(1), 27–44.

Reuer, J.J. and M.P. Koza (2000), 'Asymmetric information and joint venture performance: theory and evidence for domestic and international joint ventures', *Strategic Management Journal*, vol. 21(1), 81–8.

Rumelt, R.P. (1974), *Strategy, Structure, and Economic Performance*, Boston, Mass.: Harvard Business School Press.

Rumelt, R.P. (1991), 'How much does industry matter?', *Strategic Management Journal*, vol. 12(3), 167–85.

Sako, M. and S. Helper (1998), 'Determinants of trust in supplier relations: evidence from the automotive industry in Japan and the United States', *Journal of Economic Behavior and Organization*, vol. 34, 387–417.

Samuelson, P. (1976), *Economics* (10th edn), Tokyo: McGraw-Hill/Kogakusha Ltd.

Saussier, S. (1999), 'Duration: an empirical analysis of EDF coal contracts', *Recherches Economiques de Louvain*, vol. 65(1), 3–21.

Schelling, T.C. (1960), *The Strategy of Conflict*, Cambridge, Mass.: Harvard University Press. (Reprinted 1980)

Schleifer, A. and R.W. Vishny (1997), 'A survey of corporate governance', *Journal of Finance*, vol. 52, 737–83.

Schreuder, H. (1993a), 'Coase, Hayek, and hierarchy', in: Lindenberg, S. and H. Schreuder, *Interdisciplinary Perspectives on Organization Studies*, Oxford: Pergamon Press.

Schreuder, H. (1993b), 'Timely management changes as an element of organizational strategy', *Journal of Management Studies*, vol. 30(5), 723–38.

Schreuder, H. and A. van Witteloostuijn (1990), *The Ecology of Organizations and the Economics of Firms*, Research Memorandum, University of Limburg.

Schumpeter, J.A. (1934), *The Theory of Economic Development*, Cambridge, Mass.: Harvard University Press.

Scott, W.R. (1992), *Organizations: Rational, Natural, and Open Systems* (3rd edn), Englewood Cliffs, NJ: Prentice Hall.

Sculley, J. with John Byrne (1987), *Odyssey: Pepsi to Apple . . . A Journey of Adventures, Ideas, and the Future*, New York: Harper & Row.

Simon, H.A. (1961), *Administrative Behavior* (2nd edn), New York: Macmillan.

Simon, H.A. (1991), 'Organizations and markets', *Journal of Economic Perspectives*, vol. 5(2), 25–44.

Soeters, J. and H. Schreuder (1988), 'The interaction between national and organizational cultures in accounting firms', *Accounting, Organizations and Society*, vol. 13(1), 75–85.

Stacey, R.D. (1996), *Strategic Management & Organisational Dynamics* (2nd edn), London: Pitman.

Stigler, G.J. and C. Friedland (1983), 'The literature of economics: the case of Berle and Means', *Journal of Law and Economics*, vol. 26, 237–68.

Stuckey, J. and D. White (1993), 'When and when not to vertically integrate: a strategy as risky as vertical integration can only succeed when it is chosen for the right reasons', *McKinsey Quarterly*, 3–27.

Takeishi, A. (2001), 'Bridging inter- and intra-firm boundaries: management of supplier involvement in automobile product development', *Strategic Management Journal*, vol. 22(5), 403–33.

Teece, D.J. (1980), 'Economics of scope and scope of the enterprise', *Journal of Economic Behavior and Organization*, vol. 1, 223–47.

Teece, D.J. (1982), 'Towards an economic theory of the multiproduct firm', *Journal of Economic Behavior and Organization*, vol. 3, 39–63.

Thompson, G., J. Frances, R. Levacic and J. Mitchell (1991), *Markets, Hierarchies and Networks*, London: Sage.

Titmuss, R.M. (1971), *The Gift Relationship: From Human Blood to Social Policy*, New York: Pantheon.

Usher, J.M. and M.G. Evans (1996), 'Life and death along gasoline alley: Darwinian and Lamarckian processes in a differentiating population', *Academy of Management Journal*, vol. 39(5), 1428–66.

Waldrop, M.M. (1992), *Complexity: The Emerging Science at the Edge of Order and Chaos*, New York: Simon & Schuster.

Weber, Max (1947), *The Theory of Social and Economic Organization* (original edition 1925), A.M. Henderson and T. Parsons (trans.), New York: Free Press.

Weick, K.E. (1979), *The Social Psychology of Organizing* (2nd edn), Reading, Mass.: Addison-Wesley.

Williamson, O.E. (1975), *Markets and Hierarchies: Analysis and Antitrust Implications*, New York: Free Press.

Williamson, O.E. (1985), *The Economic Institutions of Capitalism*, New York: Free Press.

Williamson, O.E. (1996), 'Economics and organization: a primer', *California Management Review*, vol. 38, 131–46.

Williamson, O.E. (1999), 'Strategy research: governance and competence perspectives', *Strategic Management Journal*, vol. 20(12), 1087–108.

Winter, S.G. (1990), 'Survival, selection, and inheritance in evolutionary theories of organization', in: Singh, J.V., *Organizational Evolution: New Directions*, Newbury Park, Calif.: Sage.

Young, R.C. (1988), 'Is population ecology a useful paradigm for the study of organizations?', *American Journal of Sociology*, vol. 94(1), 1–24.

Index

Page numbers in **bold** refer to marginal definitions.